NOMADS UNDER THE WESTWAY

Irish Travellers, Gypsies and other traders in west London

NOMADS UNDER THE WESTWAY

Irish Travellers, Gypsies and other traders in west London

Christopher Griffin

University of Hertfordshire Press

First published in Great Britain in 2008 by
University of Hertfordshire Press
Learning and Information Services
University of Hertfordshire
College Lane
Hatfield
Hertfordshire AL10 9AB

© Christopher Griffin 2008

The right of Christopher Griffin to be identified as the author of this work has been asserted by him in accordance with the Copyright, Designs and Patents Act 1988.

All rights reserved. No part of this book may be reproduced or utilised in any form or by any means, electronic or mechanical, including photocopying, recording or by any information storage and retrieval system, without permission in writing from the publisher.

British Library Cataloguing in Publication Data

A catalogue record for this book is available from the British Library

ISBN 978-1-902806-54-9

Design by Sara Chapman, www.letterg.co.uk, Harpenden, AL5 2LS

Cover design by John Robertshaw, Harpenden, AL5 2JB

Printed in Great Britain by Antony Rowe Ltd, SN14 6LH

To the memory of my parents David Griffin
and Brigid Mary Griffin (née Nolan);
to my wife Clare for boundless love and patience;
and to Freddy Bailey, Emeritus Professor of Anthropology
at the University of California, La Jolla,
for starting me on the road at Sussex.

Contents

List of illustrations   ix

Acknowledgements   xiii

Preface   xv

1   **Routes and redirections**   1
2   **Emigrés and wanderers: labourers, tinkers, Gypsies**   29
3   **North Kensington, 1800–1900**   59
4   **North Kensington, Hammersmith and Westway Site, 1900–1987**   89
5   **Mortlake (Richmond-upon-Thames)**   123
6   **Return of the native: politics, ethics and ethnography**   161
7   **Ecology, economy, habitat**   185
8   **Work and networks**   215
9   **Spouses and children**   245
10 **'Community'**   277

Epilogue   317

Bibliography   323

Index   341

List of illustrations

Sir Richard Burton's (1821–90) tomb at Mortlake	13
London Borough Map. HMSO incorporating Ordnance Survey material. Copyright granted.	14
The Potteries, c. 1850. Taken from Malcolmson (1975), 'Getting a living in the slums of Victorian Kensington', *The London Journal*, 1.	66
Last kiln in the Potteries	68
'Testimony to a slum'	68
Gypsy *tans*, Notting Dale 1861. *The Queen* magazine, 16 November 1861. Courtesy of the Royal Borough of Kensington and Chelsea public library.	73
Double tent and Romany face, Notting Dale 1861. Courtesy of the Royal Borough of Kensington and Chelsea public library.	74
Gypsies and benefactor near Latimer Road, 1879. *The Illustrated London News*, 13 December 1879. Courtesy of the Royal Borough of Kensington and Chelsea public library.	75
Vardo interior, near Latimer Road, 1879. *The Illustrated London News*, 13 December 1879. Courtesy of the Royal Borough of Kensington and Chelsea public library.	76
Map of Shepherds Bush, Notting Hill, Notting Dale and the Westway	88
General Anne Hearne's mother. Reproduced with the kind permission of Mrs Florence Allen.	96
Florence Allen, St Mary's Place, Notting Dale, 1991	100

Medfield Street, Roehampton, 2004, seen from the edge of Putney Common.	127
Map of Barnes, Mortlake and East Sheen	141
George 'Feathers' Smith, wife Lemonelia, and family	143
Grave of George and Lemonelia Smith at Old Mortlake Cemetery	146
Mitcham Smiths with donkey rides, c. 1930 (unknown location)	149
The Harris house, Christchurch Road, East Sheen, 1995	153
Mr E. Vine, sweep and general dealer, Upper Richmond Road, East Sheen, 1995	157
'Rich homes', Notting Hill, 2004	168
Jim O'Donoghue	194
Westway Site and M41 (now the West Cross Route) looking towards Shepherds Bush	200
'Triangle' and Westway Site viewed from the railway line, 1986	200
Westway Site, looking south to north, winter 1984	225
Mrs Winifred Ward	230
Irish Traveller girls, Portobello Road, Notting Hill, 1986	231
Teenage Doyles	253
Double first cousin marriage I	256
Double first cousin marriage II	256
Double first cousin marriage III	257
Dressed for St Patrick's Day, 1987	264
French Gypsies, or Kalderash, camped by North Pole Road, 1987	268
Kitty Connors	284

Westway shrine	288
Former Westway residents on the Ealing site	288
Pristine interior	293
Tom McCarthy	294
Handbill	297
Romany flower seller in Nascot Street, off Scrubs Lane, 1986	299
Part of the new sports facilities under the M40/M41 interchange, 1994	301
New (or New Age) Travellers camped between Evesham Street and the M41, 1986	302
John Doyle	308
Martin Ward and the author, 1994	314
The Westway Site, 2004, looking north west	316

Acknowledgements

It hardly needs saying that without the help and co-operation of many people this book would not have got written. It is equally obvious that it is impossible to name all these people who in various ways (both in the northern hemisphere and southern) have helped in my inquiries. Yet to all of them I extend my deep gratitude, and I ask you, the reader, to remember that none of them bears responsibility for the interpretations put on my data or such flaws that may remain.

My first thanks go to all the Travellers and Romanies I once knew at the Westway Site, especially Martin and Winifred Ward, the late Thomas McCarthy and his family, the O'Driscoll clan, the Connors, and Doyle-Keenan-MacDonough (or McDonagh) network. Secondly, my thanks go to the following people in England: for their informative correspondence, Josephine Warne and my old friend Mike Trim; for their hospitality and connections in Cambridgeshire, John and Mary Neale; in Barnes, Rebecca and Kieran Higgins; in Surrey, Anne Cunnningham; in High Wycombe, Michael and Margaret Griffin; in Devon, Paul and Sue Ring; and not least, Catherine and Arthur Ivatts in Saddleworth, Lancashire. Indeed, my special thanks go to Arthur for years of support and encouragement.

In Britain, Ireland, and Australia I have benefited greatly over the years from conversation and correspondence with several people. In England, my thanks go to Professor Thomas Acton for his ever keen responses; to Dr Donald Kenrick for tea and conversation in Notting Hill; to Dr Colm Power for valuable comments on an earlier draft; and to Jenny Loker and Margaret Woods of the Travellers Support Team, at Trumpington in Cambridgeshire, for kindly arranging site visits in 2004. In Australia, I am especially grateful to Irish anthropologist Dr Edward McDonald for counsel on modern Irish history; to Professor Alan Bittles, another Irishman, who also happens to be an international authority on genetics and close-relative marriage; and to Dr Charles Edelman, a colleague and expert on the work of Shakespeare who promptly answered my questions regarding the Bard's language. I also owe thanks to Dr Vivian Forbes,

Robert Munro, and Tuyen and Karen McDonald, all in Perth, for cartographic and reprographic advice; and to Dr Charles Eaton for newspaper clippings over the years on matters-Gypsy sent by way of a subtle reminder of how slow I was in finishing. In Ireland thanks go to the Foley family for bed, board, and their never-failing Dublin hospitality; to the McCarthys in Limerick for staying in touch with me for over twenty years by way of cards and ribbons on St Patrick's Day; and to Professor Michaél Cinneide, in Galway, for so kindly filling me in on a matter of contemporary Irish life. And, in Fiji, to Larry Thomas for timely hospitality in Suva, where the job was finished.

At the Borough of Hammersmith and Fulham's Housing Department in White City, I'd like to acknowledge all my former colleagues for their professional support in what were sometimes difficult moments as site warden. Special gratitude is also extended to Mrs Florence Allen of Notting Dale, and to her family, for granting interviews and permission to publish a family photograph. For the same reason, at Mortlake, thanks go to Mrs Joan Parsons and her family. Unfortunately all recent attempts to contact them, along with members of the Dickerson family at Barnes, have been unsuccessful. I presume they have moved out of the district. I hope they will forgive me then for not bestowing them the courtesy of seeing relevant parts of the text before it went to print. Which brings me to my editor Jane Housham, and Sarah Elvins and Helen Miller at the University of Hertfordshire for being so patient, sage and professional. Finally, thanks to all the regulars at *The Hare and Hounds*, *Charlie Butler*, and other pubs who, all those years ago, took an interest in what I did and who wittingly or unwittingly so often proved useful informants.

Preface

It has often been said, and was recently reiterated by the Chief Executive of the Holocaust Centre,[1] that no ethnic minority has faced more prejudice and discrimination in Britain than the Gypsies and Travellers. And over thirty years ago, in a seminal study of the rise of Gypsy nationalism in Britain, Acton (1974) declared that Irish Travellers suffered the brunt of this hostility, some from Gypsies themselves. It seems, today, that not enough has changed. Indeed, judging by the media, who often do little to help and all too often exacerbate the problem, the situation of Irish Travellers has worsened. In the UK general election campaign of 2005, for example, Michael Howard, leader of the Conservative Party, targeted Travellers, Gypsies and the Human Rights Act for radical reform, seemingly in that order of importance. His opponents howled him down as 'racist'.

In these circumstances, then, it may be surprising to learn that this book is not directly concerned with prejudice, discrimination or racism. Not because they are unimportant matters — on the contrary — but because I can safely leave these matters to those who are closer to the situation and more up to date on these justice issues than I am. Here, rather, I intend to concentrate on something no less important in helping to undo the negativity which surrounds Irish Travellers: namely, an examination of the complexity of Irish Traveller and Gypsy cultures and communities, which go largely disregarded or uncomprehended by outsiders who, as a result, regard Travellers either as 'victims' or as social deviants; two views which Travellers themselves find equally repellent.

There are 'problems' with Irish Travellers: *some* Travellers. Equally, there are 'problems' with non-Travellers: *some* of them. Not surprisingly, therefore, some areas of conflict between these two groups arise out of a clash of interests between, on the one hand, the nation-state, representative of a sedentary — but increasingly mobile — majority, and, on the other, a travelling or nomadic minority under increasing government pressure to settle. The increasing mobilisation of the sedentary majority is one aspect of 'globalisation', which although a relatively recent term, is not a new thing: it has been in progress for centuries. Moreover, if 'globalisation is a blanket term where sovereign national states are criss-crossed and undermined by trans-national actors with varying prospects of power, orientation and networks', as Jameson has suggested (cited in Benyon and Dunkerley 2000, 4), one would have to conclude that Gypsies have been prominent 'trans-national actors', as *traders* — a word tied etymologically to 'tread', 'track' and 'traffic' — and as *refugees* and *immigrants*, for an equally long time. If only for this reason and there are, of course, others, Gypsies and Travellers are of no small importance when it comes to understanding the important issues of global population movement.

The vilification of this particularly mobile group by a now increasingly mobile majority is not the only paradox. Since the advent of industrial capitalism nomadic Travellers and Gypsies have succeeded in keeping their nuclear and extended families intact against the odds and where many other people have failed, including some who loudly proclaim the importance of the family and 'family values'. More to the point, this is *because* rather than *despite* the fact that Travellers and Gypsies minimise their involvement as employed labour. Nor does it end there. Far from being the parasites they are often alleged to be, most Travellers and Gypsies exemplify the enterprise culture espoused by 'Third Way' political ideologies, which champion 'small government', greater risk-taking, reduced safety nets and greater individual autonomy. In post-industrial Britain nomadic Traveller society is robust and successful on its own terms *because* of its flexible *pre*-industrial social organisation. Yet it pays the social cost of this in terms of high morbidity and mortality rates, stigma and psychological stress arising from inadequate state provision of caravan sites and the refusal of local authorities to give planning permission to Travellers when (in the absence of official sites) they buy land to build their own sites.

The German sociologist Tonniës posited a century ago that, unlike land and agriculture, *trade*, *travel* and *science* were inimical to 'community' or *gemeinschaft* (Worsley 1992). He also pointed out that 'community' does not necessarily depend on *habitat* or locus. Rather, he saw it evolving out of friendship or shared religion, which transcend habitat or site, and as involving urbanites as much as country people. In fact, his ideas about 'community' are similar to later ones about 'imagined communities' (Anderson 1994), where power, communication and networks are important. Tonniës's insights into 'community' without physical loci are therefore as pertinent today as are his remarks on travel, trade and science given that so many in the global village now live 'on the move' and in some cases go so far as likening their life-style to that of 'Gypsies'. One person who has critically extended notions of community beyond the idea of mere sites of habitation to that of 'sites of travel' is James Clifford (1992) who did so in his essay 'Travelling Cultures' and which he later (1997) enlarged, on thus serving indirectly to bring the hitherto marginal field of Gypsy-Traveller Studies *per se* into the anthropological mainstream as well as other travelling cultures.

The Gypsy Lore Society (GLS) was founded in 1888 and has existed ever since in relative academic obscurity, quietly publishing papers on every aspect of Gypsy social organisation and culture. However, in 2006 the Association of Social Anthropologists of the UK and Commonwealth (ASA), established in 1946, organised a conference around the problematic subject of 'Locating the Field' and called for papers on (among other things) '"travelling" or "touring" cultures', thereby bringing travel in from the anthropological margins. Today GLS conferences are advertised in the ASA's calendar of events. Moreover, as I write this, I notice that the GLS 2007 conference is being organised with the help of the Migrations and Diaspora Cultural Study Network of Manchester University, which underlines the increasing relevance of the GLS to contemporary affairs. No longer quaint or exotic, Traveller affairs are now deemed 'relevant' to policy. And this book tries to extend that sense of relevance by deepening the reader's acquaintance with Travellers, thereby building on the major contributions made by a small number of anthropologists to the study of Irish Traveller and British Gypsy cultures, long before the ASA conference was suggested.

I first became involved with Irish Travellers and Gypsies over twenty years ago, when I began work as warden of the Westway Travellers Site, in Notting Dale, west London, close to Shepherds Bush. At the time there was nothing like the volume of literature, conferences or activism surrounding Gypsies and Travellers that exists now, which is by no means to suggest that there was none. Nevertheless, the dearth of reliable writing on Irish Travellers, particularly in Britain, was one reason why I took the job and put in two years' work there.

A full explanation of why I chose to work on the Westway, both as warden and anthropologist, is provided in Chapter 1. Suffice it to say, here, that the reasons were as much personal (in the sense of psychological) as they were professional (in the sense of career-orientated). That is to say, they were as much tied to questions of my identity as one of the second-generation, post-war 'Irish', and linked with the 'kind of chronic rootlessness' that Lévi-Strauss (1976, 67) once commonly associated with anthropologists, as they were to any academic, professional, pragmatic or ideological issue. The reader is warned, therefore, that this book is more autobiographical than most other ethnographic studies. It eschews the notion of clinical detachment, but at the same time does not recoil from the idea of objectivity. Instead, it adopts the kind of framework that Professor David Pocock (1977) called 'personal anthropology', a *modus operandi* akin to what has since been dubbed 'auto-ethnography'.

Chapters 1 draws shamelessly on what it meant to me on a personal level to grow up 'hybrid', as one of the 'English–Irish' or second-generation 'London Irish', for whom stigma was part of ethnic identity. At the same time I step outside that subjectivity to see west London, and two districts of it in particular, with as much anthropological detachment or objectivity as possible. One, North Kensington and north Hammersmith, is where the Westway Traveller Site is located, and is the subject of Chapters 3 and 4. The other district, Barnes and Mortlake (here abbreviated to 'Mortlake', in accordance with ancient tradition) is where I lived while working at the site and where I grew up before I had even heard of 'anthropology' (see Chapter 5). Chapters 8, 9, and 10 deal as objectively as possible, and in detail, with the site itself.

Because ethnography is essentially a detailed description of a socio-cultural situation or setting, the analysis contained is usually firmly embedded within it. Furthermore, because I seek as wide an audience as possible, and not just an academic one, what theory I have used to select, shape, and interpret all that I have seen and heard is unobtrusive; at least, as unobtrusive, I hope, as a tourist's travel guide. In other words, having borrowed other people's ideas about what and how to see when 'travelling' sociologically, or how to interpret things afterwards, and found them useful, I pass them on to you without undue insistence.

One reason for going into the details of two districts, one north of the Thames, the other south, where Travellers, Gypsies and other people interact, is to deepen our understanding of the social fabric of suburbs; those residential areas situated betwixt countryside and city-centre whose wealth and statuses vary greatly with location and with time. With a view to seeing Irish Travellers and Gypsies in historical *and* geo-spatial contexts I have therefore incorporated the work of historians, including little-known local historians, and leant on novelists and biographers whose neo-realism has opened my eyes to the wonder of the western suburbs, which I was only half-aware of (and felt more than a little dejected about) when as a young man I decided to escape by getting into social anthropology, only to return there eventually.

Finally, an apology and explanation for taking so long in getting this book into print to the Travellers who encouraged me to write and must have given up waiting, to those who may be wondering what value there is in a text that draws on data substantially gathered twenty years ago, and to the publisher. The excuses for slow delivery are many and no doubt some are less convincing than others, but I will mention them all the same. They include the decision to move to Australia in 1987, the demands and upheavals of university life, involvement in other research projects, time required to sift and analyse uncatalogued field notes made before laptops existed, and the need for half a dozen return trips to England and Ireland to conduct follow-up interviews and do the kind of library research necessary to fill the gaps in my original data.

In a real sense all ethnography is history. To this extent, therefore, I trust the delay is not too consequential. In addition, all ethnography is at least implicitly (if not explicitly) comparative. We 'know this' about a culture because it is different from 'that one', so if in what follows I occasional make explicit comparisons to arrangements in other cultures, I hope they are insightful and not distracting.

Notes

1. *New Scotsman*, 23 April 2005.

1
ROUTES & REDIRECTIONS

I do not think one can access a writer's motives without knowing something of his early development. His subject matter will be determined by the age he lives in — at least this is true in tumultuous revolutionary ages like our own — but before he ever begins to write he will have acquired an emotional attitude from which he will never completely escape.
George Orwell, *Why I write*, 1947

Each person's work is, to some extent, an encounter of his or her own history. The intellectual problems one chooses to dig into, the tools one employs, and the perspective one takes up are so rooted in that history, or more precisely, in the questions raised by that history. So too are the sources of inspiration that keep one going.
Carol Delaney, The seed and the soil, 1991

'... the mobility of a population is unquestionably a very large factor in its intellectual development ... What mental characteristics of the gypsy, of the hobo, and of the nomad generally can be traced to these nomadic habits?'
'The City: Suggestions for the Investigation of Human Behaviour in the Urban Environment', in R.E. Park, The City, 6th edn., 1970 (1925), pp.18–20

Anthropology is concerned with the physical and cultural evolution of *Homo sapiens* and is so big in scope — 'the human condition', no less — that it is divided into half a dozen specialist sub-disciplines, or 'small "a"' anthropologies, that, for convenience's sake, we can think of as occurring in two large streams: *social* or *cultural anthropology* (sometimes called 'socio-cultural' anthropology) and *physical anthropology*.

Cultural or social anthropology is the study of Culture and

social systems and is closely related to history, sociology and various other social sciences, and, to some extent, the humanities. Physical anthropology focuses on Nature, or the biological side of the human condition, and is more closely joined to the natural sciences. In reality the two streams are interrelated: cultures evolve in adaptive response to Nature and Nature is changed by human cultures. Understanding how and why particular cultures evolve and adapt in the ways they do to nature, or else choose *not* to adapt (Diamond 2005), is clearly one of humankind's most urgent tasks.

Probably the most important fact about *Homo sapiens* is its capacity to learn. Indeed, by 'culture' anthropologists mean all those things humans learn and share with other people, as opposed to what is given to them by biology. Through learning, humans adapt to Nature — the natural environment; through Culture, the cultural environment, humans alter aspects of that same cultural environment, either *intentionally*, because they judge it desirable to change conduct and values, or *unintentionally*, in the course of making intended changes.

Some anthropologists call the process of learning and sharing new ideas 'enculturation'; others call it 'socialisation'. Whatever term we choose, we are talking about learning to be social, learning to share ideas and practices with other individuals, and learning to be members of groups or networks from which we derive a sense of community and identity.

Most human enculturation occurs informally and unselfconsciously in the course of everyday life. Where it occurs formally we speak of education, and since education is concerned ultimately with surviving and 'thriving', the access or otherwise that an individual or group has to it is a determining factor of their life-chances and future feelings of inclusion.

It follows, therefore, that in order to 'learn' an unfamiliar culture, an anthropologist must become sufficiently socialised in it to feel a semblance of owning it, the kind of feeling that comes from being able to operate in (and with) it like natives. For anthropologists, the professional path to this kind of socialisation is what they refer to as 'fieldwork'.

Fieldwork and ethnography

A cultural anthropologist's principal (but not only) task is to produce accurate, detailed, convincing descriptions of the culture (and social system) studied. These descriptions usually take the form of monographs we call ethnographies, but can also take the form of field reports or films akin to documentaries. No matter which form is chosen, however, in these guises the anthropologist is also known as an ethnographer.

In conducting fieldwork, ethnographers aim to gather as much empirical data as possible on their topic of interest from first-hand experience: from repeated observation; recorded interviews; conversations; overheard dialogue; and from actual *participation* in the lives of those they are studying. In doing so, they try to see from a variety of 'inside' perspectives, as locals do, and not just from their own, as outsiders. In contrast to the 'detachment' sought by most social scientists, the process described above calls for a degree of trust and friendship 'attachment' with one's subjects or, at least, with a cross-section of them. Without it, it is impossible to understand what people think about their cultural environment and what it means for their identity. An anthropologist's socialisation is thus not unlike a child's. A humbling, hesitant, experience, one learns by trial and error, by acquiring a new language, and by asking questions about things one's newly made friends and acquaintances largely take for granted. Mistakes are made; offence is given; and notes are written in the hope that sooner or later, subject to interrogation, they will reveal patterns and recurring themes.

Although the goal is to collect empirical data, all fieldwork is to some extent driven by 'theory' or explanatory ideas brought 'to' the field and not simply inferred 'from' the data, and the latter, *inductive*, method is more prominent in anthropology than is the former, *deductive*, method, which is typical of some other social sciences where there is an emphasis on measurement.

Most socio-cultural anthropologists today are less concerned with the 'scientific' measurement of cause-effect relations among variables identified at the beginning in carefully worded hypotheses than they are with combining the subjective meaning of other people's worlds with their own unfolding experience and understanding of it knowing that their personal attachment as fellow human beings to the people they study must be balanced by their 'detachment' as participant-observers: an equilibrium calling for art and intuition as well as a scientific attitude in pursuit of objective truths (see Clifford and Marcus 1986; Geertz 1988; Marcus 1998). They are much more likely to be concerned with exploring and interpreting relations between persons of different status (leaders and led; men and women; educated and uneducated, and so on); between groups; between social institutions (government and the military; the Church and industry); and between categories (such as class and ethnicity). In short, their ambit is *qualitative*, not quantitative, data, although they are not averse to the use of 'objectivity' or of quantitative analysis where needed. Fieldwork is always highly personal, but it is not entirely subjective.

Delaney (1991) knows as well as Orwell (1947) did that it helps to know something about the writer's background if you are to understand the work. For this reason, and no other, I therefore need to say something about myself, before expanding on the theory and method entailed in this work, since the inspiration that has kept this project going owes as much to my own roots and journey as it does to those of the Irish Travellers whose routes crossed mine.

Roots

My parents and three of my grandparents were born in Ireland. My father's father first emigrated from a village on Kerry's Atlantic coast in the late nineteenth century and got work in London. There, in Somerstown, he met and married my grandmother, the daughter of Irish immigrants, before settling in Mortlake, London, sw14. They returned to Kerry with two young children when their third, my father, was expected, and stayed for three years before returning to Mortlake and, soon afterwards, moving a mile away to Roehampton (sw15). I mention this only because it was my residing in Mortlake throughout my time with the Travellers and Gypsies near Shepherds Bush that led me to think seriously about the Gypsies and Travellers who lived in or passed through Mortlake and Roehampton.

My mother was born in the eastern county of Carlow and was raised by her mother and an uncle and aunt when her father was forced (by dint of disinheritance) to go, as a migrant labourer, first to Scotland, then to England, and eventually to America, where he made his way out west.

Before she married, my mother's mother, an O'Brien, had also lived in America, but only for a short time, as ill health compelled her to return to Carlow where in due course she married my grandfather, John Nolan. When, after a number of years, Nolan went to work on construction sites in Scotland, leaving her with children, and in effect taking leave of his family for good, my grandmother came to London, joining up with cousins in Roehampton where she got work as a servant in one of the big houses in the village. Sometime in the late 1920s she called my mother to join her, and it was in Roehampton that the Nolans and Griffins met.

I was the third of five children. By the time I was born, in Medfield Street, just below Putney Common (about which more later), my father's father was a widower and my mother's mother a widow. Both played important roles in our upbringing; first in Roehampton where my father was raised, and later in East Sheen, in the old parish of Mortlake, where we moved after the war.

When my grandfather John Griffin died in 1951 he was buried in the cemetery of St Mary Magdelene's church in Mortlake, near the High Street. Eighteen months later my grandmother Brigid Nolan died and was buried in Sheen, near the old Mortlake parish boundary with Richmond. A few weeks later, following her funeral (and incidentally Queen Elizabeth's coronation) I was sent to Ireland in the company of one of my father's acquaintances (although a stranger to me) and for the next three or four weeks I was to live among strangers in the countryside. It was my first journey abroad, and a *rite of passage* the full consequences of which would only dawn on me years later.

Routes

Ireland was, in the 1950s, still overwhelmingly rural, and exiles returning there from London travelled either by rail from Euston station to Holyhead (Anglesey, north Wales), and from there by steamer to Dun Laoghaire, Dublin, or else they took the southern route, via south Wales and Rosslare.

The farm on which I lived in County Wexford comprised several acres of dairy pasture and an oblong-shaped, single-storey, slate-roofed house surrounded by barns and outhouses. Water was drawn from a well in the yard, cooking was done on a large black range set in an old fireplace, lighting came courtesy of paraffin lamps, bathroom there was none, and the main means of family transport (though I think there was an occasional bus service) was horse and trap. To add to my sense of wonder, my hosts were previously unknown to me, strangers all, and me to them; they were close relatives of the friend of my father who had brought me there, a member of the Augustinian order who shared an interest in bees with my father and with his father before him. And so it was, here in countryside outside New Ross, far from the austerity of post-war London, that I was first acutely alerted to questions of culture and identity.

A second and rather different journey turned out to be more prosaic, but educational in its own way, partly because it occurred so soon after returning from Ireland and provided another contrast with my life up until then. Because instead of returning to my primary school, the Sacred Heart, in Roehampton, where my father, spinster aunt, and my grandfather before them had accommodation as caretakers, I was sent each day to preparatory school in Ealing (w5), on the other side of the Thames.

Holiday freedoms and years of family intimacy at primary school behind me, I was suddenly thrust into an each-way journey by bus and Underground, via Hammersmith, to savour the rigours of stern Benedictines. It was nothing less than acute culture shock. The journey was irksome, though not entirely without interest; the destination was purgatorial. Hammersmith Broadway was a site of passage, a locus of transients and transition, a place of labour movement, of Irish recreation and worship, and a truly urban benchmark for making sense of leafy suburbs like Mortlake, Barnes, Roehampton and Sheen, and Ealing, at the far end of the District line, where teachers and fellow Benedictine students were encouraged to hide all semblance of the working-class Irish connections that so many of us had.

There are still people who talk of Roehampton 'village', despite intensive housing development and massive growth of population since the first London County Council (LCC) flats were built on the Alton Estate in the 1960s. At its southern edge the 'village' sits alongside Putney Common, an extensive area of heath and woodland. To its west lie the 2,500 acres of land enclosed by Charles I in 1637, which stretch as far as Kingston-upon-Thames and Richmond and today constitute the largest of London's royal parks (Fletcher Jones 1972). For decades Roehampton was a famously pretty place, albeit located administratively, eventually, in the less than pretty Borough of Wandsworth. Today its densely built-up eastern side melds into Putney, which in turn blends into central Wandsworth proper (SW18), which urbanised rapidly in the nineteenth century.

I spent my first seven years in Roehampton before the family moved to East Sheen, just below Richmond Park, in what was then the Borough of Mortlake and Barnes. Sheen, or Shene, is the old name for Richmond (the name was changed in honour of Henry VII, Earl of Richmond), and means 'shining' or 'shiny', no doubt referring to the river at what is now Richmond-upon-Thames. East Sheen was simply a hamlet of Sheen (or Richmond) proper.

According to the Domesday Book, the great Norman land register of England, the manor of Mortlake included the villages of Putney, Barnes and Wimbledon as well as Mortlake, and throughout most of the medieval period was just as often known as Wimbledon Manor even though the main manor house was alongside the Thames at Mortlake. Not until the fourteenth century did Mortlake, along with East Sheen, become separate from Wimbledon.

Because of the historical links between Mortlake, East Sheen, Wimbledon, Putney and Barnes, and my early familiarity with them, which was revived when I lived there again while working on the Westway, I will treat them from here on as a single district — Mortlake — in order to compare them with North Kensington and Hammersmith, the second district, where the Westway Site is located. For my knowledge of Irish Travellers and Gypsies in North Kensington and north Hammersmith emerges from and is informed by my knowledge, research and recollections of living in Mortlake. And both areas contain strong pockets of Irish migrant history.

When my grandfather moved from Mortlake to Roehampton around the time of the First World War, he moved up in the world not just spatially but socially, for Roehampton had long been noted for its private rural estates and upper-class inhabitants; its parliamentarians, aristocrats, senior military men and its growing number of leading merchant bankers. It also sheltered two important Roman Catholic institutions: Manresa College, a Jesuit seminary overlooking Richmond Park; and a convent secondary school for upper-middle-class girls run by nuns of the Sacred Heart order. Both places had strong ties with the Continent, Spain and France respectively. It was into this environment of class, religion and learning that my grandfather stepped when he was made boiler-man and general factotum at the Sacred Heart convent (and later at the Sacred Heart primary school which opened in the 1920s) and went on to buy a cottage in the village. Among the girls who attended the convent in the 1930s were the actors Vivian Leigh and Maureen O'Sullivan, Patricia Kennedy, daughter of the American Ambassador, and sister of the future US President John F. Kennedy, and Mary Tew who in due course would become better known as Mary Douglas, a major figure in post-war British social anthropology whose special interest in ritual, symbols and cosmology would have a lasting intellectual influence both within and beyond academic anthropology (Farndon, 1999).

At the outbreak of war the convent school moved its teaching activities to Hammersmith Broadway, an area with a reputation for 'subversive' continental Romanism going back to Tudor times (Whitting 1965). Two of my sisters were educated there, one later attending Roehampton convent, which by then had become the Catholic women's teacher-training college known as Digby Stewart. In the 1970s, Digby Stewart College became the Roehampton Institute of Higher Education, part of the University of Surrey. Among its staff were several anthropologists, including John Eades, whose publications cover religion and pilgrimage. In 2004 the Institute obtained its own university charter, becoming the University of Roehampton.

In summary, a path that began for me in Roehampton at the Sacred Heart primary school, opposite the convent, where my grandfather worked when he came from Ireland, not only led me to anthropology, and back again years later to west London after fieldwork abroad, but took me into 'fieldwork' with Travellers and Gypsies in Hammersmith, a place of earlier interest on my daily journeys to Ealing by virtue of the contrasts it offered with Mortlake, and at the same time made me think of Travellers and Gypsies on my doorstep in Mortlake.

After (and even before) leaving school and working in the City, the 'Square Mile', I quickly discovered that Hammersmith was more than a place of hard-working immigrants, Irish pubs and accordion showbands, and more than a hangout for derelicts; it was a portal on to the 'world' by way of Harold Davison concerts at the Odeon cinema, involving visiting American jazz bands and orchestras. It led me to hear Louis Armstrong play at the Odeon in 1959 and to discover the Original Dixie Land Jazz played the Hammersmith Palais in 1921. With other jazz greats they made Hammersmith now appear exotic.

The Hammersmith public library stands opposite what in the early 1960s used to be the Palais, and I often studied there for my A-Levels alongside other importunate scholars and the homeless men who used to while away the hours there before bagging a bed at Rowton House, a lodging house or 'spike' on the Hammersmith

Road. I did not know then, of course, that twenty years later I'd be back doing historical research for this book. Rowton House stood next to Nazareth House, another Roman Catholic institution working with the poor, on the other side of the road from the Sacred Heart School.

Prior, therefore, to embarking on a degree in sociology at Kingston-upon-Thames I had developed an interest in 'outsiders' and in social and economic disparities. I had avidly read modern novels and would continue to do so. Orwell, Waugh, Steinbeck, Hemmingway and Greene were among my favourite writers. Orwell's *Down and Out in Paris and London* (1963), a sort of auto-ethnography, had cast a strong effect, and so, for reasons more to do with its Algerian setting than its existentialism, did Camus' *The Outsider* (1946). William Davies' *Autobiography of a supertramp* (1951) also impressed me, possibly because of the questions it raised for me about my maternal grandfather, who disappeared in Colorado after working on the railroads. In college I delighted in sociology and was excited to find Conrad Arensberg's *The Irish countryman* (1937) and Claude Lévi-Strauss's *Tristes Tropiques* (1976); two disparate books, their methodologies nevertheless appealed more than some of the statistical techniques I was confronting in sociology. They were my first introduction to 'real' anthropology.

Around this time, and even before, I found hitchhiking in Europe afforded a satisfying blend of unplanned travel and encounters with strangers. It was on one such trip that I had my first encounter with Gypsies: a young girl outside Skopje in Macedonia and, between Thessalonica and Istanbul, a youth who demanded my wallet. About this time I read Allsop's history of the American hobo, *Hard Travellin'* (1972); O'Connor's study of vagrancy in England, in which Irishmen were evident (1963); and Nels Andersen's *The Hobo* (1961). Postgraduate studies in social anthropology at Sussex University led to two years' fieldwork in France, but not on the subject of transhumance that I had originally proposed (only to be advised otherwise), but on Italian immigration and integration in the *departements* of Alpes Maritimes and Var just over the border from Italy; a study that, as it happened, made me think hard about 'strangers' and people 'passing through'. During this period I worked in both urban and rural environments. In Nice, the scope for traditional participation-observation was limited, and in the village, I found the rural patois daunting. Far from feeling that I'd 'arrived' in anthropology with my doctorate, I felt I had hardly begun. The question was: 'what next?'

Redirections

The ideal option was to pursue my curiosity with 'travelling people' by doing fieldwork among Irish Tinkers. However, Irish research funding was scarce in part because two American anthropologists had recently published an article on Travellers (Gmelch and Gmelch 1974) and were soon expected to publish books (S.B. Gmelch 1975; G. Gmelch 1977). A second possibility was to find a post-doctoral fellowship that would open up fieldwork in a more 'traditional' setting than the one I had worked in (especially in the city) and in the process hone the fieldwork skills — or lack thereof — I had acquired in France. A third idea was to find a university teaching position.

In the end, the second and third ideas were both met. I accepted a lecturing position at the University of the South Pacific and in May 1975 boarded a ship at Southampton, crossed the line with the last of the 'Ten Pound Poms' and many returning young Australians, and went on to New Zealand and the Islands.

Fiji occupied me for seven years and when it came to leaving I had few plans other than to take up a short Fellowship at London University's Institute of Commonwealth Studies. However, three things with interesting consequences unexpectedly turned up.

First, a year before I left Fiji, Joseph Berland, a psychological anthropologist, came to the University to teach for a semester and complete a book on Gypsies in Pakistan (Berland 1982). My old interest in nomads was reignited by his seminars and I thought again about working with Gypsies or Irish Travellers in England. Secondly, while I was in Fiji, my youngest sister had married someone involved in Gypsy education in England and Wales who had completed a postgraduate degree in sociology and anthropology focused on Gypsies. Thirdly, I was returning to live in west London with someone who had not previously visited the northern hemisphere; someone through whose eyes and experiences, as well as my own now more distanced view, I would began to re-evaluate 'home', if indeed it still was home.[1] The roles were reversed: she, a Fijian, was now the 'anthropologist' and I the marginal 'native informant'. Furthermore, the fact our home was by coincidence a rented flat in Sheen just five doors down the road from the house in which I had grown up and my mother still resided, meant she was an outsider in 'my' territory and I was an 'anthropologist at home'.

Grave matters

Graves have a special place in the lives of the living, not least in the lives of 'travelling people'. Graves reaffirm roots, free up new paths, and become our sites of return. When my father died the year before I left Fiji and was buried in the cemetery of St Mary Magdelenes, near other members of his family, one of my first tasks on returning was to visit his grave. Once again, this is where the personal and objective dimensions collided and lent inspiration to see this project through.

My father is buried in a plot that was being reserved for clergy until it was donated to the family, and lies within a few yards of the tomb of Richard Burton, the Victorian explorer, travel-writer, linguist and translator, Islamic scholar, ethnographer and author of *Gypsies, Jews and El Islam* (1898). A man who claimed Romany descent, Burton was also the co-founder (with Dr James Hunt), in 1862, of the London Anthropological Society (Lovell 1999).

Burton's tomb resembles an Arab tent (see below) and as a boy it intrigued me; however, my father was reluctant to talk about him for reasons, I presume, which had something to do with Burton's work as a translator of erotic literature, notably the *Kama Sutra*, and his lusty reputation for sex. It was not long, however, before I was able to find a copy of the *Kama Sutra*, and afterwards learnt something of his travels and adventures as a participant-observer in Asia. Only relatively recently, though, did I discover the graves of Romanies buried not ten minutes away from Burton and my father, in the old Mortlake cemetery in South Worple Way, and come across a benefactor of St Mary Magdelenes Church, in the 1960s and 70s, called Pharro.

Sir Richard Burton's (1821–90) tomb at Mortlake

The following map shows the relative proximity of the two main areas this book is concerned with: the *inner* London Boroughs of Hammersmith and Fulham and Kensington and Chelsea, situated north of the Thames, and the district I broadly call Mortlake (in line with historic facts), south of the river, that now forms part of the *outer* London Borough of Richmond-upon-Thames, and to a lesser extent part of the inner London Borough of Wandsworth.

When a newspaper advertisement appeared in May 1985 calling for a temporary warden for a Gypsy site, we were already living in a flat at 1, Richmond Park Road, East Sheen, a two-storey Edwardian villa that I had known (along with the boy my age I remembered once living there) nearly all my life, but which was now converted

London Borough Map. HMSO incorporating Ordnance Survey material. Copyright granted.

into flats. We were upstairs; beneath was an Australian couple on work visas. The word was that the landlord liked 'colonials' because sooner or later they 'moved on', and for that reason if no other we qualified. In fact, we were all global travellers, landlord included: he was a Scotsman living and working in Sydney, who left maintenance of the house to his father who, living in Perth, Scotland, we never saw. If this was the experience of just one house in the street, it must have been replicated in many others throughout the district, and was a reflection of the demand for rental accommodation inside an hour from the West End and three-quarters of an hour from Heathrow.

In short, if in an age of globalisation this to me was 'home', and I rather doubted it was, what did it mean to other travellers and sojourners, and how did their experience of culture, community and identity in one part of the world affect their experience of these things in other parts of the world, to some of which they might one day return? A tiny part of the answer was already becoming apparent through my wife's relations with locals in Mortlake.

Initially, she was a complete stranger among the locals who drank at *The Hare and Hounds* in Sheen, where my father had been a regular; but she was soon introducing me to people who had known him (and in one case, known my grandfather), people I may never have spoken to had I been left to my own devices. Intent on crossing the line into her new community she was doing now what I had previously done in fieldwork; namely, attempting to learn a culture through the kind of privileged observation and participation that can sometimes come from being a stranger or outsider. Her ability to cross the line in ways I may not have chosen to resulted in meetings with people who later turned out to be good informants when it came to local Gypsies.[2]

Crossing the line: studying community and identity

To talk of identity is to speak about 'community', about symbolic borders (Cohen 1987), and about crossing the line from one community to another, involving a change of personal status or, failing this, a limited kind of membership. In this sense, crossing the line shares something in common with those social journeys entailing hardship and new status opportunities *within* communities that Van Gennep (1960) called *rites of passage*. If we want to understand inter-community relations in an epoch of global travel, especially inter-ethnic relations, then it helps to understand how particular communities police their borders, choosing to let some people become enculturated while keeping others out. Indeed, it was growing up in London in the 1950s and 1960s and sensing this line between the 'English' and 'Irish' that eventually led me to sociology and then across the borders into socio-cultural anthropology whose raison d'être is the study of societies, cultures and identity (as witness the title of a monograph read by all students of my generation, Firth's *We, The Tikopia* (1936)).

As a newcomer to anthropology I had little interest in doing fieldwork in London and it would be another decade and a half before I did so. In fact I can hardly overestimate how much I wanted to do field research abroad. Moreover, in those days that is generally how it was. Fieldwork at home was generally thought likely to be sharper if one had first studied a community abroad and while it is possible I might have stayed in London if I had heeded the advice of Arnold Bennett's Mr Aked to his niece Adeline (back from the country), it is very unlikely. I was simply too hungry for fieldwork elsewhere. Besides, I only stumbled on Bennett's *A Man from the North* (1973; first published 1898), his first book, late in this Traveller research when my fieldwork was near complete and I no longer needed to be sold the intrinsic social interest of suburbs, let alone be persuaded of it by a late Victorian patriarch like Aked. 'Child! — his eyes were still closed — the suburbs, even Walham Green and Fulham, are full of interest, for those who can see it... Why child, there is more character within a hundred yards of this chair, than a hundred Balzacs could analyse in a hundred years' (1973, 68).

The 'science' of suburbs

Adeline hated London: 'I know practically nothing of London, real London, she said; but I think these suburbs are horrid — far duller than the dullest village. And the people! They seem so uninteresting, to have no character!'. Not so, Richard Larch, a newcomer from the north, who overheard this. On the contrary, Larch soaked up Aked's words and set about his work immediately.

Aked's advice to the newcomer 'from the north' shows that Aked was a man of his time: Bennett too, of course. What Aked was urging on him was a 'scientific' attitude called positivism, an approach to understanding society that would dominate sociology and social anthropology for the best part of a century. Consequently it is worthwhile hearing more of Mr Aked before moving on to consider newer approaches, including both the development of Bennett's own ideas about the evolving nature of modern society and its rational social organisation, and the development of more literary and other recent approaches to the study of cultures and society recommended by anthropologists themselves. So let us go back to Aked:

> 'Speaking roughly, each of the great suburban divisions has, for me at any rate, its own characteristics, its peculiar moral physiognomy.' Richard nodded appreciatively ... People have got into a way of sneering about suburbs. 'Why the suburbs, are London! It is alone the — the concussion of meeting suburbs in the centre of London that makes the city and West End interesting. We could show how the special characteristics of the different suburbs exert a subtle influence on the great central spots. Take Fulham; no one thinks anything of Fulham, but suppose it were swept off the face of the earth the effect would be to alter, for the seeing eye, the character of Piccadilly and the Strand and Cheapside. The play of one suburb on another and on the central haunts is as regular, as orderly, as calculable, as the law of gravity itself'
> ... Already, before a single idea had been reduced, to words, 'The Psychology of the Suburbs' was finished. A unique work! Other authors had taken an isolated spot here and there in the suburbs and dissected it, but none had viewed them in their complex entirety; none had attempted to extract from their incoherence a coherent philosophy, to deal with them sympathetically as Mr Aked and himself had done — or rather were to do.
> (Bennett 1973, 71–3).

Positivism argues for the use of natural science research methodologies when it comes to the study of society: the use of hypotheses, close observation, empirical testing, measurement, and ultimately the creation of scientific laws. For Mr Aked, positivism opened up the possibility of a 'psychology of the suburbs' that took into account their *moral* nature, or what Bennett's contemporary, the French sociologist Emile Durkheim (1858–1917), called the 'collective consciousness'. Such an approach would also examine the 'concussion' of suburbs (Bennett 1973) that made London more than the sum of its suburban parts, even though each part (street or neighbourhood) had its own 'moral physiognomy'. Aked and Arnold Bennett's idea of a 'psychology of the suburbs' called for observation of a suburb's role in sustaining the city as a whole, a 'psychology' more like the sociology of Durkheim than the wholly 'psychological' approaches to the city and its problems that the Frenchman found inadequate. Furthermore, Bennett's Aked considered the 'man from the north', with his outsider's perspective, well positioned to see the suburbs with scientific detachment.[3]

The Man from the North (1898) was Bennett's first novel. Both in his novels set in the Pottery towns where he grew up and sought escape to modernity and its metropolises, and in his later 'London' novels, Bennett promoted the virtues of modern rational social organisation, the idea of progress and an end to the sort of patriarchy or sexism clearly displayed in Aked's words to Adeline. Essentially an Edwardian 'modern' writer, as distinct from a 'modernist' of the kind Virginia Wolf identified with in her attempt to embrace tradition and cut Bennett and his like off from 'Georgians' like herself, Bennett moves towards revealing the irrational basis of character and thus the underlying psychology of persons, their 'unconscious fears and secret desires that were indiscernible from the distant perspective initially employed' (Squillace, 1997, 24).

Therefore, just as anthropologists in the 1920s and 30s were embarking on first-hand observation of customs and beliefs in so-called 'primitive' societies and coming up with 'functional' theories to explaining how such strange phenomena fitted into the 'system' as a whole, so 'the man from the north' could now turn to Walham Green or Fulham and expect to find equally remarkable 'social facts' worthy of social analysis. Indeed, American sociologists and anthropologists were doing just that in Boston, Chicago and Philadelphia, while in Britain investigators using 'social surveys' pursued the facts of urban social problems.

Lévi-Strauss described the anthropological perspective as the 'view from afar... a special title expressing what I consider the essence and originality of the anthropological approach, as illustrated by field work and laboratory experiment ... bearing on a wide range of subjects' (Lévi-Strauss 1987, xi). It captures his own commitment to a law-making science and resonates both with Bennett's early 'distant perspective' and his later interest in that which lies beneath the social surface. Like that of Durkheim, Malkinowski and Radcliffe-Brown before him, this was a scientific or, as some perhaps would have it, a more 'scientistic' perspective; a far cry from more recent post-modernist approaches that are sceptical if not downright dismissive of the very idea of objectivity when it comes to experts analysing and representing cultures be they their own or those of other people. For this reason Todorov's (1988) recalibration of Lévi-Strauss' view of anthropology being lofty or 'distant' is welcome; in practise, the ethnographer alternates between being 'close' to and 'distant' from the people he or she studies.

'Writing' moral systems

Over the past eighty years sociologists and anthropologists have not ceased to ask theoretical and methodological questions as well as empirical ones. Four are relevant to the present discussion: how should sociologists and anthropologists treat history? How should they treat 'social facts' systemically without allowing the approach to distort untidy realities? How might they devise models that take equal account of conflict and consensus, system-threatening and system-sustaining action, respectively? And how should they deal with individuals' subjective meanings without entirely relinquishing the goal of objectivity? I will deal with each very briefly in turn.

History

For some social scientists 'history' demands documentary evidence: written records. According to this view, non-literate people have no records which constitute reliable history: facts are not the same as myth or narrative. This led several generations of functionalist social anthropologists and sociologists, committed to positivism, to downplay oral history, native theory and native psychology *per se* in favour of *observable* behaviour and their own 'outsider' explanations. Exceptions to this rule included American *cultural* anthropologists like Franz Boas (1858–1942), and Bronislaw Malinowski (1884–1942) in British *social* anthropology who stressed the huge importance of 'the native point of view' and formulated a psychological- and biological-needs-based functionalism that was too 'reductionist' for 'sociological' anthropologists following Durkheim. Both Boas and Malinowski were originally trained in the physical sciences. By contrast, British social anthropologists who came under the theoretical influence of another famous anthropologist, A.R. Radcliffe-Brown (1881–1954), were inclined to eschew native commentary, indigenous theory and oral history, and it would take another generation of scholars in Britain to insert history, local theory and indigenous meaning, and thereby argue that social anthropology was more like history than a natural science. This book, like most contemporary anthropology, favours an attention to history.

Social systems
The positivist 'social systems' approach to societies and cultures taught by Radcliffe-Brown, when used in conjunction with intensive fieldwork as so brilliantly demonstrated by Malinowski, resulted in three decades of unusually productive research. However, an emphasis on tribes or villages as 'closed' systems was inadequate to explain radical social change in an interconnected, decolonising world, and it took the likes of Max Gluckman, Peter Worsley, F.G. Bailey[4], and Raymond Firth (Malinowski's student) to develop concepts of conflict, class-conflict, critical decision-making, and 'social organisation', to begin undoing the functionalist paradigm – though not its 'scientific' ethos. Arnold Bennett's 'concussion of meeting suburbs' and 'moral physiognomies' in London is therefore systemic in the old-fashioned positivist sense of 'as understood by a detached observer', rather than a concussion of minds embodied in men and women, or a concussion of 'imagined communities' (Anderson 1994) dependent on flesh-and-blood actors. This book sees merit in approaching the Westway Site

as a social system, but it also sees it as a system comprising men and women whose lives are *not* bounded by the concrete walls that literally surround them.

Conflict

Functionalist investigators with a positivist mind-set portrayed peasant and tribal 'social systems' as enjoying a state of systemic balance or homeostasis. This view arose both from their ignoring history in favour of the 'ethnographic present' (a portrayal of people 'now', in which history was ignored) and from their failure to take on board conflicts of interest originating outside the 'system'. Internal social conflict was thought to be controlled by various institutional checks and balances that allowed the system to remain intact. Some, like Gluckman, regarded endogenous conflict as a safety valve (Gluckman 1966; see also Barrett 1996). Aside from mavericks like Worsley, it was not until the 1970s that some anthropologists and 'underdevelopment' theorists used Marx to explain imbalances in a post-colonial capitalist 'world-system'. Up until then, and until a more recent awareness of 'globalisation', there was a tendency to see villages and tribes, even nations, as bounded systems unaffected by conflicts induced by outside powers. That, of course, won't do. Conflict arises in all communities and conflicts arise between communities. Indeed, conflicts 'inside' often have their source of origin 'outside'. In both cases, social conflict is a measure of community relations and the imbalance of power contained in those relations. One thing we shall be doing here, therefore, is examining both the internal and external sources of power-driven conflict.

Meaning

Durkheim examined the functions of ritual and symbols as if from a distance but it was Max Weber (1864–1920), a history-aware sociologist, who saw social action in terms of people's value-orientations and sense of meaning or understanding. This appreciation underlies what is now understood as 'social constructionism' (Berger and Luckman 1967), which argues positivism is mistaken when it states 'social facts' are 'things' *sui generis*, existing 'over-and-above' people, and constrain them; on the contrary, for social constructionists social arrangements are the way they are because people cause them to be that way and derive meanings from them. The American cultural anthropologist Clifford Geertz famously expressed this in his view of cultures as 'webs of meaning' (Geertz 1973). The point is that human beings are not just socialised *into* and *by* cultures they make and remake those cultures of socialisation. Thus sociologists and anthropologists do not simply observe what is 'out there', describe and classify, and in this way scientifically explain; rather, they select, interpret, and persuade by dint of evidence (including the evidence of local people's meanings). In this regard, as Evans-Pritchard (1962) insisted, anthropologists are more akin to historians than biologists and mathematicians, closer to 'writers' than scientists.

A book that did more than any other to draw attention to the 'writing' aspect of anthropology is *Writing Culture* (Clifford and Marcus 1986). Geertz's *Works and Lives* (1988) comes a close second. Pratt's article 'Fieldwork in Common Places', in the first of these books, reminds us that a lot of anthropology developed out of travel writing (see Stocking 2001). Clifford's essay, in the same collection, compares the writing of ethnography to the storyteller's use of allegory as effective 'performance'. He later argued that the sort of communities conventionally described by anthropologists were 'sites of travel' as much as sites of habitation, though you would not know it from the way most anthropologists described communties (Clifford 1992). The present book concerned as it is with commercial nomads and a caravan site therefore places emphasis on both these characters of 'community' — sites of residence *and* sites of travel.

Geertz's influence on what has been called anthropology's 'literary turn' and its distancing from 'scientism' can hardly be overestimated. His concept of 'blurred genres' (1973), suggesting anthropology to be a meld of scientific and literary approaches, had an impact on other social sciences and fields as well. His ideas borrowed from and built strongly upon those of his teacher, Robert Redfield, who helped pioneer anthropological studies of towns and urbanisation. Redfield's books *The little community* (1955) and *Peasant society and culture* (1956), moreover, are relevant when it comes to the Westway Site, its neighbourhood and Mortlake, and Travellers' relations with 'country people' or non-Travellers/non-Gypsies. Take, for example, this passage in *Peasant Society and Culture*:

> When the anthropologist studies an isolated primitive community, the context is that community and its local and immediate culture. When he comes to study a peasant community and its culture, the context is widened to include the elements of the great tradition that are or have been in interaction with what is local and immediate. If he is interested in the transformations that take place through this interaction (diachronic studies), he will investigate the communication of little and great traditions with each other and the changes that may have resulted or come to result in one or both because of the communication. If he regards the peasant village as a persisting system, as synchronic studies (perhaps limiting his view of the lapse of time to the three generations that are sometimes said to constitute the period within which the recurrent changes that sustain the system take place), he will include in the analysis the persisting and expectable communications from the great tradition to the village as these are necessary to maintain the culture of peasant. (Redfield 1960, 52–3, my emphasis)[5]

He ends by saying 'The anthropologist who studies one of these small societies finds it far from autonomous and comes to report and analyze it in its relations, societal and cultural, to state and to civilization' (Redfield 1960, 59, my emphasis). In other words, in studying the Westway, and Irish Travellers generally, it is important to view culture and community as changing in response to changes in the wider environment: the neighbourhood, metropolis, State, and world at large. Such changes have always occurred, but we need history to remind us of this: history lends the present meaning. The anthropologist's task is to represent that meaning to readers.

In *The Little Community*, first published in 1955, Redfield spelt out a prospect for anthropology that pre-empted the 'literary turn' developed by Geertz and others concerned with meaning, and which I have now arrived at via a discussion that began with Arnold Bennett:

> Perhaps then we shall find ourselves conceiving the community in terms of values or basic assumptions about life and experience, and imagine these as arranged in a sort of hierarchy of propositions, not like a machine or organism at all, but rather like a textbook on formal logic. Perhaps, in thinking about the way people of a small settlement, long established on the land, look out upon the life or man in the cosmos they know, we shall find ourselves using words and thoughts that do not readily find acceptance in the natural sciences, but rather are appropriate to drama or other forms of literary art. There may be models for conceiving the community that come to our minds from sources more artistic than scientific. (Redfield 1960, 16)

Locality and identity

As well as identifying themselves as 'Londoners', people whose sense of Self is inseparable from the landscape and life of the metropolis, most Londoners identify closely with *particular* localities. This is true of all metropolises and even small villages. For a time I lived in a French village of 608 people for whom the word *quartier* signified houses in a few adjacent streets and alleyways identified by a saint's name that differentiated them from the villagers in other *quartiers* with whom they sometimes had surprisingly little to do. *Quartier* was arguably the village equivalent of 'city suburb', and equated with 'neighbourhood' or *vosisnage*. It is not surprising, then, that one important source of spatially defined identity for Londoners is their suburb name and postal code; estate agents know this only too well. Cardinal and lesser compass points (NW,NE,SW,SE) relative to the Thames are key indicators and so are postal codes; the lower the number, the closer generally is the area to central London.

Memory sustains spatially defined identity. No matter how it is modified, 'belonging' (or Be-Longing) is not necessarily erased by mobility, emigration, displacement and resettlement. People belong to and identify with places they no longer live in or frequent, or, in some cases, with places they have *never* lived in. They do so by virtue of remembering and recalling, including the recollection of places that other people have passed on to them. Oral histories or memories of substance and recall are, like written history, thus 'another country' and this applies as much to Travellers and Gypsies as it does to so-called settled people.

Not all Irish Travellers and Gypsies are nomadic, and most who are tend to be *seasonal* nomads. Some Travellers live in houses for years. Many combine house dwelling with seasonal nomadism and some have never been nomadic. Court (1985) notes the case of one Bridget Murphy, an Irish Traveller and a hawker by trade, whose family never travelled. The same goes for Gypsies.

At the same time a growing number of non-Travellers, 'settled people', *gorgios*, 'buffers' or 'country people', are becoming increasingly mobile, whether for work, leisure, education, adventure or spiritual reasons. Millions of people each year are on the move, regularly travelling from one 'country' to another, and for some the 'travelling hopefully' is more rewarding than the arrival. It is not a new phenomenon, to be sure; what *is* new is the scale and the motivations that drive it.

Casual observers sometimes call travellers like this 'nomads' or 'Gypsies' and, in some cases, so do the travellers themselves. However, travellers like this usually have somewhere or other they call 'home'; a place to which they feel a special sense of 'belonging', which their travelling only serves to heighten or render more complex.[6]

The term 'Traveller', which for decades British Gypsies (as well as Irish and Scottish commercial nomads) have applied to themselves, is (to borrow Howard Becker's language) in other people's hands a 'master-identity' (1996) that dominates all others by emphasising mobility, in-betweenness, ambiguity and freedom at the expense of stability, certainty and social control. Travellers recognise this 'Othering' and at times subscribe to it themselves, but are equally aware that 'being' (or having identity) is in fact tied to named places or localities: ones to which they 'Be-long' and at times long-to-be in.

Whether Travellers also realise that they are in some cases transnational agents of globalisation, border-crossers *par excellence*, bridge-builders across locality or country, is not so certain.

Arrival

The advert called for someone to fill the temporary post of Gypsy Site warden in the inner London borough of Hammersmith and Fulham, a site I later found out was in the northeast of the borough, under the Westway flyover. The Housing officials who interviewed me said they wanted someone who could achieve rapport with residents, understand their 'culture' (a word they used repeatedly), and liaise between residents and the Housing Department until the Council and its neighbouring authority, Kensington and Chelsea, got news of the fate of an application placed before the Minister of the Environment for 'designation' under the rules laid down under the 1968 Caravan Sites Act.

'Designation' was granted, the officials explained, wherever central government agreed with a local authority in England and Wales that it was unable for good reason to provide an official site (whether or not it permitted or provided some sort of halting place already) and therefore might be exempted by the government from doing so. In this case, until a decision was made Hammersmith and Fulham would install a new site warden and manage the site properly as ordered by a court in a recent case brought against the local authority by Martin Ward, a Westway Site resident. Until that time, however, the job of warden was temporary. So it was that I was appointed, and began almost immediately.

Over the next few months nothing was heard about the

application for designation, and therefore nothing, either, about the renewal of my contract. Finding it impossible to live on the low wage and, without an increase, which was unlikely before a decision on designation, I would have to leave. I resigned at the end of 1984 and took a lecturing position in Bushey, Hertfordshire, from where coincidentally many of the first Romany settlers in Notting Dale came.

Fortunately, leaving the job did not mean severing my ties with Travellers entirely. Several times in 1985 I met up with an Irish family who had quit the site the previous August, and news filtered back to the site. When my teaching contract suddenly ended in December 1985, and I heard that my replacement on the Westway Site had moved on, I contacted Housing and was immediately reappointed. The reception I received from Travellers was universally warm, or so it seemed; the only obvious sour note came from a few non-Traveller members of the Westway Support Group. This time I would stay eighteen months; two years, all in, excluding five subsequent short visits.

Notes

1. Jackson (1987) along with others was among the first to raise questions about 'anthropology at home'. See also the work of two former colleagues of mine, Ruth Finnegan (1989) and Stanley Barrett (1994), for their studies of places returned to after years of fieldwork abroad.

2. Simmel's essay 'The Stranger' (translated 1950) is of immense importance here. See also Griffin (1999).

3. 'Attention to detail is Bennett's distinguishing trait, nothing being too trivial to be investigated and described' (*Chamber Biographical Dictionary* 1994, 123).

4. Bailey (1960) examined the changing fortunes of members of tribes and castes in the state of Orissa in the context of the newly independent India. He went on to study peasants in northern Italy where local scholar Dionigi Albera (1988) in the light of Gluckman (1964) accused Bailey of being cavalier with regional history and language, and inadequately connecting the small scene to the larger.

5. Marriot (1955) explained the unity of India as a 'civilization — an historic patchwork of political communities, religions, castes, and ethnic cultures — in terms of a Great Tradition and Little Tradition; the former being an intellectual tradition based on the classic Hindu texts and latter local and non-literate variations thereof; connected to each other to some extent by the role of traders and other travellers.'

6. Research on the social and psychological impact of travel on individuals who regularly or extensively travel away from 'home' is fairly new, as is interrogation of the very concept of 'home'. In Australia, where for years it has been the practice among suburban retirees to travel by car and caravan in winter in search of warmer climes and adventure, journalists have dubbed them 'grey nomads', yet to my knowledge no one has studied them. In contrast, research into industrial 'fly-in/fly-out' workers associated with the minerals industry in remote areas of Australia is well underway. In the US, Joel Kotkin has observed of San Francisco how 'Its once diverse population is increasingly bifurcated between the *nomadic* rich and a sizeable population of *servants* as well as a large homeless population' (*The Australian*, 20 February 2006; my emphasis).

2

EMIGRÉS & WANDERERS: LABOURERS, TINKERS, GYPSIES

It is not because men are alike that they are social, but because they are different.
Robert E. Park, *The city*, 1925

To the peasants of old times, the world outside their own direct experience was a region of vagueness and mystery: to their untravelled thought a state of wandering was a conception as dim as the winter life of swallows that came back with the spring; and even a settler if he came from distant parts hardly ever ceased to be viewed with a remnant of distrust ... All cleverness, whether in the rapid use of that difficult instrument the tongue, or in some other art unfamiliar to villages, was itself suspicious ... In this way it came to pass that those scattered linen-weavers — emigrants from the town into the country — were to the last regarded as aliens by their rustic neighbours...
George Eliot, *Silas Marner*, 1861

How we see people 'now' is shaped by our previous perceptions of them. This chapter, therefore, draws on the work of historians in order to sketch in the background to Irish settlement in Britain, in which we can then situate Irish Travellers as immigrants and relate their lives to those of other people in west London with whom they interact and share certain aspects of culture.

The early history of Irish settlement in Britain was marked by Irish raids on Wales and the West country in Roman and pre-Roman times, and the settlement of Irish monks in Scotland, Wales and northern and south-western England during the sixth century; leaving these aside, our story begins in 1172 with Henry II, the Norman king of England.

1172–1600

Henry II had two reasons for invading Ireland: he wished to control and consolidate the gains made by his Norman vassals and — with papal benediction — to bring the Irish church under the authority of Canterbury and Rome. In the end he acquired part of the eastern territory and the Viking towns of Dublin, Wexford, Waterford and Cork. This laid the groundwork for future English claims on Ireland that would culminate in the Battle of Kinsale (1601) and the flight of Irish nobles to the Continent, and a further four hundred years of dispossession by the English.

In 1942 the Irish nationalist, Sean O'Faolain, shared historian David Mathew's view when he stated that '[With] England's decision to make [Ireland] her first real colony, two civilizations became interlocked that were in spirit utterly divergent ... It is the same forced juncture of modernity and antiquity that comes with every imperial conquest, whether it is the conquest of Mexico by the Spaniards, or the colonization of India by the Hanoverians, or the plantation of Ireland by the Tudors ... The mutual incomprehension of the Irish chieftains and the officials of the New Monarchy suggest that the Irish wars would have been inevitable even if Catholicism had remained the state religion of England. Doctrinal differences only served to embitter the struggle and to emphasize its cause — the fundamental divergence between the Celtic conception of a ruler and the new conception of a State' (O'Faolain 1942, 4–10).

This, then, was a 'clash of civilisations'. A head-on clash between indigenous kingdoms with a single culture and an utterly foreign feudal state with colonising ambitions; a clash of cultures in which (as so often is the case) substantial numbers of the colonised slowly ended up living in the coloniser's own land doing the work the indigenes didn't want, so long as demand lasted. Thus in 1243 a statute directed local authorities in England to expel all Irish beggars.[1]

In 1349, a year after the Black Death, an English statute outlawed vagrancy, and in 1351 the Statute of Labourers tried to prevent freemen and runaway serfs from going to the new towns and leaving the Crown and other big landowners without harvest labourers (Chambliss 1964). Perhaps because of this, and an Irish readiness to provide the needed labour to the point, later, of oversupply, that Henry V passed laws in 1413 to expel all Irish people from England except those attending university. This was a restriction on movement foreign to the Irish.

Crossing the Irish Sea for England's cereal harvest was to some extent an extension of an old form of transhumance known as *booleying*—about which I will say more in Chapter 7—that inevitably led some Irish to overstay for the next year and thus in certain cases take on the beggar's mantle. By Tudor times Irish people were found in the emerging new towns and over the course of the following years more joined them. In the eighteenth and nineteenth centuries Irish drovers bringing cattle to British markets were another part of the landscape (Evans 1966). So too, well into the twentieth, were the traditional seasonal harvesters called by some people the 'autumn boys', among whom may have been some Tinkers.[2]

Tinkers or tinsmiths
According to the *Oxford English Dictionary* (OED 1989) the words 'Tinkler' and 'tynkere' first appeared as trade or surnames in Scotland in 1175, and in England in 1265. Contrary to Gmelch and Gmelch (1974, 229) and George Gmelch who say '*tinker* and *tynkere* started to appear in written records as trade names or surnames' by 1175 (1975, 9) thereby concluding this was the case in *Ireland*, 1175 is not the date 'tinker' first appeared in that country.

Written English variations on tinkler and tynkere included tynekere, tinkere, tinkeler, tincker, tinker and tinkard. The last of these came from lowland Scottish Gaelic, *caird* or *kaird*, meaning 'artificer in metal, tinker, blackguard'. *Caird* is cognate with both the old Irish *cerd* and *cert* and the Irish Gaelic *ceard*, meaning 'artist, artificer, metal worker, tinker' (OED 1989). It is therefore apparent from this that *ceard* and *tinceir* (the modern Irish for 'tinker') are related. By the seventeenth century tynner and tynne-man were also in use in England and were later written as 'tinner' and 'tinman'.

Tinne Ceards
As well as 'smith', the old Irish *cerd* and *cert* referred to the 'artificer, artist, composer, and poet' (OED 1989), suggesting that the smith's vocation shared something in common with that of the poet, storyteller or *word smith*; the source is not hard to find. Storytellers, poets, praise-singers and bards flourish in many oral cultures and their ritual words are thought to have intrinsic power. Furthermore, like smiths working with metal, those working with words often belong to ambulant castes thought vaguely 'dangerous'.

Homer described the god Hermes as 'a smooth talker and stealthy'. In Hermes, metal and verbal artifice, trickery and 'trade', were found together. One who is 'stealthy' is thought apt to steal. The person caught stealing (or about to steal) may 'talk his way out of it' (Brown, 1990). The power of the smith as a fabricator has thus, since ancient times, been universally feared and valued (Vogel 2000). Tinkers are usually repairers or fabricators of inexpensive goods who, if they are itinerant, as indeed in most parts of the world they are, are held in low regard on two counts; first, their relative lack of skill compared to other smiths, and second because as outsiders their activities are not fully accountable to the communities they serve. A similar sentiment to the former, incidentally, also attaches to the work of the 'cobbler', a word derived from the Latin *cerdo* that is related to *ceard;* for unlike the shoemaker proper the cobbler is a mere repairer of shoes.

Artelia Court, in her book on the oral literature of Irish Tinkers, argues that the word 'tinker' has probably nothing to do with the word 'tinkling', as in a hammer striking metal (Court 1985, 212–13 n.41, 216 n.62), as has sometimes been suggested. But I would go further and suggest that the phoneme 'tin' in 'Tinker' that, to English ears, suggests *base* metal, is far more likely to derive from the Gaelic *tinne* meaning 'mass of metal from smelting furnace', 'pig' or 'ingot of gold or silver', in other words *precious* metal, not base, and is thus consistent with the label *tinne ceard* meaning 'skilled' artificer. If so, then it can reasonably be suggested, as some scholars have already hypothesised,[3] that some modern Irish Travellers at least (not all) are descended from those Irish craftsmen of the Bronze Age who combined the work of precious-metalworker and wordsmith. A far cry from the tinker whose name, Lister said, 'is a byword for shoddiness, for lack of social respectability, [and who is] often a gipsy [sic] or diddecoy, at best an itinerant repairer of pots and pans, such as may still be met with in Ireland' (Lister 1966, 92). Over the centuries after the disappearance of the great Bronze Age craftsmen and, much later, under hegemonic colonial influence, it is easy to see how the English phoneme 'tin' would in time have superseded the Gaelic Irish *tinne*, especially as the modern Tinker actually worked in tin sheet. Support for this theory is further strengthened knowing that the Gaelic Irish word for tin was not 'tin' at all but *stàn* and that the modern Irish word is *stánáim*.

According to Lister, 'The tinker is a repairer, especially an itinerant repairer of such domestic products of the coppersmith, whitesmith or tinplate worker, as kettles, pans, pots and jugs. The whitesmith himself is a highly skilled worker' (Lister 1996, 97). The whitesmith worked with tin plate, like the tinker, but, like the pewterer, turned out objects of high quality, which in turn bestowed much higher social status than that given the tinker. Whitesmithing seems to be of relatively recent origin and is 'related to the ancient craft of the armourer ... [while] its even more closely-related trades of the pewterer and the lead worker are of great antiquity'. Indeed, 'there was a company of wire-drawers in the 16th century, and it was probably out of that the Worshipful Company of Tin Plate Workers, alias Wire Workers, was formed', getting 'its Letters Patent in 1670 from Charles II ... the only city company with an alias in its title' (Lister 1996, 100). Considering how wire drawing (whether by tinsmiths or anyone else) was previously associated with the manufacture of armour, it is worth recalling Artelia Court saying 'The possibility that Tinkers' and Gypsies' work with tin plate may have evolved from a historical involvement with armory or armed forces invites further investigation' (Court 1985, 216 n.63).

Tinkers and Gypsies in Shakespeare
'Egyptians', meaning Gypsies, never appear on stage in any of Shakespeare's plays and there is no reason to think his tinkers were anything but English. Yet seeing as the first reference to Romanies in England was made in 1514, and in Scotland in 1505 (Fraser 1995, 111–112), fifty years before Shakespeare's birth, giving him ample time to have heard about Gypsies and of Henry VIII's legislation declaring them a 'problem', it is appropriate to consider his plays, if only for the sake of providing insight on the historical reputation of 'tinkers' and Gypsies.

In *Henry IV*, Hal the young Prince of Wales, in the Boar's Head tavern, summarises his social life with the lads of Eastcheap: 'To conclude, I am so good a proficient in one quarter of an hour, that I can drink with any tinker in his own language during my life' (Part 1, II,IV). The nineteenth century American gypsiologist, Leland, generally accredited with being the first scholar to identify Shelta as a distinct language, to begin with took this to mean Henry's drinking pals were Irish, but later changed his mind. Mcalister (1976), an authority on Ireland's secret languages, and Vesey-Fitzgerald (1944), also rejected the notion of Henry's friends being Irish. Tinkers employing a trade argot had lived alongside a wide variety of 'travellers' in England since at least the Middle Ages (Jusserand 1891). Which is not to say the tinkers who spoke Shelta in the slums of Victorian England were not mostly Irish, nor to say they were not socially closely connected to Gypsies. Indeed, according to Leland most Shelta-speakers in the cities knew Romani and for this reason he said, 'I class it with the Gypsy' (1882, p.v cited in Acton 1974, 89). Kellow Chesney borrowing presumably from Leland went further when having noted few Irish could have been better adapted to deal with the 'change of country or to dodge repatriation in the bitter days of the late forties' than

Shelta-speaking nomads, added 'Fairly clearly in Victorian times these people of Irish origin formed at least the hard core of the vagrant tinkers. For some years after the mid-century Shelta is said to have been so common that it was virtually impossible to take a walk through the London slums without hearing it spoken — though one may doubt if many literate observers could have distinguished it from ordinary Erse' (1972, 93). Exactly, and had Henry's tinkers been Irish their speech would have included Irish Gaelic, an identifier in England hard to overlook. There is one other matter. Henry IV reigned from 1367 to 1413, long before Gypsies are thought to have arrived in Britain, but even allowing for artistic license it is hard to think why Shakespeare would *not* have explicitly identified the king's friends as 'Irish' tinkers if indeed they were. This is all the more true considering how in other plays he readily identifies Scots, Welsh, and Irish people as members of ethnic minorities by their minority names and dialects (Lonergan 2004),[4] and is centre stage with his Jew and Moor. The same goes for Christopher Sly in *The Taming of the Shrew* (1594): 'old Sly's son of Burtonheath; by birth a pedlar, by education a card-maker, by transmutation a bear-herd, and now by present profession a tinker?' (Induction, 11) who drunkenly boasted (Induction, 1) his ancestors 'no rogues'; 'came in with Richard Conqueror' — when he meant to say 'William the Conqueror'.[5]

The Winter's Tale was written sometime between 1609 and 1613. In it the 'rogue' Autolycus, who is neither Irish nor a tinker, is 'married to a tinker's wife', goes to 'wakes, fairs, and bear-baitings', and sings of a 'sow-skin budget', the tinker's tool bag. By naming him Autolycus, literally 'very wolf', Shakespeare alludes to the Greek god Hermes, notable 'trickster' and 'god of the wasteland' or border (Brown 1990), thereby drawing that connection between stealth, tinkers and trickery which stubbornly still clings as part of the negative stereotype to Travellers.

There are no obvious Gypsy characters in Shakespeare's plays, only a few brief references. For example, Fraser (1995, 136 n.8) reminds us of the line in *As You Like It* (one of the later plays, written around 1598),[6] 'Both in tune like two gipsies on a horse'. In *A*

Midsummer Night's Dream, also from the late period, the monstrous figure Caliban may well have been inspired by Gypsies, according to Vaughan and Vaughan (1991) who say the name derives from the Romani *kali ben*, meaning 'black devil'. Not everyone agrees. According to Stokes (1970, 53) Caliban is 'a metathesis of Canibal — the Indians [reputed man-eaters] seen by Columbus as "Caribes Canibales" and their country "Calibana"'. Ben Jonson (1572–1637), Shakespeare's contemporary, is more transparent in his poem 'On Gypsee':[7]

> Gypsee, new bawd, is turned physitian,
> And gets more gold than all the colledge can:
> Such her quaint practise is, so it allures,
> For what she gave, a whore; a bawed shee cures.
> (George Burke Johnston 1962)

In *Othello* (1599–1606) the playwright deals entirely without animus with a matter Romany when he has the Moor, another outsider, declare:

> That handkerchief
> Did an Egyptian to my mother give;
> She was a charmer, and could almost read
> The thoughts of people: she told her while she kept it,
> 'Twould make her amiable, and subdue my father
> Entirely to her love; but if she lost it
> Or made a gift of it, my father's eye
> Should hold her loathed, and his spirits should hunt
> After new fancies: she dying gave it me;
> And bid me, when my fate would have me wive,
> To give it her. I did so: and take heed on't; (III.IV.54–64)

If anything there is a hint of fondness.

At this time in England Gypsies were sometimes known as 'moonmen' (Salgado 1977) because of their habit of travelling by night, intent presumably on evading some of the draconian anti-Gypsy legislation brought in by Elizabeth I and before her by Henry

VIII. One such piece of legislation from 1530, describing 'Egyptians' as 'subtyll' and of 'crafty meanes to deceyve', aimed to stop them entering the country and to expel them if they did (Fraser 1995, 113–115). In 1536, Thomas Cromwell, the Chancellor of the Exchequer and son of a Putney blacksmith, weaver, publican and brewer, criticised local authorities for not upholding this law and ordered them to execute those Gypsies who refused to leave. Further anti-Gypsy legislation followed in 1544, and again in 1550 with the Act of Tinkers and Pedlars, although by now 'most contemporary observers ... made a clear distinction between gypsies and English vagabonds' (Salgado 1977, 155). That being so, the wording of another Act is instructive. A 1562 Act 'for further Punishment of Vagabonds, calling themselves Egyptians' did clarify that Gypsies born in England and Wales could not be forced out of the country, and to this extent applied especially to those who 'pretend' to be 'Egyptian'. According to Fraser (1995, 133) the latter referred not so much to *gorgios* pretending to be Gypsies, but to people born of Gypsy parents in England and Wales (Fraser 1995, 133). Nevertheless the Act was aimed directly at ending what Fraser paraphrases as the Gypsies' alleged 'idle and ungodly life and company' (1995, 133), and approved death and confiscation of lands and property for all those caught 'pretending' to be Egyptians. While there is no clear evidence to suggest the sanctions were aimed particularly at Irish Tinkers there are Traveller advocates like McDonagh (in Sheehan 2000) who believe the Act proves Irish Travellers lived in Ireland and in Britain at this time.

Elizabeth I settled 10,000 colonists in Munster before turning her attention to Ulster (de Paor, 1986). James I added another 100,000 Scottish Presbyterians. Subsequent dispossession and displacement were followed by the enslavement of thousands of Irish in England's Caribbean plantations (Becket 1986). Between 1641 and 1652 Cromwell followed up by slaughtering half the Irish nation, reducing it to 400,000 and forcing another 34,000, under the Act of Settlement (1652), to seek asylum on the Continent. Shakespeare, who died in 1616, lived to know only half the story.

1600–1900s

In the early seventeenth century the main Irish settlement in London was St Giles in the Fields, near Holborn. Other areas in which the Irish settled were Whitechapel, in the east, and Marylebone, in the north (George 1966). Many had come to England as seasonal agricultural labourers before making their way to the city, where they got work as building labourers, porters, coalmen, milk sellers, sedan-chair carriers, hawkers and, in due course, publicans and lodging-house keepers (George 1966). Countless Irish must have been victims of the Plague (1665) and Great Fire (1666), and many must have helped rebuild London afterwards.

The 'pull' reasons for Irish emigration were the economic opportunities presented in England by rapid urbanisation associated with industrialisation, as suggested above, and the lure of the military's 'Saxon coin'. The 'push' reasons are obvious: dispossession; poverty brought about by displacement and genocide; and, ironically, cultural hegemony. William Cobbett visited Ireland in 1834 and, in a letter addressed to 'the sensible and just people of England', was scathing in his analysis of the causes of Irish poverty:

> You will easily suppose that it must be a prime object with the sons and daughters of corruption, with those who wish Ireland to be kept in the state which I have described to you in my letters to my labourer Marshall; who wish that the great landowners of Ireland may continue to draw away all the fruits of this fine country while those who till the land are driven to live upon food worse that that of the hogs which they rear to be sent away; who wish even the farmers of Ireland to be a great swarm of beggars, not tasting meat nor bread from year's end to year's end, and the greater part of them clothed worse than the common beggars in England; who wish that the landowners of Ireland may still possess the power of driving the people off the land of their birth, and compelling them to perish with hunger,

and with cold on the bare ground, or to go to foreign
lands there to perish, or perish on board a crowded and
filthy ship; who wish that the people of Ireland may
still be compelled to render tithes to a church to which
they do not belong, and which they hold in abhorrence.
(Cobbett 1984, 159)

In the second half of the eighteenth century, radicalism drawn from France and America had taken root among the working classes in England, of which the Irish formed part, as well as among the Irish at home chafing under English rule. To pre-existing cultural (including religious) differences and anti-English sentiments was thus added a democratic radicalism inspired by the likes of Thomas Paine. By the late 1700s radical organisations like the London Corresponding Society (LCS) had established provincial branches in fast-expanding towns across the length and breadth of England, including Manchester, Sheffield and Norwich (Thompson 1968, 117–18), where the Irish were conspicuous in LCS activities. When anti-Jacobin forces tried to destroy Thomas Hardy's London home in 1797 'the attack was beaten off by a guard of 100 members of the LCS, many of them Irish, armed with good shillelaghs' (Thompson 1968, 118); as well they might, considering the LCS included 'Irish coal heavers on the Thames' (Thompson 1968, 186). In Manchester LCS members included Irish soldiers in the Light Dragoons, and in Sheffield, where wire and tinplate workers became involved in the LCS, Irish people were again prominent (Thompson 1968, 171–2).

A central tenet of eighteenth-century British political philosophy owed its origins to the view held by sixteenth-century philosopher Thomas Hobbes that the State (or monarch) alone could never guarantee citizens social order and it was necessary, therefore, for both sides to enter a social compact wherein the ruled relinquished certain freedoms in return for the other's rule-of-law. On the basis of this principle eighteenth-century governments introduced laws both to curtail vagrancy or 'undesirable' travelling, and to deal with the growing problem of poverty and the costs borne by parishes in trying to alleviate it (George 1966, 116).

Corporate towns attempted to curb labour movement and resettlement and relieve the pressure on parishes in four ways, variously applied: by demolishing empty houses; by discouraging marriages between locals and newcomers; by stopping youths seeking apprenticeships outside their parishes; and by compelling strangers to go home (George 1966). Unfortunately for the authorities, these actions often had just the opposite effect to those intended, with particular consequences for seasonal Irish migrant labour. Instead of deterring travel, those best equipped to do so were encouraged to move as fast possible to the largest towns from where a good many English were emigrating to America and there become absorbed in the workforce before they were detected. Second, by forcing people back to their own villages, the laws removed labour from where it was most needed, namely those former market towns now rapidly industrialising. A third effect, though, was by the far the most ironic. Because 'vagrants' were given passes allowing them to beg on their supervised return journeys home, the Poor Laws encouraged the very behaviour that they were intended to control: a good example of those unintended consequences of cultural change I mentioned at the start of Chapter 1. Consequently it was common for the travelling Irish, who were anxious to return home with as much of their savings intact as possible, to request they be officially classed as 'vagrants' and expelled; a quintessentially 'Irish' piece of opportunism, surely, if ever there was. Meanwhile many who did not ask to be expelled, but were rounded up anyway, managed to elude their captors. The paradox, then, is that the Irish were both among the few to satisfy the criteria for application of the vagrancy laws and among those who most benefited from them (George 1966, 155-7).

In 1795 and 1796 changes were made to the Poor Laws which were designed to encourage people to remain in their parishes on local relief rather than move away and lose it. By the time the changes bit, though, in the 1820s and 1830s, the supply of labour in the countryside was greater than demand, and the demand in the towns greater than supply; a demand that the Irish rose to meet.

By the end of the eighteenth century Ireland's population was among the fastest growing in Europe. On a hefty diet of potatoes supplemented by dairy products, cabbage, other vegetables, fish and bacon, it grew 172 per cent between 1779 and 1814. By 1841 the total population reached over eight million. Then, in 1845, the blight *Phytophera infestans* struck the potato crop, blackening the fields, poisoning the air, and triggering the greatest natural catastrophe in Europe since the Black Death.

Robert Peel, the British Prime Minister, tried to repeal the Corn Laws, which protected cereal prices, in the hope of shipping grain to Ireland. He met resistance from his fellow Tories, however, and was forced to import maize, or 'Indian corn', from America. To add to this crisis, 1846 was the coldest winter in memory. By 1851 the population, which, allowing for the previous rate of natural increase, should have registered nine million, was reduced by death and emigration to 6.5 million (Woodham-Smith 1991, 411). Thousands starved or succumbed to typhus and unburied corpses littered the countryside. By April/May 1847 tens of thousands of peasants streamed into every part of Britain via Scotland and the ports of Liverpool and South Wales. In Liverpool alone, between January and June 1847, an additional 300,000 Irish joined a local population of 250,000 (Woodham-Smith 1991, 276). The city housed more Irish-born people than any other in Britain, far ahead of Glasgow, Manchester and London. The sick, alas, were often forced home under an Act dealing with Irish paupers. Thousands more headed to America, most of them on so-called 'coffin ships'.

In London they settled in overcrowded slums like that of St Giles in the city centre. In the countryside vast mobs of tramps and beggars, sometimes hundreds-strong, presented insurmountable problems for the casual wards and pauper relief. The blight recurred in mid-1848, bringing havoc the following winter. Between November and January 1848/1849, 11,000 people landed in Liverpool alone (Scally 1995). Further outbreaks of blight occurred in 1852 and 1879 (Scally 1995, 407).

Exactly how many died directly of starvation, typhus or from a cholera outbreak in 1849 is open to question. Some provinces fared better than others; Leinster and east Ulster were the least affected, Munster was the worst. In estimating the Famine's impact on demographics, one must also appreciate that the downward trend in population began before the 1840s and that putting an end to partible inheritance, alongside clearances, had already made America the destination of choice by the 1850s (McMahon 1996). McMahon puts the total figure for emigrants to America up to 1900 at around five million (McMahon 1996, 134). Altogether, perhaps 2.5 million died or emigrated between 1845 and 1849, while another five million emigrated between 1852 and 1910, a fifth to one-quarter of these to Britain (Davis 1991, 11). From this point onwards, the Irish would be found in almost every rural and urban community in Britain.

By 1841 some 400,000 Irish people lived in Britain, mostly in the bigger towns; thousands more were of the second-generation (Thompson 1968, 469). Drawn from every part of Ireland, Protestants and Catholics alike (but mostly Catholics), they 'differed greatly from each other', and this often led to sudden and bloody internal eruptions that, to the amazement of their English neighbours, were just as quickly finished and forgotten: 'Constantly fighting among themselves, they turned as one man if any individual was attacked from outside. Attempts to seize illicit stills led to use of cutlasses and brickbats, in which the Irish women were not the most backward' (Thompson 1968, 476–7). It would sound like caricature were the source not so reliable.

London, by the seventeenth century, was a 'multi-centred' city, comprising small patches of wealth and poverty not just at its extremities, the unfolding and well-planned West End and the haphazard East End, but throughout the city (Golden 1981). This metropolitan patchwork became even more evident in the course of the next two centuries, and by the 1800s one such patch stood out in Kensington. A tenement slum defined by high walls (Lovrick 1849), Jennings Building stood a mere hundred feet from the gates of Kensington Palace. Of its 836 residents, over 500 were Irish. Some were building labourers, others worked in the market gardens in Hammersmith, many were street traders, and not a few were charwomen. So bad was Jennings Building that towards the end of the century even the local authorities viewed it with alarm and on health grounds eventually decided to raze it. Meanwhile, a mile away in North Kensington two other patches of deprivation and privilege were Notting Dale and Notting Hill (see Chapter 3).

Social reformer Charles Booth described the occupants in places like Shelter Street, near Drury Lane, where in the 1880s Irish families occupied twenty out of every thirty houses (Fried and Elman 1971) as 'living like pigs'. Unlike the so-called 'little Irelands' of Liverpool and Manchester, London's Irish did not form ethnically distinct quarters. On the other hand, the use of loose expressions like 'little Ireland' may be misleading. After the first Famine influx into Manchester there was, according to some writers, little intermarriage with the English until well into the twentieth century. As one eyewitness put it: 'Until the coming of the coloured people, Irish Roman Catholic immigrants, mostly illiterate, formed the lowest socio-economic stratum. A slum Protestant marrying into the milieu suffered a severe loss of face. Such unions seldom occurred' (Roberts 1971, 23 n.8). This is not to say, however, the Irish formed ghettos.

In London they occupied particular streets, courts, and back alleys in the poorer districts (Lees 1979; Thompson 1968) but were sufficiently integrated by the 1850s for Henry Mayhew to call the second generation 'Irish cockneys' (Mayhew 1985). Most important of all, perhaps, in sociological terms, was not so much their cultural 'difference' from the English as their ubiquity. Even 'Irish Court' in Lambeth, south London, home to Patrick Hooligan in Clarence Rooks's fiction (1979), was less an Irish 'ghetto' than just another London slum, a slum where, according to Alf, the author's hero, Oxbridge toffs came to 'slum it', hoping to experience 'darkest Africa' at home. 'Fort they was going to see 'orrors ... they didn't see nuffink. I know that sort. Come down just as if they were going to look at a lot of wild beasties' (Rooks 1979, 117).

Despite racism and ridicule, as Roberts (1971, 110) recalls them at first-hand in Manchester, or being depicted as apes in *Punch* (Curtis

1985), the Irish experience in England in the 1900s was anything but uniformly negative (Davis 1991). In 'English eyes, the men and women of Ireland were a paradigm of the barbarian: an easily conquered race, apparently cheerful and satisfied in conditions of the most revolting poverty, and lacking in any ambition to exert themselves out of it' (Scally 1995, 8). However, their reception in places where labour was badly needed was often quite positive. Either way, the Irish adjusted and integrated. While most settled in established urban slums, others did so on the edge of towns amid market gardens, from where they helped to supply the central wholesale markets. Some worked as live-in servants in wealthy town or country houses, others settled down in villages, and many moved between town and country as a lot of English people did, alternating seasonal agricultural and casual city work. Thus spatial mobility and occupational flexibility were general Irish traits (Davis 1991, 110) and are not just Traveller features.

Mortlake village is situated only ten miles from central London and by the 1870s, like Hammersmith, supplied the London wholesale markets with market-garden produce. And, not surprisingly, it attracted Irish immigrants. By 1871, according to one account, they formed an 'alien colony' whose 'effect on village life' could 'be conceived if not discussed' because 'in common with most poor immigrants, [they] tended to congregate in small ghettoes' (Rose cited in Brown 1985, 34). In truth, for reasons already discussed, this is probably as misleading as it is prejudiced.

Throughout most of the seventeenth century the Mortlake parish register showed no Irish but did record one or two 'Scotch', as well as a large number of Dutch or Flemish people who had come over to work in the village's famous tapestry industry (Cockin and Gould 1954). When, occasionally, Irish people are mentioned it is as vagrants, like the four 'with passes' who were given two shillings' assistance in the winter of 1639/40 (Anderson 1983/1886). Not until 1830 does the register show the first permanent Irish settlers, their number increasing as the decade wears on, so that by 1850 they were sufficiently numerous as to warrant the building of a church. Construction on St Mary Magdelene's began the following year and when completed it served not only the working-class Irish, many of whom had worked on it as labourers, but English Catholics and a few of French or Italian origin who, judging from their headstones, were like the Burtons — frequently solid middle class. This mix of working-class families of Irish origin with a smaller proportion of middle-class, mainly 'English' families, would become the parish pattern for a century.

One exclusively working-class corner of Mortlake from 1854 to the 1930s was Hampton Square, on the west side of Sheen Lane on the parish boundary of Mortlake and East Sheen. A small area of streets containing workmen's cottages, by the turn of the century it had acquired a reputation for being 'rough', Irish, and full of tough customers who kept their coal in the bath, their donkeys in the kitchen, and gave policemen a hard time on Friday and Saturday nights when *The Wheatsheaf* called 'time'. After the Square was demolished in the late 1930s and its residents relocated, the space was eventually taken over and council offices of the borough of Barnes and Mortlake and a small public library were erected. The pub was eventually pulled down in 1954. Being just five minutes from where I lived as a child and grew up at 13 Richmond Park Road, I well remember the offices and library (now rebuilt), and also the stories my father told of the robust folk who lived in Hampton Square. However, it was not until I returned to Sheen in 1982 and began working at the Westway Site that I learnt the Square had housed not only Irish families, but also several Romany ones, some of whose descendents still lived locally. In addition, in the 1990s, I met a woman of Romany descent working in the new medical suite alongside the present library where Hampton Square previously stood, whose mother lived in Notting Dale. Indeed, I interviewed her mother, Florrie Allan, many times in connection with the Gypsies.

At the start of the nineteenth century 33 per cent of England's population was urban. By the end of the century the proportion had risen to 80 per cent (Golden 1981), most of whom were living in towns with populations of about 20,000. London was the exception because of its unique place in national life. Front door on the Empire, seat of the Empress, principal port for receipt of Empire provender — especially after completion of the West India Docks in 1805 — its population, which in 1800 stood at around 865,000 (compared to 200,000 in 1600), rocketed to 6.25 million in 1901.

As well being a country of increased urban *settlement*, Britain by the mid-nineteenth century was also a country of increased population and product *movement*, due to the development of roads, railways and canals. Coleman estimates (1972, 84) that the navvies, or 'navigators', building railways in the mid-1840s were equally divided between Scots, English and Irish. He also observes, as did Engels, that the Irish willingness to work for lower wages than the others frequently got them into fights, especially with the Scots, though one with English labourers at Penrith (Cumbria) in 1845 'was near civil war' (Engels 1987); troops were often called out to pull the sides apart (Scally 1995, 207). Not that Irishmen, who often had their families with them, sought trouble, they had seen trouble enough in Ireland. Coleman put it thus: they 'did not look for a fight, they camped with their women and children, in some of the most secluded glades, and although most of the huts showed an amazing disregard of comfort, the hereditary glee of their occupants seemed not a whit impaired. This glee enraged the Scots ...' (Coleman 1972, 84).

The presence of women and children in the navvy camps meant that the Irish workforce was not just made up of single 'itinerants'. It included families who had turned into 'commercial nomads' or, more correctly speaking, into 'industrial nomads', a category that may well have included some of Ireland's traditional commercial nomads, the Tinkers. Whether Irish Tinkers really were among the navigators one cannot say, but if expertise with horses and skills in metal repair were valued, then the notion cannot be ruled out. Besides, muscle power and willingness to toil were the qualities needed most, and if 'Gypsy Joe', identified by Coleman (1972), was a navvy then the chances are other Gypsies were too, including Irish Tinkers whose own progeny would one day help build the motorways.

Irish tinsmiths and Travellers in London

In 1742 English members of an order of the Tin Plate Workers' Company demanded that 'all the unskilled Irishmen' working in the industry be prosecuted (George 1966, 124). We cannot be entirely sure whether any of the Irishmen were Tinkers or Travellers, but since Gratton Puxon (1968, 18) reckons Travellers worked in the Birmingham metal workshops early in the following century, there is a good chance that they did so in London too. Six years before the Tin Plate Workers' incident, in 1736, violence meted out on Irish weavers and building labourers at Spitalfields led to the Riot Act being read at Tower Hamlets. Other violent anti-Irish labour outbursts in the 1700s occurred at Southwark, Lambeth, and Paddington (George 1966). And as late as the 1860s, at Kensal Green in North Kensington, 200–300 police struggled to restore order between battling English and Irish (Gladstone 1969, 200). In some cases the 'race riots' involved the desecration and near-total destruction of Catholic churches.[8]

Mayhew calculated an annual average of 354 'tinmen' among men admitted to Asylums for the Homeless Poor in London in a seventeen-year period during the Famine (Mayhew 1985, 378).[9] In light of the 1742 uproar over 'unskilled Irishmen' in the tin-plate industry, it is therefore again possible some of these were Irish Tinkers or, at least, Irish Travellers in the making.

Most of London's nineteenth-century tin-can factories were located around the East End docks (Jones 1971), and some of them were not far from one of the capital's biggest Gypsy encampments, at Friars Mount, Shoreditch, where Borrow reported seeing the 'wildest Irish' living alongside Romanies, amongst which were the London Gypsies named Lee (Borrow 1982, 155). Spitalfields lies very close to Shoreditch and it was at Shoreditch that George (1966) told of fights between English and Irish 'tin-platers' and openly wondered whether the latter might have been Tinkers. We must also remember that until the end of the nineteenth century tin cans were still made by hand (Jones 1971, 28), so it is likely some of the Irish tin-platers at Shoreditch were Irish Tinkers or 'Travellers' as we now know them (or at least ethnic Travellers in the making). This reinforces the likelihood that some of Mayhew's 'tinmen' in Asylums for the Homeless were also Tinkers or Travellers.[10]

Whether those described by the *Gentleman's Magazine* in 1763 as 'Irish travellers' who in broad daylight robbed a certain Mrs Jewell (OED 1989, 445) were the same sort of people we now think of as Irish Travellers or were simply vagrants is equally murky. Nor was George Borrow clear about ethnic identity in 1864 when he reported meeting people in Notting Dale — the second biggest 'gypsyry' in London after Wandsworth — called by the Romanies living nearby 'hindity mush' or 'hindity mengre', 'shitty people' (Acton and Davies 1984), although Thomas Acton (pers. comm.) thinks they were.

Mayhew's description of vagrant Irish camped at Gray's Inn in the 1840s is also evidence of a possible early Irish Traveller presence or of families in the early stages of becoming 'Travellers'. For it is worth remembering that any group whose usual mode of subsistence — be it foraging, pastoralism, agricultural or industry — will (if it has the mind to) adopt other modes of subsistence, including some foreign to its traditional habits and identity, if its survival as a collective becomes an issue.[11]

> Two years and a half ago, 'a glut of Irish' (I give the words of my informant) 'came over and besieged the door incessantly; and when above a hundred of them were admitted, as many were remaining outside ...' I again give the statement (which afterwards was verified) verbatim. 'They lay in camps', he said, 'in their old cloaks, some having brought blankets for the purpose of sleeping out; pots, and kettles, and vessels for cooking when they camp; for in many parts of Ireland they do nothing — I've heard from people who have been there — but wander about; and these visitors to the workhouse behave just like gipsies, combing their hair and dressing themselves. The girls' heads, some of them, looked as if they were full of caraway seeds — vermin, sir — shocking! I had to sit up all night; and the young

women from Ireland — fine looking young women; some of them finer looking than the English, well made and well formed, but uncultivated — seemed happy enough in the casual wards, singing songs all night long, but not too loud. Some would sit up all night washing their clothes, coming to me for water. They had a cup of tea, if they were poorly; they ran around like kittens used to a place. The young women were often full of joke; but I never heard an indecent word from any of them, nor an oath, and I have no doubt in the least, that they were chaste and modest. Fine young women, too, sir. I have said, "Pity young women like you should be carrying on this way" (for I felt for them), and they would say, "What can we do? It's better than starving in Ireland, this workhouse is". I used to ask them how they got over, and they often told me their passages were paid, chiefly to Bristol, Liverpool, and Newport in Monmouthshire. They told me that was done just to get rid of them. Others told me the captain would bring them over for any trifle they had: for he would say, "I shall have to take you back again, and I can charge my price then". The men were uncultivated fellows compared to the younger women. We have had old men with children who could speak English, and the old man and his wife could not speak a word of it. When asked the age of their children (the children were the interpreters), they would open up the young creatures' mouths and count the teeth, just as horse-dealers do, then they would tell their children in Irish what to answer, and the children would answer in English. The old people could never tell their own age. The man would give his name, but his wife would give her maiden name. I would say to an elderly man, "Give me your name". "Dennis Murphy, your honour". Then to his wife, "And your name?" "The widdy Mooney, your honour". "But you're married?" "Sure, then, yes, by Father—". This is the case with them still. Last night we took in a family, and I asked the mother — there was only a woman and three children — her name. "But your Christian name?" "The widdy" (widow) was the only answer. It's shocking, sir, what ignorance is, and what their suffering is. My heart used to ache for the poor creatures, and yet they seemed happy, Habit's a great thing — second nature even, when people's shook. The Irishmen behaved well among themselves; but the English cadgers were jealous of the children, and chafed them for spoiling their trade — that's what the cadging fellows did. The Irish were quiet, poor things, but they were provoked to quarrel, and many times I had to turn the English rips out. The Irish were also very thankful for what they had, if it was only a morsel: the English cadger is never satisfied. I don't mean the decent beat-out man, but the regular cadger, that won't work and isn't a good beggar, and won't starve, so they steal ... I'm an Englishman, but I speak the truth of my own countrymen, as I do of the Irish. The English we had in the casual wards were generally a bad cadging set ... As to the decent people we had but a few, and I used to be sorry for them when they had to mix with the cadgers; but when the cadgers saw a stranger, they used their slang. I was up to it. I've heard it many a night when I sat up, and likes they thought I was asleep. I wasn't to be had by the likes of them. The poor mechanic would sit like a man lost — scared sir. There might be one deserving character to thirty cadgers. We have had gipsies in the casual wards; but they're not admitted a second time, they steal so'. (Mayhew 1985, 415–17)

The parallels with contemporary Irish Traveller culture are worth pointing up. First, by likening these Irish to but distinguishing them from Gypsies, the author does what Romanies and Travellers themselves do when talking about themselves. Second, the woman giving her maiden name, not her husband's, is being consistent with modern Traveller practice (see Chapter 9). Third, wanting to assure the inquirer she was married by a 'priest' is more consistent with being a Tinker (for whom the common practice was *not* to marry within the Church) than it is with being a countrywoman. George Smith of Coalville said the same nuptial trend occurred among two-thirds of Romany Gypsies (*The Graphic*, 29 November 1879, 279). Fourth, though estimating a child's age by its teeth 'just as horse-dealers do' may not have been peculiar to peasant horse-traders, one might more easily expect it of Tinkers. Fifth, Mooney, to the best of my knowledge, is not a name found among Travellers; Murphy (albeit a common Irish name) is.

The Irish never counted for more than 8 per cent of London's population in the 1800s but were still common scapegoats whether or not they were Travellers or Irish 'Gypsies'.[12] This did not stop them enjoying upward social mobility, however; by the end of the century great numbers of them had moved up in society as publicans, hoteliers, building contractors, rag and bone wholesalers and retailers. Lots made it into the heart of the English 'establishment': the Civil Service, military, education, and medicine, both as doctors and as nurses; others improved their lot by way of the stage and entertainment (Davis 1991). And through the Catholic schools system their children would follow.

1900–1987

In 1541 a parliament in Dublin extended Henry VIII's titles of Lordship in Ireland, including Earl of Ulster and Lord of Leix and Connacht, to that of King of Ireland. It thus established the new Kingdom of Ireland, which in the words of Professor Curtis, not only "lasted in that form till the Union of 1800" but was thereby "*ipso facto* vested in whoever was king of England" (1985, 169). In 1603 following the defeat of the last great Gaelic aristocrats at the hands of the English, Ireland lost her independence and in effect became an English colony, albeit with a parliament in Dublin. However the period 1641 to 1691 was the last time (except for 1689) Irish Catholics sat in parliament. In 1692 Catholics were banned from parliamentary participation and they would remain locked out until 1829 when Westminster eventually passed the Catholic Emancipation Bill. Meanwhile, by the 1801 Act of Union, Ireland was made a part of the Union of Great Britain and Ireland. The effect was to stoke up existing rural insurrection and demands for land and republicanism in Ireland. In short, the Union created the movement for Home Rule

Irish Nationalists/British 'Patriots'
William Gladstone, the British Liberal Prime Minister, twice tried introducing Irish Home Rule, and twice was thwarted by Unionists backing the Conservative Party who for the most part came from Ulster. Following the death in 1891 of the anti-Unionist, anti-English Irish Protestant advocate of Home Rule, Charles Stewart Parnell, and with the Conservative return to power and switch to conservative liberalism under Joseph Chamberlain, hope of imminent Home Rule was shelved. Not until John Redmond of the Irish Parliamentary Party, and Arthur Griffith of Sinn Féin (who sought independence not Home Rule) took up the cause in 1906 through their newspaper, *United Irishmen*, were Irish political demands effectively recharged.

In April 1912, at its third attempt, the House of Commons saw a Home Rule Bill introduced along the lines of Gladstone's 1891 bill; amended to exclude Ulster. In Ulster the Protestant population, led by Orangeman, Sir Edward Carson, but not confined to Orangemen, called for 28 September to be designated Ulster Day. Some 218,000 Ulstermen then signed a 'Solemn Covenant' to break the 'conspiracy' of Home Rule and thereby defy Westminster (MacMahon 1996). In January 1913 the Bill was passed by the Commons but unsurprisingly was rejected by the Lords. The Commons again passed the Bill only to see it rejected by the Lords in July 1913. It could now only automatically become law the following year. Meanwhile 100,000 armed Ulster Protestants led by an English general mobilised to fight

(Curtis 1985), and an army of National Volunteers (led by Pearse, McNiell, and others), along with a Citizen Army under the authority of James Connolly, awaited orders in Dublin. Civil war appeared inevitable.

The Home Rule Bill passed into law in May 1914, but the outbreak of the First World War prevented it being implemented. It was a war Redmond supported and despite the Volunteers and Citizen Army's failed 1916 Easter 'Rising', some 200,000 Irishmen of both major religions enlisted in the British army in equal proportion (McMahon 1996); among them an unknown number of Travellers, some of whose descendents would in time live at the Westway.

Quite a number of Travellers and Romanies serving in the army[13] appear to have been used as smiths or put in charge of horses, or chosen to carry despatches because their ability (as non-readers and non-writers) to remember accurately ensured the safe delivery of secret messages (Green 1931–2). Many were killed or injured in the war, as were others in earlier wars. How many exactly, we do not know. A grandfather of Westway resident, Martin Ward, and his grandfather's first cousin, were both killed at Mons. Two uncles of another Westway man, John Doyle, died in the war. Thomas McCarthy lost uncles at Dardanelles. The relatives of other Westway people, including some of the Romanies, fought in the Boer War, as well as at Crimea where 'navvies' (who of course included Irishmen) built railways for Lord Raglan before being ordered to take up arms (Coleman 1972, 84). One young Romany at the Westway was actually called 'Crimea'.

In 1918 Sinn Féin won 73 out of 105 of the Irish seats at Westminster, and in 1919 set up an Irish Parliament in Dublin. Guerrilla war followed between members of Sinn Féin, the newly formed IRA, and British troops. A solution of sorts was eventually found in 1920 in the partition of the six northern counties of Antrim, Armagh, Down, Fermanagh, Londonderry and Tyrone. Two years later under the Anglo-Irish Treaty, brokered in part by the IRA leader Michael Collins, the remaining twenty-six counties became the new Irish Free State, a dominion within the Commonwealth. But this solution did not please anybody, and civil war erupted between pro-Treaty supporters and anti-Treaty followers of Eamonn de Valera's Sinn Féin. Lives were lost on both sides. In accepting dominion status the idea of a free republic was lost. In 1937 a constitution covering all thirty-two counties changed the name of the Irish Free State to Eire. Throughout the Second World War Eire remained neutral but that did not stop Irish there or in Britain (including the second generation) from enlisting. Depending on precise definitions it has been estimated that between 40,000 and 400,000 Irish joined up. Of these, seven (four from the South, one from Belfast, and two born in England) later won the Victoria Cross, the highest British military award, thus adding to the tally of 190 won by Irishmen (among the total of 1,356 awarded) since the medal's inception in 1856.

A number of Gypsies and Travellers left Britain at the outbreak of war and spent the next few years in Eire. Others joined up (or were conscripted) just as Gypsies and Travellers had done since at least the time of the Napoleonic wars (Boswell 1973). For example, the father of one elderly Romany woman at the Westway, the great grandfather of the young man called Crimea I mentioned earlier, served throughout the war in the Black Watch. But proud of this as she was, far from making her feel patriotic, the wartime service of her ancestors only fuelled her anger at the government's current treatment of Gypsies and Travellers. Like other nomads I heard speak of the matter, she was particularly contemptuous of the jingoism surrounding Britain's recent 'victory' in the Falklands. On the Irish side of the ledger, Travellers from the now comfortable village of Rathkeale, in Limerick, kept the English sewers working throughout the duration of the war, and cleared bombsites in London, Birmingham and Liverpool (Ross 1990). Today descendents of these men in Britain, along with other Irish Travellers, are at the blunt end of anti-nomad sentiments and action.

In 1949 Eire became the Republic of Ireland. Travellers now began reappearing in Britain in numbers (Vesey-Fitzgerald 1944, 184). Many of them had spent the war years working in agriculture (helping Ireland feed Britain) or trading horses, which were much in demand as draught animals due to petrol shortages, as well as by black-market butchers for meat. Alongside thousands of other Irish immigrants they found work in infrastructure reconstruction and the building of Britain's first motorways in the 1970s and 1980s. 'Boom and bust' marked the British economy, and large construction companies like Taylor Woodrow, Murphy, Laing, and Robert McAlpine, hitherto big recruiters of Irish labour, were forced to lay men off. According to one source over 100,000 Irish in the 1970s returned to the Republic (*The Írish Exile*, August 1991).

In early 1981 unemployment in the Republic reached its highest in decades, 232,000 in a population of 3.5 million; by 1987 the unemployed would represent 18 per cent of the population, twice that of 1982. By April 1986 net migration to Britain alone was over 30,000, comparable to the high days of the 1950s, except the immigrants now entered a faltering economy not a strong one. Unemployment in the Republic in May that year registered 230,357 (*The Irish Post*, 14 June 1986). At the same time 70,000 young Irish lived illegally in the US where most worked in building construction, restaurants and bars, those staple Irish sources of employment abroad (*The Irish Post*, 15 November 1986).

Four other elements distinguished the Irish arriving in Britain in the early 1980s, and their circumstances, from those who came in the 1950s and 1960s. Firstly, the newcomers were not just young they were well-educated — among the best in Europe. Secondly, they came as successive Conservative governments were thinning the welfare state, and this at a time when repeated surveys showed the Irish in Britain to suffer a disproportionate degree of mental illness, compared to other ethnic groups, particularly among elderly earlier settlers. Thirdly, they arrived when Catholic and IRA protestation at Britain's role in Northern Ireland was at a climax following Derry's 'Bloody Sunday' in January 1972; Provisional bombings in Birmingham and Guilford (1974); the IRA's assassination of the Queen's uncle, Earl Mountbatten, in Ireland (1979); bomb attacks on the Queen's troopers in London's Regent's Park and Hyde Park (1982); and the IRA's devastating bomb attack on the Tory Party and its leader Prime Minister Margaret Thatcher, which left several dead and many injured at Brighton, in 1984. A time of terror in the capital and the wider country, it was not the best times to be an Irish Catholic immigrant in Britain as the subsequent failure of British justice with its mistaken convictions attested. Finally, and more positively, Irish arrivals in the 1980s entered a Britain not only more ethnically diverse than ever but also one increasingly ideologically committed to concepts of multiculturalism and equity, especially in London and other major cities.

Whatever the extent to which Travellers were conscious of these matters, they undoubtedly formed part of the backcloth to the stage Travellers and Gypsies trod in 1984 in London's second largest 'Irish' borough, the Borough of Hammersmith and Fulham, a soon-to-be Conservative administration like its next-door neighbour The *Royal* Borough of Kensington and Chelsea, which rather ironically was only slightly less 'Irish'.

Notes

1. Taken from *Minceir 2000: A Travelling Pageant through the Ages* (c.1985), Minceir Misli, Pavee Point, Dublin.

2. Towns in Ireland were Viking and Norman inventions and the agricultural system was different from that in England. Large monastic communities, as opposed to the small hermitage of the early Irish monks, were also a Norman product. In eastern counties like Wexford, Carlow and Kilkenny (Leinster province), where English influence was greatest, villages had a complex division of craft labour not seen in the south-west (Munster). In one Kilkenny village alone, 'Within living memory one could have found almost every necessary craft being practised ... boat-building, nail making, weaving, boot-making, bacon-curing, the making of salt, starch and candles, tanning, a small foundry, carpenters, joiners, *tinsmiths*, backers, coopers, quilters, and so on' (O'Faolain 1981, 61, my emphasis).

3. http://news.independent.co.uk/uk/thisbritain/story.isp?story=b4047.

4. According to Lonergan (2004, 14), Cairns and Richards (in Ashcroft,

Griffiths and Tiffin 1995) believe that where the Welsh, Scots and Irish chiefs speak their own particular English dialects, as for example in *Henry V*, Act III, Scene II, where the Irish captain Macmorris's says '*ish*' for is, '*Chris*' for Christ, and '*tish*' for 'it is', the Bard's intention is to demonstrate the subordinate status of these groups to the English.

5. According to Shakespeare scholar, Charles Edelman (personal communication), most editors agree it was because he was drunk that Sly mistakenly said Richard not William. The surname Slee, incidentally, possibly related to Sly, crops up in Chapter 5. According to Stokes (1970) a family named Slee lived in Stratford in Shakespeare's day.

6. The dates of Shakespeare's plays come from Thorne and Collocott (1990).

7. Jonson is more ambiguous in 1631 in his play *Bartholomew Fair* (act I, scene v) where he pens the expression, 'Marry gip, goody she-Justice'. For Hibbard (1977, n.13) this was 'an exclamatory' oath which probably originated from 'By Mary Gipcy' ('by St Mary of Egypt') and then became confused with 'Gip' meaning (i) gee-up (to a horse) and (ii) 'go along with you' (to a person). Hibbard either forgot or didn't realise 'Gip' and 'Egyptian' could also mean 'Gypsy, and that 'gip' or *jib* refers to Anglo-Romani.

8. 'Past Notes', *The Guardian*, 4 July 1994.

9. Vesey-Fitzgerald (1994) mentions a Gypsy named Cooper who boxed under the name 'Hooper the Tinman'.

10. On the subject of homelessness and tramping, one ought not forget that a great many of England's tramps were Irish former servicemen. Large numbers of Wellington's army in India and the Crimea were Irish, as was the Duke. A large part of the British army in the eighteenth and nineteenth centuries consisted of Irishmen. O'Connor, in his 1960s study of vagrants — men who hated *employment* but not *work* (a sentiment all Travellers would understand) — found that most tramps were itinerant labourers; one was a Gypsy from north Wales (O'Connor 1963, 104), another was 'formerly an Indian army major, ex-Rugby' (O'Connor 1963, 112), and a third was a meths-addicted Irish ex-convict named Murphy (O'Connor 1963, 123). I used to see men like this in Hammersmith Broadway when I was coming home from school, or later on when I

was studying for my A-levels in Hammersmith. They slept at Rowton House, the doss-house on Hammersmith Road, just before West Kensington. Westway Travellers sometimes hired day labourers from hostels for the homeless.

11. Hope's comic novel *Darkest England* (1996) shows this in his background sketch of Bushmen in southern Africa who became commercial nomads. See also Tennant's novel *The battlers* (2002) about settled Australian families who went on the road in the Depression. New or New Age Travellers in Britain are another example.

12. George Smith estimated that a fifth of Gypsies lived in city slums (*The Graphic*, 13 March 1880). Moreover Roberts recalls that in Manchester, between the wars, there was a popular sherbet commonly known as a *kali sucker* (1971, 111, n10), which I suggest in view of *kali* being the Romanes word for 'black' suggests Gypsies made and/or sold them; further evidence of the long history of Gypsies in British cities. Incidentally, Barretts, a famous confectionary company, sold generations of British children sherbet packets with liquorice 'suckers'.

13. George Hall (1915), who used the word 'travellers' for Gypsies in the 1850s, also spoke of Gypsies in the 'militia'.

3

NORTH KENSINGTON, 1800-1900

A little country place [North Hammersmith in the early 1840s] with few shops and those very small ... the whole country was open, and only a few farms here and there ... scarcely a house to be seen.

But what a place it was when I first discovered it [Latimer Road] — comparatively out of the world — a rough road cut across the field, the only approach. Brickfields and pits on either side, making it dangerous to leave on dark nights. A safe place for many people who did not wish everybody to know what they were doing.
An 'old inhabitant', *Kensington, Notting Hill, & Paddington*, 1882

In the opening chapter I talked for two reasons about Arnold Bennnett's, Richard Larch, "a man from the North", a newcomer to London. One was to preface some remarks about the literary character of much modern social and cultural anthropology. The other was to set the scene for my own incursions into an area of west London I knew virtually nothing about when I first got there in 1982; an area known variously as Shepherds Bush, North Kensington, north Hammersmith, Notting Hill or Notting Dale; an area wherein more particularly I went to work in the small community known more vaguely — if known *at all* by outsiders — as the Latimer Road Gypsy Site or Westway Travellers Site, a 'little community' of the type Redfield (1960) referred to and to which I will return in subsequent chapters to unpack the complex matter of culture and identity.

'Little communities' in London

In the two centuries from 1600 to 1801 London's population grew from 200,000 to almost one million, thereby accounting for 11 per cent of the country's population, making it the nation's 'primate city' (Bounds 2004, 76). By 1880 there was a further five-fold increase, yet London would remain a 'walking city' and, despite the presence of the combustion engine and Underground, it remains one.

In particular, the original walled Roman city, the famous 'square-mile' or 330 square acres (Ackroyd 2001, 22) of City which, rebuilt after the Great Fire, in due course became Britain's financial and commercial centre, maintains the intimacy that comes from walking. But most of Inner London remains remarkably accessible to pedestrians (and cyclists) thanks to pre-motorcar infrastructure and the recent introduction of financial disincentives to driving cars in central London. These help retain an air of conviviality or community based on what Lewis Mumford (see Hughes and Hughes 1990) called 'relation incarnate', a relationship once evident in the City especially, where old school networks and remnants of medieval trade guilds made for trust in financial and commercial transactions. Similar small communities based on trade or occupations exist in most other parts of the city, or did so until recently, when for reasons of space or new technology some businesses were compelled to relocate further out.

North of the river, the West End stretches roughly from the City and St Paul's Cathedral in the east to Knightsbridge and Chelsea in the west, and from the Thames embankment northwards to Oxford Street, Marylebone and Euston Road. Until the eighteenth century most of what is today called the West End and considered the centre of 'town' was fairly open territory west of the City; these were areas that over the course of the next two centuries would attract people of every social class. Today some areas in this part of west London are what sociologists dub 'inner city', replete with social indicators of poverty. Others contain 'town' houses of the rich (who come to live here from every quarter of the globe), the finest hotels, private clubs, luxury shops, royal parks, theatres and cinemas. London remains a patchwork. Postal districts are only a half-accurate guide to who is affluent and who is not. The borough of Westminster, for example, includes within its boundaries Westminster Palace, the Houses of Parliament, senior government ministries of Whitehall, Pall Mall, St James and Buckingham Palaces, and the prestigious club, residential, retail and hotel areas of Piccadilly, Mayfair and Belgravia. It also contains several hundred low-income families living in flats built by the Peabody Trust.[1]

Most of the inner-city areas of London are situated only a little less ambiguously around the northern reaches of south London, about the outer edges of the West End and City proper, and along the inner borders of north London. Hammersmith, Shepherds Bush, White City, Notting Hill and Kilburn can thus also be thought of as 'inner city'. However, subjectively, for inhabitants, the least affluent included, all is not alienation. For a great many there is sense of 'little community' in their 'patch' of the inner-city suburb, much in the same way that there is in some old 'outer' London suburbs. This sense survives thanks to local memories, to limits on redevelopment imposed by ancient infrastructure and natural features, to restrictions laid down in heritage and urban planning laws, and to people ready to defend and promote their semblance of 'village' or 'little community'. The same goes for the Westway Travellers' Site.

Latimer Road Caravan Site

In 1984 outsiders also knew the Westway Travellers' Site as the Latimer Road Gypsy Caravan Site. The site, a concrete-covered roughly oblong strip of ground, stood on the north-east edge of the inner London borough of Hammersmith and Fulham, on the north-west border of the Royal Borough of Kensington and Chelsea. For decades this inner-city spot, along with its immediate surrounds, was spatially and socially marginal. Only in recent years have urban redevelopment programmes improved the vicinity, and local authorities upgraded the site itself.

Down the site's eastern and western edges concrete walls shield it from slip roads of the A3220 or West Cross Route (known as the M41 at the time I worked there). A short stretch of motorway on a north–south axis, the A3220 connects at right angles with the A40 (known hereabouts as the Westway) that carries eastbound traffic into central London and out again. The northbound A3220 slip road by the west wall of the site serves traffic from Shepherds Bush, half a mile away. Rising gently above the top of the wall the slip road turns directly over the roofs of caravans parked at the lower end just inside the site entrance, before it joins the A40 by way of a huge roundabout. On the other side of the slip road a railway line adds further definition to the site's western boundary and a sense of being cut off from White City, or at least it did so up until recently. On the east side, beyond the southbound slip road, a cluster of council flats nineteen-storeys tall with views over White City, East Acton and beyond, looms over the site. The site's only entrance is at the north end virtually beneath the flyover. For a newcomer it can be hard to find especially if one is driving. The easiest way to get there is to come down Latimer Road from North Pole Road and then turn right into a scruffy lane called Stable Way. The site lies a hundred yards down the end and forms a cul-de-sac.

Before the Westway went up in the 1960s, Latimer Road extended south three-quarters of a mile from North Pole Road to a spot just short of Holland Park Road near Shepherds Bush. For all practical purposes the road effectively marked the western boundary of Notting Dale, the small area immediately west of Notting Hill itself whose name often presumes to include the Dale. The decision by London's governing authority, known at the time as the London County Council (LCC), to improve traffic flows in and out of town by extending the existing A40 using an elevated motorway, the A40(M), therefore dealt a heavy blow to Latimer Road and scores of other streets in west and central London. Latimer Road was snipped in two. A 'little community' (and others like it) was literally ripped asunder. Many inhabitants were devastated by the demolitions that followed yet other people saw it as a chance to improve their lives, and not a few sceptics did so in retrospect. By any standard many of the streets in the area were rotting slums overdue for demolition whose inhabitants savoured the prospect of relocation to greener outer suburbs on new estates such as the LCC's Alton Estate, Roehampton, south of the river. Other people in other streets regarded the intended works as destructive to community and networks. Latimer Road was one such. One of the least contentious roads to go was infamous Rillington Place just two minutes away from Latimer Road. Already renamed by the early 1960s, the road was where a psychopath named Christie had lived in the post-war years, at house number 10. He murdered several women and a baby there before concealing their bodies in the house and backyard (Kennedy 1995). No one complained about that street being demolished to make way for the longest elevated motorway in Europe.

When the M40 severed Latimer Road it cut apart a 'little community' that owed its sense of being partly to the fact that it had long been a marginal place, a borderland, physically and socially. Well before the construction of the West Cross Route and its predecessor roads, a railway track cut off Notting Dale from areas to the west, making it something of a no-through area. Indeed some of those who came to live in the Dale and more particularly in Latimer Road in the late Victorian period *because* it was set apart were Romany Gypsies; families who, in the course of time, moved into cottages and raised their children and grandchildren there. So when Romanies and Irish Travellers arrived under the roundabout at the bottom of Latimer Road in the early 1970s (and eventually convinced the authorities to provide them with a caravan site), history was repeating itself, since living beneath the viaducts of Notting Dale was exactly what an earlier generation of Gypsies and Travellers had done.

'Comparatively out of the world': birth of an urban slum

On 13 December 1879 the *London Illustrated News* carried the following piece:

> The ugliest place we know in the neighbourhood

of London, the most dismal and forlorn, is not the
Hackney Marshes or those of the Lea, beyond old Ford,
at the East End; but is the tract of land torn up for
the brickfield clay half consisting of field laid waste in
expectation of the house-builder, which lies just outside
Shepherd's Bush and Notting Hill. There it is that the
gypsy encampment may be found, squatting within an
hour's walk of the Royal Palaces and of the luxurious
town mansions of our nobility and opulent classes to the
very west of the fashionable West End.

The question is: how had it come to this?

In the mid-nineteenth century the railways fragmented Notting Dale. In 1837 the London and Birmingham Railway (LBR) opened an east–west line across the northern tip of Hammersmith and Kensington, between the Harrow Road and the Grand Junction (later Grand Union) Canal, which had opened for business in 1801. Other lines followed. In 1844 the West London Railway (WLR) commenced operations between north Hammersmith and the Kensington Canal Basin at the west end of Kensington High Street, near Olympia. The line proved a commercial failure but remained intact, later forming part of the Channel Tunnel goods and motor line that runs beside the Westway Site.

In 1864 the newly established Hammersmith and City Railway (H&C) made its own contribution to social disconnection by connecting Hammersmith and Shepherds Bush to the Great Western Railway (GWR) terminus at Paddington, and to the burgeoning City, whose workforce wished to live in the new suburbs. One of the stations on the new line was Latimer Road, in Notting Dale; the next one up the line was Ladbroke Grove. Both still function, although the line is now the Metropolitan and City line, known usually as the Met. The viaduct of the H&C line, sweeping through the Dale and Notting Hill and displacing people as it did so, nevertheless proved attractive as a sheltering place for Gypsies and itinerants in the same way that the M40 would a century later. One inhabitant was Ryley Bosvil, from

Yorkshire, also known as the 'Flying Tinker', who lived most of his life and died in Notting Dale (Borrow 1982, 154-62).

Another track to carve up and redefine the 'little communities' in (and community of) Notting Dale was an H&C branch line running between the Latimer Road and Uxbridge Road stations, the latter at Shepherds Bush. Uxbridge Road station did not last long, though, because in 1901 it became Shepherds Bush station, on the Central Line (Goudie and Stuckey 2000), not to be confused with another station of the same name on the Met.

The lines of the WLR, H&C, and GWR running across the top of the district came together at Willesden Junction, a remote area made that much bleaker by the development of major gas works and a swathe of cemeteries in the Harrow Road in the second half of the nineteenth century. Together these constructions further helped to enclose and confine Notting Dale, which already had a shabby reputation before the mid-century, as this observation by a resident of nearly forty years' duration makes clear:

> But what a place it was when I first discovered it
> — comparatively out of the world — a rough road cut
> across the field, the only approach. Brickfields and
> pits on either side, making it dangerous to leave on
> dark nights. A safe place for many people who did not
> wish everybody to know what they were doing. (Old
> Inhabitant 1882, 27)

Notting Dale's transformation from fields and scattered cottages to a place of ugly brickfields, a slum area without parallel in west London, rivalled only by the East End, all began in 1818. In that year Samuel Lake, a scavenger, chimney sweep and nightsoil man, arrived from Tottenham Court Road, near St Giles rookery, pleased no doubt to have escaped it (see Gladstone 1969; Sheppard 1973; Evans 1975). Clearly an innovator, Lake saw an opportunity in raising pigs from household scraps discarded by the rich who had recently moved out from the West End. So successful was Lake that when he was joined by poor people displaced by the building of the Great Western

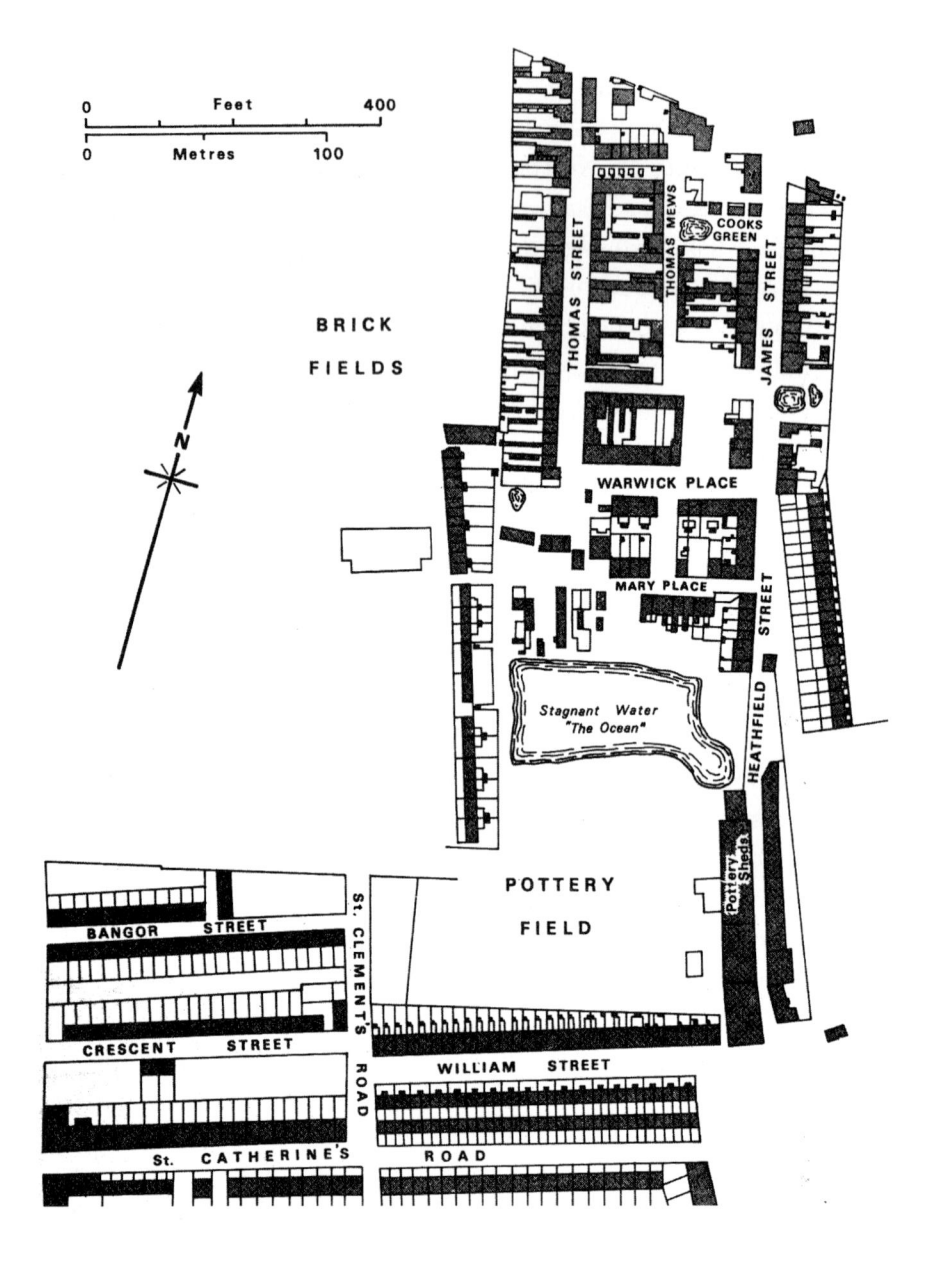

The Potteries, c. 1850.
Taken from Malcolmson (1975), 'Getting a living in the slums of Victorian Kensington', *The London Journal*, 1.

Railway on the Bishop of London's Paddington estate, Tyburnia (later to become Marble Arch), they quickly took his lead (Sheppard 1973, 340).

As well as providing a source of pig food, the rich also provided sources of employment. Houses needed building; buildings required bricks, tiles and chimney pots; and the local clay proved perfect for the job. In no time Notting Dale became known for its brickfields and potteries. Housebuilding also required labour and, what is more, according to Gladstone and Barker the brickmakers were 'chiefly Irish labourers of a low type' (Gladstone 1969, 70). Other Irish found work in the brickfields around Brook Green, not far from Shepherds Bush (Draper 1989), and others as domestic staff and drivers. Inside a decade of Lake's arrival Notting Dale was commonly known as 'the Pigs and Potteries'.

By 1850 laundering and carpet-beating had also established themselves as Dale industries. The district, from Notting Dale to the northern reaches of Hammersmith and Kensington, was also known as 'Laundry Land' and 'The Land of Soap and Suds' or, in the case of Latimer Road, 'Soapsud Island' — a tag that captures the isolation to which I have already referred. In 1895, in one street in Kensal Green alone, Beethoven Street, there were at one point seven laundries, five of them adjacent. By 1899 there were in the entire district around 200 laundries, sufficient for many men simply to be 'kept' by their wives (Malcolmson 1975).

Pigs, brickfields subject to flood, immigrant influxes and a total absence of building regulations had already made Notting Dale a dreadful place in which to live before 1850. Conditions were among the worst in London. In 1849 the local mortality rate was 60 per 1000 living persons, compared with a London average (1846-1850) of 25.4 (Sheppard 1973, 342). Influenza, cholera, diarrhoea, dysentery and smallpox outbreaks were common. The rate of smallpox infection in Notting Dale was double that in other parts of North Kensington. Dickens, in his weekly, *Household Words*, referred to it in 1850 as 'this pestilential locality'. 'In a neighbourhood studded thickly with elegant villas and mansions – named Bayswater and Notting Hill,

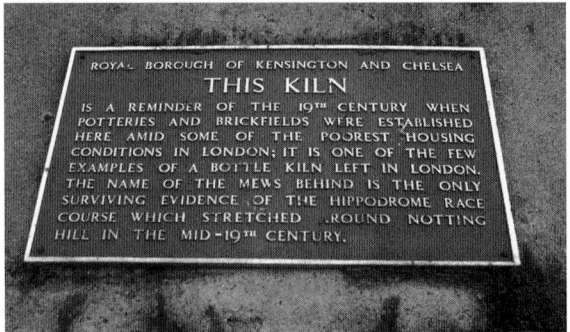

Last kiln in the Potteries and
'Testimony to a slum'

in the parish of Kensington – is a plague spot scarcely equalled for its insalubrity by any other in London: it is called the Potteries. It comprises some seven or eight acres, with about two hundred and sixty houses (if the term can be applied to such hovels), and a population of nine hundred or one thousand ... pigs, ducks, and fowls are kept in an incredible state of filth. Dogs abound ...' (Dickens 1850, 403).

Others said the Potteries covered four acres, not seven or eight, so that, with a population of 1056, the density rate was 264 people per acre, twenty-six times that of Kensington as a whole, more than enough to substantiate Dickens' description of the area as 'pestiliential'. According to *The Builder* magazine (1856, 43–4), 'some of the dwellings are not houses at all, but caravans which had become too old for service at the country fairs and were placed here in a line with ill-shaped erections of bricks and mortar; adjoining them their unwholesome accompaniments'. For some observers, the Potteries after 1860 was no longer confined to its original eight to nine acres, but had spread west and south as far as St James' Place. Whatever the differences of opinion about the area of the Potteries (and there is no reason to wonder at it), it is pretty clear that the eastern boundary ran down Pottery Lane, where in 1860 the Irish opened St Francis of Assisi church, while the western border was Counter's Creek, also known as Billingwell Ditch, the old parish boundary with Hammersmith, on the west side of Latimer Road. Counter's Creek rose in Kensal Green and flowed into the Thames at Chelsea, and was the cause of regular outbreaks of rheumatic illness among those living along its banks (Smith 1983). It was covered over long ago, but presumably runs underground not far from the Westway.

Following the Famine years, the Irish population increased greatly throughout the whole of Kensington, but not least in Notting Dale where they went on to build St Francis', as noted above. A small neo-Byzantine gem designed by the architect who drew up Westminster Cathedral, set amidst scenes of poverty, it must have been a source of strength and consolation to the immigrants. It still is, although the newcomers now come from elsewhere. Among the Irish who arrived in Notting Hill and Notting Dale during the last quarter of the nineteenth century were many who had fled slums in central London, such as St Giles, which was demolished in 1878–9, or Jennings Building in Kensington High Street, pulled down five years earlier (Malcolmson 1975; Jones 1971). By the 1860s the Irish had settled in most parts of Kensington and Hammersmith, but some parts of North Kensington were considered particularly 'Irish': St Columb Road, east of Portobello Road, for one, and Kensal New Town, for another. Here, during the 1860s, fights with the English sometimes erupted into full-scale riots, including on one occasion in Middle Row, next to East Row (Gladstone 1969, 207). It was there, on ground between East Row and Boswell Row,[2] that Romanies regularly camped regularly in the 1880s and 1890s; one year joining in seasonal festivities at the local Agricultural Hall, which itself says something of its distance from the Potteries (Gladstone 1969, 203). *The Builder* of January 1856 confirms it: 'On the outskirts under the shelter of a wall several gypsies were comfortably encamped. The gipsies seem to have the best of it, they are at a distance from the putrid gutters and other refuse, and ready at an hour's service to tramp off to a more favourable site, if the health of the neighbourhood becomes affected.'

In the last quarter of the nineteenth century many churches, city-missions, temperance societies and philanthropic organisations sprang up to help alleviate the social ills associated with the unplanned and exceedingly rapid growth of Notting Dale. Two prominent 'city-missions' (both still in existence) sprang from two of England's most prestigious public schools, Harrow and Rugby. Harrow opened premises in Latimer Road, in 1883, under William Law, at the behest of its headmaster the Very Reverend Henry Montague Butler (Burnett 1983). Addressing Old Harrovians, Dr Butler expressed a hope that 'the strong tide of brotherly feelings which flows through generations of Harrow men may find one new and not uncongenial channel in ministering to the wants of the poor and neglected and so contributing to bring together classes of our fellow countrymen who know far too little of each other' (Burnett 1983, 2). Law was blunter: 'Nothing could have been more forlorn, neglected or desolate than the condition of this district at starting. The station of the Metropolitan Railway, which bears the name Latimer Road, was familiarly known as 'Piggery Junction' from the miserable and unwholesome establishment of the feeding of those animals, which then occupied the site of our Church and Mission Room. The livelihood of the men — brick makers, costermongers, casual labourers — was always precarious, while the women, the real bread-winners of the families, were mainly employed in steam laundries away from their homes and children. Rich inhabitants there were none; the moderately poor were scarce' (Burnett 1983, 3).

Among those who attended mission meetings in Latimer Road at this time, though whether it was Harrow mission or some other is slightly unclear, was one Cornelius Smith, the father of the famous Gypsy evangelist Rodney Smith who was born in 1860 in Wanstead, not far from Epping Forest (Smith 1902). Having vowed he had 'done with the roaming and wrong-doing, and that he meant to turn to God', Cornelius had gathered his wife and small children and, along with his brothers and their wagons, had gone to Shepherds Bush, where he 'placed them on a piece of building land close to Mr Henry Varley's Chapel' (Smith 1902, 49). One evening soon afterwards, Cornelius was converted to Christianity at a mission hall in Latimer Road, and by the next morning thirteen other Gypsies had followed his example (Smith 1902, 54).

In an 1889 survey of an area covering Notting Dale and a bit beyond, the social reformer Charles Booth estimated that 36,236 people lived hereabouts: 119 to the acre, 47.4 per cent of them in abject poverty and insanitary conditions. Toilets and washing facilities were virtually non-existent until municipal baths were built in Silchester Road at the north end of Walmer Road. In an adjacent area that included the northern end of Latimer Road the density rate was 145 to the acre. Looked at together with the Potteries, more narrowly defined, it meant that out of 134 areas Notting Dale was by far the most impoverished in west London, and the fourteenth most deprived in London as a whole.

One thing that clearly emerges from this overview is that the 'little communities' found in this part of west London were 'sites of travel' and 'travelling cultures' (Clifford 1992) as much as they were sites of residence, and this is how it was perceived at the time. Not without reason, for example, did the Rev George Hall (1915) describe the general population of North Kensington in the 1850s as made up of 'travellers', and Draper, borrowing from a contemporary observer, speak of Hammersmith's 'inevitable migratory tendencies' (Draper 1989, 80).

Gypsies and Travellers

Though we have no precise date, one of the earliest Gypsy camping places in Notting Dale was on the corner of Latimer Road and Oxford Gardens (Taylor 1983, 2) just inside the Kensington border, 100 yards from what is now the Westway Site.

By the mid-century Black Hill, in the centre of the Potteries (Gladstone 1969) not far from the Hippodrome race track on Notting Hill, on or close to what is now Avondale Park, was well known for its Gypsy tents, carts and 'vans'. The track lasted only four years before local authorities closed it in 1841 because of disputes over rights of way, a contemporary noting that the 'pathway people ... seemed as a rule to have been orderly enough, but gypsies [sic], prigs (thieves) and hawkers did not neglect the opportunity of mingling with the nobility and gentry' (Gladstone 1969, 84–5).

The streets about Avondale Park are still home to people of very varied social status. A row of town houses labelled 'Hippodrome', built opposite the park some time in the 1970s, evidently houses comfortably-off people. The fact that they stand behind the last remaining brick kiln in the area, in Walmer Road, where a National Trust plaque testifies to the extreme poverty of the old Potteries, merely lends heritage kudos to the town houses. Meanwhile, a short stroll from the kiln, which faces various kinds of old council housing, some of it of the 'cottage' variety, and by no means short of charm, there are even more prestigious properties. Here in the 'Crescents', behind St Francis of Assisi's, Regency houses which owe their lines to

Gypsy *tans*, Notting Dale 1861.
The Queen magazine, 16 November 1861.
Courtesy of the Royal Borough of Kensington and Chelsea public library.

Double tent and Romany face, Notting Dale 1861.
Courtesy of the Royal Borough of Kensington and Chelsea public library.

the sweep of the old Hippodrome are now mostly converted to flats. They lie beyond the means of all but the very affluent.

As early as 1861 *Queen* magazine was helpfully explaining to its readers that Notting Dale was 'a gypsy emporium before it became a suburban emporium of pigs ... but became their fixed location after the ground had been leased to pig-breeders'. This would suggest that Romanies were coming to the area by 1820 at least, and possibly as far back as the eighteenth century. In fact Borrow, writing in 1864 (see Borrow 1982), reckoned Gypsies called Lee were 'natives of the metropolis or neighbourhood' (Borrow 1982, 154), which, allowing for three generations, would push the date of arrival back to around 1800. Meanwhile, Dr Donald Kenrick, a noted scholar on Romany and Traveller affairs who also lives in the area, thinks Gypsies were probably there long before that.[3]

Gypsies and benefactor near Latimer Road, 1879.
The Illustrated London News, 13 December 1879.
Courtesy of the Royal Borough of Kensington and Chelsea public library.

Vardo interior, near Latimer Road, 1879. *The Illustrated London News*, 13 December 1879. Courtesy of the Royal Borough of Kensington and Chelsea public library.

A third stopping place for Gypsies in the 1850s was ground 100 yards north of Black Hill on that part of Bird's Brickfield where the church of St Clements was built in the 1860s: at the corner of Treadgold Street and Sirdar Road (Gladstone 1969). By coincidence, it was through its vicar that in the 1980s I got to meet Mrs Florrie Allen of St Mary's Place, a woman in her sixties, and her next-door neighbour, 94-year-old Miss Kate Adams, who had lived in the Dale since 1915. Florrie Allen's late husband came from a well-known local Romany family, as we shall see in the following chapter.

Between forty and fifty Gypsies were regularly camping in or around Latimer Road by 1862 (Gladstone 1969, 43). Two years later Borrow (1982, 151) described the Potteries as the biggest 'Gypsyry' in London, except for the one at Wandsworth (sw18), and listed, among the families stopping there, Hearnes or Herons (*Ratzie-mescroes*), the odd Black Lovel (*Kaulo Camlo*), the Tinker Bosvils (*Chumo-mescroes*), Stanleys (*Beshaleys*) from Hampshire, Shaws, Deightons, Smiths

(*Petulengros*) and the London skewer smiths or *esconyemengres* called Lee.

Wormwood Scrubs, a tract of land in Hammersmith on the north-west side of the Potteries, was another favourite stopping place and in the 1980s it remained so with visiting Irish Travellers. The Gypsies erected stalls on the Scrubs on bank holidays the way that they did at other fairs in London, including St Giles Fair, where they ran drinking booths and sold snuff boxes before the event was eventually disbanded in 1914 (Alexander 1993). A favourite Gypsy speciality at Scrubs fairs was the boxing booth and some of the fights were rugged. In the 1870s a Potteries Gypsy was killed in the ring and so raucous were the fairs generally that Parliament brought in a special Scrubs Bill to rein in the events' excesses (Gladstone 1969).

A fifth site for travelling people in the 1800s was an area of five or six acres known as Latimer's Green, located somewhere not too far from Shepherds Bush, a no man's land on the north-west side of the Potteries. The Green was 'a great resort of vagrant people, less of Gypsies than those who call themselves travellers, and are denominated by the Gypsies Chorodies, and who live for the most part in miserable caravans, though there is generally a Gypsy tent or two to be seen there, belonging to some Deighton or Shaw, or perhaps Petulengro, from the Lil-engro Tan, as the Romany call Cambridgeshire' (Borrow 1982, 152-3). I do not know exactly where Latimer's Green was; it may have lain somewhere between Latimer Road and Scrubs Lane, Hammersmith, or further down Latimer Road, near the present Westway Site, somewhere around the 'nomans' land at the back of Evesham Street alongside the West Cross Route where, in the winter of 1986/7, New Age Travellers camped in old buses, vans and a teepee.[4]

Apart from those people the Romanies called *choridies* (thieves), another sort of travelling person was the one they called *hindity mengre*, or Filthy People (Borrow 1982, 146), or else *hindity mush* (Borrow 1982, 153), a class of wandering Irish who played a role in the area's 'migratory tendency' mentioned previously, and who may have been — or at least included — those we now call Irish Travellers. They were a type of worker important to the London labour market, which, unlike northern cities, never developed heavy industries (Jones 1971; Chesney 1972).

London's economy revolved around its docks and the seasonal arrival of raw materials, particularly foodstuffs, from the Empire that needed a revolving supply of unskilled and semi-skilled labour for the purposes of refining, packaging and transporting. As the seat of Court and government, London was also main home to the professions, and was thus, in terms of trade and manufacture, a centre for small deluxe goods dependent on specialist 'finishing trades' (Jones 1971). It was the docks, however, with their seasonally fluctuating demand for labour (depending on the materials arriving: molasses one month, wheat another, and so forth) which caused the ebb and flow of individuals and families between countryside and town, blurring the distinction between 'settled' and 'travelling', 'rural' and 'urban', 'sedentary' and 'nomadic', as one labour historian made clear long before any anthropologist drew attention to communities as 'sites of travel':

> Travellers in nineteenth-century England played a much greater part in industrial and social life than they do today. Among them were to be found some of the country's major occupational groups, as well as many hundreds of callings and trades ... The building trades were chronically migratory ... The summer harvests depended to a considerable degree upon travelling labourers, most of them recruited from the countryside, but some come out of the towns. James Green met one of these on the road to Hitchin [Surrey].
>
> 'He seemed to be a decent sort of man, and for a wonder, was not an Irishman. He lived and walked all the winter, at the Potteries, Shepherds Bush, he told me, and every June set on a tramp, working his way at any kind of field labour and winding up with the northern late corn harvests, when he returned home

with a pound or so in his pocket, beside he was able to send from time to time, to keep his old woman.'

At the heart of the wayfaring constituency were those Mayhew called the 'wandering tribes', people who had either been born or bred to a roving life (like the gypsies [sic] or travelling showmen) or forced into it when settled occupations failed them, like the travelling Irish, who came over each year for the harvests... (Samuel 1975, 124)

A moment ago I suggested some of Borrow's *hindity mengre* in the Potteries were Irish Tinkers, Travellers, or Travellers-in-the-making, and in the previous chapter I argued it was likely some of Mayhew's 'tinmen' found in Asylums for the Homeless were Travellers. Borrow's descriptions of London's major 'gypsyries' now add weight to this probability, so it is worth spelling out the evidence once and for all.

For a start, Borrow is very clear on one thing: some of the *hindity mengre* were tinkers. In addition, they appear to have lived in family groups but so for that matter did many Famine refugees, and many Irish navvies before that. So far, then, the evidence is circumstantial. Next, some of the Irish tinkers at the Wandsworth 'gypsyry' could fake gold rings 'little inferior to that of the work of a first rate working goldsmith' (Borrow 1982, 147). Mick, the eldest brother of three such tinkers, made a particularly strong impression on Borrow. Educated in hedgerow schools and possessing little in the way of formal literacy skills, Mick had been an apprentice blacksmith in Ireland before enlisting to fight in the Peninsular Wars after which he returned to Ireland for a while and resumed his trade as a tinsmith. Some time later Mick came to England and there fell into the company of 'certain cunning smiths' who taught him how to make false gold coins and buttons (Borrow 1982, 148); who these 'cunning smiths' were exactly we are not told.

After his wife died in child-birth, leaving him seventeen children, Mick remarried, this time 'to a nice, elderly *ban* [woman] from the County of Cork who could [tell] fortunes, say her prayers in

Irish' and 'was nearly as good a hand at selling her lord and master's tin articles and false rings as her predecessor' (Borrow 1982, 149). Indeed Borrow also mentions the hawking activity of *hindity mengre* wives in Wandsworth.

All of this, the extremely large number of children (even by Irish standards of the day), the fact the first wife was an adept hawker and that the second wife was scarcely less so, as well as being a fortune-teller, therefore strongly suggests what we are looking at is an early variety of the commercial nomadism we have now generally come to associate with Irish Travellers *per se*. To be sure, we can reasonably say if these were *not* traditional Irish Tinkers of the times, and they most probably *were*, then they were people in the process of becoming what we now call Irish Travellers. This is further borne out by the fact we are told that Mick and his brothers were so highly regarded as smiths by the Gypsies that the latter 'immortalised' them in verse, praise indeed, and such that it also speaks indirectly of perceived wider cultural affinities. Finally, all of Mick's children travelled widely and one is said to have ended up a Senator in America, yet Mick and his *ban* lived the whole of their lives in a caravan. None of which would come as a surprise to anyone who knows anything about Irish Travellers. In sum, the evidence of Irish Travellers living alongside Romanies in the Gypsyries of nineteenth — century London is inescapable. In consequence, many of their descendents live all around us.

Leland is sometimes accredited with being the first scholar to identify Gammon, cant, or Shelta (as it is sometimes known), the secret language of Irish Tinkers, being spoken in the London slums. Considering an encounter he had near the British Museum with a Potteries Gypsy called Divius Dick or Wild Dick (Leland 1882, 165) it is therefore very likely he included the Potteries when he said this. But once again it is Borrow (1982) who provides the clearest evidence of Romanies and other Travellers in north Hammersmith and North Kensington:[5]

The second great Gypsyry is on the Middlesex side of the river, and is distant about three miles, as the crow flies from that of Wandsworth. Strange as it may seem, it is not far from the most fashionable part of London; from the beautiful squares, noble streets, and thousand palaces of Tyburnia, a region which, although only a small part of the enormous metropolis, can show more beautiful edifices, wealth, elegance, and luxury, than all foreign capitals put together. After passing Tyburnia and going more than halfway down Notting Hill, you turn to the right, and proceed along a tolerably genteel street until it divides into two, one of which looks more like a lane than a street, and which is on the left hand, and bears the name of Pottery Lane. Go along this lane, and you will presently find yourself amongst, a number of low, uncouth looking sheds, open at the sides, and containing an immense quantity of earthen chimney pots, pantiles, fancy bricks, and similar articles. This place is called the Potteries ... presently turning to your left, you will enter a little, filthy street, and going someway down it you will see, on your right hand, a little, open piece of ground, chock full of crazy battered caravans of all colours, some yellow, some green, some red. Dark men, wild-looking, witch-like women and yellow-faced children are at the doors of the caravan, or wending their way through the narrow spaces left for transit between the vehicles. You have now arrived at the second great Gypsyry of London — you are among the Romany Chals of the Potteries, called in Gypsy the Koromengrescoe Tan, or the place of the fellows who make pots; in which place certain Gypsies have settled, not with the view of making pots, an employment which they utterly eschew, but because it is convenient to them, and suits their fancy ...

> Though the spot which it has just been attempted to describe, may be considered as the head-quarters of the London Gypsies, on the Middlesex side of the Thames, the whole neighbourhood, for a mile to the north of it, may to a certain extent be considered a Gypsy region — that is, a district where Gypsies, or gentry whose habits very much resemble those of Gypsies, may at any time be found. No metropolitan district, indeed, could be well more suited for Gypsies to take up their abode in. It is a neighbourhood of transition; of brickfields, open spaces, poor streets inhabited by low artisans, isolated houses, sites of intended tenements, or sites of tenements which have been pulled down; it is in fact a mere chaos, where there is nothing durable, or intended to be durable; though there can be little doubt that within a few years order and beauty itself will be found here ... At present, however, it is quite the kind of place to please the Gypsies and the wandering people ...
> (Borrow 1982, 151–3)

Someone who must have known the *hindity mengre* better than most was a Gypsy named Hearne who lived locally in 'an old advertising van with a tin pail for a chimney' (Gladstone 1969, 144), had fought in the Napoleonic wars, and was known in the district as 'King of the Gypsies'. Hearne would have known many Irish families and not just *hindity mengre* either, for many of the Irish were costermongers (Mayhew 1985) and, as Orwell (1970) would document, were prominent as seasonal hop-pickers in Kent. In one of his annual reports the Headmaster of St Francis of Assisi school observed how small his classes were between late August and October because of the hops (Thomas 1985, 13).[6]

To get a closer look at 'Travellers' in Notting Dale as individuals and as families I will finish by casting an eye over two censuses (1871 and 1881) for the area lying between St Anne's Road and the lower part of Latimer Road (later Freston), on the west side, and Pottery

Lane, up as far as Walmer Road, on the east.[7]

Individuals and Families

In 1871 William Cooper and his wife Esther lived with their 3-year-old son William at Day's Cottages. William senior was born in Biddiford, Kent and, like his wife, who was born in Hertfordshire, gave his trade as hawker. Little William was also born in Kent. Their neighbours at Day's Cottages were Phoebe Chernpiloner,[8] aged 43, a chair-caner, her 16-year-old daughter also called Phoebe, and three other children aged 3 to 9; all four children were born in Kensington. Six Romany families lived in tents next to them.

Shadrack Hern, 47, a chair-mender, was born in the county of Buckinghamshire, just to the west of London. Famous for its beech woods and furniture-making, it has always had a significant Romany population. At Burnham Beeches, near Chalfont St Giles, for example, an area of the woods is still called 'Egypt' and has a stream running through it called the Nile. Shadrack's wife, 41-year-old Mary, was born in Norfolk, and gave her trade as hawker. Ambrolaine, their 16-year-old son, is listed as a domestic servant and, like his sisters Providence, 13, and Betsy, 6, was born in Notting Hill. A sixth member of the household, described as a 'boarder' but obviously a relative, was 7-year-old Unity Williams, born in Fulham.

Another family living in tents were the Smiths, Woodlock and Jessima, both 37, their 15-year-old daughter Salsh, and sons Owen, 5, and Hajikiel (Ezekiel), aged 3. Woodlock, another chair-mender, was born in Herefordshire, on the Welsh borders. Jessima was born in Suffolk. Their children were born in Norfolk. This gives us some idea of their mobility. The Smiths' immediate neighbours, also in tents, were William and Lydia Taylor, 37 and 24 respectively, their children Lydia and Betty, and a 12-year-old 'step-daughter' called Mary. William Taylor was born in Watford, Hertfordshire, just north of London, and caned chairs for a living. His wife was born in Wandsworth, and their children in Hammersmith, Kensington and Chelsea. By 1881 the Taylors had four more children and had moved into a caravan in Thomas Mews next to some other Romanies. The census also shows William Jack, a gardener, and his wife Fanny and three children in a caravan on the corner of Treadgold Street, one of the original Romany camping grounds.

James Smith, a 49-year-old basket maker from Portsmouth, lived in a tent with his 28-year-old Suffolk wife, five children and a step-child, whose ages ranged from 4 months to 14 years; the children were born in Kent, Surrey, Essex and Middlesex. John and Maria(n) Hern and five children John, 14, Nanny, 10, Mary, 7, Christopher, 5, and James, 2, all born in Notting Hill or Hammersmith, lived beside the Smiths. However, by 1881 the Herns numbered eleven and had moved into wagons in Gorham Place. Nanny Hern (or 'Annie', as she was now listed) followed her father's trade of basket-maker, while Mary did dressmaking. The household also counted three other children not included in 1871: Edith and her married sister Comfort, who were laundry workers, and a married brother, Thomas. Other family members included Thomas's wife, Priscilla, 21, — another laundry worker — and their baby, also called Thomas. In a caravan beside the Herns in 1881 lived 55-year-old George Smith, a general labourer, and his wife, Alice, 53. They were probably relatives of the Herns. Ten years before this, the Herns' neighbours included James Lovell, 35, a horse-dealer born in Kensington, and his wife Atheline and two children, Betsy and James; also Richard Gray from Aylesbury in Buckinghamshire, and his Middlesex-born wife, Hannah, and 18-month-old daughter of the same name.

In a tenement in Thomas Street around the corner from Mary Place (where Mrs Florrie Allen lived in the 1980s), 25-year-old Joseph Boswell roomed with his Fulham-born wife, Susan, a hawker. So did Frank Wood, 21, another hawker, whose wife Eliza came from Somerstown, near Euston, where my paternal grandmother lived with many other Irish at the end of the 1800s. Plastoe Boswell, 48, born in Worcestershire, another hawker, also lived in Thomas Street with his wife Freedom, 30, from Surrey, and three sons: Joseph, 11, born in Wandsworth; Canney (or Carney), 10, listed as a 'working servant' and born in Middlesex; and Isaac, 3, born in the Potteries. Other residents were chair-mender Joseph Williams, 30, born in Surrey, his wife, from Essex, and her 9-year-old daughter who, for reasons one can only guess at, was apparently born in Spain. Benjamin Hearn, a 45-year-old basket-maker, and his mother Alice, 71, both born in Bushey, Hertfordshire, also lived in the tenement with five children aged 1 to 16 years, all born in Kensington.

In 1871 Henry Taylor, 47, a chair-caner born in Watford, lived with his wife Mary in another tenement further down Thomas Street. So did 22-year-old Walter Hearn from Newmarket, Suffolk, his wife Phillis and her brother; and next to them lived William Cooper, 25, and his spouse Esther, both born in Plymouth, Devon. In 1881 in Thomas Mews, at the back of Thomas Street, 49-year-old chair-mender Thomas Herne occupied a caravan with wife Frances and son Christopher. Local-born John Lovell, a labourer by trade, and his Surrey-born wife lived at 12, St Mary Place. Thirty-seven nearby abodes housed, among others, seven Irish families, eight female laundry workers, one chimney sweep, a mender of broken china, a pig-feeder and a brick-maker.

In 1871 three young Romany hawkers, John Davis, Henry Taylor and Christopher Taylor, lived in tents in the Kensal Road area. Joseph Taylor, a basket-maker from Bushey, his wife Henrietta from Alton, Hampshire, and three children lived alongside them in a caravan. Two more Taylors, Albert and Henry, born in Putney and Malden, also had tents and, close to them, in another caravan, lived Plato Taylor, 47, a chair mender, with his wife Elizabeth, from Bedfordshire, and their children: Henrietta, 14, born in Kingston, Surrey; and Amy, Jeremiah and Delilah, born in Hendon, Kensington and Chelsea respectively. The proximity of all these Taylors indicates a single family or extended family.

Other caravan-dwellers in Kensal Green were chair-menders Sidney and Catherine Smith, born in Buckinghamshire, and their baby Phoebe, and a family of three named Stone, with whom was living a girl by the name of Smith, who is listed as a 'servant'. There was also a family of four, the Simpsons, chair-repairers from Kent; an older couple of the same name with another child, probably grandparents of the Simpson children; and hawkers Francis and Augusta Light, with four children aged between 9 and 17, three of whom were born in Notting Dale or Hammersmith.

Conclusion

These data on 131 people refer to only a fraction of the Romanies living in or visiting Notting Dale and Kensal Green in the last years of the nineteenth century. They exclude Romanies residing in and around Latimer Road, let alone those in other parts of North Kensington or north Hammersmith, and say nothing at all of Irish Tinkers or Travellers. Nevertheless, they serve to give some idea of the sense of 'little community' such agglomerations inevitably entailed in the second biggest 'gypsyry' in London, the population of which George Smith, in the *London Illustrated News* of 29 November 1879, estimated around 2,000 even though the actual composition of individuals and families would have been constantly shifting.

Notes

1. George Peabody (1795–1869) was an American merchant and banker who established himself in London in 1837 and donated millions of pounds to good causes on both sides of the Atlantic.

2. Boswell is a Romany name, and Bosvil a version of it. Ryley Bosvil, the 'Flying Tinker', who lived locally, has already been mentioned. There may or may not be a nominal connection between 'Boswell Row' and the Gypsies.

3. Pers. comm.

4. In 1986 Hammersmith and Fulham council suggested this piece of wasteland as a place to build a new Traveller site as an alternative to the Westway, but nothing came of it, and instead it was developed for commercial premises.

5. George Hall (1915) was already using the word 'traveller' to refer to English Romanies of the 1850s.

6. The boys' school was opened in 1886, and the girls' in 1892.

7. The 1871 data are taken from microfiche 132, pp.24–89, which covers

Mary Place, Thomas Street, Goreham Place, Day's Cottages, tents thereabouts, and Kenilworth Street. Note that the census was taken in April, just before the start of the 'travelling' season. Other files on Gypsies in the Kensington and Chelsea Public Library with information on tent dwellers come from the 1871 census, book 41, pp.88-9, and, in the case of Gypsies at Kensal Green, from book 91, pp.78-9.

8. This surname was difficult to read.

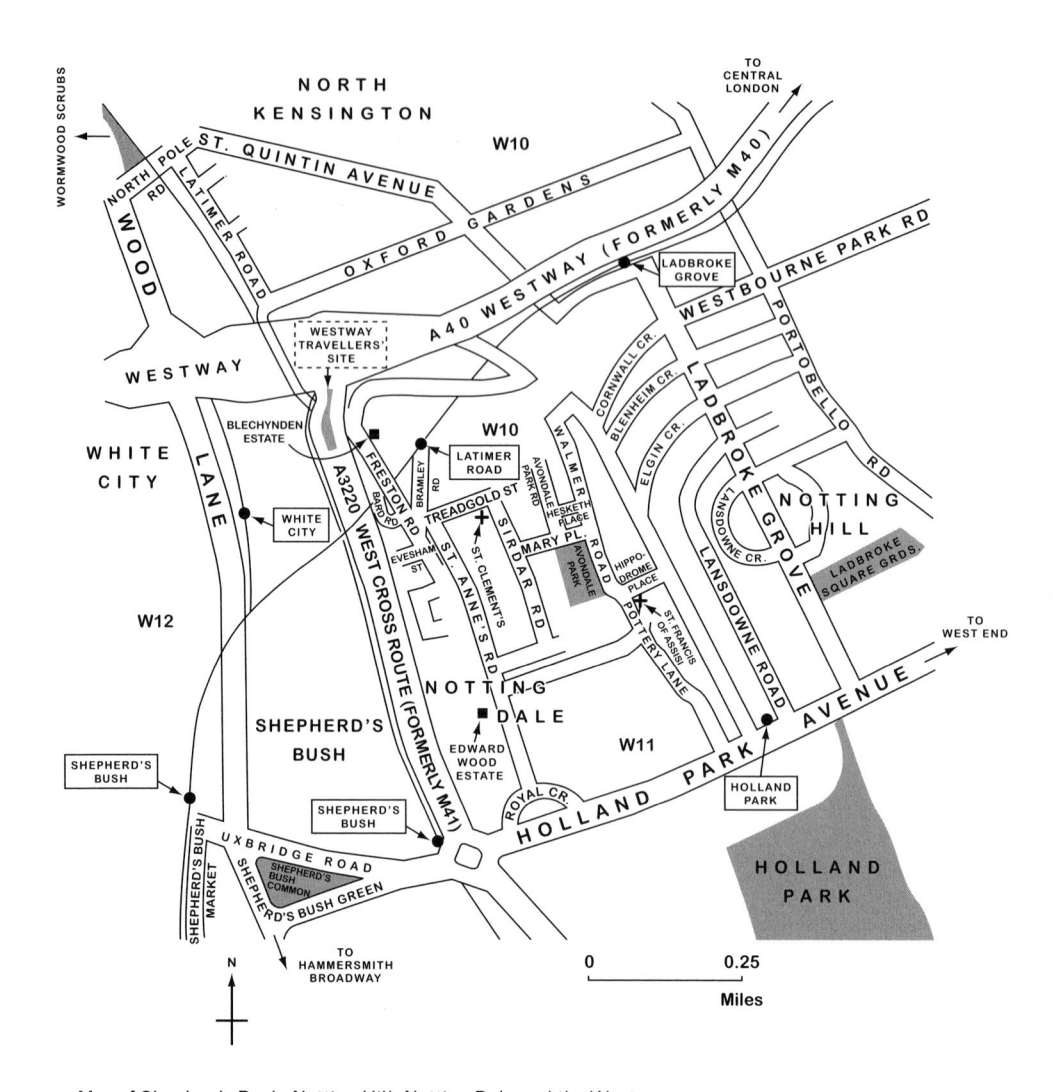

Map of Shepherds Bush, Notting Hill, Notting Dale and the Westway

4

NORTH KENSINGTON, HAMMERSMITH & WESTWAY SITE, 1900-1987

All the gypsies in the country are not upon the roads. Many of them live in houses, and that very respectably, nay even aristocratically. Yes, and it may be, o reader, that thou has met them and knowest them not, any more than though knowest many other deep secrets of the hearts and lives of those who live around thee.

C.G. Leland, *The Gypsies*, 1882

South Kensington is the aristocrats and we're working-class, that's the difference. The landlords have made a good thing out of it.

Kate Adams, 94 years old, Notting Dale resident, 1987.

No Dogs, No Irish, No Coloureds

Common sign in 1950s, Hammersmith and Kensington

People of one race and similar habits would have difficulty living in peace in such an environment; but the difficulties are greatly increased when one group, the West Indians, have different habits from their neighbours ... Almost more exasperating still, instead of being the downtrodden inferiors of whom their white neighbours read at school, they are assured, enterprising and in other ways superior to at least some of the English and Irish with whom they find themselves living ... Clearly there is a tinder here waiting for a spark ... a brew for Moseley to sup.

Labour MP J.P.W. Mallalieu, 'Background to trouble', *New Statesman*, 11 July 1959 [reprinted as '35 years ago', *New Statesman and Society*, 15 July 1994]

This chapter examines the Westway Site's struggle for existence from 1970 to 1984 in the wider context of immigration and the neighbourhood. A full account of life at the site between 1984 and 1987 is given in the last three chapters of the book, but some occurrences during that time, as well as since then, unavoidably slip into this one.

Immigrants

By 1987 North Kensington and north Hammersmith included not only British and Irish-born people, some of whom were Jewish, Romany or Traveller, but others of Spanish, Serbian, Italian and Caribbean origin, as well as relative newcomers from Morocco, Greece, Portugal, the Philippines, Pakistan, India, the Middle East and sub-Saharan Africa. Furthermore, since that time there has been an infusion of immigrants from eastern and central Europe, and even from Russia.

Irish
Irish Republicanism, it may be said, was born of the Irish rebellion of 1798 led by the Protestant nationalist leader Wolfe Tone. Over a century later it gave rise to the failed Easter 'Rising'; Britain's 'martyrdom' of fifteen 'Rising' leaders; resurgence of the movement under Sinn Féin in 1919; and its partial eclipse in 1922 as the Irish parliament in Dublin, *Dáil Eireann*, ratified the nation's dominion status and allegiance to the King, while Northern Ireland (as it now was) remained integral to the Union. Despite the Treaty and years in opposition to the ruling *Fine Gael* party, de Valera's *Fianna Fáil* was elected and in 1937 ushered in a constitution declaring *Eire*, meaning the whole of Ireland, a sovereign national territory.[1]

The 1916 Easter Rising did not endear the Irish to the British people, especially some of the Irish in London. Nor, one may imagine, did an IRA bombing campaign in Britain in 1938 (Coogan 2002), during the course of which it tried to blow up Hammersmith Bridge, do the migrant cause much good. Nor presumably did Eire's declaration of neutrality in 1939. But to consider these effects on the London Irish we need to go back a little.

After the Catholic Emancipation Bill was passed in 1820 the Catholic Church in England grew sufficiently confident to speak out against 'mixed marriages' and so reduce their frequency (Fielding 1993, 70). As an index of social integration, however, the rate of intermarriage between English Protestants and Irish Catholics differed from place to place according to the gender balance of migrants. Where Irish Catholic men and women settled in roughly equal measure the proportion of inter-faith marriages was less than it was where Irish men or women formed a gender minority. For instance, in London in the early 1930s females born in Ireland accounted for 61.5 per cent of all the Irish-born, making it necessary for many of them to look for English partners, preferably Catholic, but failing that non-Catholic. Generally speaking the percentage of mixed marriages increased after 1914. In Bermondsey, south London, for example, where in 1881 mixed marriages accounted for 25% of unions, by 1928 the proportion had doubled (Fielding 1993, 73). Here class played a role, with educated Irish 'professionals' proving more conservative than their working-class compatriots.[2]

In North Kensington and Hammersmith, as elsewhere in Britain, many Irish had begun moving up the social ladder before the turn of the twentieth century. They were helped by the fact that the 1922 Treaty acknowledged the Irish in Britain as 'British' while at the same time waiving the need of newcomers for passports. This is not to say newcomers were not confronted by discrimination. When it came to housing, jobs and career progression many Irish faced problems. Coogan cites O'Connor (1972), pointing out that, outside of Scotland and the north-east, Irish workers suffered badly in the 1930s from a lack of leadership from older established Irish and that after 1916 the same was true for many professionally qualified immigrants. He even goes so far as to say 'The sector which might have provided community leadership, the Irish professionals, tended to hive itself off into a ghetto of its own' (Coogan 2002, 121-2). The term 'ghetto' is loosely used here; what is clear is social differentiation along class lines.

In working-class North Kensington oral history attests to local sectarianism and ethnic prejudice[3], especially in the inter-war years, but it was not confined to this period. Racial discrimination in housing lasted well into the 1950s as evidenced by the 'room to let, no Irish' signs in front bed-sitter windows or on the advertisement boards of newsagents. It was not until the Race Relations Act came into effect in 1959, aimed primarily at stamping out discrimination and racial hatred directed at Britain's new 'coloured' immigrants, that such matters were officially addressed, but even then racial discrimination against individuals, including Irish people, continued well into the 1980s. To its credit *The Irish Post*, a media voice for the Irish in Britain, went a long way to draw attention to such matters, including discrimination enacted against Irish Travellers by individuals or public authorities. And well it might, because national tabloid media like *The Daily Mail* and *Evening Standard*, in the 1980s, regularly ran florid stories with accompanying pictures on the alleged misdemeanours and atrocious conduct of Irish Travellers.

Jews
In the early years of the twentieth century Russian and East European Jews moved to Notting Hill from the East End and ran small textile businesses. By 1910 the area around Kensington Park was popularly known as 'Little Israel' or 'Jews Island'. A decade or so later, following the Wall Street crash, national unemployment rose giddily, thousands of families in the capital were affected, and Jews became scapegoats. Many men were also thrown out of work in North Kensington when London's horse-drawn omnibuses became motorised. Anti-Semitic demonstrations organised by the British Union of Fascists took place in the 1930s, but were met by local resistance, especially from members of the Communist Party. New racist hostility arose in 1955, when the fascist leader, Sir Oswald Moseley, stood as parliamentary candidate for North Kensington on a platform of stopping Caribbean immigration (even though many of the first to arrive were British ex-servicemen), and here it was local Jews who often provided the resistance and lent practical support.[4]

West Indians

When West Indians arrived in North Kensington in the late 1940s and 1950s, drawn by its location and the availability of low-rent accommodation, it was local people's first experience of 'coloured' people. Their arrival would herald the first 'race' riots in North Kensington since Irish and British fought each other in the Kensal Green area in the 1860s, and it led in time to the development of an extremely ethnically diverse neighbourhood where 'coloured' faces were no longer 'minority' faces.

By 1900 a stock of large sturdy houses built by speculative developers in anticipation of aspiring middle-class buyers remained unsold when these buyers chose instead to take advantage of London's new public transport systems to live in suburbs further out. Developers and absentee landlords (frequently one and the same, and often residents of central Kensington) were consequently obliged to divide their houses into flats and rent them to low-income families, and then allowed them to become run down as the local authority, Kensington Vestry, looked on. By 1945, as people moved away from what by now were 'slums' to 'New Towns' and estates in and beyond the 'Green Belt', landlords were pleased to see their vacant flats taken up by West Indians. Unfortunately for the newcomers, their fortune was short lived, as inside a few years the local borough had drawn up plans, in line with Victorian intentions, to transform North Kensington into the sort of prime real estate already found in central Kensington. To see these plans through, slum landlords first had to get rid of sitting tenants and, in 1957, Harold Macmillan's Rent Act made this easier, though other factors colluded, including the post-war emergence from austerity which helped fuel a consumer youth culture, youthful rebellion across class lines, and a more strongly extolled British and 'English' identity. England, after all, had won the war.

It was also a time of gang wars, especially in the East End where the Kray twins ruled, but it was not confined there. 'Violence was building up in Paddington and Notting Hill as rival groups horned [sic] in to milk the gambling, prostitution and rent rackets of West

London' (Pearson 1976, 129). Not that the Krays were interested in Notting Hill. 'There was no money here for them and from the press exposés of the time it was clear that the law would soon be cracking down' (Pearson 1976, 129). All the same, it was a hostile place in which to be a post-war immigrant, especially one with a black skin, and although the fascist leader Moseley failed at the ballot box in 1955, his henchmen at street level had plenty of young raw material to work on.

Absentee landlords, some of whom were socially well connected (Peter Rachman, for example, had played a part in the Profumo affair that helped bring down Macmillan), allowed their properties to deteriorate further as a means of forcing out tenants, Caribbeans especially. The worst resorted to stand-over tactics and in many cases actual violence. West Indians in Notting Hill were not helped by the 1957 Act, which made it easier to evict tenants, and came under increasing attack in their homes, in pubs and clubs, and on the streets. This was vastly different from anything the Irish had ever faced. Finally, on Whit Sunday 1958, a young Antiguan named Kelso Cochrane was stabbed to death by whites.

When over 800 people of different ethnic origins attended Cochrane's funeral at Kensal Green it appeared the district had finally awoken to the need to confront racism. In 1959 the first Race Relations Act passed into law; not that this brought an immediate end to violence, let alone other forms of discrimination. Right-wing organisations like the Union of Fascists and the White Defence League continued to foment hatred. In 1960 and 1961 white gangs targeted West Indians and their social clubs; at times they grew to mobs[5] of between fifty and a hundred. Ironically, the rock and roll music fast taking hold in Britain in the mid to late 1950s had largely Afro-American roots, but these were discerned mainly by other musicians. At venues like Notting Hill's 'Rio Club', 'black' dance music like calypso was already entrenched.

In 1959, not long after his famous 'Winds of Change' speech in South Africa, Harold Macmillan, architect of the 1957 Rent Act, an Edwardian to his boots, became Prime Minister. Four years later, at the very height of the Cold War, Macmillan was forced to resign on health grounds, broken by the scandal of sex and lies surrounding his Minister for War, Jack Profumo. By the time Harold Wilson's Labour Party came to power at the next election the West Indian community of North Kensington had already taken initiatives: they had established tenants' associations to combat racism; formed a Coloured Peoples' Progressive Association; and proposed an annual carnival. Tenants' Associations in streets like Colville Square, Colville Road and Powis Square aimed, however, not only to protect West Indians but also the interests of poor Irish and English.

Although by 1965 most landlords, under pressure of the law, had ceased their worst forms of exploitation, many had turned their attention to more lucrative markets in other parts of the borough thereby forcing new Conservative administrations to take up the provision of more public housing. This they did reluctantly and inadequately despite their borough being London's richest. For instance, in the mid-1960s Kensington supplied merely 5,381 low-cost dwellings compared in 1966 with the 922,391 provided by the borough of Southwark (Owusu and Ross 1988, 61).

The first Notting Hill Carnival was held in 1963. Intended originally as a neighbourhood event for people of all 'races' it would in time become a rallying point for a burgeoning 'black British' identity, but not before it ended on several occasions in race riots, including a particularly bad episode in 1976. A subsequent inquiry into the 1976 riots placed much of the blame on the crowd-control tactics of the police whose racial prejudices and other institutional failings had earlier been exposed by an independent investigation into the circumstances surrounding Kelso Cochrane's death in 1958.

Since the 1970s, in partnership with the Notting Hill Amenity Trust (NHAT) (Duncan 1992) and with funding from the Greater London Council (dissolved by Margaret Thatcher in 1987 and revived in 2003 under its former leader, the then Mayor of London, Ken Livingstone), the Carnival has become the biggest in Europe, a celebration of multicultural policies (see Cohen 1993) and a national focus for multiculturalism. Furthermore, an eloquent speech

General Anne Hearne's mother.
Reproduced with the kind permission of Mrs Florence Allen.

delivered by Livingstone shortly after the London bombings in July 2005 served to reinforce the Carnival's nationwide significance.

Totters and Costermongers
Totters (the word is of late-nineteenth-century origin and comes from the verb 'tot', meaning 'to go rag picking' or 'scavenge') are general dealers in material waste. Sometimes called 'rag and bone' men, their business is urban foraging and recycling. Up until the 1960s and 1970s the totter, with his barrow or horse and cart, was a familiar sight around all residential parts of London; North Kensington had many of them. The TV characters Steptoe and Son, who were supposed to live in Shepherds Bush, were totters. And quite a few still live there.

Costermongers (derived from 'costard' — a species of apple) are street sellers of fruit and veg, and also fish and poultry. As noted earlier, Mayhew (1985) found many of them to be Irish. Rough and showy, they spoke a cant or back slang. Bangor Street in the Potteries, especially, was full of them, just as it was also full of totters with their gaily painted barrows.

The costermongers and totters of Bangor Street shared, in the early 1900s, not just deprivation but also a sense of 'little community'. So when its houses were pulled down after World War II as part of 'slum clearance', just as houses were in other streets, most of that feeling went too. In place of terraced houses with steps up to their front doors came a low-rise block of council flats named Henry Dickens Court, and though some families remained, most did not. They either went to other flats in the area or to flats and houses on the White City Estate, in north Hammersmith, or to East Acton. The 'lucky' horseshoes hanging outside the front doors of several Henry Dickens Court flats in 1984 (and possibly still) hark back to those simpler, harder times when all the narrow streets hereabouts resounded to the clatter of horses' hoofs, the cry of traders, and the sound of children playing.

Notting Hill and Notting Dale still have their small traders and dealers, including totters and costermongers. One lot of totters have stables a few yards from the Westway Site in Stable Way. The

Portobello Road is famous for its street-market, which is by no means confined to bric-a-brac and old clothes. Most of the stalls and shops lining each side are given over to fruit and veg and other foodstuffs, though there is every other kind of retail interest besides, and cafes galore. Less apparent, except to those who know them, are Romany and Irish Traveller women from the Westway and other sites, who go there periodically both to shop and sell. Speaking of small traders, I should not overlook the fried fish vendor vans, the ice-cream vans, the man who from time to time sold whelks and winkles from a stall in St Anne's Road alongside the Edward Woods Estate, the small army of carriers and removal men, and the owner of the horse van in Freston Road.

Gypsies, Travellers and friends
According to older Travellers at the Westway Site the flats around Latimer Road are 'full of Gypsies'. The same claim was made in a letter published in the Kensington Post in May 1976, signed 'A Gypsy', who reckoned that 85 per cent of council house tenants in w10 (the area around the site near Latimer Road station) were Gypsies and then went on to explain that 'It doesn't matter if he lives in a flat, a house, a caravan, or a palace, a gypsy will always be a gypsy and proud of it'.[6] It was the sort of remark Travellers and Gypsies often made to me; one that opens up the whole question of identity and one we can start answering now by examining the evidence of Romanies and Travellers, not just from historical records but directly from the Travellers themselves and from their *gorgio* (non-Gypsy) friends and acquaintances.

Joe Hearne, a cousin of Gypsy evangelist Rodney Smith, came to the area in the 1870s. After his wife died, leaving him with four children, Joe re-married, this time to Marian (or Mary-Anne). In the 1870s the family, for a while, occupied a tent in the Potteries before moving into a wagon parked in Hesketh Place, near Bangor Street, an area the locals called 'the Puzzles'.

Joe Hearne, like many other Romanies living there at the time, was a caner of chairs and, according to Florence Allen, whose husband was a grandson of Joe Hearne,[7] the old man's clients included two well-known West End department stores, John Lewis and D.H. Evans. Joe's daughter Anne, Marian or Mary-Anne, also known as General Anne, used to help him. General Anne Hearne married a *gorgio* called William Davis and had a baby boy, but her husband died while still only in his twenties and in due course she married again, this time to George Allen, a *gorgio* she met one Saturday night at a dance at the Rugby Clubs in Walmer Road.

For a time, Anne Hearne and George Allen lived at Bushey, in the county of Hertfordshire, to the north of London, where a son was born to them whom they called George. When Anne's mother died, the couple and their children went back to Notting Hill to help Joe mend chairs and run coconut shies on Wormwood Scrubs fair-days late into the 1930s.[8] This reveals three things: that contrary to norms Romanies marry *gorgios*; that *gorgio* partners sometimes adopt Romany values, ways and mores that, as in this case, involved Gypsy modes of livelihood; and that when they do, their identification with Romanies may be passed on through socialisation to later generations — as in the case of George Allen (junior), the General's son, and to George's *gorgio* wife, Florence Allen (my informant) and Florence's own offspring.

The first time I met Florence Allen was in 1986 at her home in Mary Place, opposite Avondale Park. Florrie by then was probably in her mid- to late sixties. Originally a Gallagher, Florrie was born in Talbot Road, off Portobello Road, one of eight children. Her father had been a leather worker. One of her uncles had been a totter who collected rags and remnants from the Jewish tailors, which he then made into children's clothes to sell at the Sunday 'rag and veg' fair in Bangor Street. 'They was all totters and dealers then, rough but honest', said Florrie, who often went out totting with her uncle, or, failing that, went hunting for rabbits with him on Wormwood Scrubs to sell later in the market.

The Gallagher family deplored Florrie's marriage to George Allen and loathed her going to work with 'Gypsies', but Florence 'loved the Hearnes' and what they stood for, especially her mother-

Florence Allen, St Mary's Place, Notting Dale, 1991

in-law, who taught her to cane chairs and how to hawk and charm as only she could. General Anne Hearne 'talked lovely' and she valued 'style'. Knowing how and when to dress up and go 'on the town' and spend was something Florrie's mother-in-law had taught her. Pride and self-respect demanded one spent freely occasionally without undue fear of tomorrow.

Joe Hearne, or Dad-Joe as she called him, ran coconut shies with his brother Jack on Wormwood Scrubs. Their cousin Nini sold the fleshy cracked shells afterwards in the Potteries. Fair stall licenses went to the highest bidders, making it necessary sometimes for the Hearnes to first pawn their rings and other valuables. Setting up public latrines at Pinner Fair, Middlesex, and at Ascot Races, was another scheme: 'Piddle and poop, a penny' was the cry.

Among Joe Hearne's contemporaries on the Scrubs was the Smart family who went on to own one of Europe's biggest circuses, rivalled in England only by Bertram Mills, whose Big Top was a Christmas fixture at Olympia, west Kensington, in the post-war years. Other contemporaries in the Dale were Billy Hearnden, 'the Kangaroo Boxer'; Billy Nolan, 'the copper basher'; Billy Upper, whose speciality was smashing raw marrow bones on his chest; 'Old Born-Drunk'; Ginger Elmer the undertaker; and Old Mother George of Thresher Place, otherwise known as 'Old Mother Dirty Belly'. The nicknames reveal something of the familiarity and intimacy that came with living in a 'little community'.

Like all Romanies in Notting Dale, the Hearnes had many ways of making money beside the ones already described. One of Anne's younger sisters, according to the 1871 census, did dressmaking. And Anne herself told fortunes until her father was converted by the Salvation Army and took up preaching at the Four Square Gospel Church at Notting Hill Gate.[9] Dad-Joe sold old clothes as well as fresh vegetables from a painted barrow, the like of which brought colour to what 94-year-old Kate Adams unhesitatingly called 'a real slum in those days'.

General Anne Hearne and George Allen's clients included families in Westbourne Grove and people in 'Millionaires Row' on the other side of Holland Park Avenue; nor were they alone in servicing the rich. Until royalty lent its patronage to the Royal School for the Blind, who taught their pupils cane-work, one of Anne's brothers-in-law by her first marriage repaired cane bed-heads at Kensington Palace, Buckingham Palace and St James Palace.

George Allen junior hid his 'Gypsy' identity and got a clerical job in a solicitor's office, yet Florrie revealed he never lost his 'Gypsy' ways. Nor did their son, an accountant in the City before he switched to general dealing, including trading in second-hand cars, and went on to own an appartment in Monte Carlo. Further proof in Florrie's eyes that 'Gypsies narf clever people'. I shall come back to her in a moment.

Nobby Buckingham resided in St James Place, also known as 'Devils' Alley', a street he described as 'full' of totters, Buckinghams, O'Shaughnessies, and Reagans,[10] and though he never said so there is good reason to think he was a Romany himself, or at least of Romany descent. Nobby father's father was born in 1850 and was a blacksmith by trade. He was also a totter of brass and rags; traded at Barnet Fair and was 'a good judge of horses'; ran a coal shop; sold cracked china; kept a monkey (presumably for performances); and in his spare time, built carts and barrows for costermongers.

Growing up in the Dale before World War I, Nobby Buckingham played 'two-up', a very simple gambling game involving the toss of two coins, which I occasionally saw Irish Travellers play on the Westway (and nowhere else until I came to Australia where it used to be popular in the bush and is now played in casinos). As a young man Nobby went hop-picking in summer, enjoyed pub songbird competitions,[11] and boxed for cash prizes on Sundays at the Scrubs. At the outbreak of war in 1914 he enlisted in the army on the same day as his friend Frank Penfold and his brother Judd, who was another 'good judge [and handler] of horses', so good in fact that despite being non-literate he was quickly promoted to sergeant, an achievement not uncommon among Romanies.

Penfold is a well-known English Gypsy surname. Before the arrival of the M40, Gypsies named Penfold had lived in houses on the west side of Upper Latimer Road. In the 1960s they moved to King Street, off the Broadway in central Hammersmith, and stayed until forced to move again, this time to make way for the Hammersmith Flyover, which now links south Kensington and Earls Court to Chiswick and the Great West Road (Taylor 1983). Until this happened Mrs Penfold, the widow of Jim Penfold (whose father Tom lived in Latimer Road until his death in 1949), sold flowers in the market opposite the Met station. In the 1970s others named Penfold lived in a wagon behind the Harrow Club, on the corner of Latimer (Freston) Road and Wharf (Bard) Road.[12] In 1986 Billy Hunt, a Stable Way totter, confirmed that Gypsies called Penfold used to live in Latimer Road. It is therefore likely they were related to the Penfolds behind the Harrow Club who, in turn, through Frank and Judd, knew Nobby Buckingham. That being the case, one may fairly deduce that Nobby was also a Gypsy.

Billy Hunt was a *gorgio* who had worked out of the stables in Stable Way since the M40 was completed in 1970. The stables had replaced ones that had previously stood in this section of Latimer Road before demolition began. Before 1970 Billy Hunt kept horses in Norland Gardens on the south side of Notting Hill and, until the downfall of communism in Hungary, had traded ponies with its State Circus. On one visit he attended a Roma wedding.

Mrs Allen's identification with Gypsies was evident not just in what she said but also in what she did. Her kitchen mantleshelf and wall above the hearth were hung with brass and copper. Her small front room contained a display of porcelain, bone china, horse figurines and hunting prints; perhaps not uniquely 'Gypsy', but certainly in keeping with things Roma. Indeed, it resembled the 'clean room' of the house-dwelling Hungarian Vlach Gypsies that Stewart portrays in his ethnographic film, *Across the Tracks*. In Florrie's front room a studio photograph showed a handsome, dark-haired, woman who I guessed was in her thirties. She was Florrie's daughter, and Florrie put her looks down to General Mary-Anne Hearne's genes. Another time, close to Christmas, I spotted in one corner of the room an intricately decorated handmade Gypsy cart, some 18 inches high, awaiting a lucky grandson.

Ten years after first visiting Florrie Allen, on one of my return visits from Australia, I got around to interviewing the daughter in the photograph. By coincidence she happened to be living in Mortlake, not far from where I was staying, and only a few minutes' walk from where another Gypsy family ran a florists' shop in Sheen Lane, opposite the station. Florrie's daughter had previously run a pub, *The Jolly Gardeners* in Ship Lane, probably the oldest lane in Mortlake. I knew it well and had sometimes drunk there in the 1980s, not knowing who the tenant was. She was now working as a receptionist in the medical suite at the Civic Centre built over Hampton Square where (unknown to her) several Romany and Irish immigrant families had lived before World War II, including close relatives of the flower shop owners.

Proud as she was of her Romany background, Florence's

daughter did not appear to count it more important than any of her other possible ethnic identities, though I could have been mistaken. This was also the impression I got from the woman's young nephew who by chance I happened to meet while I was visiting his grandmother at her home in Mary Place. 'John'[13] was 21 and lived in Hounslow, not far from Heathrow. The 'heath' in Heathrow refers to Hounslow Heath, which was once a favourite camping place for Gypsies and is not far from Northolt aerodrome, on the Great West Road, where Irish Travellers often used to stop illegally in the 1980s. Heathrow is also not far from Hanwell where, according to Florence Allen, several Hearnes are buried alongside other Romanies, including some named Jones and Parker. John is Florence's grandson, General Anne Hearne's great-grandson, and Joe Hearne's great-great-grandson. Yet in conversation he said he knew various people with Gypsy connections, including some 'showmen' of Argentinean background named Ayres (Aires). Together with the toy cart present (awaiting him or possibly a brother or a cousin), this knowledge, this interest, albeit in a small way, suggests a lasting identification as 'Gypsy' even though the *gorgio* side would appear to provide a more compelling identity, simply judged rationally.

One of the most interesting 'nomad' phenomena of the second half of the twentieth century was the appearance in the 1970s and 1980s of a new kind of Traveller, one for the most part without generational ties to Romanies or Irish Travellers, namely New Age Travellers or, more simply, New Travellers. In the winter of 1986/7 six New Traveller domestic units (neither 'families' nor 'households' seem quite the right word) pulled onto land behind Bard Road, off Freston Road (old Latimer). They were not the first to do so; ten years earlier New Age Travellers calling themselves 'The Republic of Frestonia' lived here. In 1987 another group in converted lorries and various other commercial vehicles, including an old showman's caravan, parked on ground at the back of Galena Road, off King Street, Hammersmith. Some of them had links with former so-called Frestonian Republicans who now called themselves the Mutoid Waste Disposal Company and recycled vehicle parts as sculpture

(Griffin 1995). In 1987 Galena Road ran at right angles to a row of derelict cottages in Glenthorne Road where Irish Travellers had until recently squatted. About the same time, on the other side of King Street, near Hammersmith Broadway, two caravans belonging to the Penfolds (or Pinfolds) had parked up for more than a year. To my knowledge, though, the Penfolds and New Travellers did not mix. Indeed, the latter said they preferred to keep their distance from both Gypsies and Irish Travellers. Unfortunately the Penfolds moved before I had a chance to meet them.

In 1911 the Reverend George Hall remarked you could tell a house-dwelling Gypsy living in the streets around Latimer Road station (which an MP in the 1930s called '"Piggeries Junction" the worst, the ugliest, and the dirtiest station in the whole of London' (Burnett 1983, 34)) just by their physiognomy. Such remarks, of course, are full of the dangers of stereotyping; as Leland's remark at the start of this chapter indicates. All the same, it would be silly to dismiss physical appearance out of hand, for the fact is that, put alongside other factors, 'physical appearances' may indeed lead one to correctly identify a Gypsy, though the method is far from foolproof. Successfully identifying people this way tells us nothing about all those who were *not* so-identified. 'Identity' is a complex, contingent and multi-layered matter. That said, I remained curious to test George Hall's remark; particularly given comments made by Westway Site residents about the numerous Gypsies living in local flats.

My opportunity came one afternoon in 1986. The setting was Hall's or, to be more precise, the actual foyer of Latimer Road tube station. My 'experimental subjects' were two women I presumed to be mother and daughter and (from their appearances) flat or house-dwellers. My 'research technique' was simple: a quick approach and the question, 'Excuse me, but do you *rokker* (speak) Romanes?' The result came in parts: a look of puzzlement, a moment's hesitation, and a request from the older woman that I repeat myself. Aware of a train approaching, I did so, adding, 'Are you Romany by any chance?' Further hesitation. 'Why,' she asked, 'I don't look like one do I?' 'Well,' I replied, 'there is surely no harm if you do?' This time a smile: 'Yes,' she replied, her mother was a Romany named Browning and with that she wished me a pleasant goodbye and hurried up to the train. Hall was partly vindicated. In terms of appearance I found hairstyle (see also Court 1985, 41), gait, dress and jewellery helped me identify Travellers — Irish and Romany. Asked whether they thought they ever *failed* to recognise a Traveller, some female Irish Travellers replied they usually 'picked it up', though it sometimes took a moment or two. And did they ever want to hide their identity and, if so, how? 'Oh yes,' they replied in chorus, 'take off the jewellery and leave behind the handbag.'

On another occasion, as I happened to walk past Foreland House flats in Walmer Road, just behind Latimer Road station, my attention was drawn to the sound of Irish country music emanating from a car parked with its doors open outside a ground-floor flat where two small children wearing gold earrings were playing with an elderly woman I guessed to be their grandmother. At the same time, a young woman obviously related to the family, wearing earrings of a sort much favoured by Travellers and Gypsies, came down the street with a robust rolling gait. Without hesitation I asked her straight out, adding I worked on the Westway Site. 'Yes,' she said, she was a 'Traveller'. Her father was a Stanley and her mother was a Lane and one or both of them came from Bushey.

Donald Kenrick, mentioned earlier, was an activist in the early days of the Westway Site. According to him, sometime around 1936–7 about a hundred Gypsy families used to camp on ground lying between Latimer Road station and White City, but they later moved into houses on the east side of Portobello Road. This adds weight to the notion of a substantial number of Romanies or Travellers living here in houses. So does a facsimile 1911 street directory for Notting Hill.[14] Information on residents printed on the back included, for Latimer Road: at numbers 1 and 17, two persons called Shaw; one a removal man, the other a slate roofer. William Dean, a chair-mender, at 28; at 118, by the railway arches towards Shepherds Bush, Edward Lovell; at 151 Hannah Lovell ran a laundry; at 219 a Mrs Cooper lived next to *The Britannia* on the corner of Wharf Road; Harry Cooper, a wheelwright, resided at 271; Herbert Shaw at 301; Charles Lovell at 34; and in St Anne's Road, near what is now the Edward Woods Estate, Charles Buckingham, who was surely a relative of Nobby. Other 'Gypsy'-sounding surnames found in the street were Harris, Wright, Green and Wells.

Clear evidence of Irish Travellers living in the neighbourhood between the wars is harder to find. The nearest thing was what the parish priest of St Francis of Assisi, Oliver McTernan, recalled concerning one of his former parishioners, a 90 year old Mrs Hickey, who had died not long before. She related that as a child she had been brought up in the Potteries in a wagon. This would suggest that some of the Irish Travellers who had lived in wagons about the turn of the century later moved into houses, which they still occupied in the inter-war period and after.

'Prince' Gypsy Lee, who was a snowy-bearded Romany who favoured head-scarf and earrings, lived for years in the 1970s in a wagon parked on ground in Barby Road, on the west side of Latimer (Freston) Road. His apparel went down well with his fortune-telling clients in the Portobello Road. By the time I arrived Lee had been gone a long time but his name was still visible in paint on an old corrugated iron fence. Other evidence of Lee are words attributed to him in the *West London Observer* of October 1974, on the eve of his marriage to a *gorgio* woman, not long after the arrival of the first Irish Travellers under the motorway. 'These are not our kind of people ... They are not proper Romany gypsies'. Most locals agreed with him, *gorgios* and Romanies alike. As one Gypsy woman put it to me, years later: 'the thoroughbreds have gone'. Bred out. Now they're all 'hedge-crawlers', 'didikais' and 'Tinkers'.

By this last view Gypsies are 'born', not made. People do not 'become' Gypsies, Gypsies only perpetuate themselves or die out, what counts is 'blood' or genes. Yet, as argued previously, the situation is really more complicated than this. People *can* become 'Gypsies' and do so, though never easily or quickly, for identity is bound up with both biology and culture and 'biology' itself is a matter of how cultures frame it. What is (or who are) 'blood' in one society is not necessarily the same in another set of people, which is why anthropologists distinguish between patrilineal and matrilineal societies. Thus, on the one hand, identity depends on breeding and gene pools, and on the other breeding practices (like all other practices) are shaped by notions of what behaviour is culturally appropriate to one's identity. Therefore, as long as Romanies and Irish Travellers, and many *gorgios* for that matter, continue to think of Romanies and Travellers as living in close-knit bounded communities, they will for the most part latch on to biology rather than culture as the thing which most 'makes' Gypsies or Irish Travellers; or, in the case of the Irish, they think of them as a biological sub-set of the 'settled' population which has escaped the latter's norms.

Development in North Kensington and Hammersmith

Changes to the physical environment of North Kensington have been going on for decades as historians have documented. But aside from the Westway and the high-rise flats that appeared forty years ago, the 1990s brought a vigorous program of urban renewal and gentrification to the Dale as community development programs, often conducted by the NKAT sought to reduce urban blight and wasteland. Emerging around the time of the A40(M) project, the NKAT has helped set up numerous small businesses and community projects in premises located beneath the A40. It has been responsible for the development of public gardens, paved walks, cycle paths and BMX tracks, as well as state-of-the-art recreational facilities. It has put up children's playgrounds, used graffiti artists to cover ugly concrete, and helped sponsor the now world-famous Notting Hill Carnival. In the process it has created jobs and helped relieve the boredom and frustration of thousands of young people of various ethnic origins living in the tower blocks, other council housing, and on the Westway Travellers Site.

Since 1987 the boroughs of Kensington and Chelsea (K&C) and Hammersmith and Fulham (H&F) have also played important roles in enhancing the environment. Improvements are particularly noticeable around Latimer Road tube station. Here K&C have upgraded public housing precincts by building well-designed low- and medium-rise housing; redesigning public spaces to return 'ownership' to residents thereby reducing litter and vandalism; upgrading streets and paths on housing estates; planting trees; and by installing CCTV and better street lighting. At the same time K&C has increased its income from rates by attracting new enterprises to marginal spaces. So where oil-streaked car-breaker yards and the like abounded there are now businesses involved in the high-tech and design industries. Finally, recent steps taken to connect Notting Dale to White City by an overpass across the A3220 are helping to undo the sense of semi-isolation that for a century and a half has characterised the Dale and Latimer Road.

The Westway Site

The history of the Latimer Road Gypsy Site, which opened for business in April 1974, is part of the history of Gypsies in the area and the history of post-war Irish immigration, and is bound up with the arrival of Irish Travellers and Gypsies beneath the Westway flyover in the weeks before Christmas 1972. It also belongs with the history of Gypsy caravan site legislation going back to 1968, and to the vexed business of 'designation'.

Site legislation
When in 1968 Parliament passed an Act obliging all local authorities in England and Wales to provide caravan sites for Gypsies living or resorting within their municipal borders, it defined 'Gypsies' as 'persons of nomadic habit of life, whatever their race or origin, but does not include members of an organised group of travelling showmen, or persons engaged in travelling circuses, travelling together as such' (Forrester 1985, 1). It also stipulated that where a London borough, county council or other authority could prove it had no 'suitable' land for the purpose or, in the case of a county council, that in the five years before 1968 it had negligeable numbers of Gypsies living in or

'resorting' to its territory, such that it made the notion of 'provision' look foolish, then that authority could apply to central government for exemption. This remained the law until 1980, in which year passage of the Local Government Planning and Land Act removed the proviso, voided numerous central Government controls and repealed all previous exemptions — though none had actually been granted in London — which went far to explain the record, hitherto, of inadequate site provision (Forrester 1985, 34). Forrester also points out that something the 1980 Act did *not* change was the Minister's power to 'order' local authorities to provide sites where he saw fit, and it is a point he returns to when he discusses court instructions to H&F in 1973 regarding the Westway Site (Forrester 1985, 34)

According to Section 9 of the 1968 Act any local authority meeting its minimum legal requirement to provide ten caravan pitches could apply to the Secretary of State (or Minister) for the Environment for 'designation' (Forrester 1985, 34).[15] If granted, the authority could then issue summonses to Gypsies stopping anywhere other than on its official site. 'Designation' also allowed the authority to evict caravan owners and their vehicles and, if necessary, eject them beyond its municipal borders and impound the caravans. That power was further strengthened by the 1980 Act, which allowed several district councils covering large swathes of country, including entire counties, to apply collectively for designation. Where granted, this would permit authorities not only to evict and move on named individuals, but also entire, un-named, groups. Thus the two Acts together effectively restricted large numbers of commercial nomads from legally practising nomadism.

As already noted, to be eligible to apply for 'designation' a local authority had only to provide ten pitches. However if on application the Minister considered it 'not necessary or expedient' (Forrester 1985, 37) for an authority to provide a site, 'designation' — without provision — could still be granted. Consequently, councils allegedly *intending* to apply got away without providing anything in the meantime. Another consequence of designation was that where evictions occurred families faced the prospect of being shunted back and forth across municipal borders as separate authorities acted in their own interests. To make the situation even more ridiculous, where councils impounded caravans, making families homeless, they became statutorily obliged to find and fund 'emergency housing'. Since Irish Travellers arriving as immigrants or choosing to be nomadic anyway (no matter how long they'd lived in Britain) tended to be more mobile than Romanies, it is they who bore the legislation's brunt.

Most Irish Travellers arriving at the Westway for the first time between the early 1960s and late 1980s were young couples with small children. Mobility, as a means of finding much-needed shelter, whether in a caravan or a temporary stay with relatives in houses, was important. Those arriving for the first time after 1980 were particularly at risk, while those who had come earlier (or had been born in England) were more inured to the vicissitudes of British law.

When in December 1972, therefore, a dozen Irish Traveller and Romany families with caravans drove onto ground on the east side of Woods Lane, opposite the White City Estate, north Hammersmith, their arrival reflected the national shortage of 'Gypsy' caravan sites. Moreover, when they moved on in January 1973 to land under the M40 at the bottom of Latimer Road, just inside the borough boundary of K&C, they did so following the Minister's rejection of K&C's application for 'designation with nil provision' in 1970.

The campaign

Roy Wells was a Romany who had already been effective in getting local authorities in south London to provide Gypsy caravan sites. In 1972 Wells turned his attention to west London and took K&C to court for not providing pitches according to the 1968 Act. A court of appeal subsequently ruled in favour of K&C, stating that since only the Minister could 'insist' on councils providing sites, there was nothing the court or any authority could do about it, so K&C had acted within its legal rights when ordering evictions. The Gypsies and Travellers who moved beneath the flyover near Latimer Road station in January 1973 (whether all of them realised or not) thus formed part of Wells' already proven 'rolling campaign'.

In 1967 the Gypsy Council was established. Its founding members included Irish Travellers; Johnny Connors, for example, was a Vice President (Acton 1974). Furthermore, by 1970, under the leadership of its Secretary, Gratton Puxon, a *gorgio* with a history of campaigning on behalf of Travellers in Ireland, the Council was 'the strongest organisation of its kind in western Europe' (Acton 1974, 175). Later that year its educational section, the Gypsy Council Trust (Education), comprising Romanies, Irish Travellers and *gorgios* (including its chairperson Lady Plowden), renamed itself the National Gypsy Education Council (NGEC). Splits in the Gypsy Council appeared.

By 1971 the Gypsy Council was racked by factionalism based on personal and parochial agendas. Inside a year it split when a faction backed by certain members of the NGEC set up a rival body called the Romany Guild (Acton 1974). In 1973 Lady Plowden, supported by most of the NGEC and Gypsy Council, created the Advisory Council for the Education of Romanies and other Travellers (ACERT). The following year, Hughie Smith, the Gypsy Council's President, a northerner, split the Council further by creating the Northern Gypsy Education Council. Others responded by creating the Southern Gypsy Education Council (SGEC), a body that quickly set about building ties with the Inner London Education Authority (ILEA).

Roy Wells later became Secretary of the Gypsy Council and Donald Kenrick and Thomas Acton led the SGEC. Under Acton's influence the SGEC set up the Inner London Education Group (ILEG), aimed at addressing the educational needs of Gypsy and Traveller children in inner London. It quickly put pressure on H&F and K&C to provide a site for the Travellers parked under the Westway.

That H&F should have agreed with its neighbour K&C's application for designation in 1970 is not surprising.[16] Both were Conservative-led authorities, which considering rate-payers' reactions to the appearance of Travellers under the motorway in January 1973, regarded Gypsies and Irish Travellers as an electoral liability. Not that any of this deterred the likes of Wells and Acton. After twelve months of ILEG and Gypsy Council pressure, rumours of site construction began circulating. The campaigners were emboldened and their opponents were enraged. In October 1973 when the authorities tried evicting thirty families from under the flyover, fighting ensued. However, site proponents, believing H&F had land well-suited to a site, turned up the heat by planning a demonstration at the town hall in central Hammersmith to coincide with a crucial council meeting. The council relented. It agreed to consider a site. As Christmas passed and 1974 rolled in, campaigners like Irish Travellers Martin Ward and Roger Slattery[17] had reason to feel hopeful. Not so the other side. *The Latimer Arms* pub at the bottom of Latimer Road barred Travellers and Gypsies from the premises which now became the meeting place for a local residents' Action Group. Many members of the Group lived in K&C's tower block flats, Kelfield House and Silchester House, overlooking the proposed site, and in February *The West London Observer* (7 February 1974) reported the Group's complaints of fetid conditions under the flyover, including a rotting donkey carcase: though the ownership of the animal was (as usual) assumed. At a council meeting in Hammersmith in March of that year police ejected people on both sides of the argument. However, what had started as Wells' 'rolling campaign' now proved to be unstoppable. H&F and K&C finally agreed to provide a site.

It was to be built on 1.1 acres of unused land belonging to the Greater London Council's transport section just inside the Hammersmith border, between the 'up' and 'down' ramps at the junction of the M41 and M40, and it would have twenty pitches. H&F would pay for the lease and manage the site, and both authorities would share in the construction and ongoing running costs. The twenty pitches proposed were more than most sites provided (the legal minimum was fifteen), but were five fewer than the thirty normally expected of two separate authorities. Another caveat was the announcement that, once it was built, the authorities would apply for 'designation'.

Even as work began on the site, the Action Group, claiming to represent 2000 local residents, sought a court injunction. It was unsuccessful. On 21 March 1975 *The Guardian* reported a victory for the 'gypsies and tinkers' under the M40 who, it estimated, made up some sixty families. The site opened a year later, in April 1976, and Martin Ward and his family were among the first to move in. He could hardly know that his battles were only just beginning.[18]

Wars and wardens

As families under the roundabout in 1975 weathered opposition and waited for their site to open, their children had the benefit of a volunteer teacher and a caravan 'classroom' funded by the ILEA. When the Travellers moved in 1975 so did the teacher.

Rosemary Gibb had taught Traveller children in Ireland before taking up her job at the Westway, which involved preparing children for primary school in nearby Oxford Gardens. She also played a role in appointing the site's first warden, a man called Bruce McKenzie. Once he had weathered some initial set-backs (including seeing his caravan vandalised), he proved hard-working and effective. By 1978 Gibb and McKenzie had helped establish the Westway Travellers' Support Group (WTSG). Its members included some of the site's residents; one or two H&F Housing Department officials; a social worker; Fr Oliver McTernan, the parish priest of St Francis of Assisi's; and solicitors from the North Kensington Law Centre (NKLC). The NKLC, the first neighbourhood law centre of its kind to be established in Britain, was founded in 1970 by local resident, Lord Gifford QC, who saw the district as 'teeming with injustices' (*The Observer*, 20 July 1988).

By late 1982 the number regularly attending WTSG meetings was about eighteen. Chaired by Frieda Schicker of the Save The Children Fund (SCF), its other members included two on-site SCF project workers (Ms Terry Suddaby and Mr Tim Muirhead), two health visitors, two representatives of the Irish Welfare Bureau, a teacher from Oxford Gardens school, two teachers from Holland Park Secondary School, a social worker, an NKLC solicitor, a local resident who happened to be an architect, a member of the Society of Friends (or Quakers), several Romanies and Travellers and two Housing officials. The precise number of people attending and the regularity of meetings varied.

Of the site residents regularly attending Support Group meetings in the early 1980s most were women, the single male exception being Martin Ward. After 1982 the Support Group decided to exclude Housing Department officials. It also no longer included Oliver McTernan, who had withdrawn, arguing that his pastoral duties to the site's Irish ought not be compromised by site politics. So by the time I started in May 1984 the WTSG, now smaller than before and led largely by SCF personnel, was not an organisation open to me, and reasonably so, given the site's robust political history.

As far as I know I was the eighth warden in seven years. If there were others then records and memories failed to show it. Bruce McKenzie, the first site warden, left after eighteen months, some say out of frustration at H&F's negativity, which seems likely given the notes he left behind in Housing which reveal an intelligent, hardworking man who empathised with Travellers, something always apt to annoy conservative authorities. The second warden was a woman who combined her work with other duties in Housing and who quit, according to some residents, under mental pressure of the job. Incumbent number three claimed to be a Traveller and may well have been, but his alleged know-it-all attitude annoyed residents who denied his claims to Traveller identity. His line manager at the time observed he 'failed in his role as resident warden and was not a strong, dominant, natural leader', while noting 'the job is not considered overly attractive and is difficult to fill'. This opinion of what it takes to be a site warden is way off the mark, for the idea of playing the role of 'leader' to a disparate collection of Traveller and Gypsy families ignores their deep sense of family independence and self-regulation. This is not to suggest that the role of warden is one for shrinking violets, nor to deny that the job indeed holds little attraction to local government officers set on a Housing career, nor yet to deny the need of Traveller site-management pro-activity whatever the incumbent's ethnic origins. When warden number three left sometime around late 1980 or early 1981, his replacement, an ex-soldier or policeman, according to Travellers, lasted only a few days. A resident Irish Traveller woman then took over for six months before she too ran into difficulties and quit. Her replacement was social worker, Pat Hamilton, who combined her social work with other site duties under her job title of 'Gypsy liaison officer', and was by all accounts very effective. When she in turn moved on after about two years, conditions on the site deteriorated quickly. For a long time the community had no warden and it was not until July 1981 that Michael Stewart (who had done voluntary work on the site with the teachers and children the summer before) was appointed. I followed him in May 1984.

Except on small sites, smaller than the Westway Site, where residents are likely to be closely related to each other and thus politically self-regulating, it is usually considered not advisable to appoint a Traveller or Gypsy to the management duties of warden; an outsider is better. Nor does the outsider's own ethnic identity enter greatly into it, what matters is his or her effectiveness which comes in large part from the ability to empathise or what anthropologists have long spoken of as 'establishing rapport'. Of the three wardens who followed me into the position (one in 1985, before I returned in 1986 and the others in the late 1980s, 1990s and early 2000s), the last two were of Caribbean and West African origin and neither were disadvantaged because of it. On the contrary, many Westway Travellers and Gypsies saw both men's ethnic minority status as a bonus; at least they did so eventually.

Stewart, my predecessor, was both popular with the Travellers and committed. Too much so on both counts according to some of his blue-collar colleagues in the technical services section of Housing responsible for organising clean-ups and repairs on site. Older Westway women, both Romanies and Travellers, particularly liked him, some more so than others, and youth of both sexes spoke well of the way he 'joined-in' with them. Only a few men were critical of him, alleging he was either 'not strong enough' when it came to decision-making or else suggesting he neglected his duties, which was often code for saying he was not around when the speaker wanted something sorted out in his favour when other families were involved. In this regard

I quickly discovered that working in a situation of endemic interfamilial contest is not easy and that no warden remains blameless for long. Indeed, that is why Travellers prefer outsiders, non-Travellers or non-Romanies (*gorgios*) as site wardens or liaison officers, for they can make decisions that individual site residents dare not. Moreover, Travellers can blame them for decisions that go against their individual or family interests without doing further damage to their own inter-relationships (cf Frankenberg 1975). Stewart eventually departed in April 1983 after a year and eight months service — the longest-serving warden since Bruce McKenzie in the 1970s.[19] Twelve months would now pass before I entered the scene, and in that time physical conditions once more deteriorated, but first I need to backtrack to recount the legal battles preceding my appointment.[20]

The battlefield

In 1981 Martin Ward, with the help of the Notting Hill Law Centre, got H&F to answer for six offences under the 1936 Public Health Act. Four concerned the accumulation of rubbish and two addressed more fundamental issues about the site's viability as a safe environment. In court, Ward's counsel referred to the site as a 'slum' that was 'a source of shame to any civilised society', where high lead levels threatened children's health and in two cases in particular may have contributed to intellectual impairment. Magistrate Geoffrey Noel responded, 'You make it sound like part of the Somme battlefield' (*Guardian*, 7 August 1981) and immediately arranged to visit the site. He subsequently upheld the injurious to health allegation but dismissed the others, though not before ordering the council to take immediate steps towards improving the site. As H&F moved in the direction ordered, Ward appealed to a higher court for a writ of *mandamus* to compel the authorities to find the Travellers an alternative site.

At the beginning of 1982, nine long months after Stewart's departure, a Divisional Court granted the *mandamus* writ and ordered the case back to a lower court for 'expert' testimony on the site's intrinsic health risks to be heard. That court dismissed the allegation on a legal technicality. Ward once more appealed the decision and in November that year the High Court returned the case again to a lower court while at the same rebuking the authorities for not properly managing their site. So the battles raged on. Next, the Support Group, which had always played an important role in Ward's contests with the municipal authorities, upped the *ante* and in February 1983 was able to share in victory celebrations when a magistrate's court found H&F culpable on various nuisance counts and ordered it to provide covered rubbish skips, reinstate a regular garbage collection service, reduce lead levels in surface dust and appoint a new warden as quickly as possible.

H&F immediately set about launching a counter-appeal and in April 1983, through its main policy-making body, passed four radical resolutions: to reaffirm its previous position that it had no land available for an alternative caravan site; to accept Ward's argument that the Westway Site was totally unsuited for human habitation, and for this reason would therefore return it (as proposed the year before) it to its rightful owners, the GLC, when the lease expired in June; to support its western municipal neighbour, the Borough of Ealing, in arguing that the long-term answer to Traveller sites did not lie with 'local' authorities; and, for this reason, to tell the GLC about its intentions and advise it to ask central government to find long-term 'regional' solutions instead.

The boldness of the resolutions stunned Martin Ward and made a direct appeal to the Minister of the Environment for personal intervention his only option. Unfortunately for Ward, his plea failed. H&F, he was told, was not actually threatening to 'evict' anyone, it was merely returning the land (and everything on it) to its owners when the lease expired; in the meantime, the local authorities were obliged to go on managing the site. With June fast approaching, a battle-weary Ward sought an injunction in the hope of obtaining a judicial review.

On 5 October 1983 a court of the Queen's Bench heard Martin Ward's case against H&F and K&C for a judicial review that would prevent the two boroughs from closing the site and returning it to the GLC in accordance with H&F's April decision. In granting that review,

Mr Justice Woolf now ruled that under section 6 of the 1968 Act H&F had a continuing responsibility for running the site. He further ruled that as the Secretary of State had not acted improperly or unreasonably in having claimed there had been no pressing need for him to issue directions at the time, it would be improper for the court to intervene with that discretion. In short, H&F as site managers, along with K&C as co-financial providers, were ordered to resume their legal responsibilities. But H&F did not give up. Even when compelled to improve living conditions and install a warden, it aimed to get rid of the site. It would seek 'designation' *without* site provision. In the meantime it would do what was minimally required, which is how I came to be appointed temporary site warden.

What met my eyes on that first visit to the site is something I cannot forget. The filth and destruction were unimaginable. I had seen urban squatter settlements in Fiji and been in Algerian shantytowns or *bidonvilles* along France's Côte d'Azur, but as poor and shockingly provided as those places were the mark of human order and dignity stamped on them by their residents was plain to see. Here habitats were hellish. Physical chaos ruled half the site. An avenue of garbage had led me into the place. Rotting detritus lay in piles on pitches just inside the entrance. So did the wrecked bodies of a bus and caravan lying amid broken glass, smashed plywood and twisted metal. Two amenity blocks on pitches beneath the flyover ran awash with sewage; toilets smashed. Here and elsewhere (but mostly on pitches near the entrance) showers had been ripped from walls, and few residents if any had had hot water for months. Steel poles carrying electric cables to caravans leant at crazy angles; bare wires snaked across the concrete in easy grasp of playing children. Slab perimeter walls on the west side between trailers and the railway line had been pulled down and the triangle of ground in-between used for fly tipping. The triangle belonged to the North Kensington Amenity Trust and was full of building rubble dumped from lorries, and a sea of household waste. In a word, it was mayhem, and hard to believe such living conditions existed outside the worst slums of the Third World.

Conclusion

Viewed in the context of H&F's decision in 1982 to return the site, its infrastructure and inhabitants to the GLC when the lease expired, this was a shrewd tactic on the council's part. In any case, these were the circumstances of my appointment and they would continue to evolve as the weeks and months unfolded. Together with the older history of Gypsies and Travellers locally, and of Irish immigration, discussed above, they form not just the 'background' to my tenure but a 'foreground' to my entire involvement in Notting Dale, and would provide an important point of comparison with Mortlake, from where I would now travel each day.

Notes

1. *SBS World Guide*, 9th Edition (South Yarra, Australia: Hardie Grant Books).

2. For interesting and humorous autobiographic insights into what it was like for second-generation Irish growing up in post-war London, see Keaney (1985) and Walsh (1999). Irish Catholic ambivalence towards the Jews, and the Vatican's nebulous position towards Jews during the war as far as many Irish Catholics were concerned, plus Eire's neutrality, may have helped rekindle anti-Irish sentiments in sections of the English population.

3. See Owen (1987); North Kensington Community History Series (?1987); Adams and Bartlett (1990). Before 1919, when the Irish conducted their outdoor religious processions in the Portobello Road area, children would taunt them by chanting 'Dare to be a Protestant, Dare to be Alone, Dare to say the Bible's True, And Dare to Make it Known'. None of these publications, incidentally, mentions the local Gypsies and Travellers.

4. See note 3.

5. Journalist Colin Eales says that he was oblivious at first to 'the seething pot that was Notting Dale' when he visited Ladbroke Grove in Notting Hill one evening. It was only after a crowd set off in chase towards Latimer Road tube station from Bramley Road, Notting Dale, screaming 'Kill the niggers ... let's get the blacks ... [and] the coppers, let's get on with it' that he realised what was happening.

He later learnt that a crowd of 700 had previously been listening to fascist speakers in Bramley Road as officers from the nearby police station looked on. Later 150 people were arrested in the main trouble spots, which included Bramley Road, Latimer Road, Blechynden Street, Portobello Road, Blenheim Crescent, Talbot Road and others; North Kensington Community History Series (?1987).

6. This and other material was taken from files in the Urban Studies Centre attached to Harrow Mission in Freston Road. The Centre opened in 1974.

7. I interviewed Mrs Allen several times at her home in Mary Place in the 1980s and 1990s. Much of what she said about Joe Hearne matches up with information found in the 1871 and 1881 censuses.

8. Leland (1882) recalls seeing 'a large flourishing community of the black blood [Romanies] ... set itself up in the *pivlo* (cocoanut) [sic] or *koshta* business' at one of the Thames regattas.

9. It is unclear whether General Anne was called 'General' from a child (as Florence Allen said), or whether it was added later.

10. Information on Nobby Buckingham comes from an Urban Studies Centre file.

11. An Irish Traveller who sometimes visited the Westway Site described going to illegal songbird competitions and dog-fights at secret locations around London, most of them pubs.

12. See Taylor (1983, 13), an invaluable booklet. Mike Taylor ran a Christian mission in a building under the M40 flyover 100 yards north of Latimer Road station. I would particularly like to acknowledge the help he gave me in a conversation twenty years ago.

13. Given the lapse in time since most of these events took place and the date of publication it is unlikely naming people now would offend anyone. Even so I have acted on the side of caution and disguised most identities by using false names (indicated by single quotation marks around the first use of the name) or simply omitting names where possible. However where I thought there was little or no chance of giving offence, and/or where individuals played major roles (and possibly still live) at the site or elsewhere in the districts described in this book, I have kept people's first names and surnames for the historical record and possible future interest of their descendants. Martin Ward's name is one of them; Florrie Allen's is

another. I've also kept the names of most of the people who lived south of the river, which is to say in Barnes, Mortlake, East Sheen and Roehampton; names like those of the Smiths, Parsons, Sharps, Fares, Pharos and Dickersons. In still other cases, for essentially the same reasons, I have played safe by changing first names while retaining family names. I therefore hope I have caused no one undue upset and if I have, I sincerely apologise. Finally, 'sorry' to anyone who is disappointed because I have *not* identified them; it was not because I undervalued them.

14. Godfrey, A., *Old Ordnance Survey maps, the Godfrey edition* (Gateshead, 1986).

15. At the time of writing, responsibility for Traveller sites comes under the Office of the Deputy Prime Minister (ODPM).

16. The original east–west *parish* boundary between Hammersmith and Kensington was Counter's Creek, which became the *borough* boundary before World War I (Barton 1982; Draper 1989). The northern boundary of both boroughs is Harrow Road. Wormholt Scrubs (originally spelt 'Scrubbs'), which was originally a wooded area of about 200 acres, lies below the Harrow Road on Hammersmith's eastern boundary (Whitting 1965). Most of the woods have long gone and the area is generally known as Wormwood Scrubs.

17. Slattery has recently been prominent in Traveller affairs at Smithy Fen, Cambridgeshire, a place which gained national notoriety in 2004.

18. In 1995 changes by the Boundary Commission placed the Westway Site inside K&C, instead of H&F. Day-to-day management, however, remained the latter's responsibility.

19. Long after I resigned I discovered that Stewart had read anthropology at university and had gone on to study and write about Gypsies in communist Hungary (1989; 1997). We eventually met in the 1990s at one of Professor Acton's Greenwich conferences.

20. Readers interested in a recent report on the problems of caravan sites and social policy should see the Commission of Racial Equality's *Common Ground: Equality, good race relations and sites for Gypsies and Irish Travellers. Summary* (2006).

5

MORTLAKE (RICHMOND-UPON-THAMES)

Where observation is concerned, chance favours only the prepared mind.
Louis Pasteur, 7 December 1854

The centre of the parish [Barnes] is almost wholly occupied by an open space, tolerably level, and covered with gorse or furze, a favourite haunt of gypsies [sic] and itinerant hawkers since they were driven from the green lanes about Wandsworth, and a pleasant open recreation ground for the Londoner of the south western districts. It comprises an area of about 120 acres.
Edward Walford, *Greater London*, 1885

Why is Mortlake like a piano? It's all Sharps and flats.
Local saying

Borders and crossings

Long before the Norman Conquest the manors of Mortlake and Barnes belonged to the 'hundred of Brixton' in north Surrey. Barnes manor appears to have been in existence by AD 939 (Brown 1996, p. 11). The Norman land survey, the Domesday Book (1086), shows that Mortlake manor and its lesser manor of Barnes also included the parishes and minor manors of Putney and Wimbledon, the latter's 'living' being a 'peculiar' of Mortlake[1] (Walford 1885, vol. II, 470).

The manor house in Mortlake stood at the centre of the village to the east of Ship Lane on the banks of the Thames, in an area today occupied by the Budweiser brewery, and before that by the Watneys brewery. Beer has been made in Mortlake since 1487 and the sweet smell of yeast and malt is an embedded memory for generations of Sheen and Mortlake people.

The principal church was originally four miles to the south, on the other side of the manor, at Wimbledon. Mortlake people by the river wanting the sacraments either had to take the path up through the hamlet of Roehampton or else wait for a priest to come from Wimbledon. Not until 1348 did people around Ship Lane and the village green get their own chapel. This explains why, until the fourteenth century, Mortlake manor, along with its minors Putney, Barnes and East Sheen (which became a 'subordinate' a century earlier)[2] was often called Wimbledon manor (Brown 1996, 12).

All communities define and differentiate themselves by their boundaries. Barth (1969) explored this for 'ethnic groups' and Cohen (1985; 1987), Clifford (1997), Donnan and Wilson (1999) and Herzfeld (2001), among others, subsequently examined how the symbolic boundary separates 'us' from 'them', locals from strangers, and insiders from outsiders.[3] Other anthropologists have examined the notion of 'boundary' in terms of what they do to bridge communities through the practice of cultural 'translation' (Pálsson 1994). This interpretive approach to cultural anthropology owes its origins to earlier scholars, to some of whom I want to briefly refer.

Anthropologists and sociologists have long talked about (social) 'systems' and their means of boundary maintenance. The idea of 'borders' was implicit, for example, in nineteenth-century social Darwinist theories that subscribed to the notion of social structural (as well as mental) difference between people in so-called 'primitive' societies and the inhabitants of more evolved societies, and hence in the ability or otherwise of the former to adapt to change. It was present and made more explicit in the paradigm that early the next century displaced social evolutionism and in the hands of anthropologists like Franz Boas highlighted the fact that thinking about cultures as bounded entities was simplistic. The concept of border was also evident in the concept of the 'moiety', as recorded by Spencer and Gillen (1899) for the tribes of northern and central Australia, in which natives conceived the tribe as organised into two large sections: both distinct and 'different' from each other in terms of collective identity but necessary to the other when it came to marriage. As well as leading Durkheim towards exploring the importance of symbol and ritual (1915), the moiety idea led him to distinguish but connect the 'sacred' and 'profane' generally. Since then Peterson (1976) and others have gone on to discuss the numerous problems of trying to specify Australian tribal boundaries. Van Gennep's (1960) analysis of 'rites of passage' is another major piece of work concerned with social boundaries, and Frankenberg's *Village on the Border* (1957) is oriented towards both the problems of geographic marginality and the status of outsiders in a small community. In fact, the idea of the boundary or border has occupied a great many social scientists from structural-functionalists to post-modernists, including Talcott Parsons, whose theoretical concern with the relationship between 'the social system' and the 'cultural system' was profoundly influenced by Clifford Geertz, for whom the 'interpretation of culture' (1973) is anthropology's core business.

The following passage from Parsons clearly articulates the importance of boundary and boundary-maintenance for social systems and personal identity:

> Relative to non-members, which category may be very important to its environment, a society exhibits the property Durkheim called solidarity. This may be characterized at the level of what one might call collective identity as above all expressed through the collective pronoun 'we' ... Readiness to use the concept 'we' seems to indicate both that the collectivity referred to has some kind of relatively definite identity and that the individual participant has a sense of belonging to it, that is, of membership. (Parsons 1973, 34)

In summary, both from *emic* (insider) and *etic* (outsider) perspectives, or what Geertz (1993) calls 'experience near' and 'experience far' viewpoints that require cultural interpreters to seek a balance, there has proved to be an enduring interest in the way symbols and symbolic action are used to express ideas of border and identity. With this in mind, therefore, I hope that when I speak of Mortlake in the same breath as Barnes or East Sheen, which is how many locals (particularly those at the border) talk about them, or indeed when I speak of Barnes and Putney, or of Putney and Roehampton, or Roehampton and Wimbledon, or (as I have already) of Wimbledon and Mortlake (as many people in this part of 'north Surrey' once used to) that what is envisioned are co-existent notions of 'difference' and 'sameness', and thus of emic notions of identity, culture and community.

If I am successful I trust I will also convey to you, the reader, something of that same sense of travelling from 'familiar' to 'foreign' that I felt in my youth whenever I crossed the Thames at Barnes for Hammersmith, from Surrey to Middlesex, or what in today's civic labels are respectively the Borough of Richmond-upon-Thames (which takes in Barnes, Mortlake, and East Sheen) and the Borough of Hammersmith and Fulham (H&F). If so, perhaps then I may also succeed in conveying how these sentiments were revived returning to Sheen after seven years abroad, when I travelled to-and-fro each day to my job under the Westway on the border or north Hammersmith and Kensington.[4]

Mortlake and its others

From the eleventh to fifteenth centuries Mortlake — otherwise known as Wimbledon manor — and its main manor house belonged to the Archbishops of Canterbury (Brown 1996). At the time of the Reformation, Henry VIII gave it as a gift to his Chancellor, Thomas Cromwell, and then, when Cromwell was executed, to Catherine Parr. Throughout this period and up to the seventeenth century Mortlake was famous throughout Europe for its tapestry works and, during the later period, many Flemish artisans came to work here. From the seventeenth century to the late twentieth century the title of Wimbledon manor lay in the hands of the Spencer family; a pub called *The Earl Spencer* stood opposite the house in which I was born at the foot of Medfield Street in Roehampton village (SW15), just below that part of Wimbledon Common sometimes called Putney Common. In 1996 the fifth Earl Spencer auctioned off the Lord of the Manor title. As for the pub, it is now an off-licence.

MORTLAKE (RICHMOND-UPON-THAMES)

Medfield Street, Roehampton, 2004, seen from the edge of Putney Common. The multi-storeyed housing in the distance forms part of the Alton Estate built by the LCC in the 1960s. The pillar and dome structure at the end of the street is a public fountain erected in 1882.

By the 1880s Wimbledon was a 'very extensive and scattered' parish (Brown 1996, 470). To the south it bordered on Merton and Cheam and to the north it abutted Putney and Wandsworth. Its eastern boundary was the River Wandle (from which Wandsworth takes its name) and along whose banks many small industries sprang up in the nineteenth century as London expanded. The parish's western boundary with Mortlake parish was another watercourse, Beverly Brook, which later formed the modern municipal boundary of the Borough of Wandsworth under whose authority Wimbledon falls.

The western boundary of Mortlake parish runs more or less northwards in a straight line from the gates of Richmond Park at the top of Richmond Hill, and across the Upper and Lower Richmond Roads to meet up with the Thames at Chiswick Bridge. An old plague pit stands on it on the Richmond Park side of the Upper Richmond Road, almost directly opposite the *Black Horse* pub. Beverley Brook, Mortlake's eastern parish boundary, rises in Sutton, to the south of

Wimbledon, and flows north along the eastern edge of Richmond Park below Roehampton before it forms the boundary of Mortlake and Barnes parishes, and the borough boundaries of Wandsworth and Richmond-upon-Thames. It then wends its way through Barnes and across the Common and Barn Elms before entering the Thames at Putney. Like all symbolic boundaries, Beverley Brook divides what is otherwise obviously connected. Even today, as roads and railways and suburban sprawl have helped obliterate or radically alter senses of local identity in much of London by removing the space between 'things' which functions to define them (and thus, as a result of this blurred connection, also reducing 'travelling' to 'commuting'), most Londoners still acquire a sense of Self from their locality or neighbourhood. And in south-west London this scope for feelings of 'different' local belonging and identity is helped by a great many big 'open spaces' in the shape of parks and commons. A glance at a map of London, for example, will show the area covered by the ancient manor of Mortlake (roughly speaking SW13, 14, 15 and 18) to be among the greenest 'spaces' in the capital. At the same time specific suburbs or localities (the city's *quartiers*) stand out within the district.

Except in open spaces like Richmond Park and Barnes Common, the symbolic value of Beverley Brook as a marking edge of collective identity has largely disappeared beneath roads and behind buildings. Today Barnes and Mortlake are now more likely to be thought of as dividing and connecting at White Hart Lane, which is a few yards to the west of the stream, and then what marks their separation is not the watercourse but the post codes SW13 and SW14. Yet over 600 years ago, before a separate church was built in Mortlake, priests travelling from Wimbledon crossed Beverley Brook into Mortlake at a point known then and ever since as Priests Bridge where, for most of the twentieth century, a pub there bore the apt name *Halfway House*. Anyone who cares can still look over the parapet next to the pub (whose name has unfortunately changed) and watch Beverly Brook flow out from under nearby flats on the Upper Richmond Road. Here too, around Priests Bridge, alleys between the houses lead directly to the heart of old Mortlake where there are more alleys that owe their origins to medieval land tenure and historic rights of way (Hailstone 1983; Grimwade and Hailstone 1992).[5]

In its south part Mortlake parish takes in East Sheen and part of Richmond Park, but the sense of unity and connection that once existed in these areas was severely affected when the Richmond Railway Company[6] laid tracks across the fields in 1846 to facilitate suburbanisation. The line connected hitherto remote parts of Surrey with London's new Waterloo Station by way of stations east of Richmond, which included Mortlake, Barnes Junction, Putney, Wandsworth Town, Queen's Rise (Battersea), Clapham Junction and Vauxhall. As in Notting Hill, the new connections came at the expense of severing old ones.

Two hundred yards south of the river the railway acted as a demarcation line between Mortlake and East Sheen, adding something extra to a line that admittedly already existed in the form of the Upper Richmond Road, a main road running across the district midway between the river and Richmond Park. An old coaching route, the Upper Richmond Road joined Richmond to Clapham and Wandsworth in south London. In the mid-twentieth century this main road constituted part of London's South Circular Road, which joined up at Ealing with the North Circular Road, to make what was then the city's principal ring road. And, like the railway, the Upper Richmond Road in time came to divide Sheen and Mortlake along class lines.

Areas south of the railway, and even more so south of the main road, on ground rising up to Richmond Park, were unambiguously identified as 'Sheen', solidly middle class, and in the case of one road on the Park's perimeter (Fife Road) distinctly upper-middle. That is how 'we' who lived there saw it and that is how 'they' saw it. In the 1960s or 1970s, for example, the Irish Ambassador lived in Fife Road. The Sheen Lawn Tennis Club was also located there. Localities on the north side of the main road, especially ones between the railway and river, were unambiguously identified as 'Mortlake' and were predominantly working class. The principal area of ambiguity over status was the one between the Upper Richmond Road and railway. That is to say, the area that was officially in Sheen but on the Mortlake side of the main road, where the closer to the railway one lived the greater the likelihood of one's address being identified as Mortlake.[7] The fact that both areas shared (and still share) the postal code sw14 added to the ambiguity and made status-seeking edgy throughout the twentieth century.[8] Sheen was politically to the right. Mortlake was politically to the left. Sheen tended towards high Anglicanism. Mortlake tended towards Protestant non-conformism and Roman Catholicism. Together, this mix of class and religion lent Mortlake in particular an ethnic dimension: an Irish one.

Some of these class and ethnic differences have disappeared over the course of the last twenty-five years. Gentrification in the Thames areas of Mortlake and Barnes has seen middle-class professionals buy out the cottages and terraced houses of working- and lower-middle-class people who now either occupy the council flats that Mortlake — unlike Sheen — has always had, or have moved away entirely. Today the near boundaries of river and railway, along with gentrification and a large middle-class presence, and the astronomic rise in London house prices have only added to the caché that comes from living in an urban 'village' with cafes and restaurants that imitate the Continent, and this has helped to flatten the old socio-economic differences between Barnes and Mortlake and East Sheen.

Greater ethnic diversity is another feature of the area today. Whereas in the late nineteenth and the twentieth centuries, up to the 1970s, the Irish stood out in Mortlake as being virtually the only ethnic group distinguishable from the English or British, today the 'English' and British include people from a wide range of former colonial territories and cultures. Borough of Wandsworth council flats on the Roehampton side of the Upper Richmond Road, between Priests Bridge and Priory Lane, for example, contain many such families, along with a good number of South Africans and immigrants from the European Union (EU).[9] Some of the youth from these flats in 2004 qualified for the slang descriptor 'chavvies', a Romany word for 'kids', though the Londoners who applied it appeared not to know its origin. The presence of all these immigrants and their offspring in the streets and schools, shops and sports fields, around Mortlake and Sheen, indeed, throughout the entire district that was once the manor of Mortlake, has consequently helped to create an almost seamless suburbia.

Roehampton used to be a hamlet of Putney. Situated between Wimbledon to the south, Barnes to the north, Mortlake and East Sheen to the west, and Putney and Wandsworth to the east, it has abundant open space nearby in Wimbledon Common, Putney Common (or Putney Heath), Barnes Common, Palewell Park (East Sheen) and Richmond Park. Throughout the eighteenth and nineteenth centuries Roehampton village was renowned for its rustic picturesqueness, big aristocratic houses and handsome estates. Home to more than its share of statesmen (including William Pitt the younger), blue-bloods, judges, admirals, and banker millionaires like Baron Hambro and the American John Pierpont Morgan (who in 1913 left a legacy of seventy million pounds), Roehampton stood out as 'a cut above the others' (Loose 1979).

After 1850, when many of the estates were sold and subdivided for new housing development, substantial numbers of labourers and domestic servants living in tied cottages had to find accommodation in the village, which basically consisted of two streets, the High Street and Medfield Street. Between 1851 and 1886 Roehampton's population more than doubled, growing from around 950 to over 2,000, and, by 1911, to around 2,500 (Loose 1979). Housebuilding continued apace between the two world wars and included the London County Council's (LCC) Dover House Road estate on the east side of the village, below Putney Heath. Alarmist forecasts of 'slums' on the doorstep proved to be unfounded, while the commons and Park provided a buffer to suburban development. The elites did not disappear overnight, either. Two Lords of the Admiralty, Admirals Domvile and Larkin, lived there in the 1940s and 1950s and were friendly with my father and grandfather, the former through Lady Domvile's conversion to Catholicism and both through a shared interest in bees.

In the 1950s the LCC opened the Alton East and Alton West council estates on the site of the Jesuits' Manresa House estate overlooking Richmond Park. A mix of high-rise flats and low-rise 'maisonettes', the estates housed over 2,600 families who had been displaced by slum and bomb clearances elsewhere in London or living up until then in emergency prefabricated housing. Bureaucrats from the Soviet Union liked to visit this experiment in 'socialist' public housing. Other flats were later erected in and around Bessborough Road area at the junction of Roehampton Lane and Kingston Road. By 1971 Roehampton's population had reached 21,000 (Loose 1979) and today it must be many times that number; even so, the old village still retains some of its charms.

The shops and terraced houses built in the 1860s and 1870s in Medfield Street, with their yellow brick walls and black slate roofs, have changed little in the near century and a half since. In the High Street *The King's Head* and *Angel* pubs retain their unusual nineteenth-century black wood shingle walls, and continue to serve ale made at Young's brewery in Wandsworth, which used to be delivered by drays. St Mary's Convent, further up the High Street, which I remember being full of fresh-faced Irish country sisters after the war, is still a Catholic institution of some sort. On the other hand, the shops are now much like those in any other English high street. Atkinson's, the ironmongers, is now a protected building but given over, I think, to the blandishments of real estate. The fishmonger's, with its huge slanting slab of marble streaming water over cod and haddock, has long gone. So have the riding-stables behind the *Angel*. In their stead, out of twenty-one shops there are now six restaurants, cafes or takeaways, among them two Tandooris, a Chinese takeaway, and a Vietnamese noodle bar. A few yards away, below the High Street, facing the late Victorian Italian marble fountain and horse-trough opposite St Joseph's Catholic Church in Roehampton Lane, *The Montague Arms* advertises 'Indian food'. Whether the African woman in *hijab* I saw walking down Medfield Street on my last visit, where full-robed Catholic nuns and sisters once walked, felt 'at home' here, I did not stop to inquire. Instead, I hastened to the public library to see what it might reveal about Gypsies.

Romanies

In and about Wimbledon and Roehampton
The view of London from Wimbledon Common and Putney Heath was magnificent until recent times. St Paul's Cathedral was clearly visible, as I remember it used to be also from Richmond Park. Today such views are confined to those living in the tower block flats, and even tall buildings get in the way. Nevertheless it is still plain to see why the Common's elevation and airiness, not to mention its ample supply of rabbits and hedgehogs, attracted Gypsies possibly long before they were forced out of Wandsworth, the biggest 'Gypsyry' in London, in the nineteenth century.

In the late 1700s Wimbledon Common was notorious for highwaymen. The most infamous of all was Jerry Abershaw, a man the authorities in due course caught and hanged, before slinging his corpse in a roadside gibbet as a warning to others. Well into the twentieth century part of the old Portsmouth Road that here runs across the Common was known as Abershaw Hill. By the early 1800s Wimbledon Common was also known for horse-racing, a Gypsy attraction, at roughly the same time that Norwood, near Croydon, south of London, was known for its Gypsies, as an unknown poet mentioned by Walford records (1885, vol. II, 490):

> The wrinkled beldame there you may espy,
> And ripe young maidens with glassy eye;
> Men in their prime, and striplings dark and dun,
> Scathed by the storm and freckled with the sun,
> Their swarthy hue and mantle's flowing fold
> Bespeak the remnant of a race of old.

However, not all was bucolic on Wimbledon Common. In 1837 a report stated that some parts of the commons were in 'a deplorable state of devastation as a consequence of people dumping night-soil and tipping muck from pig-sties' (Gerhold 1994, 89). In 1864, the same year Borrow talked about the Wandsworth Gypsies, a Roehampton clergyman complained of Gypsy acts on the Common 'so atrocious that it had been impossible to put them on paper' (Gerhold 1994, 89). One can only guess what might have stirred the clergyman's moral outrage. Shortly afterwards, the fifth Earl Spencer, Lord of the Manor, declared that because of 'the evils of drainage, rubbish dumping and gypsy encampment' the Commons had become 'unmanageable' (Gerhold 1994, 91), a line that might surely have been commissioned a century and a half early for H&F was it not for the Earl's vested interest in making sections of the Common private by blaming the dumping on Gypsies (Gerhold 1994).

One of my sisters remembers a Gypsy knife-grinder calling periodically at Medfield Street in the years after the war. Whether he came from the Common or from Wandsworth, or possibly from Mitcham, my research does not show. What we do know is that between the wars, Romany families lived in houses in Wardley Street and Lyddon Grove, off Garrett Lane, in Wandsworth, where according to one eyewitness it was not unusual to see a horse's head sometimes poking from a front-room window (Stanley and Griffiths 1990, 91). The same source mentions Queenie Godfrey who, though not described as 'Romany', almost certainly was.

Queenie Godfrey — the surname is found among Romanies — was born in Bullen Street, Battersea, in 1911 and later moved with her family to Sheepcote Lane. The Godfreys were costermongers who bought their fruit and vegetables from the central London wholesale market at Covent Garden before selling it in Battersea Park Road. They also sold fish bought at Billingsgate by London Bridge, watercress from Mitcham, and lavender (see Evans 2004), her mother's catchcry for the plant being 'Who will buy my sweet smelling lavender, sixteen branches for a penny?'

Pubs around Clapham Junction were an outlet for sales of the Godfreys' fruit and peanuts (Stanley and Griffiths 1990), as, no doubt, was Epsom on Derby day, since the Godfreys, like most other Londoners, did not confine themselves to the 'little community' in SW18 but worked and played outside the 'manor'.

At the beginning of the nineteenth century Norwood (now SE27) was popular with Gypsies because it was secluded but within striking distance of Croydon and London (Walford 1885, vol. VI, 314). By the 1700s Londoners were regularly going out there to have their 'life foretold by the palmistry of the Zingari folk' (Walford 1885, vol. VI, 314), and in 1808 a writer for *Gentleman's Magazine* wondered whether Gypsies hadn't lived there since they first arrived in England in the sixteenth century. On one occasion the writer met a Romany called Sarah Skemp who was so infirm she could only crawl, and in the nineteenth century, in the area known as Gypsy Hill, a pub called *Queen of the Gypsies* was named after Margaret Finch, who died in 1760[10] aged 109 (Walford 1885, vol. VI, 314). Sarah Skemp and Margaret Finch were almost certainly one and the same person, because it is said of Finch:

> For half a century she lived by telling fortunes in that rural and credulous neighbourhood. She was buried in a large square box, as from her constant habit of sitting with her chin resting on her knees, her muscles had become so contracted that at last she could not alter her position. 'This woman', observes Mr Larwood, in 'History of Signboards', 'when a girl of seventeen, may have been one of the dusky gang that pretty Mrs Samuel Pepys and companions went to consult in 1668, as her lord records in his 'Diary' the same evening, the 11th: 'This afternoon my wife, and Mercer, and Deb went with Pelling to see the gypsies at Lambeth and have their fortunes told; but what they did I did not enquire'. 'A granddaughter of Margaret Finch', Mr Larwood adds, 'was living in a cottage close by in the year 1800' (Walford 1885, vol. VI, 314).

By the time she died, Finch had travelled the length and breadth of England, an inveterate boundary crosser at a time when the law discouraged such behaviour. 'Her funeral was attended by two mourning coaches, a sermon was preached upon the occasion; and a great concourse attended the ceremony' (Walford 1885, vol. VI, 102).

Another gathering place for Gypsies 200 years ago was Epsom

Downs, south of Wimbledon, and it remains so today. Each Spring Romanies and Irish Travellers come here for one of England's great racing carnivals, the Derby. King James I (1566–1625) introduced it to Banstead Downs and by 1700 it had become 'a great gathering centre — dancing, music every evening, horse races on the downs at 12:30 pm daily, wrestling, cudgel playing ... raffling shops' (Walford 1885, vol. VI, 245–50). In other words, it was a site of playful interaction across class boundaries, and between Romanies and *gorgios*: 'Look at that young dandy to whom a black-eyed houri of the gipsy tribe offers a spring blossom, and the stately dame in the carriage behind listening to the sugared prophesies of the old crone' (Walford 1885, vol. VI, 260).

One other location for Romanies in the nineteenth century was Mitcham Common, three miles from Wimbledon. Lavender was an important Mitcham industry and Gypsy women hawked it all over south and south-west London far into the twentieth century. Some of them even came and settled in Barnes and Mortlake. A photograph from the 1920s or 1930s shows two lavender hawkers in Mortlake.[11] Further west, south of Kingston, Gypsies with suburban London accents camped at Esher and on Cobham Common in the early 1900s (Parker 1919), in what today is regarded as the 'stockbroker belt'.

In Putney and Barnes
Only six roads in Greater London carry the word Gypsy. Three are in Norwood, one is in Welling, towards Kent, another one is in North Acton, in the Borough of Ealing and the last is off the Upper Richmond Road, half a mile from Roehampton Lane, between the main road and Barnes Common. It is called Gipsy Lane.[12] In the 1950s and 1960s it was a short, quiet, leafy road with big double-fronted detached houses down one side only. An Irish family with many youngsters lived there. It lies on the border of the three old parishes, Putney, Barnes and Roehampton, where up until 1836 the Barnes workhouse stood (Anderson 1983).[13] With its horse chestnut trees and the Common with blackberry bushes close at hand one can understand how it acquired its Gypsy association. It also lay near

Barnes Junction railway station, where goods trains dropped off coal that (as we shall presently see) was of no small interest to one Gypsy family in Barnes.

In the second half of the nineteenth century William Lobjoit ran a market garden at Barn Elms, half a mile from Gipsy Lane, near to where Barnes becomes Putney Common, and he often employed Gypsies (Grimwade and Hailstone 1992). One of them was William Pharo, who went on to set up his own business and, in 1868, run a market garden near a pub called *The Strugglers* (Anderson 1983). The pub was pulled down at some point after he sold the business, and was replaced by the *The Red Lion*.

Another site for Gypsies in the Barn Elms and Putney Common area was opposite Ranelagh Gardens, between old Barnes cemetery and what later became the Rocks Lane tennis courts and council recreation ground (Attwell 1996, 40-1). It was very close to the Ranelagh Club where Empire aristocrats played polo. Gypsies could also be found next to ponds on the Common, dug out in 1846 when the railway line was built (Anderson 1983).

Mignonette Lovell lived with her family on Barnes Common towards the end of the century, as one Barnes resident remembers:

> A very handsome clean woman, she used to go about hawking laces, cottons and clothes pegs. We would often meet her with her basket tramping up to Castelnau with her wares to dispose of them at the better class of house up there. Sometimes the gipsies [sic] sold little brooms — 'buy-a-broom' as we called them — and little baskets made of peeled rushes from the Common. I remember there was once a smallpox scare among the gipsies and we were forbidden to buy these much-coveted treasures for fear of infection (Attwell 1996, 41).

One of Mrs Lovell's nieces, Lemonelia Smith, was among the first Romanies from the Common to move into houses in Barnes village. She was born on Putney Common, baptised in the parish and raised on the Common. Attwell remembers seeing her and the family dressed up 'to the nines' setting off by horse and cart to Epsom in Derby week. The Gypsies' single-storey wooden houses were at the bottom of Archway Street in an area still known as Westfields, located between Beverley Brook and Railway Side (that is to say, between Beverley Path and the railway arches carrying trains from Barnes Junction to Chiswick over Barnes Bridge), and were dubbed by locals 'Uncle Tom's Cabins' (Grimwade and Hailstone 1992). When the 'cabins' were demolished, *The Manor Arms* went up there. Slightly off the beaten track, this originally very local 'local', redesigned and renamed, is now patronised by members of the middle classes, who first began coming here thirty years ago when estate agents hit on calling the area 'little Chelsea'.

A general practitioner, Dr Benjamin Ward Richardson, arrived in Barnes about 1845 and often visited the Romanies. Ward went on to write a book inspired by those visits, called *The Diseases of the Child*, which helped him to a knighthood (Attwell 1996, 60). Other visitors to the Romany tents were the Methodists who came to Barnes in 1860 and built a chapel by the railway crossing in White Hart Lane (Barnes and Mortlake History Society n.d.). The last time I saw the building it belonged to the Barnes Healing Church.

In Sheen and Mortlake
The earliest suggestion of Gypsies in Mortlake village is found in the Parish Register for the years 1599–1678 (Cockin and Gould 1954). Here it is recorded that on 4 May 1666, at 'Mortelack Chappel', one Hesther Hedges of Mortlake married Ric Wood of Richmond, and while it does not say that either of them was Romany there is good reason to think that it was the case. To start with, there is a poem at the start of one of Donald Kenrick's books (Kenrick and Clark 1995) written by a modern Romany (or Romanichal) called Hester Hedges (spelt without the middle 'h'), and the name is so unusual there may be a link. When I put this possibility to Kenrick, he agreed.[14] Besides, Hesther Hedges' husband was a Wood, a not uncommon Gypsy surname. That, however, is not all. Eleven years before Hedges and Wood tied the knot, on 21 May 1657, Thomas Brazier (originally

a trade name)[15] married Mary Smith (a trade name usually adopted by Gypsies in lieu of Petulengro), before the bride's mother, William Thornton, Alice Slee and one Henry Haley who only ten days later married Margaret Wood with Thomas Brazier a witness. In view of this obvious close friendship between the Braziers and Hayley, not to mention Slee, it is more than likely that Margaret Wood was herself a relative of Ric Wood who had earlier married Hesther Hedges, and that the Braziers and Woods (along with Alice Slee[16]) were Gypsies.

On the west side of Mortlake, not far from the towpath at Kew Meadows where old Kew and Mortlake parishes meet, there is a spot that in the nineteenth century was known as Gypsey Corner. It was slightly west of the site of Chiswick Bridge, which was built in 1931 to allow easier access to Chiswick and Hammersmith than that provided by Hammersmith Bridge, which itself came into use in 1827 to allow (in the words of a local paper) 'direct passage from Hammersmith, to Barnes, East Sheen and other parts of Surrey without going over either Fulham or Kew Bridges' (Draper 1989, 56).[17] During the twentieth century the area about Gypsey Corner was variously used by the Mortlake Dust Destruction Works, the Hammersmith Cemetery, the Mortlake Crematorium, and the Borough of Barnes municipal rubbish tip (before the borough became the Borough of Barnes and Mortlake and, later, the current Borough of Richmond-upon-Thames). The polluted nature of these activities reflects the marginal status of the Gypsies who previously camped here on the border almost 200 years ago, and the marginal status of the young Irish Traveller I met on the tip here in 1984.

We know something of Romanies who camped at Kew Meadows in the early 1800s from an account, cited by Hailstone (1983, 32), left by Sir Richard Phillips in his book *A Morning's Walk from London to Kew* published in 1817:

> As I proceeded from the stile towards their tents, the apparent chief of the gang advanced with a firm step, holding a large knife in one hand, and some eatables in the other; and he made many flourishes with his knife,

seemingly in the hope of intimidating me, if I proved an enemy. The old woman who was engaged in smoking her pipe, took it from her mouth, and said: 'I ayn't told so many gentlefolks their fortune to no purpose, and I'll tell yours, sir, if you'll give me something to fill my pipe'. I smiled and told her I thanked her. 'Aye, sir,' said she, 'many's the lover I've made happy, and many's the couple that I have brought together'. The ground served them for a table and the grass for a tablecloth. Their tents were formed of a pole at each end, with a ridge pole, covered with blanketing, which was stretched obliquely to the ground by wooden pegs. I felt it my duty to give the old woman a shilling to buy some tobacco for her pipe. (cited in Hailstone 1983, 32)

Until 1840 Gypsies were also linked in Mortlake minds with Snake Alley, just a few minutes' walk east from Gypsey Corner and west of Ship Lane. 'The most notorious of the lost alleys of Mortlake' (Hailstone 1983, 48), Snake Alley led 'off Williams Lane, across Watney Road through Chertsey Court and the cemetery into Mortlake, it was apparently on the ancient way from Mortlake to Richmond'.[18] Rumour had it that either a Gypsy 'chief' or someone drowned in the river was buried there (Hailstone 1983), which only added to the alley's notoriety; this was a reputation that eventually led to its being closed by the authorities in 1840. In the 1930s the LCC built Chertsey Court, a large block of council flats on land once partly occupied by Snake Alley, and several Gypsy families moved in; some of them were from Hampton Square in Sheen Lane. At about this time an 'exorcism' was performed in one of the flats to rid it of a 'poltergeist' (Hailstone 1983), but it did not stop Gypsies (and individuals of Gypsy descent) from going on living there into the 1990s.

Between the wars another place associated with Gypsies or *didicais*, as an 83-year old Acton born informant, now long residing at Priests Bridge put it, was Devonshire Road, Chiswick (W4), not far from Chiswick Eyot, on the Middlesex bank opposite Lonsdale Road

MORTLAKE (RICHMOND-UPON-THAMES)

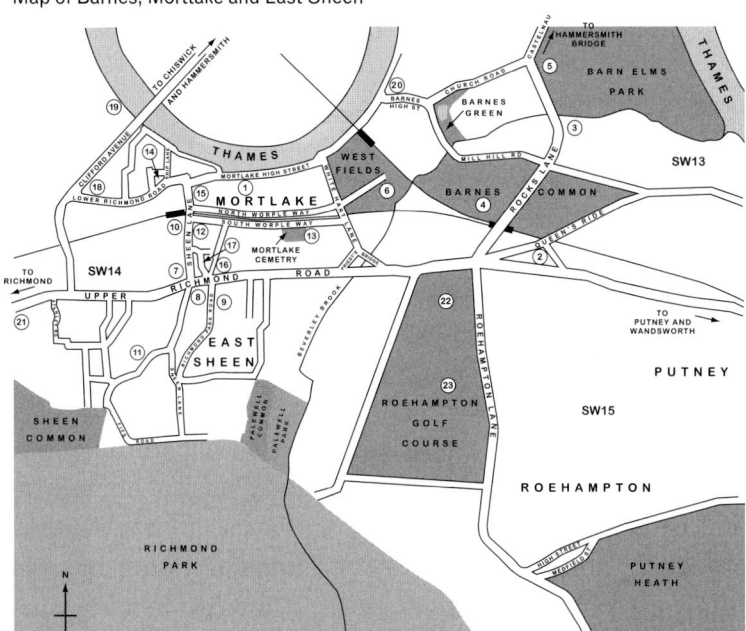

Map of Barnes, Mortlake and East Sheen

1. Sir Richard Burton's Tomb, St Mary Magdelene's R.C. Church.
2. Gypsy Lane (19th cent. stopping-place).
3. Lobjoit's market-garden.
4. Gypsy camp spot, Barnes Common.
5. William Pharo's market-garden, Barn Elms.
6. 'Uncle Tom's cabins', Westfields.
7. Hampton Place.
8. Meadows of Sheen House (Gypsy grazing).
9. Author's home.
10. Sharp's coal-yard.
11. Harris's house with equine adornments.
12. Mrs Parsons' flower-shop.
13. Old Mortlake Cemetery (resting-place for the Smiths, other Romanies, and relatives).
14. The Jolly Gardeners.
15. The Charlie Butler.
16. The Hare & Hounds.
17. Lemonelia Smith's flower-stand.
18. Chertsey Court flats and approximate site of Snake Alley.
19. Gypsey Corner, formerly Kew Meadows.
20. Sharp family's original home.
21. Stable of Fares' brothers.
22. Roehampton Club.
23. Digby Stewart College (today the University of Roehampton); also the Sacred Heart Convent.

in Barnes. Here Huxleys, Dixeys, Williams — including one Barty Williams — lived, as well as a Yonky Hearne and various Italians or Spanish. They owned donkeys and barrows and sold cut flowers in the Chiswick High Road that joins King Street, Hammersmith.

Cut flowers, sharp knives

Older people remember Hampton Square, off Sheen Lane on the Mortlake side of the Upper Richmond Road (comprising Gloucester Place, Brighton Place, William Street, Agate Yard and Queens Place (Barnes and Mortlake History Society 1983)), as a rough quarter inhabited by Irish families and Gypsies. I had heard for myself from my father about the boisterous antics of the Irish on a Friday night, but it was not until I was working at the Westway and began asking questions locally that I was to hear about the Gypsies. The fact that Hampton Square (demolished in the 1930s) was only three minutes from where I grew up and now lived only added relish to doing this 'anthropology at home'. So too did the realisation that some of those plying trades in and around Richmond Park Road in the post-war decades were Gypsies related to the Hampton Square families.

Lemonelia Smith, Mignonette Lovell's niece, was a 'very big dark gipsy with a stentorian voice' (Attwell 1996, 41), and well she might have been considering that she was born in a bell tent on Barnes Common and survived a strike by lightning before going on to marry a Romany from Mitcham, George 'Feathers' Smith, in 1860 and raising all but one of her children on the common. Lemonelia's only child *not* born in a tent on the Common was Patience (or Paisha as she was known), the youngest, who was born in Westfields, Barnes, in 1911. When Patience grew up she married a *gorgio* called Tom Parsons, a general dealer and coal merchant from Richmond, and in 1995 I talked with two of the couple's children, Ivor and Janet Parsons, and also with Ivor's wife, Joan (originally a Webb). The conversations took place in the Parsons' flower-shop by the railway crossing in Sheen Lane, a shop that had originally belonged to Harry Turner, a man my wife and I had earlier got to know at *The Charlie Butler* in Mortlake

George 'Feathers' Smith, wife Lemonelia, and family

High Street. What transpired revealed a network involving people with an unexpected range of trading interests in common.

Ivor and Janet Parsons, grandchildren of Lemonelia and 'Feathers', son and daughter of general dealer Tom Parsons, themselves had married people with Gypsy or (as some locals saw it) *didicoi* connections. Ivor had married Joan whose maternal grandmother from Northamptonshire, named Moore, was a Spanish Gypsy who had worked in service for the Duke of Wellington who later presented her with a testimonial and two goblets. Whether she entered the Duke's service during his Iberian campaigns, and whether Moore was a play on Moor, or even derived from the name of General John Moore of Corunna fame, I forgot to ask and left too late to find out subsequently, but something in Joan's appearance suggested she had inherited her grandmother's genes.

Ivor's sister, Janet, is married into a Westfields family named Dickerson; her father-in-law, Albert, having been a well-known general dealer and trader. Mary, another sister, married another of Albert Dickerson's sons. As for Ivor himself, although he said he no longer considered himself a 'proper Gypsy', and by way of example said he owned pieces of china he had inherited from his mother that he would never sell but which his brother would have smashed long ago in accordance with Gypsy norms. Nevertheless he networked with Gypsy horse-dealers at Southall market, Middlesex; knew totters in Stable Way beside the Westway Site (as had Albert Dickerson); and had earlier that day spoken with 'Eddie' Harris, a general dealer from Sheen who began his career as a coalman working for Gypsies, and about whom I shall say more in a moment.

According to Joan and Janet, Patience Parsons' sister Lol had married George Pharo a Gypsy knife-grinder from Mitcham.[19] This confirmed my suspicion that William Pharo, who in the 1860s ran a market garden at Barn Elms, was also a Gypsy. Still more importantly the pair confirmed what others had already told me about Patience Parsons being the person I remembered in the 1960s and early 1970s selling flowers at the junction of Milton and the Upper Richmond roads. Joan used to help her. I also discovered the woman I used to see selling flowers on the corner of Richmond Park Road, in sight of the family home when I was young, was Ethel Ballard (born 1898), a friend of Patience, and wife of Percy Ballard, another pair with Romany connections. Whether wild or cultivated, sprigs or bunches, the sale of cut flowers is a staple trade for many Gypsies. Unfortunately, rocketing rentals forced the Parsons to close their shop for the last time in 2006. It is one further sign of change in Mortlake and Sheen's streetscape and the people once long connected with it, but before we move on let us look more closely at the name Pharo and others who were knife-grinders.

Pharo (and its variant spellings) speak loudly of 'Egypt' and 'Egyptian' whence the word 'Gypsy' comes, and in the 1990s the London telephone directory turned up several of them, mostly in south and south-west London, where some worked in branches of the motor trade. In 1996 the sw London (Richmond) telephone directory listed three *Pharoahs*, one each in Roehampton, Fulham, and Kingston-upon-Thames; two examples of *Pharo*, one in Isleworth and another in Teddington; and a *Pharro* in Feltham. There was also a *Pharo* in North Kensington. In 2004 the Richmond directory showed up two *Pharoahs* in Roehampton, one in Kingston, a *Pharoahan* in Richmond, two *Pharros* in Feltham and Twickenham, and examples of *Pharo* in both Teddington and Isleworth. The largest concentrations of *Pharoahs* in England are found in Newcastle-upon-Tyne, in the Isle of Wight and adjacent southern counties, and in south-east Essex and Surrey, where *Pharos* show up strongly in the towns of Farnham and Guildford.[20]

Ellen Pharo (1890–1963) is buried near 'Feathers' and Lemonelia Smith in the Old Mortlake Cemetery in South Worple Way, an annexe of the St Mary's Anglican churchyard in Mortlake High Street. In the 1950s and 1960s other Pharos were parishioners of St Mary Magdelene's (R.C.) Church in North Worple Way; one of them, Reginald George Pharo, was listed as a benefactor, though I did not put all this together until I returned to London in 2004. And even then it only happened by chance.

Grave of George and Lemonelia Smith at Old Mortlake Cemetery

Back in 1994 on one of several visits I made to London in the 1990s I had bumped into an old acquaintance from my St Mary Magdelene days whom I'll call 'Ted'. Ted was wheeling his bike not a few yards from Joan Parsons' flower-shop when I spotted him and knowing him since childhood immediately went over and asked him what if anything as a parish stalwart he knew about the family known as Pharos. Just then one of those things happened that is pure serendipity but is by no means uncommon in fieldwork, especially fieldwork carried out over a long duration. For no sooner was my question put than Ted pointed with a sense of urgency over my shoulder to a passing car saying, 'That's Pharo *now*, an engineer; he lives in Chertsey Court'.

Almost as surprising and certainly no less rewarding when it happened, a decade then passed before I'd stumble across the name of Reginald George Pharo's for the first time, scribbled in a thirty-year old diary kept at the back of St Mary Magdelene's Church where it did rough-and-ready service (considering Sir Richard and Lady Burton's tomb outside) as the Visitors' Book. To this day I am still unsure whether Ted's Pharo and the Reginald George Pharo referred to in the 1970s section of the Visitors' Book were one-and-the-same; they probably were, but even if they weren't they were without question part of the same family.

Thus did luck or 'chance', as Louis Pasteur had it, 'favour the prepared mind', just as hunch and intuition do. In short, luck can play an important part in empirical research no matter whether the observer is a physical scientist, social scientist, or for that matter neither but rather a Traveller on the lookout. What is important in each case is preparedness.

The Hare and Hounds in Sheen and *Charlie Butler* in Mortlake often brought small anticipated, but unplanned, rewards. According to a 78-year-old customer of *The Hare and Hounds*, for example, Gypsies grazed donkeys in the fields of Sheen House, between Richmond Park Road and Sheen Lane, in the area of Muirdown and Shrewesbury Avenues, right up to the 1930s; literally a minute's walk from where I lived. Furthermore, considering that 'Feathers' had lived in Hampton Square it is more than likely the donkeys were his. When Sheen House and its land eventually came to be sold for housing development its stables were left intact and used by well-off riders, who rode in nearby Richmond Park. The stables were eventually torn down in the late 1960s or early 1970s and replaced by townhouses.

At the same pub, I got to know a second-generation Irish woman who had grown up in the 1950s in Garrett Lane, Wandsworth, where her father spoke Romany with Gypsies called Penfold and Hughes living there in LCC flats. In both *The Hare and Hounds* and *Charlie Butler* I met patrons who had known or heard of people named Pharo, of whom they often remarked that if they were not actually 'Gypsy', they were somehow 'mixed up' with them. Other people 'locals' thought to be 'mixed up' with Gypsies, if not actually 'Gypsies', were people with names like Bailey, Fairbrother, Gurney, Kilsby, Locke, Lee, Mitchell, Reid, Sharp, Harris, Smith and Dickerson. Bailey, Locke, Lee, Mitchell and Harris, as well as Smith and Pharo (of course) *are* 'Gypsy' surnames, and it is likely that Fairbrother and Reid are too. 'Eddie' Harris, who many people thought might be 'Gypsy', but who turned out not to be, nevertheless started his career working with Romanies called Sharp, one of whom I was eventually able to speak with. Conversations with customers in *The Hare and Hounds* also led to my meeting with Ron Kilsby, Barnes flower-seller whom some suspected was of Romany 'blood'. I will come to him and others presently.

The question is: what did locals mean when they said these individuals were possibly 'mixed up' with Gypsies? Did they mean married to, worked with, something else entirely, or did they simply not know? The answers are surely important when it comes to identification and 'border crossing', and when it comes to bestowing and withholding the label 'real Gypsy' on others.

Ron Kilsby was one of those who 'locals' thought might have been 'mixed up' with Gypsies. He ran a flower stall in Stanton Road off Barnes High Street, which had been started by his grandfather in 1901 after buses running between the village and Barnes Junction put his hansom cabs out of business. When Barnes became a municipal authority in the 1930s the village had around sixty street vendors, but the authorities quickly set about discouraging open-air trading and left it to the existing licensees to see out their times. As far as he knew, Ron was not of Romany blood. Nor I think was the other open-air flower-seller who to Ron's amazement had managed to set up a stall in Barnes. This individual sold flowers outside *The Sun Inn* across the road from the village pond and green where fairs and circuses attracted 'mountebanks, charlatans and quacks' in the 1830s (Anderson 1983), and without doubt Gypsies too. (In fact it was here in 1995 that I spotted Irish Travellers selling rugs at one of the community's fairs.)

Ernest Jacobs, who married Lemonelia (Lol Pharo's daughter, named after her grandmother), was apparently a *gorgio*. However, another Jacobs, whom I'll call 'Alan', was the friend of a neighbour of mine in Richmond Park Road who I used to drink with at *The Hare and Hounds*. He reckoned Alan was a 'pikie': someone of Gypsy 'blood'. A swarthy silent man, Alan was a 'dealer' from Brentford who shared an interest in river-craft and all kinds of collecting with my neighbour-friend, an ex-river policeman. Knowing I worked with Gypsies and Travellers, when we met Alan would often amuse himself by testing my knowledge of Gypsies gruffly without comment. Though his 'character' seemed 'Gypsy', Alan neither admitted nor denied being Romany. The nearest thing he ever came to revealing anything about his family was to say his father had been a 'gamekeeper'.

Mitcham Smiths with donkey rides, c. 1930 (unknown location)

Another person whose background was unclear was Frederick Gryce who, in the 1950s and 1960s, sharpened knives at the bottom of Richmond Park Road using a treadle grinder he pushed from Roehampton. An elderly man with a grey walrus moustache and large trilby hat, Gryce lived on the Dover House Road Estate and, according to one informant, came from a family of bargees who used to carry bricks from London to Belgium. Gryce may or may not have seen himself as a 'Gypsy', and I forgot to check with people like the Parsons, but he surely would have mixed with them.

Similarly, a Mrs Deacon sold flowers in the 1970s and 1980s at the corner of Penrhyn Crescent and Upper Richmond Road, where her van and buckets were a familiar sight opposite the whitewashed premises of Mr Vine, the chimney sweep. Heavily bundled in headscarf and overcoat, her early daffodils and tulips promised warmer days ahead, but I am not sure whether she had any 'Gypsy' connections. Vine, on the other hand, whose business included bicycle repairs and second-hand bike sales, admitted to the likelihood of 'Gypsy blood' mixed in with the blood of his East End Jewish forbears. The question of Romany 'blood' had often arisen in the course of family conversations it seems.

Rag and bone men and carriers

Albert Dickerson (1910–1983), his wife Emily (1909–1990) and their children lived in Cross Street, Westfields, not far from *The Manor Arms* and *Rose of Denmark*, where Albert used to enjoy a sing-song. Today he is buried beside the Smiths and Pharos in the Old Mortlake Cemetery in South Worple Way. Several times Albert had carted stuff in his van from Roehampton to Sheen for my father, and on one occasion his sons (about my own age) turned up at a Sunday evening youth club in Castlenau, causing mild alarm by their cheeky banter. Albert was one of those people others often refer to as a 'character'. Thickset, gravel-voiced, and nearly always decked in an old cap pushed to the back of his forehead, he was one of the cockney 'bulldog breed'; a man who would stand out in a crowd anywhere but nowhere more so than among the streets and small working-class cottages around his home in Westfields which since the early seventies had steadily been taken over by middle-class professionals. So it is not surprising that travelling through Barnes to work at the Westway I had reason to remember the Dickersons and wonder whether they might not be of Romany blood. There was certainly something in Albert's ways to think he might have been. Passing their house one evening in 1986 or 1987, coming back from Hammersmith, I was therefore interested to see a van parked in a small yard at the side of their house, which looked to have at one time been a stable, the only one of its sort amid the gentrification. The chance to check, though, did not arise until 1996, on one of my short field trips from Australia when, on my way to keep an appointment with Joan Parsons and her sister-in-law Janet at their flower shop in Mortlake, I suddenly saw Micky, one of Albert's sons, come out of the shop. Not realising then that Micky was married to Janet, I seized the opportunity. He did not remember me but, because Barnes and Mortlake retained something of the 'little community', he was happy to answer my questions, especially when I said I was only visiting from Australia. 'No', his father, who had been dead and buried several years, was *not* a Gypsy but he had mixed with them. Other details, including his marriage to Janet, only emerged when I went into the shop.

Albert Dickerson was born in Cross Street, got married to Emily, who came from East Anglia, and then moved to Willesden, below Harrow, before returning to Cross Street where he worked with horse and cart as a totter and carrier and enjoyed a reputation as an expert builder of carts. One of his 'trolleys' had been used in the BBC television series *Steptoe and Son*, about a rag and bone man in Shepherds Bush coincidentally called 'Albert' and his brow-beaten bachelor son, Harold. Still more remarkably, I learnt that some of the outdoor scenes for *Steptoe and Son* were filmed in Stable Way, in the totters' yard beside the Westway Site. There Billy Hunt (see Chapter 4), a member of the yard, later described Albert as 'straight as a dye' and a good 'letter-out of horses'. I was hardly surprised. Joan and Janet told me another Dickerson son had married another of their sisters: the kind of brother-sister 'exchange' common, in fact, among Romanies and Irish Travellers. In the meantime, Micky has established his own carrier/courier business.

Fruit and veg

In the 1950s and 1960s, two brothers named Fares or Fairs lived in Stanley Road, East Sheen, opposite the home of a close friend whose mother was Irish. Most of the properties in the road were workers' cottages built in the last quarter of the nineteenth century. The only commercial business apart from that of the Fares', who delivered fruit and vegetables to customers by horse and cart (before they graduated to motor transport), was a private coach service. The brother I remember best, simply because he delivered produce to my aunt in Roehampton Lane, had a sallow complexion and wore a trilby hat. Whether he was a Gypsy I am unable to say but since he and his brother rented stables in the road from his neighbour Mick Sharp, who was a Romany, there is a chance he was. It is also possible Fairs or Fares is related to the surnames Pharo and Pharoah which show high rates of frequency in the counties south of London and along the south coast. Thus Farnham is the town in Great Britain with the greatest number of people named Pharo, and Guildford (Surrey) the top area, while Dorking is the town with the highest frequency of Fairs, with Redhill (virtually next door to Guildford) the top area. Pharoah occurs most often in the area of Newcastle-upon-Tyne, but back in 1898 did so in Portsmouth where Pharoahs are still well represented.[21]

Coal and plate china

In the upper part of Sheen Lane, at the junction with Christchurch Road, a few minutes' walk from my home in Richmond Park Road in the 1980s, there was an intriguing house that, again, coincidentally, stood next door to one previously owned by a friend's family. The walls of this two-storey semi-detached Edwardian building were now decorated with various equine accoutrements: a wrought-iron manger, the near-life-size bust of a horse, a weathervane depicting a horse and jockey, and a carriage wheel. A Mercedes Benz was sometimes left parked in the paved garden. Was this a 'Gypsy' house? Once more, it would take me time to find out.

The girl who first answered the door was strangely unfazed by this inquiry from a total stranger. 'No,' she didn't '*think*' her father (who no longer lived there) was a 'Gypsy', but (and here she offered the thought as if it might be relevant) the front room was still full of brass he had collected. I declined to step inside to see it but instead said I'd call back later when her mother was at home. I did so and through her eventually spoke over the phone to her husband, the young girl's father, 'Eddie' Harris, to see whether he'd agree to an interview. Eddie readily agreed but limited time and a full schedule on my side meant it was another two years before I returned to England and met him.

Harris lived in a large house in a road off the Upper Richmond Road on the Mortlake side, and no sooner did he open the door than I found myself bundled upstairs to view the state of rooms vacated the day before by a couple of young men Eddie had rented to as a favour. The men had fled without paying. Perplexed and incensed, Eddie talked as if we'd known each other ages and I wondered again at the privilege that comes from being a passing stranger.

The Harris house, Christchurch Road, East Sheen, 1995

A man of middle years, Harris talked straight and lived without frills in a downstairs backroom. This came as a surprise given the double-fronted house's desirable location, impressive entrance and spacious hallway, where a pair of fine new doors led into a room housing an unexpected collection of special items.

He was the youngest of eight children, and had been born into a dirt-poor family from Richmond. A self-described 'wheeler-dealer' who found it 'easy to make money, but harder to hold on to [it]', he enjoyed the trappings of success. In his case, they included ownership of several properties (which he rented out), membership of the Sheen Lawn Tennis Club, foreign holidays, cruises, horse-racing and expensive motors — including at one stage, a Rolls Royce. Harris enjoyed 'style' in the same way that Florrie Allen and her son with the apartment in Monaco did. He also displayed 'character', the sort of 'get up and go' that urban foraging requires, and which had seen him interviewed on commercial television about his life. He promoted himself as:

Edward Harris
Property Letting Units & Services
Fully Furnished Flats, Houses and Cottages
Personal and Private Maintenance

and had began his career carrying hundredweight sacks of coal for a local firm of coal merchants called Sharp. Indeed, at my father's instruction I had often counted off the sacks Sharp's men delivered to our house, in case one or two were held back for sale to someone else on the side. The Sharps, I learnt, were Gypsies, and had given Harris his start in life. The hallway and room behind the smart doors told something of the story.

The first thing to catch my eye in the room Eddie led me to after we had talked in his back bed-sitter was a cabinet of statues carved exquisitely in coal. Nine or ten inches high, they depicted coalmen carrying loads; some wore old-fashioned leather caps with upper-back and shoulder protectors. Other cabinets held shelves of brightly painted enamel miniature coal-lorries amounting to a history of the vehicle, and tiny shiny black horses and donkeys, also carved in coal, a memoir of the pit days. In the hallway outside framed paintings of ships and collections of nautical material filled the walls and further cabinets, and I was shown a special collection of old postcards. There was money to be made in postcards, it seems, though this clearly didn't stretch to one somebody had sent to his Christchurch Road house in Sheen, asking if he was a 'Gypsy'. To my surprise, Eddie was insulted, so I was glad I had not made much of it myself.

With their father William S. Sharp — and, presumably, their mother — Bill, Charlie, Jim, Joe and Tom Sharp arrived in Barnes village from Swan Bottom, Aylesbury, Buckinghamshire, sometime between 1865 and 1870, and rented ground between the Terrace and

Barnes High Street from the Duke of Northumberland's estate.[22] Like other Gypsies in Barnes, the Sharps worked for a time in the local market-gardens alongside Irish immigrants. They also did cartage and hauling before going on to buy steamrollers in order to — in the words of 85-year-old Dicky Sharp — 'build half the roads in Barnes and Mortlake'. The coal business followed.

Dicky Sharp lived in a block of mansions by the river next to Barnes Bridge. Through Eddie I was able to talk to him twice on the phone, and from the conversation and Eddie's information I pieced together the following. William S. Sharp's son, Bill Sharp, along with *his* son, set up a scrap metal and demolition business at 5, Sheen Lane, opposite Mortlake Green. With Tom and some of his other brothers Bill also opened up a coal delivery business next to the station.[23] Joe Sharp married a Kensington woman, and their son Dicky did well in property. Mick Sharp, the son of another brother, lived with his family in Stanley Road, Sheen, in the 1950s, from where at one time he ran a paraffin delivery-business (though according to one informant Mick never seemed to have a 'real' job) and rented out stables and storage to the Fares' brothers. Mick's brother, Mush, was a coalman at the family yard alongside Mortlake station. In 1981, following the adoption of domestic central heating and the ban on coal fires, the Sharps closed their business in Mortlake and the small Victorian office became a junk shop before being upgraded to antiques and 'collectables'.

Gypsies value good china and Tinkers among them used to mend customers' broken china with wire. Others sold chipped or cracked china plate. Charles Henry Mitchell ran a china shop on the Upper Richmond Road opposite *The Hare and Hounds* from the 1920s to 1960s, and all his china was new. Mitchell was dark-haired, dark-suited, and bespectacled; he and my father, two small businessmen together, were pub friends. I have no evidence to suggest that Charles Mitchell was any more Romany than the quiet, dark-skinned Lees who lived next door to us, but certain people said that some of the local Mitchells (some of them in the building trade) were of Gypsy origin, and Mitchell is a name found among Kalderash. If he was

Romany or had any Gypsy background, Mitchell obviously saw fit to keep it to himself in much the same way that my father (an otherwise unabashed Catholic) tended to hide his 'Irishness'. In those days, some in Sheen thought such discretion was the better part of valour.

Conclusion

In discussing Gypsies and their traces in Mortlake I have fallen back on history books, interviews and observation. Far from yielding 'thick description' (Geertz 1973), the descriptions tend to be 'thin', for Gypsies and Irish Travellers rarely reveal their ethnic identity to outsiders and often deny it when asked. On top of this, the daily lives of most Londoners outside their families, neighbourhoods, and 'urban' and 'suburban' villages consist of passing encounters with strangers; surface encounters at most, facilitated by trade and market place and the simple routines of going about 'one's business'.

Gypsy women still door-knock in Sheen and Mortlake as they did when I was young, when they collected old clothes and begged a bob or two 'for fags'; some of this business has changed, though some remains. In 1985 a Romany woman up for the Derby read my palm on the pavement outside my house and gave me a 'lucky' charm in the shape of a tiny cowry shell (probably taken off a necklace). Many others Travellers live in houses and their ethnicity — unless deliberately questioned — is no more important to their normal social interactions than it is for most metropolitan and cosmopolitan people. Someone whose identity surfaced only because of deliberate inquiry was Rose K, a Surrey Gypsy, who worked with my wife at the Royal Star and Garter Hospital in Richmond. Another was the Irish Traveller in Sheen called Murphy, who drove mini-cabs and 'came out', when, driving my wife home one night, their conversation turned to identity and place of origin. Such 'thin' encounters can but call forth 'thin description' yet, thin as these encounters are, it is in this way that people in the metropolis connect outside the manor.

Mr E. Vine, sweep and general dealer, Upper Richmond Road, East Sheen, 1995

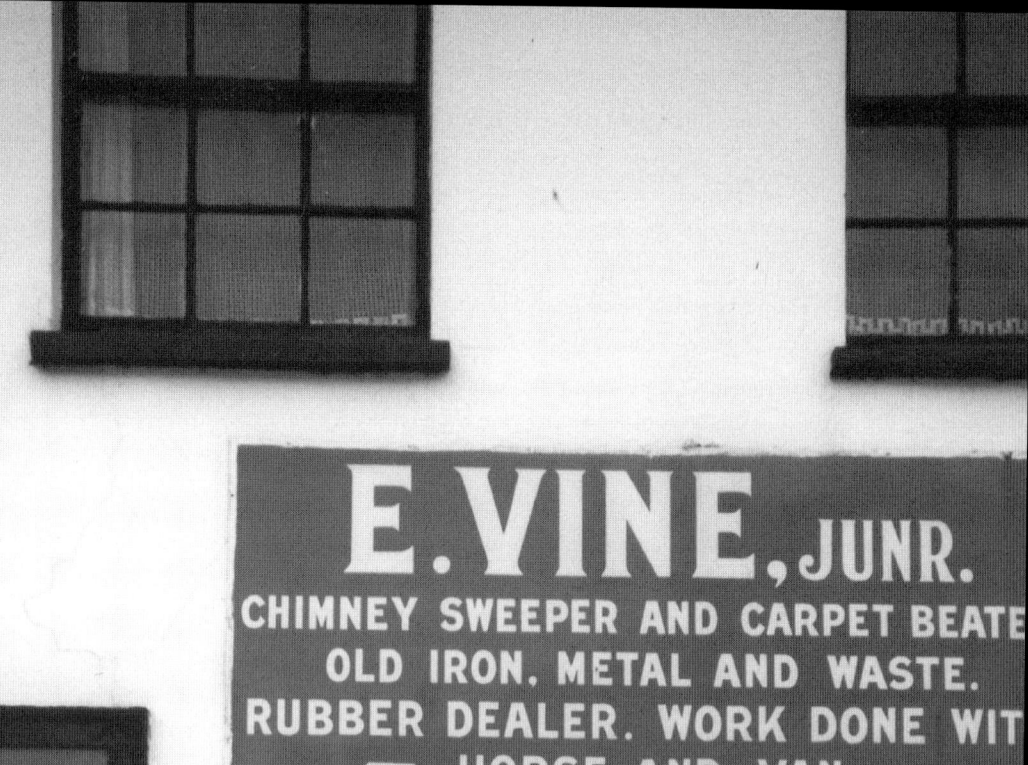

E. VINE, JUNR.
CHIMNEY SWEEPER AND CARPET BEATE[R]
OLD IRON, METAL AND WASTE.
RUBBER DEALER. WORK DONE WIT[H]
— HORSE AND VAN. —

298

Notes

1. 'Peculiar': a parish exempt from diocesan jurisdiction.

2. The manor house at East Sheen was situated near the modern junction of Sheen Lane and Christchurch Road.

3. In the French village where I did fieldwork this difference was expressed by the contrast terms '*gens du pays*' and '*étrangers*' ('*éstranger*' in patois); alternatively, '*nous*' and '*les autres*', 'us' and 'the others', or simply '*nous*' and '*les eux*' ('them').

4. I have kept to the boundary between Kensington and Chelsea and Hammersmith and Fulham as it was in the 1980s. The boundary in the vicinity of Notting Dale and the Westway site was slightly modified in 1995, resulting in certain administrative shifts.

5. Some of these alleys lay close to the homes of relatives I stayed in when I did this research.

6. In 1847 this firm was taken over by the London and Southwest Railway Company.

7. Two vehicle level crossings link Sheen and Mortlake: one in Sheen Lane, SW14, next to Mortlake Station, and the other in White Hart Lane, Barnes, SW13, near Priests Bridge. Three railway footbridges also connect them: one at Mortlake Station; one at the Mortlake end of Church Avenue (an extension of Church Path, an ancient way connecting East Sheen and Royal residences in Richmond Park with the parish church of St Mary's in Mortlake High Street); and another, Spur Bridge, midway along the line between Sheen Lane and White Hart Lane. Further west, there are other railway crossings and a bridge for motor traffic at Clifford Avenue (part of the South Circular).

8. From 1948 to the 1980s the family home was at 13, Richmond Park Road, a minute from the Upper Richmond Road, and during my time on the Westway I lived at number 1. Throughout the last century, however, and even today we have had family ties across the tracks in Mortlake. And by the strangest of coincidences close kin have recently returned to live at number 13, though the family no longer own it.

9. On my last trip to the area in 2004 I also noticed many Poles working (not necessarily living) in the area as labourers, cleaners and nannies. According to one newspaper more than 230,000 Poles have entered Britain since Poland joined the EU in 2004 (*Weekly Telegraph*, August 2006, 17).

10. Or possibly 1740, since Walford gives two dates.

11. Originally published by Barnes and Mortlake History Society (1983 (orig. 1979)).

12. All six spell 'Gipsy' with an 'i'. In Norwood (SE10 and SE27) there is a Gipsy Hill, Gipsy Road and Gipsy Gardens. In Welling it is Gipsy Road, and in Ealing (W3) Gipsy Corner.

13. Wedged in a triangle formed by the Upper Richmond Road, Queens Drive, and Gipsy Lane, the workhouse building, dating back to 1778, was converted to the Manor Hotel in 1837; see Barnes and Mortlake History Society (1983 (orig. 1979)). From memory, the hotel was demolished in the 1950s or 1960s. Today the area contains flats.

14. Pers. comm., October 2004.

15. See Thompson (1983 (orig. 1939)), in which the author associates 'braziers' (portable fires) with the travelling tinkers of Oxford.

16. Earlier we came across Shakespeare's 'Peter Sly', a friend of Autolycus; the name is related to Slee. There are Gypsies in Australia called Slee.

17. The 1827 bridge was replaced by the existing one in 1882.

18. The location is at odds with Anderson, who says Snake Alley connected the north side of the Lower Richmond Road to a point near the river where it ended by a gravel pit. In another book, *Rambles through Mortlake*, also cited by Hailstone (1983), Anderson described the vicinity as a place where 'A number of tramps used to sleep under those trees in the summer time and hang pots and pans, clothes ... [here] river thieves ran their goods ashore and took them through Snake Alley ... a lurking place and place of concealment for depredators and petty thieves as well as an excuse for their trespassing on the adjacent ground' (Anderson 1983 (orig. 1886), 75).

19. In her account of rural Oxfordshire in the 1880s, Flora Thompson describes 'Travelling tinkers with their barrows, braziers, and twirling grindstones, razors or scissors to grind? ... anything in the tinker's line ... old pots or kettle to mend' (Thompson 1983 (orig. 1939)). As she did not say they were Irish we may safely assume they were not. Nevertheless, we know that Irish tinkers were travelling around Britain at this time because the artist Augustus John, who mixed with Romanies and Irish Travellers, learnt their languages and was a close friend of John Sampson, mentions meeting Irish tinkers 'rich in the wisdom of the road' (Holroyd 1987, 357) at Haverford West in South Wales in 1897, in lodging houses in Liverpool's Scotland Road around 1901 (Holroyd 1987, 143), and even in Marseilles in 1910, where they were camped with continental Gypsies (Holroyd 1987, 409). Though Thompson, like John, thus distinguished Romanies from Irish Travellers, she was disdainful of Gypsies, whereas he was enthralled by them 'The gypsy lot' (as she referred to them) who lived in the hamlet outside her village were clearly looked down on by the villagers, and this contradicts the claim often made by *gorgios* that while they have no time for Irish tinkers or Travellers they admire 'real Gypsies'.

20. http://www.spatial-literacy.org/UCLnames/Surnames.aspx.

21. http://www.spatial-literacy.org/UCLnames/Surnames.aspx. Consulted 11 July 2007.

22. This land, or part of it, later became the site of Barnes Police station and the Metropolitan Police's motor section. A pub called the *Duke of Northumberland* also stood for years on the Terrace in front of the Thames, virtually next to another pub, *The Bull's Head*. Throughout the 1960s and 1970s *The Bull's Head* was one of London's premier modern jazz venues; it continued to be so for many years, and possibly still is.

23. For a long time coal was delivered by rail from Feltham (near Hounslow) to Barnes Junction. In 1984 I supplemented my income on the site by teaching 'life-skills' part-time at Feltham Borstal, a prison for young men, where one of my students was a Gypsy. Anecdotal evidence suggests young Gypsy and Traveller men are over-represented in prison (and see Power 2003).

6

RETURN OF THE NATIVE: POLITICS, ETHICS & ETHNOGRAPHY

The actual evolution of research ideas does not take place in accord with the formal statements we read on research methods. To some extent my approach must be unique to myself, to the particular situation, and the state of knowledge when I began my research.
William Foote-Whyte, *Street Corner Society*, 1973 (Appendix)

On the long journey doubts were often my companions. I've always admired those reporters who can descend on an area, talk to key people, ask key questions, take samplings of opinions, and then set down an orderly report very like a road map. I envy this technique and at the same time do not trust it as a mirror of reality. I feel there are too many realities. What I set down is true until someone else passes that way and rearranges the world in his own style.
John Steinbeck, *Travels with Charley: In search of America*, 1965

Introduction

At the start of this book I examined my motives for working at the Westway, the sources of these motives, and why they have sustained me. Three sources stood out: my personal experience of growing up in post-war London, questioning the meaning of Irish identity for immigrants and the second generation; the ambivalence — or stigma — surrounding that identity; and the growing realisation that being an 'outsider' 'in', but not 'of', the group is a strong position from which to examine Irish and English identities.

In Chapter 2 I looked at Irish Travellers in England in the

context of Irish immigration and a Gypsy presence. In Chapter 3 I narrowed the focus to look at Irish Travellers and Gypsies in North Kensington and north Hammersmith, a district with a significant history of Irish and Gypsy immigrants, before 1900. Chapter 4 took that examination into the twentieth century and included a history of the Westway Site up to May 1987, the point at which I resigned as warden, although I have since returned there six times.[1] In Chapter 5 I turned my attention to Mortlake, south of the river, the district I grew up in, returned to after some years in the Pacific, and lived in while working with the Travellers. Here I illustrated the localised sense of space by which Londoners derive some of their identity, a sense which in some cases involves notions of 'little community' or the 'suburban village'. By examining these two districts over the course of three chapters I hoped to show how my understanding of Travellers and Gypsies in one district triggered my surprised appreciation of their existence in the other.

This chapter has three parts. The first takes up the sense of personal journey discussed in Chapter 1 and describes the feelings of 'foreignness' and 'culture-shock' encountered when I first arrived in w10 and w11, the postal districts around Notting Dale and Notting Hill, and links it to what I felt about Hammersmith as a boy. Some social scientists, including Bochner and Ellis (2002), call this approach auto-ethnnography. The second part sets out the political and ethical dilemmas faced while being simultaneously a local government employee and an anthropologist, especially as I was not officially employed as an anthropologist. The final part describes my research methods.

Familiar or foreign

In 1982 Margaret Thatcher had been in power for three years with the Opposition in tatters, still reeling from the defection of thirty-plus MPs to the newly formed Social Democratic Party. Market deregulation, industrial reorganisation and 'privatisation' were the mantras of a new generation of City brokers, bankers and businessmen (see Hutton 1996). Unemployment rates were rising, notably in manufacturing and mining. With the country inflated by revenue from North Sea oil and puffed up by victory in the Falklands, voters in 1984 returned the Conservatives to power.

As unemployment in the north and the midlands increased, so did surplus labour flow into London and the south-east, just as the government's commitment to reducing welfare and community services began biting. Thousands in need of help, including many whose mental health had previously warranted residential care, now found themselves 'returned to the community', an idea that hardly squared with Thatcher's dictum of 'there being no such thing as society'. West End shop doorways quickly became night shelters for the homeless. Busking and begging flourished in the Underground. Waterloo and the South Bank sprouted cardboard cities. The Victoria Embankment and gardens of the Temple — elite home to the legal profession — filled at dusk with cardboard groundsheets, sleeping bags, tents and makeshift shelters. I even saw beggars in comfortable outer suburbs like Richmond. Mayhew and Dickens' London was come alive again. Meanwhile, deregulation in banking and the easier availability of credit forced up house prices, causing the average price in England to double in the decade 1980-90, with still more dramatic rises in London (Hutton 1996, 71).

Riots in Brixton in April 1981 involving black Londoners of Caribbean origin and the Metropolitan police were the worst seen in the capital since the Notting Hill riots of the 1960s. And although Lord Justice Scarman, in his 1982 report, cleared the Metropolitan police of conscious prejudice — particularly among senior ranks — and ruled that its behaviour was not an instrument of racist government, he found evidence of potentially damaging police activity at street level (Scarman 1982, 105). He recommended special programmes for ethnic minorities be implemented only where the need was utterly beyond doubt, and then such programmes should proceed even if it risked a white backlash, which in Scarman's view was rarely a product of institutionalised racism (Scarman 1982, 170). All this I had 'come home' to.

Through the late autumn and winter of 1982/3 I was a Visiting

Fellow at London University's Institute of Commonwealth Studies. The daily journey involved either taking a bus to Hammersmith and then the Underground to Tottenham Court Road or Russell Square, or driving to Hammersmith and Shepherds Bush and from there up the short stretch of the M41 and onto the M40 for the run into Bloomsbury. The first option was less a case of 'travelling' than 'transport'. Here the London Underground obliterates a sense of the world above. The dark side rendered by Victorian tunnels deep beneath the earth eradicates sky, city lights and buildings. Or, at least, the Piccadilly Line does. One is literally displaced, lacking all referents or landmarks excepting ingenious abstract Underground maps and station signs. Arriving at one's destination is magical and certainly more enchanting than the journey itself, and must be even more so since the Islamist bombings of July 2005. Starting 'there', by way of crowded stairs, tunnels, tiled labyrinths, lifts, escalators and sleek carriages one is suddenly — 'here'. The second option, going by car, had the opposite effect. Here displacement felt like 'travel' (even though 'travel' is always so much more than that), but the arrival disappointed.

Travel, a cognate of the French *travail* (work), implies effort and brings it own reward. To travel hopefully is a better thing than to arrive, it is said, and true success lies in the labour, according to the 'Story Teller' or *Tusitala* (in the language of Samoa where he lived and died), R.L. Stevenson. And so it was that, via unfamiliar, traffic-choked routes through 'foreign' parts of London, I slowly acquired what, in another context the anthropologist Jenkins (1994, 434), citing Rorty (1991), calls 'habits of action for coping with reality'.[2] In other words, it was the mental connections I made between alien pockets of the city as I moved through them that allowed me to get to 'know' the spaces or pockets themselves, by learning their names and realising their connection with other pockets, even as areas spreading laterally from the journey's route remained as much a mystery as ever.

Driving east down the M40 under a wintry white sky looking roughly south from where I had come, I saw meaningless buildings, senseless roads, and numberless strangers. Tower blocks in the middle distance, which presumably meant something (even 'everything') to those who lived or worked there, meant nothing to me. I felt deep pangs of nostalgia for Fiji and at such moments it was impossible to imagine that some of this alien landscape would soon become a source of intellectual and emotional nourishment.

One distant slate-grey monolith, taller than the rest, would in time acquire a name and location on my emergent mental map. Trellick Tower, Golborne Road, off the Portobello Road, was the highest block of council flats in Kensington and Chelsea (K&C). Another pair of dusky high-rise blocks turned out to be the nineteen-storey towers of K&C's Blechynden and Silchester estates, overlooking the Traveller caravan site (that had yet to register at all). These glass and concrete giants, as well as the terraced brick houses around them, would eventually become as much part of 'my London' as other corners of the earth had become permanent parts of 'my world'. Indeed, if history is another country, so is memory. And the memories and stories anthropologists hear and retell in their own fashion are countries that anthropologists abide in permanently.

Among the giant towers were council flats on the Borough of Hammersmith and Fulham's (H&F) Edward Woods Estate, near Shepherd's Bush, a few minutes from the Travellers' site. The authorities had an Estate Housing office there and its officers, not without reason, saw Edward Woods as a 'problem estate'. Numbers of people with mental illnesses and alcohol problems (who had previously been in sheltered care) lived there. Suicides were not uncommon and amnesiacs not infrequently left taps running, flooding flats below. I once watched water pour down the outside of a tower block as if it were some clever design feature. Along with official reports that came my way, it did little to soften those first distant impressions from the M40. Nevertheless, the challenge of learning to see the occupants of that estate and surrounding neighbourhood as locals in all their diverse opinions, and in the process become changed myself, was a prospect I looked forward to, even though I was not enticed to live there when the chance momentarily arose. Instead, the Edward

Woods' estate Housing office would be my bolthole in times of stress and ennui.

The place that would in time take on the greatest meaning was, of course, the caravan site itself. No longer a space glimpsed without thought from above as I drove from Shepherds Bush onto the M40 in a convoy of commuters, caravans barely registering, within twelve months it would unexpectedly become part of my life. No longer a 'space' or gap between 'places', it would be a 'place' in its own right, a space with a name. A named place full (sometimes far *too* full) of people with names, sometimes reluctantly divulged; people with real lives about which most were slow to speak, thus making the eventual business of writing this book difficult and more devoid of local voices than ever I have previously encountered. Still, they would be seen in time, I hoped, not just from above or 'afar' (as Lévi-Strauss once described the anthropological perspective) but both from ground level *and* 'afar'. For, as 'a man from the South' (to subvert Arnold Bennett's phrase) — south of the Thames, the southern hemisphere, and before that the south of France — it could not be otherwise.[3]

Looking north from south

In his portrait of the capital (2001) and his historical novel *Hawksmoor* (1985), Ackroyd reveals his fascination with London's wanderers and homeless, who are not entirely disconnected in terms of social history from the those contemporary nomadic Travellers and Gypsies, numbering in their thousands, who are compelled to live in illegal encampments if they are not to think of themselves as homeless.[4] However, it is the following passage I draw attention to here:

> Each area of London has its own unmistakeable character, nurtured through time and history, together they resemble a thousand vortices within the general movement of the city. It is impossible to look at them all steadily, or envisage them as a whole, because the impression can only be one of opposition and contrast. Yet out of those oppositions and contrasts London itself

> emerges, as if it sprang into being out of collision and
> paradox. In that sense its origins are as mysterious as
> the beginning of the universe itself. (Ackroyd 2001, 535)

How different and complex is this view of the juxtaposition of confused, competing and changing physical, social and cultural forms found in any district of London, when compared with the view of Arnold Bennett's Mr Aked a hundred years ago. Is the difference explained by changes happening in the city between these times, or is it due to the way we have come to think about cities? No doubt it is something of both. Moreover, a common thread joins these writers. Aked recommended Positivism — the social science paradigm of his day. A century later, Ackroyd reflects his own era. Historicity is attuned here to continuity, evolution *and* very rapid change. The prolix or messiness of value-differences, of cultural diversity, of conflict, contest — as well as consensus — are emphasised. The attention is on persistence amid change and on the virtual impossibility of grasping London in its entirety. But, like Bennett's Aked, Ackroyd still regards London as a whole. For Ackroyd, the capital's 'oppositions and contrasts' mean 'hundreds of Londons all mingled' (2001, 777), making it hard 'to look at them all steadily, or envisage them as a whole', even though out of such ill-fitting parts 'London itself emerges' (2001, 535). This is surely consistent with Aked's observation of the 'concussion of suburbs in the centre of London' (Bennett 1994, 47).

Though conscious of these 'oppositions' and 'concussions' *within* North Kensington (w10 and w11) and Hammersmith (w6) in 1984, as well as *between* them (singly or collectively), and Mortlake (sw14) with its own oppositions, East Sheen (sw14), Barnes (sw13), Putney and Roehampton (both sw15), I could not deny that all these borders were porous and their populations mingled. For me, coming from 'the south' and comparing the two zones still involved 'culture shock' and, more than this, harked back to that view from my younger days which, as I would later discover, was akin to that of the travel writer Eric Newby whenever as a child, between the two world wars, he crossed from Barnes (sw13) to Hammersmith (w6).

Travels at home

Eric Newby's earliest memory of home was a mansion flat in Barnes overlooking the Thames, downstream from Hammersmith Bridge. I know the road and knew the flats. A friend of a friend once lived there and during one school holiday I worked a short distance away at the Sunlight Laundry, in Glentham Road, on the upstream side of the bridge. Except for the boiler man, myself and another boy from school (who went on to become a senior civil servant), the workers were all women, many of them from Hammersmith, Shepherds Bush, West Kensington and Notting Hill. It seemed even then as if the laundry had dragged its anchor and become stranded on the wrong bank, and was in need of towing back to Middlesex, though I was quite unaware that Notting Dale and Shepherds Bush were once famous for their laundries.

'Rich homes', Notting Hill, 2004

For Newby, too, travelling and cultural 'differences' began at Hammersmith Bridge, under whose girders, at the outermost margins of north Surrey, the infant Newby encountered what he called his first 'real travellers':

> It would not have been much of a night for the homeless poor, their clothes stuffed with newspaper, who slept rough on the towing path down by the river all through my early childhood and who would certainly have been there that night. Most of them were terrifying-looking women; some were 'tramps', the first 'real' travellers I can remember seeing, pointed out by my nurse. But not many of them would have been tramps because most tramps were too solicitous of their personal comfort to share the appallingly draughty, unspeakably filthy but more or less rain-proof camping places used by these unfortunate outcasts, up against the reeking abutments of Hammersmith Bridge, only about fifty yards from where, a boisterous baby, I was now giving tongue.
> (Newby 1983, p. 14–15)

At the age of 5 his travel-guide nanny took him further:

> Whether it was in pursuit of whatever she was in pursuit of, or we were simply on a new, adventurous walk, on the afternoon on which the happenings which led up to my nightmare took place, Lily pushed me in the mail cart up the towing path from Hammersmith as far as the Chiswick Ferry ... Having reached the ferry, as she usually did, Lily turned left down a narrow, unmetalled lane between two reservoirs ... This lane led to Lonsdale Road, the road up which the police used to push the drunk and disorderly on their handcart to Barnes Police Station. At Lonsdale Road she normally turned left for Hammersmith Bridge and home along the pavements. But on this particular day instead of doing this she crossed Lonsdale Road and continued to follow the

alignment of the lane into what was, for me, unknown territory.

It was an eerie place. To the left of the lane, which was also unmetalled, a rather dreary expanse of fields with a farmhouse on the edge of it, what must have been one of the nearest farms to central London stretched away towards the semi-detached developments that but for the war would have already engulfed them, as they would shortly. In these flat fields, some distant off, a line of what looked like men but I later discovered when I was older were rough-looking women wearing cloth caps and sacks in lieu of aprons, worked away, bent double among the vegetables ... [Nearby] ... thick pollarded trunks grew, or rather rotted, for most of them were in the last stages of decay. The surface of the road was full of potholes with water in them, and in the ditches on either side was some of the detritus of civilization ... It was therefore not surprising that when the fields were built over some years later and the lane became a respectable suburban road, whoever was in charge of naming roads in Barnes gave it the name it bears today, Verdun Road. Against the largest and most decayed of these ruined trees a fire was burning, eating its way into the heart of it, and sitting close to the fire, although it was late afternoon it was still warm, were three of the hideous hags who, when the tide was right, slept up against the abutments of Hammersmith Bridge. And on the fire was an iron pot. They were so blackened by smoke and smeared with filth that it was difficult to identify them as human beings. One of them was singing in a wild, tuneless way and another was screeching at the third member of this ghastly triumvirate, while picking away like a monkey in her long, lank hair. The third one was tending the pot ...

> It was too much for me and I began to bellow; and it was too much for Lily who kicked up her heels and fled ... until she reached the corner of Madrid Road where we were once again on a real, made-up road and enclosed by comforting suburbia. (Newby 1983, 30-2)

Finally, in a chapter he called 'Journeys through Darkest Hammersmith (1928–1936)' — a phrase Clarence Rooks would not have forgiven if uttered by toffs, Newby:

> These journeys from Three Ther Mansions over the bridge and through the streets of Hammersmith altogether continued for eight years of my life (not including the period when, as a small child, I attended the Froebel kindergarten in Baron's Court). In me they engendered some of the feelings of excitement, danger and despair that some nineteenth-century travellers experienced in darkest cannibal Africa and in the twentieth century in the Central Highlands of New Guinea. And even today and now with even more reason, I sometimes experience a chilly sensation when walking down a narrow south London street. (Newby 1983, 73)

So what is my point? It is simply that a comparable sense of adventure born of contrast and cultural difference gripped me as 10-year-old on my journey each day to school in Ealing (w5), and has remained with me ever since, not merely as a memory. It says much for the symbolic power of rivers as borders that help to define communities. Thus both memory and the actuality of re-encountering London in 1982, in vague anticipation of doing 'fieldwork' at home, reinstated this feeling. Perhaps, too, some of that thrill came from living in a metropolis where most people are oblivious to the lives of people in districts they have never visited nor are ever likely to, and where accordingly, when excursions do occur, the event is something of an adventure.

Raban, in his book *Soft City*, which calls up material from Notting Hill, captures the idea admirably:

> We map the city by private benchmarks which are meaningful only to us. The Greater London Council is responsible for a sprawl shaped like a rugby ball about twenty five miles long and twenty miles wide; my city is a concise kidney-shaped patch within that space, in which no point is more than about seven miles from any other. On the south, it is bounded by the river, on the north by the fat tongue of Hampstead Heath and Highgate Village, on the west by Brompton cemetery and on the east by Liverpool Street station. I hardly ever trespass beyond these limits, and when I do I feel I'm in foreign territory, a landscape of hazard and rumour. Kilburn, on the far side of my northern and western boundaries, I imagine to be inhabited by vicious drunken Irishmen; Hackney and Dalston by crooked car dealers with pencil moustaches and goldfilled teeth; London south of the Thames still seems impossibly illogical and contingent, a territory of meaningless circles, incomprehensible one-way systems, warehouses and cage-bird shops. Like any tribesman hedging himself in behind a stockade of taboos, I mark my boundaries with graveyards, terminal transportation points and wildernesses. Beyond them nothing is to be trusted and anything might happen. (Raban 1988, 166–7).

Following Ackroyd (2001) and Jenkins (1994), one sees how Londoners (and London's commuters) inhabit 'many Londons' and, through their observations, acquire the 'habits' that allow them to operate effectively in and identify with those Londons. Belonging to, knowing and identifying with the metropolis is the result of a process somewhat resembling the patchy and selective process air travellers go through when flying from A to G they look down on B, D, and E as *places* they know already, and upon C and F as *spaces* about which they are more or less totally ignorant.

Until 1984 my knowledge of London was framed by the Thames, by particular public transport routes, by walking and by bicycling, as well as indirectly by literature, the visual media, education and a personal predilection for maps.[5] 'My London' in 1984 was therefore composed of slabs or patches, some of which I knew more intimately than others. Among the areas north of the Thames with which I was reasonably familiar, were, from east to west: the City from the Tower to St Paul's; Holborn; Embankment; Whitehall; Westminster; Piccadilly; Charing Cross Road; most of the West End up as far as Knightsbridge; south and central Kensington; and Hammersmith. Beyond here, with the exception of parts of Ealing and Greenford, I knew little. I was also ignorant of most of north London, aside from bits of Regents Park and the area around Lords. The East End was equally foreign to me, and so was most of south-east London. Beginning vaguely for me at Battersea, south London quickly became the south-west and blended into the familiar postal codes SW13, 14 and 15. Thereafter 'my' London became Surrey.

Arriving on the Westway Site (W10) in 1984 thus presented an opportunity for me to study an 'unknown' part of London using the south-west postal districts as my baseline for comparison. Better still, Travellers and Gypsies would involve me with a section of that larger Irish community out of which my earliest questioning of identity arose but which, in this case, embraced nomadism and dealt with stigma on a level that, even at the darkest times, most Irish immigrants have never encountered.

Politics and Ethics

No Traveller, Gypsy, or member of the Westway Traveller Support Group (WTSG) was involved in my appointment on either occasion. The decision to employ me was taken by H&F Housing Department officials who, at the interview, stressed their need for someone capable of establishing 'rapport' and taking an interest in the culture of the

Gypsies and Travellers so as to provide a better line of communication between themselves (the Council) and the site inhabitants. The words 'culture' and 'rapport' were theirs, not mine. I made it clear at the outset that my advocacy and partisanship on behalf of Travellers should be presumed. I would take on the six-month job providing it was understood that as a matter of principle I'd support the Travellers first, the Housing Department second, and the Council as a whole, third. I also indicated that I was an anthropologist. After my appointment, I made three resolutions.

The first of these was that in order to understand the history and conditions of the Westway, which had led to the need for a temporary warden in the first place, I would observe not only how Travellers and Gypsies behaved but how non-Travellers behaved towards them. And to do this I knew I would have to act covertly; that is to say, I would have to breach one of the basic rules of normal fieldwork. In connection with this I vowed to disclose my status as an anthropologist and writer wherever identity concealment would have breached the principle of 'good faith' which is the starting point for most social relations, be they, in this case, those between me and fellow Council employees, other 'professionals', or the Travellers. I also vowed not to be evasive should people ever inquire about my background. It is therefore remarkable (and, to be honest, fortunate) that in the course of two years nobody apart from Travellers and Gypsies themselves ever *did* inquire: my alter ego stayed closeted.

Second, contrary to the first vow, I resolved to *reveal* to as many Travellers and Gypsies who cared and had a right to know, all they wished to know about me. As one traveller of a sort to another it seemed the only and obvious thing to do. Besides, I realised that should revelations about my 'scholar' status filter back to the non-Traveller 'professionals' from whom I deliberately concealed this information, it would teach me something important about Traveller/non-Traveller 'professional' networks. Indeed, I would learn something important about those networks even if such information did *not* — or rather *appeared* not to — get back to the professionals. And not least, since reciprocity or gift giving (Mauss 1974) is a necessary though not sufficient condition of friendship, I hoped that by being open with Travellers some might be open with me.

Thirdly, I resolved to do the obvious, which was to aim to treat every individual as an individual, without prejudgement. It would be essential given the torrid history of the site.

Balancing the role of warden, anthropologist and potential ethnographer was problematic technically and ethically. For instance, whenever private conflicts between Travellers threatened harmony elsewhere it made my management decisions difficult. Following the first rule of wardening, which is not to interfere in private family matters, I therefore usually chose to delay intervention and await internal resolution, even though this was not always what *particular* Travellers wanted at the time. Nor was it always in accordance with the rules of bureaucracy applying to professionals — either in Housing or in the advocacy and 'helping professions' working behind the scenes in the WTSG, where *not* acting by the 'letter of the law' was a normative infraction sometimes quickly picked up on.

Anyway, I preferred instead to learn the *art* of management by way of observation, listening, learning by trial and error, and by not asking too many questions. In short, being the sort of fieldworker who does not see 'knowledge as a matter of getting reality right' so much as a fieldworker who sees it is important he or she acquires habits suited to dealing with the real world (Jenkins 1994, 434); in this case acquiring them as Travellers and Gypsies themselves do, as much by intuition as by an adherence to rules (Griffin 1999).

My role as warden could also be difficult when Traveller politics *on*-site collided with the political stratagems of bureaucrats *off*-site. For example, in 1986, after consulting with me, the Housing department's Estates Management section decided to evict a squatter family that had overstayed its welcome despite my many requests that it leave. Matters came to a head one afternoon when a burly Irish Traveller, on return to his caravan, found a summons pinned to his door by one of the Council's legal officers. I was aware of the summons and wondered, as I sat in my office, how the man, a father of several teenagers, would respond when he saw it. Then I heard a sudden ear-splitting bellow: 'Where's the f***ing warden?' As I came out the door I saw him striding towards me wielding a shovel. We met in the middle of the site, now conspicuously devoid of people, and at once I attempted to reason with him. I was aware of the silence now fallen over the site outside my immediate uncomfortable zone of intimacy, and equally aware of the judgements about to be made by all those peeping from their windows. It was both momentarily absurd and indelibly grave. Fortunately, a calming voice came from a trailer: 'Leave the warden alone, he's only doing his job'. I don't know who said it, but this lifeline did the trick. The circuit was broken. I walked away, stayed ten minutes, and decided to call it a day. Fortunately such confrontations were rare, and in this case the squatter and his family broke camp before an eviction was necessary.

I never enjoyed comprehensive trust, presuming that such a thing is ever possible. The social dynamic of families in a closed and politically charged environment made sure of it. Bearing silent witness is the *sine qua non* of Westway co-existence, both for Travellers and for wardens, and should the code of Traveller silence and studied indifference be seriously breached the consequences can be serious: threats of violence and actual violence to property, persons, or both. Such violence, in turn, may then be avenged.

The simplest Traveller way of managing conflict is by avoidance and, when that fails, by retreat. During my time several Travellers upped and left suddenly and so, it seems, had one or two earlier wardens. To avoid giving cause for disputation or irritation one thing I had to learn to do was not to mention to third parties what others had told me, no matter how seemingly anodyne, for any hint of gossip on my part was apt to lay seeds of doubt about my trustworthiness. I learnt quickly from my mistakes.

People in the advocacy and helping professions outside the Council's employ were also obliged to develop habits of confidentiality and secrecy, and this had unexpected consequences for their — or I should say 'our' — levels of co-operation. Different professional practices involve different habits and ideologies, which in turn give rise to different 'definitions of the situation'. At the same time the code of silence expected of us all limited the practice of reflecting on our mutual epistemologies and thus on our capacity for joint co-operation with Travellers who, at the best times, operate as autonomous households or individuals and not as a collective. Let us examine this more closely.

As each Traveller and Gypsy family or (more correctly-speaking) each domestic unit operates fairly independently of its wider kin-network (both on and off the site), it invariably keeps its own counsel. At the same time, in line with this, professionals who periodically visit the site according to clients' needs (such as social workers, health practitioners, education support officers) deal on a one-to-one 'casebook' basis with *individuals* or *individual families* and not with problems of the site as a 'community' arising out of *inter-familial* conflict. By contrast, other professionals, working on the site for continuous extended periods of time and with a larger cross-section of people, as Save the Children Fund's (SCF) kindergarten teachers did, had a wider and more 'political' perspective. They saw themselves as advocates as much as service-providers. Yet even here, an involvement with particular *categories* of people, small children and their mothers, and not young fathers, men in general, or unmarried adults, meant their outlook was at times restricted. For my part, from the privileged viewpoint of a warden-cum-anthropologist observing and dealing five days a week with individuals and every family, as well as with Council officers, the aforementioned professionals, and many other sorts of people, the outlook was different. In a word, our professional *habits* differed and with it our different kinds of knowledge. Small wonder then that SCF as one sort of advocate and myself as another often held conflicting 'definitions of the situation'.

The longer I stayed at the site the greater, generally speaking, was the trust between myself and the Gypsies and Travellers. It grew pronounced with seven or eight families. And as I remained some people quietly encouraged me to write, usually suggesting it before I did.

My return to work on the site in 1986 after a year away marked a real turning point. News of contacts I had kept up with a large family of Irish former site residents who had moved away in 1984 did me no harm with one of the older Romany women of influence who happened to be one of their friends. Another matriarch, an Irish woman, who had moved away with her family the previous summer but was visiting, remarked, 'You must like the Gypsy folk [to have come back] ... and if you weren't married perhaps you'd join us'. Charm, of course, and kindness surely, but also a small sign of progress.

Making headway with men was in some cases more difficult than with women. Certainly they were often less approachable. Consequently, when not long after I got back to the site in 1986 I noted in my diary that I had the impression that a young mother I had been talking to that day 'was deliberately educating me, so I didn't feel inhibited about putting to her some very straightforward questions', it was written in order to record the gender difference. And yet five days later a man I had spoken with several times at length in previous weeks, and to whom I'd lent a copy of Sharon Gmelch's (1975) book, said he wanted to work with me to tell his own story. Unfortunately nothing came of it because not long afterwards this somewhat 'marginal man' (his mother was a Traveller but his father was not) pulled off the site. A week later, on St Patrick's Day, while drinking with Travellers and Gypsies at *The Latimer Arms*, someone suggested I should join up and work with them, and in that way earn more money. And though it was only beer-talk it was passing comfort and emboldening. The next day in the same pub, this time in the company of the man who had suggested telling me his life story, his cousin, and a young Romany from the top of the site, I was telling them what an anthropologist did when another Irish Traveller, overhearing, suggested I should give up the job of warden and go and work with them. The message was clear: being warden was a mug's game. Needless to say, the offers were not that serious, but from this moment on (although I was sometimes still treated as a 'non-person') several people told me to write. By Spring 1987 even Martin Ward, who had stopped speaking to me about ten months before, began to lend me his backing. Having come to feel jaded about the WTSG, he started to support me from here on.

Research methods

At the start I decided to observe and *listen*, watch and keep my ears open, and to participate wherever the chance arose, rather than ask questions, except where questions were necessary to my role as warden. Reading Rehfisch (1975) very early, sometime in the summer of 1984, I also decided against absorbing too much literature in order to circumvent the risk of unconsciously seeing and hearing what others before me had suggested.

My 'master-status' (Becker 1996) as warden involved four lesser statuses and duties: on-site day-to-day manager; caretaker; cultural mediator or broker; and counsellor. Together they presented opportunities for participant-observation with Travellers (and non-Travellers) both on and off the site — socialising in pubs, attending rites of passage and visiting markets and fairs, and for asking the kind of questions that were initially impossible. However, unlike the work of Judith Okely (1983), which benefited from her going out to work with Gypsies, mine does not; nor does it benefit from having accompanied families on their travels.

In Mortlake I relied mainly on speaking and listening to local people, on personal memory and on the memories of family and friends, as well as upon observation. Some conversations are more deserving of the word 'interview' than others, and some 'interviewing' was done by way of later correspondence. In Mortlake, as in North Kensington and north Hammersmith, I used secondary historical sources, and in North Kensington and Hammersmith I utilised local and central government reports, censuses, newspaper archives, housing records, and early WTSG and Southern Gypsy Education Council minutes. Novels and autobiography have also been used and so, to some extent, the Internet.

In practice, what I saw and heard was usually committed to memory and written up soon afterwards in notebooks and diaries. This goes for practically all conversations at the Westway and in Mortlake, although by 1986 I was able to openly take notes with some site residents, while taking great care not to arouse the suspicions and wrong impressions of neighbours. Data from public records, reports and newspapers were filed and cross-referenced roughly according to topic. However, it would be another two to three years after leaving London before I was able to catalogue and reorder the information from my notebooks — personal computers were still some years away.

The office at the Westway Site where I spent most days was a metal 'portakabin' parked near the entrance. On Travellers' advice steel shutters were made for the door and window, and hardened shackles used to lock them whenever I departed. There were no attempts at break-ins and in two years it remained remarkably free from graffiti. The office contained basic furniture and the usual tools and paraphernalia of a caretaker.

Every week a few Travellers dropped by either to use my telephone (mobiles were virtually unheard of and landlines owned by only two families) or request I phone the Department of Health and Social Security (DHSS) for them. Others occasionally stopped by to chat but most adults who needed me simply waited till I passed them as I swept the site or went about other duties. Then I would be invited into trailers. A certain amount of pride also stopped people from coming to me. Better I should go to them than it be seen that they should come to me. Only short conversations took place inside my cabin. And only boys up to the age of 14 or 15 years regularly dropped in, usually because they were bored, and then either to quiz me about my knowledge of their culture or tease me by picking up my things and hiding them. Boys aged between 6 and 11 did the same, but also liked to draw pictures (usually of caravans, lorries, horses, and little houses with smoking chimney pots) on the paper I provided. Girls of over 8 rarely stopped by, never alone, and when they did it was usually to deliver a message from a parent that I should go and see them.

As I noted above, my return in January 1986 marked a turning point of a kind not unusual in fieldwork (Barrett 1996). For providing people were bothered or cared to know (and that is no small proviso), what I had done in my year away as a college lecturer served to widen their knowledge of me. A second turning point, though I did not see it as such at the time, occurred ten months later when having told some Travellers I was migrating to Australia (where some of them told me they had relatives), I then had to wait six months for our visas to be issued. Those months subsequently turned out to be marked by a greater sense of urgency and a devil-may-care attitude. Increasingly, the only people I remained 'undercover' with were the professionals, including the SCF teachers with whom, in their capacity as WTSG activists, my relations had become decidedly uneasy. To explain this situation I need to backtrack a little.

By January 1986, due partly to battle fatigue, partly to the desire of most Travellers to avoid confrontation with one another, and partly to higher morale on account of improved conditions on the site, the number of participants at WTSG meetings had dwindled to a handful of non-Travellers and an even smaller number of residents. By mid-year only two or three domestic units out of about twenty still talked about needing a new site. Most were indifferent or satisfied with the status quo.

Apart from the WTSG, which as a Council employee I was not eligible to join as far as the group was concerned, a newer group calling itself the Westway Traveller Site Inter-Agency Group (WTSIAG) was open to people from every social agency at the Westway. Eligible members included the SCF teachers, health workers, educational support officers, and Housing Department officials (myself and the Housing Estate Manager or his deputy included) within whose 'patch' the site fell. The only difficulty I had with this arrangement was that as the Housing Department was the only organisation in the agency group excluded from the WTSG, where strategy was developed (a point not missed on Travellers, who urged me to attend *both*), my participation in the WTSIAG was hobbled from the start. In addition, because agency meetings were held in the SCF classroom and chaired by one of its personnel, it became increasingly difficult to differentiate the SCF from the WTSIAG, and the SCF from the WTSG, especially since the SCF also took the minutes and guided the agenda. Therefore it was in my capacity as a member of the WTSIAG, rather than as warden, that I challenged these procedures in early 1986.

I also challenged the rhetoric of 'crisis-management' and the teachers' allegations of my personal mismanagement. The talk being put around in agency meetings was that Travellers and Gypsies were in an uproar about Housing's failure to manage the site, and therefore also in an uproar with me. In February 1986, for example, the SCF reported that a 'delegation' of male Travellers were angry at learning news of H&F's intentions to evict squatters having heard that a visit was about to be made to the site by Princess Anne (now the Princess Royal) in her capacity as President and patron of the SCF. How many men formed this 'delegation', who they were, and why they had not spoken directly to me as they normally would and rarely hesitated to do, was not explained. As far as I knew the Council had no plans whatsoever to evict anyone. In fact my line manager had already told me that H&F had decided against *any* special clean-up before the royal visit. How, then, to explain this apparent talk of crisis, evictions, and accompanying high dudgeon?

As I began to hear more of this sort of rhetoric I suspected, though could not prove, that the head of household (whose brother-in-law had previously threatened me with a shovel) was now feeling the pressure of having to engage with SCF teachers and the Council in order to secure the long-term future of the site, and as result was also under pressure from his family to 'ease-up'. Either panicked into action or led disingenuously by the Support Group that stood behind him, loose talk by the Support Group about the Council's intention to carry out 'mass evictions' seemed a cynical tactic. My hunch was soon reinforced, when, a few hours after one agency meeting ended, the complainant's younger brother came to my office (something unusual for him) and demanded I evict another squatter who had earlier pulled in beside him. This was clear evidence of words being used tactically in the interests of *one* family (and the SCF) rather than the community, and in this case intended victory over me.

I was unimpressed by the rhetoric and, having challenged agency procedures while standing behind the eviction order of the 'shoveler' whose angry relative ('Mr Angry') the SCF had always stood by, I now feared being 'outed' as a 'research anthropologist' should any members of the WTSIAG, WTSG or SCF discover this aspect of my identity and convey it to 'Mr Angry' and his brothers with the intention of having me thrown out. By that autumn my concern proved founded when the teachers announced that the SCF had commissioned a 'consultant anthropologist' to conduct an independent study of conditions on the site and of their impact on children, and for this reason the consultant would need to interview me. Matters were becoming increasingly bizarre. And so it was that at the next WTSIAG meeting — where the consultant's presence now further fogged the boundaries between the three groups — that I happily agreed to talk to the consultant, full knowing that I would now have to reveal myself as a fellow anthropologist, while at the same time realising that when this information got back to the SCF it would only enhance their power and influence.

As it happened, there was *no* interview. Over the next few days I watched the consultant visit families at the top end of the site but, as far as I could see (and as my neighbours reported), none at the bottom. Moreover, that was the last I heard of the consultant, whose departure was even more sudden than her arrival. As a result my other identity remained safe and it was only at the moment of leaving, when a social worker inquired about my plans and was bemused by the revelation, that I was ever called on to reveal that identity. This raises two questions: would my relationships with the professionals have been better if I had revealed my other status, and would it have resulted in greater cooperation advantageous to the site's inhabitants? And was acting covertly with the professionals to observe their 'normal' behaviour with Travellers and other parties justified both from the point of view of local government and academic anthropology? The answer to the first question is, I think, already evident. I doubt very much that this particular revelation would have been helpful because at the heart of the matter lay three conflicting cultures of power: the *culture of bureaucracy* — that of the Council proper, characterised by its reluctance or inability to dialogue directly with Travellers and Gypsies; the *culture of the Travellers and Gypsies*, whose lack of cohesion undermined their collective negotiating power; and the *cultures of professionals*, whose separate occupational habits resulted in a competition for knowledge, power and authority that undermined their chances of cooperation. As for the second question, in view of H&F's long-term aim to shed itself of the site, I believe my covertness was justified, for without concealing my identity from non-Travellers it would have been impossible to see how Travellers and Gypsies were 'used' as well as aided by them. The fact that I was as open as possible with the Gypsies and Travellers themselves serves to support this, I hope.

The Westway Site still exists and since 1987 there have been substantial improvements to its infrastructure, although not everyone living there today would necessarily agree with this assessment. Indeed, it remains open to question whether anyone should be still living there at all.

In all, I came to know some fifty or sixty families or 'sections' of extended kin networks, and maybe twice that number if I include those people who came and stayed only a few days. Of those fifty or sixty, I got to know eight well, or at least I *think* I did. This goes especially for those I caught up with again in the 1990s and in 2004, when I was able to talk to and question them again more thoroughly.

Notes

1. In 1991, 1993, 1994, 1995, 1996 and 2004.

2. This chapter borrows from Jenkins (1994) and his case material of peasant markets in south-west France.

3. Geertz (1993) calls these angles 'experience-near' and 'experience-distant'.

4. In March 2006 the Office of the Deputy Prime Minister estimated that in England over 4,000 Gypsy and Traveller caravans were parked illegally.

5. When I was young we never owned a car.

7

ECOLOGY, ECONOMY, HABITAT

Ecology. The science of the economy of animals and plants; that branch of biology which deals with the relations of living organisms to their surroundings, their habits, their modes of life, etc. (F. G. Oikos House).
Oxford English Dictionary 1989, 58

I believe that seasonal nomadism (transhumance) between bally and booley is an important and neglected aspect of Irish social history, and one which goes far to explain many features of traditional life. It is significant that the Irish word for a boy (buchaill) originally meant a herdsman. The charge of nomadism, using the word in its worst connotation, which English writers made against the Irish, finds some justification in the prevalence of a pastoral economy which was, in fact, more comparable to that of the Swiss peasants or the Norwegian milk-girls.
E. Estyn Evans, *Irish Folk Ways*, 1966

In this sense, the difference between such [English] villages and the bailia was precisely the difference between citizen and colonial subject.
Robert James Scally, *The End of Hidden Ireland*, 1995

At the heart of this chapter and the next lies the question 'Why is a people as committed to family, "family values", entrepreneurship, the free-market and virtues of small government as are Irish Travellers, the subject of so much vitriol from conservative liberals who essentially extol the same principles?'

Taking an ecological approach, I turn first to the Westway Site as it was in the 1980s —and largely still is. To see social organisation and culture at the Westway in terms of change and evolution, I then examine Ireland's traditional rural economy, the Celtic year, and the phenomenon of spatial mobility that was once not just part of Tinkers' lives but the lives of Irish country people in general. Having done this, we will then be in a position to appreciate, in the chapters that follow, the nexus between families, mobility and economic activity at the Westway.

Pitches, proxemics, power and principles

The Westway Site stands in the middle of the A3220, partly under the flyover. As previously described, it is a concrete-covered, roughly oblong strip of land, 1.1 acres in size, comprising twenty pitches ('plots' or 'bays'): ten either side of a central road barely wide enough to permit two cars to pass. Pitches are distinguished mainly by their shape and proximity to the entrance and overhead road.

Behind the slab concrete perimeter wall on the site's west side, the north bound section of the A3220 slip road rises over pitches at the Latimer Road end. Here in the 1980s four plots (one of them occupied by a mobile home used by SCF as a kindergarten school) backed directly onto a walled triangle of waste ground belonging to the North Kensington Amenity Trust (NKAT). Families living on these plots frequently discarded household waste over the wall. Other residents used it to fly-tip. Two iron waste skips stood at the entrance alongside the first plot on the west side, while plots on the opposite (east) side enjoyed airier positions, especially ones distant from the entrance.

Proximity to the entrance conferred strategic as well as ecological advantage. Pitches at the 'top' of the site enjoyed marginally more privacy than pitches at the bottom. Location at the top end conferred powers of surveillance denied to people at the bottom by dint of the fact that those living at the top observed those living between themselves and the entrance every time they entered or left the site. And since family reputations rested partly on the respect they showed for other families' privacy, adults rarely walked beyond the limits of their pitch other than to visit close relatives. The further one's pitch from the entrance, the greater, therefore, one's potential knowledge, power and status, and it was thus no coincidence that the longest-residing families lived at the 'top' and enjoyed more authority in consequence. In addition, this spatial advantage was further enhanced by their pitches being less vulnerable to encroachment by illegal squatters than were pitches at the bottom.

The terms power, status, influence and authority are used cautiously here. There were no leaders, formal or informal, with 'power' over others generally. Still less were there people with official or unofficial 'authority' over others generally. There were, however, individuals with rather more 'influence' than others in the community and that influence came from a mix of spatial advantage, length of residence and personal histories of influence built up over the duration of that residence. With 'influence' comes status, but 'status' refers here not to economic status so much as to 'honour', and 'honour', or an honourable reputation, depends on principles other than cash or class.

Showing other families *respect* by 'respecting' their privacy while at the same sufficiently interacting to signal respect for their status as moral equals was an important Westway principle, no matter where one's pitch, and it called for a careful balancing of sociability and social distance. Occupants of pitches in the middle section of the site, with people opposite them and on both sides, but also with good views up and down the site, had both the greatest need *and* opportunity to achieve that balance and were particularly likely to do so if relatives lived next door to them.

Throughout the 1970s and 1980s easily the longest-resident and most influential people on site were Martin Ward and his wife, who lived on pitch 10 at the top of the site. From 1984 to 1987 the Wards, their two married sons, and *their* wives and children, along with a bachelor friend 'adopted' by the Wards years earlier, occupied three or four pitches in the upper half of the site, depending on circumstances. At times one or more of Martin's married siblings, along with their families, joined them, usually on contiguous plots. The combination of sheer numbers, adult masculine presences, residential longevity and plot locations hinted strongly at *power*. Add to this Martin's literacy, reputation for toughness, way with words, battle record with local authorities, prowess as a tradesman, and success as a father of many children, one may then understand why Martin was respected and had more influence than other people.

My cabin stood inside the entrance on the east side. Being a large and irregularly shaped pitch, I shared it for most of my stay with an extended family comprising two or sometimes three domestic units living in three or four small trailers. This arrangement, along with my proximity to plots 2, 3 and 4 and, to a slightly lesser extent, with 19 and 20 (facing), made for my closest ties, though I took every opportunity to mix as much as possible with people further up.

Hammersmith and Fulham (H&F) rented pitches on the basis of one per family or domestic unit of up to three generations. Most pitches were about thirteen yards wide by twenty deep. Concrete bollards slung with chains at one time separated pitches but licensees had long ago judged them ineffective or a nuisance and removed them. Settled top-enders surrounded by kin did without fences. So did bottom-enders who, being more recent arrivals, planned either to move on entirely or move to better pitches within the site at the first opportunity. It was in the middle section, especially on pitches 14, 15, 16 and 17, that families erected their own barriers, especially if they didn't have relatives next-door. Had Travellers and Gypsies been consulted in the first place on matters of design this may not have been necessary. The same can be said with greater certainty about the washhouses, or so-called 'amenity blocks'.

An 'amenity block' was a semi-detached pair of washrooms (with lavatories) situated by the back wall on the boundary of two pitches, each pitch having its own facility and access. In principle the design allowed for privacy but in practice each was subject to encroachment by the neighbour's children, by vandals, or by anyone else who decided to use it. It would have been much better if instead of one block serving two pitches, each had had its own.

Poor internal washroom design and the shoddy installation of cheap fittings were other sources of trouble. The supply of electricity could also be problematic. As well as electric lighting and thermostats in the washrooms, pitches were equipped with 13-amp power points for their trailers. Each power point was housed in a metal box on a nine-foot iron pole, but the single point and output were inadequate in winter when household demand for heating, lighting and cooking power increased, and squatters added to the population. Poles then became overloaded with makeshift adaptors and overnight fuses were often fixed with silver foil from cigarette packets. Minor burns and electric shock were not uncommon. Delays in the repair of poles by qualified electricians resulted in further family hardship and more overloading elsewhere. Exposed wires on wet concrete were a special cause for worry, but fortunately there were no serious accidents, although, shortly after leaving the job I heard that a small girl lost part of a finger in an electrical accident. Yet as long as H&F remained intent on 'designation with nil provision', no lasting solutions were likely. An electricity sub-station housed in the Shepherds Bush ramp immediately behind my pitch became another cause for concern after I found a young boy wandering inside, who had pushed the unlocked iron door open.

Rents and other hazards

Licensees paid £12.15 a week in rent for their pitches and, for water and electricity, a set £7.35 a week in winter and £4.35 in summer. These sums were nearly always paid on time and were considered fair by residents when services functioned, but 'unfair' when they didn't.

Washhouses were crude and culturally insensitive. Multi-purpose aluminium sinks ignored Traveller and Gypsy washing practices and ideas of purity and pollution (Sutherland 1975; Okely 1983; Griffin 2002b), which normally call for an array of vessels. So while some people simply added buckets and basins as needed, some found greater value in selling their sinks for scrap-metal, while others gave their unrepaired broken showers (or showers devoid of privacy) over to storage or kennelling puppies. Concrete floors, broken pipes, broken locks on washroom doors, cheap plastic fittings and irregular water flows also deterred some people from using the showers. Neighbours' gazes in some cases deterred others, women especially. Some said just seeing a woman on her way to shower could cause men embarrassment.

Water tanks on low amenity block roofs often failed to provide an adequate 'head' of water. Pipes developed airlocks. Insufficient lagging led to water tanks and pipes freezing in winter, forcing residents to use their neighbours' facilities. Plastic pipes hastily installed or used before the cement hardened fell away. Flimsy lavatory cisterns gave up the ghost. And most of this was not the fault of residents. On the other hand, some of it was, and some partly was.

Teenage vandalism had reduced some of the washhouses to ruin before I arrived. China pedestal lavatories, for example, were smashed beyond repair. Others were blocked and unusable because squatters or licensees sharing with squatters were unable or unwilling to take responsibility for flushing and cleaning. At times I had to call in industrial cleaners to put matters straight. However, these conditions prevailed mostly at the bottom of the site at the start of my tenure and the blame cannot be entirely pinned upon the Travellers. A lack of close management and the absence of a warden for most of the previous year meant small problems had been allowed to build up into big ones, leading to residents' anger and resentment. Once I was appointed and had attended to these major tasks, the demand for repairs slowed and sub-contractors usually saw to whatever needed doing quite promptly.

Irish Travellers and Gypsies are caravan-proud and except in cases of extreme poverty or dysfunction keep their trailers bright and shiny inside and outside. This responsibility falls entirely to women and so it was women who most often used the fire-hoses on site to hose trailers and pitches down, washing off traffic grime and cooling roofs in summer. Not surprisingly, this could also lead to horseplay and damaged hoses, so it was periodically necessary to check them.

Caravan blazes were another concern. It would have proved

impossible for any fire tender to get so much as halfway into the site at night, especially in winter, without bulldozing vehicles parked in its way. The habit of burning off electric cable for copper was of less concern, but the occasional arson of stolen vehicles beneath the Interchange by young men once necessitated my calling the fire brigade to deal with the billowing smoke.

One of the site's most serious incidents occurred in 1979 and in its tragi-comedy bore a resemblance to the events found in Compton McKenzie's novel *Whiskey Galore*.[1] An articulated Customs and Excise lorry carrying a cargo of bonded whiskey crashed through the flyover and teetered on the parapet above two of the caravans, before the cabin crashed to the ground, killing its occupant. It is said that Travellers, Gypsies and policemen enjoyed liquor for weeks afterwards and that a bottle could be bought very cheaply in the neighbourhood.

One of my first tasks in 1984 was to restore essential services cut off when providers said it was unsafe to come on site. Starting with a sweep-up and clearance of putrefied rubbish and a cannibalised bus and caravan around the bottom of the site, we moved fast to reinstate a regular skip service and begin the fumigation and repair of several washhouses. Imperfect though the skip service was — and it was not the regular municipal service — the system worked reasonably well for the next three years, despite a few Travellers' persistent habit of filling the skips to overflowing with builders' rubble at night after I had gone home, making their removal and proper use next-to-impossible. So one problem begat another.

Other missing services, the like of which other people take for granted, were, for example, regular postal deliveries and (as housing tenants) reasonably swift Council repair work. For the best part of a year postmen had refused to serve the site because of the presence of dogs or the frustration of trying to deliver mail to people who had changed pitches or moved away. The postal workers' union was also fed up with its members being blamed for the wrong delivery of social welfare cheques. It was all too much for the postmen and I could see why. I could also sympathise with council workmen, who declared the site a 'no-go' area after having their tools stolen from the back of their vans or seeing their vehicles being interfered with. I witnessed some of it myself.

To overcome the problems I proposed two solutions not entirely devoid of self-interest. I would collect and deliver the mail each day myself, earning some goodwill and discovering more about families in the process. I would also assure sub-contractors I would be on site when they were, in order to reduce the likelihood of theft and uncalled-for interruption. Together with the weekly rubbish collection, these arrangements in the end worked out quite well.[2]

Other hazards were lead and noise pollution levels, which the Council monitored at least twice yearly. At this time leaded petrol was still in wide use, so lead poisoning, particularly in children, was a matter of special concern to groups like the SCF and the Westway Travellers Support Group (WTSG), who argued a connection between lead poisoning and Traveller delinquency arising from the site's location. Council environmental specialists argued that the surface lead levels detected resulted more from Travellers' scrap metal activities and the break-up of car batteries than from air-borne pollution, which they said was no worse here than in many other parts of the borough. In 2001, however, long after the introduction of unleaded petrol, carbon monoxide and atmospheric lead levels in the vicinity of the site (postal district W10 6BP) compared poorly with comparable measurements in Mortlake (SW14 8SZ) where I was staying.[3] As for noise, my impressions then and in 2004 (and impressions are all they are) were that, despite its location, the site is no worse in this regard than a great many other residential addresses in London, and that this was probably due to the fact the site is slightly *below* the level of its surrounding roads, and is walled off. For example, it seemed considerably less affected than the upper levels of the tower-blocks flats in Freston Road, overlooking the site, where noise seemed excessive.

In addition to residents' legitimate grievances over the inadequate supply of sites generally in England and Wales, all the above fuelled disharmony among residents themselves and (unless they were of the stoic 'resigned' sort) between residents, outsiders and H&F. It also led to mutual stereotyping. *Some* young Irish Travellers, for example, made verbal scapegoats of 'blacks', while *some* adult Travellers and Gypsies ignored their children's vandalism and sought to blame it on the prejudices of non-Travellers. For their part *some* Council employees, in *some* departments more than others, fell to comparing 'Irish tinkers', 'half-castes', and 'hedge-crawlers' with 'real Gypsies' and blaming the former groups for all the caravan-dweller problems in England, while absolving the latter. Equally, however, I found Irish Travellers who were defenders of 'blacks' and other minorities, and defenders of Irish Travellers and Gypsies among council employees and the police.

As to whether the Westway Site really was (and is) an *incomparably* poor environment for Travellers and Gypsies because of its location, this was something disputed by Travellers themselves and was subject to shift in an individual's opinion.

For a West Indian bus driver on the Harrow Road the entire district was 'as rough as hell' and its inhabitants were 'animals ... especially those Gypsies down Latimer Road'. The man didn't know I worked there but some Westway residents would have agreed with him. As far away as Ireland the Westway Site is notorious by reputation and first-hand experience. For some Irish Travellers it contains 'the unfriendliest people in the world ... rough and full of blackguards'. Others hold more measured views. In short, residents judge the site not just in terms of its physical environment but also its moral ecology.

Moral ecology

Some Westway families compared the site favourably with other London sites and council housing estates. The Harrow area was often described as 'very rough', the official site at West Drayton was said to be 'appalling', and the Bashley Road site in the Borough of Ealing, where many Westway families have at some time lived (or to where some even chose to move from the Westway), was likened by one woman to Long Kesh, the high-security prison in Northern Ireland best known for its IRA prisoners. In other words, opinions about the Westway varied even if most were negative. Perhaps the clearest differences of opinion lay along gender lines, with men being less critical than the women obliged to spend most of their time there. While men felt as much need to escape from the site as women, and could do so providing they had work, women with daughters old enough to look after younger siblings were freer to leave the site than younger mothers, and sometimes did so to visit relatives living elsewhere.

Generally speaking, younger women were more likely to complain of their 'nerves' and about their children's health and, for this reason, among others, they were more likely than older women to seek respite in 'emergency housing'. In the words of one young Gypsy, 'to come here is to have your heart and spirits drop'.

Jim O'Donoghue

Several Travellers, including Martin Ward, described the Westway Site as the 'best site in London', providing that it was 'managed properly' and the numbers living there controlled, as far as possible restricting licenses to 'respectable' families. Moral judgements, as previously mentioned, shifted to and fro, and I was often at a loss to know whether the grosser contradictions reflected an individual's mood-swings or personality, and whether it made sense to diminish the psychological component in order to make the sociological connection, that most social scientists of my generation still believe in, between what C.W. Mills (1959) called 'private troubles' and 'public issues'. At the same time it became increasingly apparent that shifts in moral judgement and statements made about the site's physical viability corresponded with personal crises as individuals negotiated that balance between sociability and social reserve, a balance which is a universal feature of life in all small communities, but which is especially hard to achieve and maintain in competitive, egalitarian, individualistic, face-to-face communities like this one. Thus I was frequently reminded by Irish Travellers that what he or she had just told me was for my ears only, and represented his or her viewpoint only, no one else's, and that to safely generalise I should talk to as many Travellers as possible. One man put it most eloquently: 'to speak of the Travelling People you'd need a thousand spokesmen, the finest and the worst'. He also knew how difficult it was for the non-Traveller to capture those spokesmen and how dangerous it was for him to express the problem.

Having examined the Westway ecology, I want now to turn to the 'traditional' Irish rural economy, in order to put the economic activities of the site's Irish population (who made up 85 per cent of the total) in their proper cultural context and determine how traditional rural ecology has influenced behaviour and identity in Notting Dale.

Traditional ecology, economy and habitat

From ancient times until very recently Ireland has been a rural place; a place of bog, lakes and mountains where the bulk of viable agricultural land comprised thousands of small, ill-defined, temporary land-holdings cultivated under a system known as *openfield* or *rundale* (Evans 1966; 1973).

The openfield or rundale system
Before the arrival of the Vikings and Normans, Ireland had no towns or market places. Communities were dispersed and this

pattern largely persisted thereafter. Until the 1800s most of the Irish population inhabited hamlets of scattered houses known as *clachans* or 'townlands' averaging half a square mile (325 acres) in size, with populations of around fifty people who were usually closely related kin. If the land was fertile the townland could be bigger. Without church or shops or other services it was typical of the *rundale* land-tenure system. The measure of land was not seen in terms of what was ploughed, but rather in terms of 'the cow's grass' (Evans 1966, 28–9): the number of cows (or fraction of an animal) that a piece of land could support. Townlands bore little resemblance to English villages. They were laid out loosely, without much sense of 'plan', and so were sometimes referred to as 'throughothers'. The word probably derives from the scattered nature of outfield plots, which were commonly allocated by a lottery run by a headman — sometimes called 'the king'. Cultivable land around the houses was called the 'infield' and was subject to heavy manuring.

Sometimes referred to as the *bally*, *bailly* or *baile*, meaning home-place, the *clachan* provided people their primary sense of Self and social identity. Their social needs were met by fairs, markets and other seasonal gatherings, and many of their economic needs by itinerant tradesmen and nomadic 'tinkers' (Evans 1966, 31). Marriages united *clachans* into wider senses of neighbourhood, yet with these bonds there also came competition, feuds and factional fighting — especially on fair days.

Except where agriculture required the intensive removal of rock and stone, hedges (of stone or blackthorn) only made their appearance in the mid-1700s and, because Ireland was sparsely wooded, hedges other than stone were frequently torn down for firewood. By the mid-nineteenth century the openfield and *clachans* started to disappear, to be replaced by bigger field systems and isolated cottages which managed to survive in some places up to the 1920s and even beyond. The new farming practices and habitats led to greater social isolation and increased 'fortress mentalities', tendencies exacerbated further by continuing emigration and the passage of various Land Acts between 1869 and 1925 (Evans 1966, 21).

Cattle and booley

Tillage and pasture constituted the main elements of the *rundale* system: potatoes, turnips and cabbages, dairy cattle and sheep, poultry, a pig or two, and where possible, fishing. Together, tillage and pastoralism gave shape to Irish social structure and social organisation. Cattle, in particular, were central. From early times, as we see from Celtic mythology, the Irish were engaged in the seasonal migration of cattle to summer pastures, which geographers call 'transhumance', about which we shall say more presently. Migrations were 'local' rather than long distance and the herders were usually one or more of the family's young men who stayed with the cattle throughout, though occasionally it was done by young women.

The *bally* and infield/outfield system were intensely social. People not merely lived and worked in close proximity to each other, they as often as not owned sheep and horses in common (Evans 1966), with the movement of cattle and trampling of the infield a common source of conflict. Lord George Hill, an English observer, in 1841 likened it to an 'Arab mode of life' (Evans 1966, 31), and perhaps not without reason seeing as the virtual absence of roads in Ireland might have given the cross-country transfer of grazing animals an exotic, caravan-like, quality to foreigners like Hill.

The favourite farm vehicle up to the 1700s was a sledge-like contraption known as a slide-car, a 'humble vehicle [that] is well suited to simple societies, whose transport needs are few, and to country, especially hilly country, without made roads, where the wheel would be out of place' (Evans 1966, 174). Not until the eighteenth century did block-wheeled cars (wheels comprising two semi-circular blocks joined by battens) make their appearance (Evans 1966, 175), bringing status to their owners. The principal beast of burden was the horse, even though Penal Laws in the late 1700s and early 1800s forbade Irish people from owning a horse valued over £5. Made roads were hardly needed. Most people walked. It was not until wheel-cars were invented, followed by sprung, spoke-wheeled, jaunting cars, in the nineteenth century, that narrow lanes (*boreens*) began to connect the isolated cottages.

With regards to travel and transportation the country's Tinkers were no different from most Irish people. Moreover, they made up but a section of a wider 'travelling' community that included *booleys*, drovers, itinerant tailors, other tradesmen, and agricultural labourers known as *spalpeens*.[4] To understand with open minds contemporary Irish Travellers and their cultural evolution, we need to review what Travellers historically held in common with — as well as in contrast to — country people, and decide what we mean when we use words like nomad, transhumant, itinerant and peripatetic. To this end we will begin with the *booleys*, who were integral to the Rundale system (Evans 1966, 21).

Wherever *booleying* existed 'life began and ended with the herding of cattle' (Evans 1973, 80) and, like the herding Nuer and other East Africans to whom the label 'pastoralists' has been applied, or did until recent drastic climate change, herding was the job of bachelors, while infield cultivation was left to others (Power 1976, 54), though women and children did *booleying* in pre-Norman times and in parts of Donegal up until the 1840s (Evans 1966, 31).

Whether *booleying* is best spoken of as a type of nomadism or, in Estyn Evans's words, as 'extended transhumance' — 'a complex form of transhumance' (Evans 1966, 80) — is unimportant. Having a townland address thought of as 'home' no more precluded the Irish countryman from 'pastoral nomadism' or 'extended transhumance'[5] than does living in a house or on a caravan site rule out commercial nomadism for Travellers.

Nomad, transhumant, itinerant
'Nomad' comes from the Greek *nomas*, meaning pasture, and originally applied to one who travelled with grazing stock. It is not hard to see, then, why urban Greeks or 'citizens' considered nomads no more than barbaric outsiders, and why this urban bias in western civilisation has persisted and become even more pronounced as the world becomes more urbanised.

Some anthropologists apply the word 'nomad' to a range of people whose means of subsistence entails significant spatial mobility. Rao (1987) conceived of nomads as *groups* occupying different positions on a spatial mobility continuum from 'high' to 'low' that intersected a food production and extraction continuum also running from high to low; the subsequent quadrants described four types of nomad. Pastoral nomads were minimally involved in food production, grazed animals and lived off animal products, and did a lot of travelling; hunter-gatherers produced no food but undertook considerable amounts of travelling in order to hunt animals and collect plants; swidden agriculturalists practised food production and also periodically shifted their gardens and villages; commercial nomads (or peripatetics) such as Gypsies did not produce food but instead traded goods and services to settled people (who demanded their services spasmodically) and so were spatially mobile.[6]

Irish Travellers, like all commercial nomads, are intensely family-oriented or 'familistic'. Their economic and social means of survival are inseparable from each other and are acquired by intergenerational learning. Their facility for flexibility and adaptation focuses not only on the physical environment but also on the 'total environment, one aspect of which can be demand and supply' (Rao 1987, 3). Plasticity ('moulding under heat or pressure'), mobility, multi-skilling and kinship networks are essential parts of Traveller social and cultural capital, as is the preferential endogamy (marrying within the community) and 'social character' or psychology that support them.

Settled Irish people, called by Travellers 'country people' or 'buffers', often refer to the Travellers as 'itinerants' but for sociological purposes there is something to be said for reserving the word 'itinerant' for other social types whose economic activities, while involving extensive travel, do not include features found in commercial nomadism *per se*. To begin with, the itinerant does not involve or require the backup or support of a mobile working family, and is usually a solo traveller. The Gypsy or Traveller does require this backup, and does not travel alone. Second, while occupationally mobile, the itinerant has not usually learnt his or her occupation, and the character that drives it, from a previous generation of relatives,

Westway Site and M41 (now the West Cross Route) looking towards Shepherds Bush

'Triangle' and Westway Site viewed from the railway line

nor are they expected to pass these things on to their children and grandchildren. The Traveller has done and does all of these things. Third, itinerant workers do not usually practise preferential endogamy. The Traveller does. Fourth, because of all the above, the itinerant's means of subsistence does not amount to being a component of his or her 'traditional culture'. For the Gypsy it does and so, on most counts, it did for *booleys*. In summary, we should keep the terms 'itinerant' and 'nomad' separate and, for that matter, 'peripatetic' and 'commercial nomad' too. Itinerant and peripatetic could then be thought of as synonyms and would apply to a great number of occupationally mobile types, including pedlars, hoboes, some tinkers, some New Travellers, long-distance lorry drivers, airline pilots, trans-national labourers, merchant seamen, backpackers, even business executives, politicians, movie stars, diplomats and anthropologists.

Lord Hill left this account of *booleying* in Donegal just before the Famine.

> It often happens that a man has three dwellings — one in the mountains, another upon the shore, and the third upon an island, he and his family flitting from one to another of these habitations as the various and peculiar herbage of each is thought to be beneficial to the cattle ... This change usually takes place upon a fixed day, the junior members of the family perform the land journey on top of the household goods, for which the pony may often be seen so loaded, and at the same time so obscured, that little more than the head can be observed; and thus the chair or two, the creels, and the iron pot, the piggin, and the various selected et cetera — as if invested with a sort of dull locomotive power — creep along the roads. The little churn is slung on the side of the animal, into which the youngest child is often thrust, its head being the only part visible; and in this plight it resembles in various particulars, a sweep peeping and screeching too, at the top of a chimney.
> (Evans 1973, 89)

If this is not pastoral nomadism what is? George Hill, for one, realised that *booleying's* origins derived from the old Celtic calendar and its 'fixed days'. In other words, ancient custom and in particular the important six-month period beginning 1 May, which was important not just to Tinkers but to 'foot-free "travelling men" of all kinds', including agricultural labourers (*spalpeens*) and even 'coastal traders' (Evans 1973, 80). Small wonder J.M. Synge first thought of titling his play not *The Tinker's Wedding* (Synge 1992) but *The Movements of May*; and it is to that calendar movement that we now turn.

Movement and habitat
According to Barnes (1975), Travellers only began using carts at the end of the Boer War (1899–1902); Gmelch (1977) broadly agrees. Until the twentieth century most Travellers or Tinkers walked everywhere, though some owned flat carts drawn by horse or donkey, which could also give protection from the rain. Wagons with bunks and stoves came later and were possibly introduced by English Gypsies.

A two-wheeled flat cart propped against a raised stone bank or parked over a ditch provided basic shelter not dissimilar from a house style that itself resembled an ancient habitat in which unmortared stone and turf was built directly into an embankment or the slope of a hill (Evans 1966, 43), giving it a 'semi-underground' look (Scally 1995). The cart and bank habitat may in some ways have also resembled the sod and ditch principle of the hovels erected by outcast unmarried mothers in Clare in pre-Famine times (Connell 1996, 57).[7]

An alternative habitat to the flat cart and wagon was the barn, abandoned house or outhouse, and not only for Tinkers. An itinerant labourer slept in the stable on the farm I stayed at in New Ross, Wexford, in 1953. Finding him there at dawn on my first morning came as a shock to both of us.

Another Traveller option was the bender-tent. A favourite with Travellers up to the 1960s, it consisted of twelve hazel wattles placed opposite each other in the ground, six on each side, their top ends placed in holes in a central ring-board or rigging-pole, over which a tarpaulin was thrown. Some Travellers say the idea of bender tents, like the wagon, came from English Romanies, but this ignores the history of indigenous portable shelters and the fact that Scottish Travellers, with whom the Irish came in contact decades (if not centuries) earlier, also used bender tents. Outlawed Irish in seventeenth-century Ulster used portable frame houses called *creaghts* and, at a later date, turf cutters used windbreaks of bent and tied birch rods that they then thatched. Hazel rods and pins were also used in regular thatching (Evans 1966, 48).

The first covered wagon was probably no more than a covered four-wheel cart: a portable shelter on wheels. Cabins near Newry, in County Armagh, in 1690, were said by one observer to be 'built so conveniently of hurdles and long turf that they can remove them in summer towards the mountains and bring them down to the valley in winter' (Evans 1966, 37). It is therefore worth noting that one type of wagon used by Travellers in the twentieth century, according to an informant, was called a 'Newry'. There may or may not be a connection here but I think we have shown sufficient evidence to argue that while contemporary Travellers have a culture distinct from that of settled people (and in some cases from that of their ancestors 200 or 300 years ago or more), both their travelling habits and habitats were importantly connected with aspects of mainstream agricultural/pastoral society. This further suggests that it has been mainly in the course of the last century that Travellers in Ireland have come to be regarded as outcasts or arch-outsiders, and in Britain as something worse.

Travellers are familistic, egalitarian in ethos (stratified in practice), opportunistic, competitive, good-humoured and argumentative; yet it should not be argued in the cause of upholding the authenticity of Traveller culture, and thus their right to 'ethnic' status, that in these regards they are entirely different from other Irish people. As we said earlier, 'community', by definition, enjoins 'difference'. Unity *presumes* 'difference'. And in this case much of that difference comes with nomadism and the mental character involved.

Celtic calendar

The Celtic year was divided into two seasons, the 'hot' season and the 'cold' (Sjoestedt 1982), or the 'light' season and the 'dark' (de Paor 1985); each lasted exactly six months. In view of Ireland's latitude this is hardly surprising.

The year began on 1 May with the feast of *Beltaine* (or *Beltene*) signalling the onset of the warmth and the drying out of the land. A day for families, it was also a time of anxiety as people anticipated the harvest and worried about the summer milk since the summer (July especially) was the period of greatest scarcity. On this day the cattle, before being led out to summer pasture beyond the infield, were driven between bonfires symbolising purification and rebirth, or taken through the ancient forts and fairy *raths*.

On 31 October/1 November, the feast of *Samain* (or *Samhain*), the cattle came home and the cold/dark season began. *Samain* was the occasion when families remembered their relations with the *sid*, or subterranean fairies, who, if not placated, might annoy the cattle and cause the milk and cream to curdle. It was also the day dead relatives came home. *Clachans* being close-knit, these family events turned into neighbourhood events. Today this day is known as Halloween, the eve of 'All Souls Day' (1 November), which was once an occasion for markets, fairs and racing, but is now mainly confined to bonfires, children's games, mischief-making, dressing-up and singing rhymes to neighbours in return for sweets. Green put it well when he said that *Samain* was 'a time of ritual mourning for the death of summer and a period of great danger, a boundary between two periods, when time and space were temporarily frozen and normal laws suspended. The barriers were broken: Otherworld spirits could walk on earth and humans could visit the underworld' (Green 1993, 55). In other words, *Samain* was a dangerous time when temporal and spatial thresholds called for careful negotiation.

The two seasons were subdivided. The midpoint of the cold/dark season was *Imbolc* (1–2 February), which celebrated the lactation of the ewes, or flow of midwinter milk. With the arrival of Christianity this day became the double feast of the Purification and feast of St

Brigid, the patron saint of smiths, poets and healers (Sjoestedt 1982). As with *Samain*, the family nature of *Imbolc* led to its spilling into the wider neighbourhood. The festival called *Lughnasa* (or *Lughnasad*), midway through the warm/light season on 1 August, celebrated the ripening of crops. Remnants of it survived into the twentieth century in the form of fairs always well attended by Tinkers (MacNeill 1962). Midsummer's eve (31 July) was associated with fairies, fire and mischief, and, with the coming of Christianity, became St Peter's Eve. *Lughnasa* was associated with springs, streams, hill-tops, and wide vistas — the 'threshold of plenty' or 'feast of filled fields' — and was literally a 'high-point' in the old Celtic calendar, when townland people socialised with strangers on the hills where community boundaries met (MacNeill 1962).

All these fixed dates involved a mix of familistic magic and small *community* fun: recreation in its true and broadest sense. Sacred music, song, dance, drink and games were essential aspects of Celtic religiosity (and Irish Catholicism) until the mid-nineteenth century, and nowhere were these things more apparent than in the customs of the wake. But most of the close-knittedness and ritual reaching out to others (as noted above, particularly with regard to *Lughnasa*) was damaged by the Famine and land clearances, and was replaced by an inward-looking individualism, as Professor Scally has described:

> ... in the process of trying to survive in isolation, townland society employed both a moral stigma and wilful ignorance of the outside world as part of its strategy ... In its struggle against a contending ethic of commerce and individualism, this set of intuitions was the identifying core of the townland community. The townland did not wish its poverty on itself but unable to escape it, made it work for a while as a unifying banner ... So, it is not unexpected to find in that generation a rising incidence of violence, rural 'outrages', and conspiracies against those felt to be outside its moral boundaries, including many of their own class and kin

> ... Traditional forms of cooperation among neighbours in labor and landholding, like meithall or 'cooring', joint holdings in both land and animals, and 'booleying' were also adaptable to the struggle with scarcity and, perhaps, equally as important, they could help restrain the annual panics and the inevitable internal squabbling and 'defections' that came with them. (Scally 1995, 35)

According to MacNeill, the major authority on this subject, by modern times *Lughnasa*, or rather its remnant, was generally a family affair, with faint memories of communal celebrations in only a few places (MacNeill 1962, 58). She had this to say about *booleying*:

> Gaelic oral tradition says that only the younger women of the community stayed on the hills to attend the stock. If it is to be inferred that in earlier times *the whole commmunity or large part of it* removed to the hills for the summer pasturage, Lughnasa would have been an important date on the booley, for at the beginning of harvest an exodus from the hills would have been necessary. While this remains hypothetical for Ireland, Scottish references suggest that it was the custom there. (MacNeill 1962, my emphasis)

What *did* survive *Lughnasa* into the twentieth century were the August or Lammas fairs that attracted large crowds from far and wide, leaving individuals with feelings of 'community' that extended way beyond the moral bounds of their normal, separate, multiple small communities. Feelings arising from interaction with passing strangers, which Turner (1969) calls *communitas* or ritual-community — the kind with which Travellers are familiar. Puck Fair (August 10–12), at Kilorglin, Kerry, is probably the most famous of these fairs. Moreover, where they coincided with *pattern* or patron saint days they were also places of pilgrimage and another example of Irish religiosity's combination of fun and fervour.

Without claiming 'proof' for what is actually no more than a working hypothesis, I'll summarise these features of the old calendar and its contemporary reformulations using the three inter-related concepts given by Van Gennep (1960) in his work on rites of passage: rites of separation, liminal rites, and rites of segregation. In doing so, I draw attention to the different ideas of 'community' and community-border involved in the Celtic year. To this purpose each festival is therefore followed below first by its range of community-inclusion (either predominantly kindred or reaching out to strangers), then by its dominant collective mental state, symbolic physical element, iconic life-form (e.g. cattle, crops, fairies, ewes), and it human/supernatural locational focus. To help the reader compare, the festivals' alternate items are shown in italics followed by the Van Genep category of rite that each festival most resembles.

Beltaine   kindred, *anxiety*, fire, *cattle*. HOME
               RITES OF SEPARATION

Lughnasa   strangers, *vistas or wider outlooks*, water, *crops*. MARGIN
               LIMINAL RITES AND COMMUNITAS

Samain   kindred, *danger*, dusk, *fairies*. UNDERWORLD
               RITES OF REINTEGRATION

Imbolc   kindred, *danger*, dawn, *ewes*. NEIGHBOURHOOD
               RITES OF INTEGRATION

At *Lughnasa* and August fairs the normal bounds of townland and kindred (and Self) were thrown open and challenged. At *Samain* the normal human/spirit border was openly acknowledged and crossed ritually. At *Imbolc* and *Beltaine* the borders of the small community, home and neighbourhood, were (respectively) ritually reinforced and then prised open. In summary, the Celtic year in its old form, and its form up to the mid-nineteenth century, not only marked the passage of the seasons and its meaning for agriculture and cattle, but it also marked concomitant shifts in social horizons associated with mobility and sedentism thresholds that ended for most people — other than Travellers who were permanent outsiders — with the fading of the townland and rundale.

Fairs and markets[8]

Changes in the seasons involve changes in nomadic social organisation (Evans-Pritchard 1940; Mauss 1979). The dry/light months are invariably the ones for travelling and this is best conducted in separate small family groups living in scattered camps. The wet/dark months curtail movement, call for good camping grounds, and thus allow for bigger gatherings of people and the compensations of ritual. Something of this was obvious at the Westway Site in the weeks around Christmas and the New Year, when men's work routines were temporarily suspended. The markets and big fairs that were once gathering sites for all manner of strangers and hubs of social and economic activity throughout the Irish 'summer' (and English too, for that matter) have by no means totally disappeared, however. Ballinasloe Fair (in Galway), Goose Fair (at Nottingham), Puck Fair (in Kerry), Appleby Fair (in Cumbria) and Epsom (in Surrey) remain important to Travellers, Romanies and *gorgios* or buffers alike.

Irish fairs are much older institutions than Irish towns and markets (Evans 1966). *Aonac*, the modern Irish for 'fair', comes from *aon* meaning 'one', 'one thing', or unity. A Celtic word that pre-dates towns and coins, *oenach*, meaning religious gathering, suggests assemblies where gossip, fun and excitement were *de rigueur* (MacNeill 1962). In short, the fair was sacred. What is more, its events were organised in ritual sequence, the sale of goods and livestock being followed faithfully by sporting contest, match-making, horse-racing, and in many cases a free-for-all or 'Donnybrook'. Puck Fair is still organised in three parts, Gathering Day, Fair Day and Scattering Day (Evans 1966), reminiscent of Van Gennep's (1960) rites of passage (above; Turner 1969). By bringing hilltop fairs under the authority of the State and Church, the Normans literally brought Celtic Catholicism to town and made the Church accountable.

At a fair held on the last Sunday of July at Cullen Well, Dunhallow, Cork, in the 1800s, 'The village thronged with people. Hucksters were there to sell sweets, sea-grass, mineral drinks and fruit ... The taverns, of course, were full, and the usual rustic entertainers, the thimble-riggers and trick-of-the-loop men were there to quicken the pulses and lighten the purses of the country people gathered in from far and wide in Dunhallow and even from beyond the Kerry hills' (MacNeill 1962, 269). According to my informants Travellers ran 'trick-of-the-loop' stalls at fairs in the twentieth century. At St Brigid's Well, Liscannor, County Clare, a likely old *Lughnasa* site, Travellers further provided an essential component according to a nineteenth-century witness:

> If the tinkers were not there with their women and children it is not yet a day! The world of noise from them by afternoon when the grown tinkers had a good drop past the tooth! Some of them in a fighting humour and more of them without power in foot or hand but lying in a heap all the day. (MacNeill 1962, 281)

The three days of Lammas, or Ram Fair, at Greencastle, County Down, was a venue for all sorts of travelling people. In the 1880s Michael Crawford said 'Every road led to the Fair, and every road was black with people ... the sea too ... from the Louth shore and distant places outside the Bar, far along the coast' (quoted in MacNeill 1962, 301), and at the gathering there were (in MacNeill's own words) 'all the usual participants and amusements of a country fair: tricksters, tinkers and gypsies, booths and side-shows' (MacNeill 1962, 301).

The market (*margaigh*), by contrast, was a smaller and more local affair and was more concerned with the buying and selling of livestock than with sport, matchmaking and inter-communal contest. Cattle markets took on more importance after the Famine, and the total number of monthly fairs increased steadily up to the early twentieth century, when improvements in transportation resulted in the appearance of more shops. Even so, markets marked key turning points of the year. February and March markets were noted for horse sales, July and August markets for sheep and wool, May and November for cattle and the hire of servants, and Ballinasloe market, County Galway, in October (5-9), for the sale of sheep and cattle (Evans 1966). Travellers were conspicuous at all of them and they still go to Ballinasloe, which stands at the western end of an esker or gravel ridge that stretches across Ireland to the east coast. Drovers had long used the ridge to get their cattle to Scotland[9] and to fairs at Carlisle, Norwich and Barnet (north of London), and by the late nineteenth century they had added goats and donkeys.

> The drover-dealers ... were colourful characters whose experience stood them in good stead in the wider world. These dealers in the unwanted residues of the countryside in rags and scrap as well as asses and goats have often set up as rag[10] and scrap merchants in the larger towns along their routes from Belfast and Dublin to English fairs, and one of them became Lord Mayor of a Scottish city. Others made big names as pedlars of cloth in America or Australia. Most of the 'pahvees', as they are called were born in the mountain country of Slieve Gullion [near Newry], in County Armagh, and adjoining the rich plains of the Pale, where their ancestors sharpened their wits on the English settlers. Many stories are told of the tricks by which 'the goatmen' disposed of their animals before they reached their goal at Barnet Fair. (Evans 1966, 258–9)

Given the recent connection between Travellers and rag and bone merchants in west London and the totting done by Romanies, it is probable that similar relations existed between Tinkers and dealers like the 'goatmen', and possible they also intermarried.[11]

What proportion of Travellers turned to trading horses in the early 1900s we can only guess, but informants say many of them sold horses to the British army during World War I, and others sold to French butchers. One way or another, it is fairly clear such opportunities presented themselves. Eamonn de Valera's push for more tillage and agricultural self-sufficiency in 1932 may have encouraged some Travellers, as may the Travellers' own switch to living in wagons. Rationing in Britain during World War II also presented Travellers with opportunities in Ireland as farmers there (mostly unmechanised or without petrol) sought to supply food to the British market and English butchers diversified into 'alternative' meat products. Two Travellers at the Westway said they had cashed in on this wartime demand for horses.

In the course of time, especially following the declining demand for tin work, when it came to horses some Travellers had as good a knowledge — if not far better — than farmers, and took advantage of it. Status parity or superiority in the matter of bargaining was reinforced by the status of the animal itself. Unlike animals bred intentionally for meat or other by-products, horses are bred to partner humans. Like working dogs, horses are honorary members of the family, 'friends' in a way that other animals are not (see Leach 1973). Whether ridden or used for draught purposes, the horse is big, strong or fleet; the perfect symbol of things masculine, the more so if it is a stallion. It takes a man to handle them, and handling powerful horses makes for the theatre Travellers relish. Horses and horse markets are thus essentially men's business (see Stewart 1997; Jenkins 1994), countrymen and Travellers. In County Clare, Arensberg and Kimball (1968) tell us, horse markets drew more men from greater distances than any other market. In the play and drama of the horse market Traveller men come into their own, winning respect and from peers and farmers alike. Racecourses, too, have long provided the setting for Traveller activity, albeit in this case more in the capacity as support-actors rather than major players.[12]

Subsequent changes

At the beginning of the nineteenth century 95 per cent of land in Ireland was owned by people of English or Scottish descent. By the 1870s 90 per cent of the country's 500,000 agricultural tenants farmed properties under twelve hectares and made annual 'arrangements' with the landlord to do this, in circumstances that also gave landlords the power to evict tenants after six months' notice (Hussey 1995, 304). Not until Gladstone's 1881 reforms, the 1891 Balfour Act and other pieces of legislation in 1896 and 1903, did these conditions improve. Consequently, when the Irish Free State was formed in December

1921 its leaders saw the economic future not in a return to small-scale arable farming but in an agricultural sector based on intensive cattle rearing and dairy production. Ireland was slowly moving towards the industrialisation and urbanisation it had so long avoided, bringing with it new challenges and opportunities.

Not all Travellers were or are as adept or as lucky as others. Poverty has racked the community, and alcoholism, domestic violence, and obscene rates of sickness and premature death have followed in its wake, as invariably they do. As roads and transportation improved in the 1950s and 1960s, facilitating rural access to the towns and cities and enabling the transport of consumer goods to country shops, and as agriculture became increasingly mechanised, cutting the need for seasonal labour, so inevitably did growing numbers of Traveller families gravitate towards towns. Semi-skilled and non-literate, in essence urban hunters-and-collectors (Gmelch 1977; Court 1985), usually with big families to feed, some resorted to begging, to the annoyance of settled people who (having chosen *not* to leave the country in search of work themselves) now struggled with the added sin and guilt of *not* being charitable while resenting the beggars for making them feel that way. For these Travellers, to the status of arch-outsider was now added the status of social outcast.

Conclusion

Urban forager, trader, dealer, artisan — these are words that aptly describe Irish Travellers on the Westway Site in the 1980s and probably most commercial nomads then and since. Coping with the slings and arrows of outrageous fortune directed at them by sections of the British population, who have even less grip on Traveller history and culture than they have on Irish culture and history in general, the Travellers have survived (and even begun to thrive) by grasping opportunities for marginal returns that other people either do not see or care to take, and ironically in the process they uphold many of the virtues and values that hostile society claims to hold dear.

Notes

1. In which the crofters of a remote Scottish island come into a bounty of whiskey after a cargo ship is wrecked.

2. Late in 1986 the trade union responsible for municipal garbage collections agreed to resume its service of the site. The union rep was a sympathetic Irishman. As of May 1987, though, the agreement had still not taken effect.

3. In 2001, in postal district w10 63p, the area under the motorway just outside the Westway site, air emissions of lead and carbon monoxide were 6 and 453 tonnes per annum per square kilometre respectively, compared with 1.3 and 147 for sw14 8sz, the corner of Mortlake where I lived in 2004 when I retrieved these data. Comparable emission figures in the two areas for benzene were 2.2 and 0.91; nitrogen oxides, 107 and 59, and particular matter (pm10) 7.7 and 3.3. By all these counts the area around the Westway was notably more polluted than the part of Mortlake I was staying in. www.naei.org.uk./emissions/postcode_2001.php?.f_postcode.

4. An Irish dictionary defines *spalpeen* as 'rascal' or 'mean fellow'. The stigma of being an itinerant worker was obviously not restricted to Tinker *nomads*.

5. 'Transhumance' comes from the Latin *trans* (go across) and *humus* (ground), and is defined as the 'seasonal movement of livestock to another region'. The definition allows that not all transhumance (of bees, for example) involves humans staying with the stock.

6. Other trades practised by Irish Travellers, apart from tin-smithing, were trading horses, music-making and agriculture, included chimney cleaning, repairing umbrellas, castrating farm animals, fortune-telling, and hawking cloth and small domestic trifles.

7. An eighteenth-century English view that Irish rural dwellings confirmed their inhabitants' cultural and moral inferiority overlooked the dearth of building timber and hence the use of uncut stone with turf and moss as mortar. The oldest and very finest examples of dwellings of this order are the prehistoric 'beehive' houses, or *clochans*, still to be seen in parts of Ireland. In historical times, more so in the mountainous west, semi-underground houses bore a resemblance to house types found in other parts of the

north Atlantic, including the *shiel* or *shieling* used by transhumant Hebridean crofters, and even the Inuit's igloo. Shortage of firewood for cooking and heating purposes was made up for by use of turf or, in extreme circumstances, by burning household furniture (Evans 1966), a practice Gypsies and Travellers have sometimes been accused of as if it were totally beyond reason.

8. Readers are cautioned here about the author's limited fieldwork in Ireland, lack of familiarity with fairs and markets, and over-reliance on published texts and deductive reasoning.

9. Regular steamer services across the Irish Sea began in the 1830s.

10. A song sung by the group *The Dubliners* (one of whose members, Luke Kelly, was a Traveller), 'The Ragman's Ball', wonderfully captures the rag dealers' 'colourful' ways.

11. According to one informant, a Stable Way totter had brothers who were married to Travellers in Ireland. The totter himself never mentioned it to me when I interviewed him; rather, he spoke disparagingly about Travellers.

12. Scally, speaking of the post-Famine Irish midlands, notes 'Then as now, racing and wagering on horses was a craze that cut across class and sect. It was often ruinous for high and low, but was high point of rural life, expressing the universal love of horses and belief in luck' (Scally 1995, 56).

8

WORK & NETWORKS

From all these facts, we cannot conclude with complete assurance that there is absolutely no tribal organisation among the Eskimo. On the contrary, there are a number of social aggregates that definitely appear to have some of the features which ordinarily define a tribe. Yet at the same time, it is apparent that more often than not these aggregates assume very uncertain and inconsistent forms; it is difficult to know where they begin and where they end. They appear to merge easily and to form multiple combinations among themselves; and rarely do they come together to perform common activities. If therefore the tribe exists, it is certainly not the solid and stable social unit upon which Eskimo groups are based.

Marcel Mauss, *Seasonal variations of the Eskimo*, 1979

Having looked at the Westway as a microenvironment and at the ecology of rural Ireland up to modern times, with its slow post-war transition to an urban society (which became more rapid in recent times as globalisation took effect), the time has come to see how Travellers have adapted to west London and the Westway Site. In this chapter we will look, in particular, at patterns of work and family within the wider context of the Irish in Britain.[1]

First we would do well to remember just how much more urbanised England was compared with Ireland 150 years ago because, for all its recent urbanism, Ireland's culture is still steeped in rural ways, and landscape. Memory and the story of landscape are deeply ingrained in people's mentalities. Estyn Evans once again: 'the whole of Gaelic society was opposed to urban living'; in 1841, 'when the population was approaching its maximum of about 8,500,000, nearly twice its present [1957] size, only fifteen per cent lived in towns, most of them very small, at which time nearly half the population in England was urban, Dublin alone reaching a quarter of a million' (Evans 1973, 82).

Second, let us recall some of what Mauss said about the social organisation of the Eskimos (see above), because the similarities with Travellers are highly instructive. For the Eskimo or Inuit, some of whom live on or below latitude 54 degrees north, the same latitude as counties Mayo and Louth, the 'settlement or camp' is:

> The true territorial unit ... a group of assembled families who are united by special ties and who occupy a habitat in which they are unevenly distributed, as we shall see, at different times of the year, but which constitute their domain ... a concentration of houses, a collection of tent sites, plus hunting grounds on land and seas, all of which belong to a certain number of individuals. It also includes the system of paths and harbours which these individuals use and where they continually encounter one another. All this forms a unified whole that has all the distinct characteristics of a circumscribed social group. (Mauss 1979, 27)

Next, we need to get some idea of the economic circumstances facing Irish people at the time this research on the Westway was conducted.

Metropolitan ecologies and habitats

In 1926 around 670,000 people in Ireland made a living from agriculture; by 1961 the figure had dropped to 393,000 (Hoppen 1990, 215). In 1971 a quarter of the population worked in agriculture and by 1990 that proportion had halved. Emigration and rural migration account for most of these changes in the sixty years from 1926; globalisation, EU membership and the implementation of new technologies to build new industries have done the rest. As Hussey (one of the sources of the above figures) put it not long ago, within a few years 'an inward-looking, rural, deeply conservative, nearly

100 per cent Roman Catholic and impoverished country has become urbanised, industrialised, and Europeanised' (Hussey 1995, 1). Let us clarify these concepts, since they are often used rather loosely.

By 'urbanisation' we refer either to the total proportion of a population, living in towns or cities, or, more likely, to an *increase* in that proportion. Where the total population in towns and cities increases only by the same proportion — or less — than the rural population, we should not talk of 'increased urbanisation'. 'Urbanism' refers to the character of town or city social institutions; it can increase, therefore, without any increase in urbanisation *per se*. To put it otherwise, whereas urbanisation necessarily involves urbanism, the reverse is not true. 'Industrialisation' refers to changes in technology that bring about concomitant changes in the *scale* of goods production and typically connotes factories, a good deal of unskilled or semi-skilled labour, and *mass*-production of the sort associated with 'modernisation'. Changes in technology and shifts to smaller, more highly skilled, workforces and the use of multiple sub-contracted specialists means that this particular vision of 'modernisation' is rapidly changing. Irish industrialisation, for example, has centred on high-tech industries, such as computer manufacturing. 'Europeanisation' refers to the increased sense of national belonging to the wider 'community' that flows from membership of the EU (known in previous incarnations as the Common Market, the European Community and the European Economic Community).

Although the number and proportion of people working in agriculture have declined over the last fifty years, agriculture remains very important. Furthermore, compared with Britain, the Republic *looks* a dramatically less urbanised society. Agriculture still accounts for 5.7 million hectares of the total 6.9 million hectare landmass (Hussey 1995, 306). On these grounds alone emigration to Britain offers scope for culture shock.

In 1981, when only people *born* in Ireland qualified as 'Irish' in the British census, 300,000 people in London qualified, making them the biggest 'ethnic minority' in the city (and this excluded 54,000 people born in Northern Ireland). In 1994 a report done for the Commission for Racial Equality, titled *The Irish in Britain*, established that the Irish were Britain's largest ethnic minority, with 1.4 per cent of the population having been born in Ireland. That figure increased to 4.6 per cent when the second generation was included, and rose to 11.5 per cent in the case of Greater London (Commission for Racial Equality 1997b).

Of the capital's fourteen inner-city boroughs, Hammersmith and Fulham (H&F) was second only (by the finest margin) to Islington in 1981 when it came heads of households born in the Republic. At 10.1 per cent, the Irish in H&F led Afro-Caribbeans (or West Indians) at 8.2 per cent. Kensington and Chelsea (K&C) was ninth in the league, with 5.6 per cent of heads of household 'Irish' compared with 3.2 per cent Afro-Caribbean. Taking all thirty-three London boroughs, outer and inner, H&F was third only to Islington and to Brent when it came to being 'Irish'. The council officially recognised this when, 1987, it acknowledged the Irish as a distinct 'ethnic group' and culture. Once again, the percentage would have been higher if the second generation had been included. Indeed, a *Policy Report on the Irish Community* (Greater London Council 1984) concluded that a sixth of the metropolitan population could be classified 'Irish' if ethnic identity included everyone who acknowledged Ireland as being 'significant' to their identity — a broad umbrella, admittedly. It is nevertheless somewhat remarkable that it was not until 1994 that the Commission for Racial Equality (CRE), recognising the Irish as a 'distinct ethnic group' under the terms of the Race Relations Act, recommended their inclusion as a separate category in the 2001 national census.

Much of the credit for this public recognition of the Irish as a distinct identity must go to the Irish press in Britain. Throughout 1986, buoyed by Greater London Council support for multiculturalism, *The Irish Post* reported a string of anti-Irish racism accounts and brought pressure to bear on the Inner London Education Authority to recognise the 'cultural needs' of children of Irish descent. The editorial of 24 May 1986, under a banner heading 'Discrimination' could not have been plainer:

The fault is, of course, very largely our own. Down the generations the Irish did not press for recognition within the educational establishment of their children's special requirements. Instead, they, in the main, allowed their children to grow up without their Irish consciousness being sustained by an educational base.

Still, the Irish built schools wherever in Britain they settled. They did this to ensure that their children got a Catholic education. The running of the schools was in the hands of the Catholic authorities and they, by and large, favoured washing out the Irishness. Irishness was a liability. It conflicted with Britishness and the Catholic authorities desperately needed to manifest their loyal Britishness.

So it was that in former times Irish parents blindly contributed to the eradication of Irishness in their own children.

But things are changing and, significantly, much of the demand for a change is coming from young, educated, second generation Irish who, having themselves suffered at the hands of the system, are in adulthood, fighting back...

A paper titled 'Irish in London' (c.1986) written for The Irish Employment Conference also provided some revelations about the status of Irish immigrants in London. It examined their social mobility from 1966 to 1981 and its main conclusions, set out below, provide a useful set of benchmarks against which to evaluate the position of Travellers on the Westway.[2]

In 1981 51 per cent of Irish immigrants in London were in paid employment, and 3.4 per cent were unemployed, compared with an unemployment rate of 10 per cent in the general workforce. By December 1987, when, according to *New Society* (5 February 1988), after nineteen successive adjustments to calculation method, government figures put the total number of unemployed at 2,696,000, or 9.7 per cent of the workforce, 19 per cent of the Irish in London were primarily involved in household duties, another 17 per cent were retired — the highest for any ethnic group — and over 12 per cent worked part-time, double that of the British or any other ethnic group. The single largest occupational category, at over 11 per cent, was 'catering, cleaning, and personal services', a notoriously low-paid sector that the paper said demonstrated the disadvantage faced by Irish immigrants, especially women, who found themselves in the same situation as that of Afro-Caribbean and Asian women. Many Irish men also experienced diminished labour conditions, including lots of 'self-employed' men working 'casually' for sub-contractors without the safety net of insurance and superannuation contributions; many made redundant by large construction companies in the 1970s.

Between 1966 and 1981 Irish immigrants experienced a 3 per cent *increase* in the number working in the 'skilled manual and non-manual' job category compared to a 1.1 *decrease* among the British. At the other end of the occupational scale the Irish experienced an increase of 0.4 per cent in the 'professional' category and of 1.3 per cent in the 'intermediate' category, compared to 1.3 per cent and 8 per cent respectively for British people.

Comparisons with other ethnic groups are also revealing. In 1981 over 60 per cent of Irish immigrants worked in some form of manual labour, compared with 67 per cent of Afro-Caribbeans, 65 per cent of 'Asians', and 39 per cent of British. In other words, the Irish were *well* represented, along with other ethnic groups, in dirty, dangerous and physically demanding work, and *over*-represented compared to the British. In 1981 35 per cent of Irish were employed in 'unskilled and semi-skilled' jobs, down from 43 per cent in 1966, but this still compared unfavourably with the 20 per cent of British in this category, down from 26 per cent in 1966. Overall, the report concluded, Irish immigrants in 1981 were three times *more* likely to be employed in the 'worst' jobs than the best ones, as compared with eight times more likely in the case of Afro-Caribbeans, while at the same time the Irish were *less* likely than immigrants from India,

Pakistan, Bangladesh and Kenya to be engaged in the 'best jobs', that is to say the 'professional' and 'intermediate' categories, where 5 per cent and 8 per cent of sub-continent and East African (Indian) migrants were employed. Other records show that in 1986, except for Afro-Caribbeans, the Irish in H&F occupied more of the worst jobs than they did in any other London borough,[3] had the highest rate of unemployment for men aged 25-44 among all ethnic groups, and experienced a disproportionate degree of homelessness.

The problem of 'living rough' was a major concern for Irish organisations throughout London during the 1980s and 1990s. The Irish housing organisation CARA found that 1 in 4 of those applying for accommodation in the Borough of Westminster were new immigrants from Ireland. In 1989 the Salvation Army estimated the homeless in London (including people in hostels, temporary local authority 'bed and breakfasts', and squats) at around 75,000, of whom 2,000 'lived rough', or on the streets. It gave no ethnic breakdown. An article on homelessness in the *Observer* (5 June 1988) titled 'No Way Home', based on a report by the charity Centrepoint, put the number of young people under nineteen in temporary accommodation in London at 50,000, and saw the number 'living rough' growing daily because of the way social security was paid. Many of them were reduced to prostitution. In a survey of 231 homeless young people who sought its assistance, Centrepoint found that 30 came from the north of England, 19 from London, 14 from the Republic of Ireland, 14 from Scotland, and 4 from Northern Ireland (the newspaper didn't account for the balance). In H&F the Irish Welfare Bureau found that all its first-time requests for housing came from those recently arrived from Ireland. The situation was no better in 1990. One estimate put the number of Irish living rough in London at 5,000. In 1995 the *Guardian Weekly* (26 February) reported on a paper called 'Time to Move On', put out by the organisation Single Homelessness in London, and another titled 'Out of Sight: London's Continuing B&B crisis', published by Char, which reckoned that 15,000 individuals and families were living in these conditions, six times the government estimation. The same *Guardian* article reported the number of people reckoned by the organisation Crisis to be sleeping rough in Britain at 8,000, with another 60,000 in emergency hostels.

Finally, in this attempt to put life on the Westway Site in context, it should be noted that in a flyer for a report entitled *Discrimination and the Irish Community in Britain* prepared for the Commission for Racial Equality (1997a), the authors highlighted 'evidence of inequality and a powerful sense of hurt and unjustified exclusion from an equal place in British society' among many people of Irish origin. It went on to say that 'deep-seated anti-Irish stereotypes affected many areas of interviewees' lives, including workplaces, access to housing, treatment at benefits offices and interaction with neighbours and the police'.

This was the metropolitan milieu in which Irish Travellers found themselves in the 1980s; the London to which the Westway belonged. The statistics cited refer, of course, almost entirely to the first generation — to adult immigrants and not to members of the second and third generations. Nor do most of them take account of age and gender. What is both remarkable and clear is the degree of discrimination experienced by the Irish, despite their sharing the same skin colour, language and Christian faith (as opposed to 'denomination') as the majority native-born population, and despite centuries of immigration and labour history and decades of intermarriage. This being the case, it is then surely critical to ask: what of Ireland's own outcasts — the Irish Travelling People?

An estimated 8,000 Irish Travellers lived in England and Wales in 1987 and another 15–20,000 in Ireland as a whole (Kenrick and Bakewell 1990). Among the former, according to another estimate by Kenrick,[4] 6,000 (1,000 families) were nomadic, 3,500 of these living on official sites, the other 2,500 (400 families) on unapproved ones. Among the official sites thirty-one were located in boroughs in Greater London, where they served 415 Romany and Traveller families. In 1995 Kenrick and Clark estimated the number of Irish Travellers in Britain at 19,000. Other reports put the number at 15,000, with another 25,000 in the Republic (where they accounted for 0.5 per cent of the total population. There were a further 1,500 in

Northern Ireland[5] and 10,000 in the USA[6]). In January 1984 fourteen inner London boroughs (including the City proper and K&C) out of twenty-two were absolved from providing caravan sites for Travellers and Gypsies. The other eight supplied 115 pitches between them; one of these boroughs being H&F.

Westway work

All Westway work is organised on gender lines. Most paid work is men's work. Most unpaid work is women's. Women are also important family 'providers' through receipt of welfare benefits. In the short to medium term there was a degree of occupational specialisation among Traveller and Romany men, but over the longer duration there were few men who hadn't earned a living in numerous different ways. All the men were multi-skilled, jacks-of-all-trades, individuals for whom the line between work and leisure was not clearly differentiated, 'amateurs' in the Marshall McLuhan sense. For McLuhan, "the expert' is the man who stays put'. 'Professionalism' *is* environment. 'Professionalism merges the individual into patterns of total environment' whereas 'amateurism is anti-environment' and 'seeks the development of the total awareness of the individual and the critical awareness of the ground rules of society' (McLuhan and Fiore 1967, 92). To the extent that Travellers and Gypsies emphasise the person's and each family's autonomy they do *not* merge the individual with the environment. On the contrary, they stand outside 'the ground rules of society' both by choice and by force of historical and current circumstances and, from this position, they see *themselves* as 'outsiders'. Living diurnally, without 'professional' routines, Travellers do 'their own thing' like the consummate amateurs they are. To say the Traveller is 'anti-environment' is but another way of saying he is a 'stranger', as the sociologist Simmel (1906) used the word: 'in' but not 'of' the mainstream, expected to move on, and well situated to see critically the ground rules of society.

Men's work
The work of the Westway Site men was of four principal kinds:

trades, asphalting or tarmacking, rubbish collecting and scrap metal recycling, and general dealing.

Only three men had specialist trade or craft skills, which they practised more or less continually: an Irishman who did roofing and chimney repair work; a Gypsy who did bricklaying; and an Irish Traveller who did fencing and garden work and was often away for weeks at a time. Of these three only the Gypsy had formal trade qualifications and for that reason was probably economically better off than the other two. Both the roofer and brickie were in regular work and none of the trades called for much capital outlay; the major running costs being fuel and the need, in some cases, to hire a day labourer.

Asphalting required more capital outlay than the other types of work. In 1984 buying a second-hand three-ton tipper truck (also useful in rubbish collecting) and heavy roller cost between £500 and £900. It also called for a gang and the kind of skills some of the older men had picked up in the 1960s working on the motorways and later passed on to others. Small amounts of raw material were usually collected from supply yards, while the seller delivered larger amounts direct to the job. Three yards of asphalt could be bought for £80, which meant that on a 'good day' a man working with three or four others earned between £50 and £80, over twice the average unskilled Londoner's £27 net *per diem*, or £80 take-home a week.

Two Irishmen with lorries did regular asphalting. 'Pat' was a middle-aged married man with a grown-up family scattered around England who sometimes had one or two children and grandchildren staying with him. 'Billy' was in his twenties, the father of three infants, and, with his wife 'Lily', 'squatted' with a trailer alongside Pat until eventually they got a pitch of their own. Billy was motivated and energetic — a successful boxer and member of the extended Ward family — and offered me a fee if I would agree to take his business calls, as he had no phone. I agreed to take the calls, but not for a fee as I didn't want to compromise my neutrality. However, things never amounted to much and after a few weeks Billy pulled away to go travelling for the sake of his children's health.

Westway Site, looking south to north, winter 1984

The Traveller doing asphalt hired relatives or friends by the day or else got a 'dosser' from a hostel for the homeless. Pat once hired a young West Indian man and for two weeks let him sleep in the washhouse; no one seemed to mind.

Twenty-five years ago men from the small town of Rathkeale in county Limerick began going to Germany in the Spring for tarmacking and in some cases to sell old furniture bought off farmers or from religious houses. No one on the Westway had been to Germany but men I once knew who subsequently returned to Ireland have gone there since for this purpose, as well as to Austria, Denmark, Sweden, Norway and eastern Europe, and in some cases to Spain and France to pick grapes with the 'Arabs'. Some of these same men had already made several trips to America, where they did asphalting.

Collecting and disposing of rubbish, such as building rubble and vehicle parts, was the most common sort of work under the Westway and there were few men who had not done it. Metal recycling was one of its spin-offs. The capital outlay involved was minimal and a man could do some jobs by himself. For these reasons it was often the work of first choice for Travellers newly arrived from Ireland and for men just married or recently out of prison. Dirty, laborious and not particularly lucrative, the work was plentiful as gentrification went ahead and homeowners in the western suburbs opted to renovate and rebuild rather than sell and move further out. The problem with this kind of labour was the uncertain future posed by firms specialising in the hiring-out of kerbside waste-skips. As a temporary measure, however, small-scale rubbish removals offered new arrivals from Ireland a quick means of cash. This is how it worked.

Single or married, alone or with family, the man off the ferry made his way to the site to 'visit' relatives. Thus acquiring an address that he soon claimed was 'permanent', the man now registered for unemployment benefit, which the DHSS sometimes tried checking with me, and within a few weeks had saved enough for a cheap vehicle and small second-hand trailer. If he was married and had children his wife applied for a family allowance. All he needed now, if his first vehicle was unsuitable, was a small 'pick-up' with which to collect rubbish. After deducting, say, £3 for petrol, £10 for the help of a relative if he needed it, and £15 for the municipal-tip fee, £50 cash-in-hand yielded a clear £22, or £37 if he chose to fly-tip in the 'triangle' or elsewhere. From here on his income depended on his alertness, opportunism and luck, and upon his social network.

Speaking of such matters, some months before I began on the site, H&F's Housing department, following the court's order to clean and manage the site properly, hired a firm to do the work who, in turn, hired sub-contractors who employed two Romany labourers to do most of the dirty work. The Westway residents were greatly amused when they found out. 'Where there's muck there's brass', the Yorkshire saying goes, and Gypsies and Travellers know it. The question is: was there the element of an 'inside job', or was it just coincidence that Travellers both dirtied and cleaned up?

As far I can tell there was no collusion in the clean-up, either between the residents and the two Gypsy labourers or between their boss and the man in Housing ultimately responsible for hiring the firm, who was himself a Romany on both sides (his mother being a Benson and his father a Gypsy from Mitcham who once worked the fairs on Wormwood Scrubs), though it is doubtful his team knew it. If they did know, then judging by their sarcastic (not to say disparaging) remarks about 'Travellers', particularly 'Irish' Travellers, uttered within earshot of their boss whenever I turned up, they appeared to have forgotten. Re-runs of the tired 'they're not real Gypsies' argument make it possible to suppose that their anti-Irish Traveller opinions (and withering remarks about 'Tinkers') were shared by the boss, but there was no way of being sure, and it may not have been the case. Nor was I able to confirm whether the one woman on this team was the Romany I suspected (in which case she, at least, would have known her boss also was), for she was resolutely unforthcoming when I started probing.

Nobody depended on scrap metal. Falling prices of the most common metals, the time-consuming nature of the work and the space needed to store viable quantities made it relatively unattractive. For these reasons it was mostly left to youths, to Romany women who went out totting, or even to little boys, who were sometimes given presents of rubber-covered copper wire to strip for pocket-money. In 1986 lead such as that contained in car batteries fetched £9 a hundredweight, brass £20, copper £30, and aluminium a good deal more. For most men scrap metal was a sideline interest; if it came their way, so be it; a bit of aluminium taken from an old trailer-caravan was worth having but hardly a serious consideration. For one man, an old pantechnicon bought for £600 and worked on slowly eventually yielded a profit of £300. But 'Mick', a Traveller married to a Romany, had other sources of income, so he could afford to wait for a return. The owner of a three-ton lorry, which allowed for removing rubbish on a larger scale than most other men, Mick was older, more established, and with less of a cash-flow problem than the rest. In the days of horse-drawn travel he had built wagons and even now he occasionally built model carts to sell. He lived at the top end of the site and he and his family owned two of the best trailers on site, a five-berth 'Meridian' that he had paid £5,500 cash for, and a second-hand 1985 'Marshall Supreme' that had cost him £12,500. He was a handsome craggy man who kept himself to himself; people respected Mick.

Every Traveller is a trader or dealer of some kind, confident of his earning capacity; some, of course, are more confident than others and some are more widely travelled. A handful of Westway traders, relative newcomers to the site and men of the same extended family network, were long-distance carpet dealers, a trade that involved being away for weeks at a time so that wives and children were left to cope as best they could, often copping flak in the process from neighbours resentful of the slightly larger pitches (especially as they also had smaller families) that by good luck had come the carpet sellers' way. Several of the older men had travelled extensively in Ireland and other parts of the British Isles, and a number of the younger ones had recently worked in America where they (like some Travellers who had never sold carpets) formed gangs for laying asphalt. More itinerant than 'nomad' they appear to have gone abroad as much for adventure and pleasure as for hard cash. Disneyworld and casinos figured on itineraries involving journeys from Chicago to Mexico and Florida, from Boston and New York to San Franciso and LA. Several spoke of meeting American-Irish Travellers who spoke an arcane form of Gammon (see Harper and Hudson 1971; Andereck 1992) and whose suspicion of outsiders, even the Westway men, deemed 'ignorant'. Yet, like these particularly mobile individuals, men who had lived on the site longer and established themselves in London's west as rubbish-removers, tradesmen, or asphalt specialists, dealing with people and 'making deals' as opportunity arose, trade was regarded as no less challenging, less daunting, less satisfying or sufficiently rewarding.

No Traveller regularly traded horses, but one or two men took an interest in them. Jimmy McCann was known for his prowess as a sulky driver and kept one at the back of his plot. It was said that Travellers from other parts of England used to close off motorways for racing at dawn before the police found out, and that others had even used Heathrow Airport's perimeter road; something hard to imagine even then, but inconceivable today.

In the suburb of Southall, on the Uxbridge Road not far from Heathrow Airport, a weekly horse market is held that dates back to the seventeenth century. A high percentage of the people who live thereabouts come from the Indian sub-continent or are Indians from East Africa, many of them Punjabis, but off the High Street down at the horse market are people with more remote links to India; English Romany Gypsies who come to reignite values and networks, as well as admire the horses and ponies, and stock up on saddlery and harness. So, occasionally, did Travellers like Jimmy McCann, who periodically grazed a horse on a pocket of grass at the end of Stable Way opposite *The Latimer Arms*. Billy Ward, too, had a liking for horses and at one point tethered a pony under the Interchange that he had bought for his 3-year-old. The North Kensington Amenity Trust asked me to get him to remove it. 'Son' McInerney, with whom I went to Southall, came from a well-known family of horse dealers. An elderly customer at *The Charlie Butler* in Mortlake said his father used to buy donkeys off the McInerneys in London before World War II.

Other than the incidental trading of motor vehicles, the only other kinds of dealing were illicit minority activities, and were the province of one or two young unmarried men who, with friends from other sites, dealt in drugs, stolen goods and were into 'ringing' cars. Conspicuous in their latest-model high-powered saloon cars, and with a predilection for 'burning rubber', they annoyed neighbours fearful for their children's safety and irritated others for drawing the unwanted attention of police. Drugs at that time were new to the Traveller community and a cause of concern to parents and to social workers who saw them as the source of an emergent 'generation gap' not seen before in Traveller society.

Women's work

For generations Romany women in Notting Dale were breadwinners, as, in Ireland, were Traveller women. At the Westway, though, Irish women with few exceptions were financially dependent on their husbands, except for what they got by way of welfare payments. Gypsy women, on the other hand, were more likely to go out working — either hawking or telling fortunes. No Westway woman worked in regular waged employment, although a few of the younger Irish women had held down jobs in the past. Romany wives aged 30 and above were slightly more likely to work outside the site than married Irish women, but not as employees. Rather, it was young unmarried Irish women who were more likely to seek or hold down regular employment, although, as I have noted, none did so during my time at the site. The fact that the Irish formed the majority on site also skews this observation. Overall, there was little difference between the two ethnic groups when it came to work other than the older Gypsy women's greater tendency to go out working, compared with Irish women of similar ages.

Mrs Winifred Ward

Irish Traveller girls, Portobello Road, Notting Hill, 1986

Traveller women were not in regular employment for a variety of reasons, of which the most obvious were lack of formal qualifications, limited literacy, and the compounded fear of being identified as 'Gypsy'. However, they also disliked working under supervision, keeping regular hours and having to pay income tax on low wages. One 18-year-old Irish girl for whom I wrote a reference threw in the job as a hospital cleaner after only two days, complaining that the £2.30 per hour she was paid was not worth the effort. Her family laughed. Two girls who visited relatives among the carpet traders on the site had a decent level of secondary education and used to work in a baker's shop in Hammersmith. One of them was the Assistant Manager and brought home £80 a week. Because of their education they were never taken to be 'Travellers' and though educated they never revealed their Traveller identity. Billy Ward's wife, Lily, worked as a chambermaid in a West End hotel before she married, but left because of unwelcome advances from 'Arab' guests. One Irish Traveller had been employed as a telephonist-cum-receptionist, and another worked for years as a cook in a workman's café in White City. Both hid their 'Gypsy' identity from their employers. Another kind of wage labour undertaken by Westway women, Traveller and Gypsy, in recent years although, as far as I could tell, not while I was there, was seasonal agricultural work like soft-fruit harvesting in Cambridgeshire and picking peas and hops in Kent.

Irish women of various ages from other sites periodically sold old clothes and knick-knacks in the Portobello Road which they had collected out 'calling' or at jumble sales. A day's stall licence cost £3. Some sold plastic clothes pegs door-to-door in Shepherds Bush, White City, East Acton and Kensal Green and reported being amused when the householder turned out to be a Traveller or Gypsy. But, again, it was not a Westway Irish Traveller activity. Nor as far as I know, were telling fortunes or reading palms, tea-leaves or a crystal ball. The owner of a small art gallery in Fulham once told me she paid an Irish Traveller £10 for a palm reading and was delighted with the service, but young Irish Westway women thought fortune-telling 'old fashioned' and something best left to older women or, better still, to Gypsies. For their part, Gypsy women sometimes said they envied the way Irish Traveller men took care of their women financially, but they were not always so positive.

Gmelch (1977, 113) thought that Traveller women in post-war Ireland probably enjoyed less economic independence and social interaction with country people than they had done previously, and put this down partly to the advent of welfare payments, which sounds entirely plausible. She also suggested that begging may have increased by the time she came to do fieldwork because it offered a little independence. To my knowledge no Westway women begged, and if they did, they were careful to do so well away from the site where the prevailing attitude was that begging was shameful, though 'there's a time and place for everything'. Only small children had to be actually discouraged from begging from non-Travellers on or near the site. That they had to be restrained at all indicates how the hunt-and-collect mentality is acquired very young. A woman with a baby in her arms who begged from me in Malet Street, near London University, quickly withdrew the request when I told her I worked with Travellers. Another woman, a site resident, expressed outrage at the Gypsies she saw begging at Lourdes. It was a 'sin' the way they came 'after every penny and your jewellery and even faked humpty backs'. How she would have judged the fairground Travellers' 'wheel of fortune' (Court 1985), or three-card trick (*tri carta lubair*) mentioned by MacNeill (1962) and one of the Westway men, is something I neglected to ask.

Demography and mobility

Adult work choices never depended purely on the market. Domestic requirements, domestic arrangements, age, order of birth, gender and personality all came into it. Individuals' desire for travel or possession of a pitch license were added factors.

Travellers move around as individuals and families not only for economic reasons, but also for more social or cultural reasons. Indeed, we have seen this already in the case of the carpet sellers and those among them who combined that line of work with laying asphalt (or for that matter some other trade), but it is actually true of all Travellers irrespective of their trade. This goes a long way to explain why in the case of male breadwinners (who in normal circumstances are the main earners within the family) 'work' is not easily placed in a category distinct from non-work (including such a thing as 'leisure'). Nor are summer 'movement' and winter 'settlement' entirely divorced from the old Irish calendar which, as we have seen, had important social and religious dimensions. Thirty years ago a Traveller told Sharon Gmelch 'St Patrick's Day [17 March] I start to get restless, Easter I get itchy heels, and May Day I'm on the road' (S.B. Gmelch 1975, 124). In 1990 Ross reported Rathkealers going off to Germany in May and returning in time for Christmas (Ross 1990), and I was able to confirm this when I visited the town in 1995. Travellers come and go today, for sure, for many reasons unrelated to economics and the seasons.

At the Westway the pattern of 'seasonally' connected mobility (whether for economic reasons or any other) was one of *slight* movement between May and August, and *little* in winter, with the majority of families choosing not to move at all. In addition, however, to seasonally-related movement among licensed dwellers, which is to say, relatively 'permanent' residents (though that word is misleading), there was a small amount of mobility throughout the year involving people leaving for good and others arriving unexpectedly for diverse reasons.

Some — like Billy Ward and his wife — moved on account of their health and wellbeing. Among these, some sought benefits from the actual act of 'travelling'; others from relocation. Some left to escape conflict with neighbours, others arrived for the same reason. Some moved to evade the police or feuding. A few left to attend graves in Ireland. Some arrived having fled a place where a close relative had just died. Some left for short holidays, others turned up to have a holiday among friends. Some left the Westway permanently because they'd become bored with the site; others arrived ostensibly for a wedding or funeral and then remained as squatters. Some arrived to lend a hand with aging relatives; some left to help aging relatives elsewhere.

The following data convey the extent of *seasonal* movements for whatever reason on the Westway. In February 1986 I counted 157 men, women and children in residence, although the true number may have been somewhat higher.[7] Of these, 44 individuals (28 per cent), representing 10 families, were squatters. Most of these had squeezed their trailers and vehicles onto the four plots nearest the entrance: pitches 1, 2, 19 and 20, but others doubled up with relatives on pitches 6 and 16, midway up the site. Given the 20 pitches available on site, the average number of people living on a pitch in February 1986 was 7.8, which is not excessive until one takes into account that the average pitch was not only taken up by two or more trailer-caravans but also by several cars and commercial vehicles, which were also parked in the road — and usually for most of the day at that time of year.

Records for 1984 show that summer populations sometimes slipped below 90. The difference between this and the 157 in February 1986 thus represents a 56 per cent increase, and one almost entirely due to families who had just arrived from Ireland squatting on the site. However, the change in numbers by season was not always as obvious as this. During some days in winter the population size was hardly different from that in summer. Moreover, 'peak' or 'low' days in winter were sometimes little different from 'peak' and 'low' days in summer, as is seen from data collected in the summers of 1983, 1984, 1986 and 1987 and the winters of 1983/4, 1984/5 and 1986/7. The lowest summer count for these years was 96, on one day in 1984. The highest summer count was 119, on a day in 1986. The lowest winter count was 99 in November 1986, and the highest winter count was 163, in January 1983. The average winter peak for the three winters listed above was 153, a number which meant the site was very overcrowded. The average summer low was 101, which was a 50 per cent reduction on the average winter 'peak', but that still represented a substantial number of people. The explanation for this was a growing feeling on the Westway that, in the local climate of uncertainty over the future of the site and the national climate of inadequate site and pitch provision, travelling had become increasingly risky; going away risked permanently losing one's place. Consequently, licensees who did choose to travel went only after they told me they were leaving and I was able to reassure them I would evict anyone who invaded their pitch. Although the 50 per cent increase between the average summer 'low' and average winter 'peak' was an indicator of mobility and overcrowding, even the lesser increase of 23 per cent (or 25 people) between the average winter 'low' of 135 (for 1983/4, 1985/6, 1986/7) and the average summer 'peak' (for 1984, 1986, 1987) of 110 was sufficient to cause problems.

One day in January 1986, soon after I returned to the site after a year away, I counted 139 people living on the site, of whom 68 (over 48 per cent) were aged under 16. Out of a total of thirty-two households,[8] twenty-seven (84.5 per cent) were Irish Travellers, four (12.5 per cent) were English or Welsh Romanies, and one (3 per cent) was neither Romany nor Irish Traveller but an English 'traveller' family of another kind. By May, the start of the travelling season, the population had fallen to 111 (twenty-six families), of whom more than half were under 16 years old, and 80 per cent were Irish. A closer look at the twenty-six households revealed the following:[9]

Single persons: 5

Couple + 1 child: 6
Couple + 2–4 children: 7
Couple + 5–7 children: 6
Couple + 8–10 children: 2

0–15 yrs 59 (53%)
16–20 yrs 19 (17%)
21–30 yrs 12 (11.5%)
31–40 yrs 9 (8%)
41–50 yrs 8 (7%)
51+ yrs 4 (3.5%)

In summary, in early summer 1986, when over 80 per cent of the residents were Irish, the population was predominantly young, with 70 per cent under 20 years of age and 81 per cent under 30. It is also clear that families were fairly large, considerably larger than the average British family; eight of the twenty-one households containing children having five or more offspring, and two having eight or more.

Yet the data tells only half the story and little about the reality of family networks. On the day the census was taken it is possible that some unmarried children were absent and therefore were excluded. Conversely, it is possible that some children who were included were not the biological sons and daughters of the head of household and spouse but, rather, were other relatives. Additionally, where different generations of families lived on separate pitches they show up in the census as separate households rather than as parts of the same 'family', thereby masking the functional interconnection of households and pitches. It is also certain that married children of Westway families who were living in other places (that is, off-site) were left out of the picture. Like all census data these are but a snapshot in the life of households, a moment in a family's life-cycle, and do not necessarily convey a true picture of a conjugal pair's 'complete' family: eventual total number of children. Such figures also convey nothing of how one household connects to others to be part of an interacting extended family that is itself part of a much larger network we may call the *kindred*.

Households and family networks

To see how families connect, it might be helpful to give an example. Simon was a married man in his mid-thirties who usually lived with his wife Ellen and nine children in Ireland. From time to time Simon and some of the children came to visit his father, Joe, a widower who lived at the Westway with seven of Simon's twelve siblings, among them Peggy and Paula, who were married and had children of their own. Now imagine what this implies for Peggy's 5-year-old Patricia.

Young Patricia lived with her parents, two siblings, and paternal grandfather Joe on the same pitch as seven of her uncles and aunts — three of her mother's adolescent brothers, three of her mother's unmarried teenage sisters, and her mother's married sister Paula — as well as Paula's husband and the couple's two children, Patricia's first-cousins. Patricia therefore had fifteen close relatives around her each day, or twenty-one when her mother's brother, Uncle Simon, and his wife visited, with four of their eleven children, Patricia's other cousins.

Yet this *group* of fifteen (I exclude Patricia herself) would have only been part of young Patricia's total family *network*; the kind of network of blood relatives (*consanguines*) and relatives through marriage (*affines*) that anthropologists normally call a *kindred*. This network, the kindred, further included five uncles and aunts (the siblings of her mother) who lived in Ireland who never visited the site, and her uncles and aunts — the siblings of her father (who for present purposes are excluded to simplify the discussion). Now let us do some projections. If we allow that all five maternal uncles and aunts in Ireland eventually married (if indeed they were not already) and that we include their spouses, and allow conservatively for each pair having four children each, Patricia would acquire another thirty relatives (five maternal aunts or uncles and *their* spouses plus twenty children). Added to the fifteen already counted at the Westway these people would bring the number of young Patricia's close kin to forty-five. If we then add six more as spouses of Pat's still-unmarried (in the mid-eighties) aunts and uncles who lived at the site, and a further four children for each of these couples (in all another thirty) then the figure climbs to seventy-five. Now include Uncle Simon, his wife and eleven children who normally lived in Ireland but occasionally visited the site with a few of their children, and the number of Patricia's immediate kin jumps to eighty-eight, a net of individuals Patricia would have every reason to interact with in the course of her next few years. Remember also this figure excludes cognatic and affinal kin on her father's side, and consider too that in kindred systems individuals reckon relatives on both sides as being of more-or-less equal importance. Descent is reckoned bilaterally and in practice lends itself to the shifting needs (in every sense) of nomads. Were we to include Patricia's paternal kin, the figure of eighty-eight would lift to maybe between one-hundred-and-twenty and one-hundred-and-fifty, but this still excludes second cousins, third cousins, eventual nephews and nieces and so forth. In short, an individual's kindred at any one time can extend well into the hundreds, and at different times in a person's life individuals and fragments of this network can be called upon for support.

Friends, networks, partial networks, nodes or web sites
An Irish Traveller word for relatives is 'friends' and it applies to all close relatives beyond the nuclear family, including one's cousins, nephews, nieces and in-laws. Travellers also speak of 'far out cousins' and 'far out friends', meaning roughly any kindred beyond second cousin. These terms are similar to the broader Irish expression 'far

out relations' (Evans 1966, 285; Messenger 1969; McGahern 1991, 22). Broadly speaking, Travellers show little interest in ancestors beyond two generations. Oral/aural tradition and the irrelevance of inheritance conspire against such interest, though this is not to say that Travellers have poor memories as such, or that identity with the place of ancestors is missing. Living relatives matter greatly in life's daily struggle, but it is precisely because they are surrounded by members of their nuclear and extended families, by 'friends', that Travellers have little need of the past; and with limited literacy skills, they have few means of recording and examining it retrospectively a generation or two later. As socio-linguist Walter Ong (1988) puts it, oral traditions reflect more on a society's current values rather than its idle curiosity about the past. And as with the Tiv of Nigeria (small-scale shifting agriculturalists) for whom 'the integrity of the past [is] subordinate to the integrity of the present' (Ong 1988, 48), so too with Travellers. Indeed not only do Irish Travellers see themselves as ultimately all connected but increasingly they see themselves connected by marriage and custom to English Travellers.

Firth's concepts 'social structure' and 'social organisation' (Firth 1971) are handy when it comes to examining the relations between individual Travellers and their extended family networks. Social structure is the shaping framework of a group's behavioural relations. Social organisation is the action resulting from individual actors' personal decisions made within that framework of relations.[10]

At one level Travellers are constrained by the duties and obligations that go with members of the kindred — all those they recognise as relatives and frequently refer to as 'friends', both on their mother's and their father's side. More of a loose network or *web* than a 'tribe' or 'clan', the kindred, seen from a specific individual's point of view, is connected more effectively at some points than others — points we will call network *nodes* or web *sites*. At another level, Travellers are individuals acting on their own terms both inside the extended family and as members of the network (or rather *partial network* or fragment of network) within the larger Traveller network, and are more connected to those within the node — comprising the nuclear family and particular members of the extended family ('friends'), who in turn form *groups* — than they are with Traveller 'strangers' outside and with non-Travellers in general. By virtue of the kindred's 'loose' structure and the tighter ties of the node or web site, Travellers thus learn and practise equality or egalitarianism. And one of the strongest sources of node or web relations on site is the married sibling bond between autonomous households living on adjacent pitches.

Equality and materialism
Family or household autonomy based on material or economic factors reinforces an implicit ideology of equality — the *moral* equality of individuals and families as groups. However, the functional connection between the individual and kindred and between the practice of equality and autonomy is very far from simple. Traveller society is patriarchal. Within the nuclear family husbands and fathers have authority over wives and children. Older children dominate the younger. Yet gender, ages, birth order, and personality also enter into sibling relations and relations between parents and children, and it is not unusual for children to refer to their parents by their first names. Outside the family children both refer to and address adults by their Christian names or, in the case of the elderly they know well, as 'Old Mammy' so-and-so or 'Old Daddy' whatever-his-name-is, as though they were their grandparents.

Traveller families consider themselves intrinsic moral equals: equally honourable, equally 'respectable' (to use their own word) and therefore equally deserving of respect providing they have done nothing seriously untoward to lose that intrinsic status respect. This is what Campbell (1964) also found to be the case when examining the concept of 'honour' among transhumant Greek shepherd families. Respect and respectability for the Westway Irish had little or nothing to do with economics. Those who had forfeited respect were described either as 'rough' or 'dirty', an attribution that came from incessant squabbling, fighting, unhygienic habits, perpetual criminality and a range of other anti-social habits. One's honour or respect had little to do with wealth. Status and class are not necessarily linked. Quiet or considerate people (all things being equal) are considered honourable. To be sure, income was a factor of stratification at the Westway and in its inhabitants' perceptions of the wider Traveller community, Irish and Gypsy, but it was not a sufficient factor nor was there a consistent correlation between class and status. Why?

Property is not conducive to nomadism and unsteady incomes have a levelling effect on families. This in turn lends meaning to ritual 'conspicuous consumption' in which acts of generosity enhance individual and family reputations while signalling a disregard for materialism. The most conspicuous signs of relative wealth among Travellers were their trailer-caravans and motorcars. New arrivals from Ireland with few or no dependents owned cheap second-hand trailers. More established families owned larger and better-equipped ones, but these were traded or swapped at short notice either on a whim or from economic necessity. Unlike conventional caravans, Gypsy and Traveller trailers do not have interior lavatories or bedrooms, and designated eating areas count for little. As with the countryman in the old days, the table is less important than the fire or hearth (Evans 1966, 88–9) and for most Gypsies and Travellers an outdoor fire in winter remains the place where men gather. For meals, members of the family consume them where they can, at the table or on a bunk seat, together or alone.

Caravans provide little privacy. Then again, the same was true of tents and some traditional Irish dwellings. In County Donegal, families in the mid-eighteenth century lay down naked under the same covers, guests included, in a 'thorough bed'; an arrangement that reminded Evans (1966, 86) of the Lapps and Mongols and, he might have added, the Inuit. Within the restricted space of the trailer Travellers and Gypsies are careful about who sleeps where, being sure, depending on age and gender, to separate children and where necessary move adolescent boys or girls into separate trailers. Only in a poor family beset by the father's alcoholism was this norm flouted.

In 1987 a new trailer in the mid- to top-quality range, such as a 'Buccaneer', cost around £9000. In 1994 a similar vehicle, such as a

'Vickers' deluxe or 'Roma', cost roughly £15,000, while a 'Nuvardo', custom-built in York and equipped with coal-fired heater, gas stove, two convertible double beds, 'silver' filigree cupboards, etched glass display cabinets, mother-of-pearl design benchtops and elegant ceiling lights, cost more than £20,000. In mid-1984 thirty of the thirty-two dwellings on the site were caravans, the other two were mobile homes.[11] By the following mid-winter the numbers were forty-six and three respectively. By December 1986 the number of mobile homes had risen to nine and caravan numbers had fallen to thirty-nine. There were two principal reasons for this change of behaviour.

Improved infrastructure and site management led more residents to think of remaining on the site, so opting for more spacious homes not only meant greater comfort but also better defence of pitches. In addition, rumours of H&F's plans to abandon the site and find a new one where priority went to existing licensees led some residents to believe their chances would be improved by buying mobile homes, which, being less manoeuvrable than trailers, conveyed the message 'we are here for the foreseeable future'. Besides, a mobile home *in situ* was a 'saleable' asset in a buyer's market because, although it had no right to, a family leaving the site permanently usually tried to 'sell' the pitch to friends or other bidders. Consequently I sometimes arrived at work to find that deals had been made in advance and a new family had moved in overnight onto the old pitch.

The Housing department did not ban mobile homes for two reasons, which were not explicitly articulated: the difficulty of policing such a policy, and the tendency of mobile homes to limit manoeuvrings and deter squatters. From the sociologist's viewpoint an argument against a general move to mobile homes is that it could give the unintended impression that Travellers on the whole are content to see an end to nomadism (though not necessarily itinerancy) when this is not really the case. To send this signal just as globalisation and trans-nationalism are making travel the *modus vivendi* for increasing numbers of working people would be ironic, even tragic, given that Travellers and Romanies who are culturally well positioned — and of the right mental disposition — could now take advantage of travelling to further lift themselves from the economic disadvantage from which they have so long suffered. For that process to continue, however, national governments for their part need to acknowledge nomadism as central to Traveller culture, recognise Irish Traveller culture as one that is distinct from other cultures, and then go on to actively support the Travellers' basic right to defend and shape their culture and identity as they see fit, by providing sufficient sites and stopping places, and vigorously upholding policies of mutually responsible multiculturalism.

Notes

1. Kyriacou *et al.* (1989) have already written briefly of the site in this context.

2. 'Irish in London Research Project: Irish Employment Profile — Evidence from the 1966 Sample Census and 1981 Labour-Force Details', an unpublished paper (no further details available).

3. *Branch Secretary's Jottings. National Association of Local Government Officers*, Hammersmith, c.Nov/Dec 1986, p.8.

4. Donald Kenrick in *Bush News* (local newsletter), November 1984.

5. Data retrieved around the time referred to from www.exchangehouse.ie/faq.htm.

6. Data retrieved from the Irish Traveller Movement website: www.itmtrav.com.

7. Counting heads was made difficult partly because I found the invasiveness embarrassing, but mainly because the constant coming and going of individuals over a 24-hour period meant relying sometimes on residents' honesty and accuracy. Even for good reasons, though, the count could be very different from day to day. One must also realise that the number of *families* or *conjugal households* counted on one occasion, and the number of *individuals within households* (i.e. families' social composition) counted on that same occasion were not necessarily the *same* families or *same* individuals counted on another occasion.

8. 'Household' refers here to persons occupying or sharing occupancy

of a pitch who regard themselves as economically self-sufficient. Thus, while a household is what we normally consider a 'family' it is better we regard it as a 'domestic unit'. A single household or domestic unit very often has more than one trailer-caravan on its pitch, while several caravans parked on the same pitch may belong to two or more domestic units. Where for instance a single person such as a widow or widower occupies the same pitch as relatives but occupies his or her own caravan and remains largely economically self-sufficient of the others, they are counted here as a separate 'household' even though they are of one and the same 'family' or domestic unit. Where persons occupy the same pitch as a single individual (widow or widower etc.) who occupies his or her own trailer but is largely economically *dependent*, they are counted as part of the same household, not separately. Most domestic units or 'families' comprised of married couples and their unmarried offspring.

9. 'Child' and 'children' refer to co-resident dependent offspring, regardless of age.

10. 'The more one thinks of the structure of a society in abstract terms, as of group relations or ideal patterns, the more necessary it is to think separately of social organization in terms of concrete activity ... of people getting things done by planned action ... Social organization implies some degree of unification, a putting together of diverse elements into common relation. To do this, advantage may be taken of existing structural principles, or variant procedures may be adopted. This involves the exercise of choice, the making of decisions. As such, this rests on personal evaluations, which are the translation of general ends or values of group arranged into terms which are significant for the individual' (Firth 1971, 35–6).

11. Compared with most homes, mobile homes are indeed ultra-mobile. But as alternatives to trailer-caravans they are relatively immobile.

⑨

SPOUSES & CHILDREN

We're like the Pakis.
A Westway Traveller

There's a proverb in rural Ireland that it is unlucky to marry for love.
H.V. Morton, In Search of Ireland, 1947, 187

'For', says I, 'the Wards are relations of mine, and I know them, and I know that none of them would marry an amadan [fool] that couldn't earn his bread...'
William Bulfin, *Rambles in Erinn*, vol. 2, 1981, 206

The nuclear family is the core unit of Traveller social organisation, followed by the extended family and wider kindred, and to grasp its sociological significance we should understand the value Travellers put on marriage and children: for while they are important to other Irish people, they hold extra significance for nomads.

Traveller childhood is short compared with the protracted dependence of children in the settled population. Boys and girls grow up fast, marry young, do not delay in having children of their own and few are those who come to marriage without having absorbed the principles making for the good or honourable family: the family life lived well. Make sure your family is fed; see that your children obey you; instil the gift of faith; ensure your daughters remain pre-maritally chaste; keep a clean home; don't speak detrimentally of or try to speak for others; and be extremely cautious of buffers.

Marriage

Before the Famine poverty led the Irish to marry early (Woodham-Smith 1991; MacNeill 1962). It was not until the second half of the nineteenth century that changes in the law led to a consolidation of scattered strips of land and ended their constant division among sons by instating primogeniture — inheritance by the eldest son. According to Arensberg (1937), the handover of the farm intact from father to one son increasingly meant sons were delaying marriage — sometimes past forty — until such time as the old man's frailty forced the inheritance, and in time produced a more 'puritanical and cautious ethos' (de Paor 1986, 258).

Thirty years ago Traveller marriages might be arranged, the result of elopement (S.B. Gmelch 1975), an outcome of being seen going out together (Barnes 1975) or the product of free choice. In nineteenth-century England, according to George Smith (*The Graphic*, 13 March 1880), only around a third of English Gypsies married according to law, and the same held true of Irish Travellers into the twentieth century (McRitchie 1889; Sampson 1891; Synge 1992; Barnes 1975; Gmelch 1977; Court 1985), as my informants attest.

Matches and arrangements
A combination of factors, including the legal changes just mentioned, the residual effects of Famine, and (especially female) emigration, led farmers who were concerned to see their name continue on the land to use the services of marriage brokers. These matchmakers would find wives for their eldest 'boys', those who were most capable of bearing heirs and most willing to look after them (the farmers) and their wives in their old age (Arensberg 1937). The man best positioned to make these matches was the man who knew most farmers and could bring individuals together, namely, the publican or livestock dealer, who was often one and the same.[1] In the case of Tinkers, for whom inheritance was not an issue,[2] the use of matchmakers is more of a puzzle.

Four elderly Westway women said that their marriages were the result of 'matches' and declared that the practice was once common, especially among the families of horse dealers. Whether they involved the services of an independent matchmaker or were the outcome of arrangements made directly by members of the two families I neglected to ask, but, if the former, the matchmaker himself would almost certainly have been a Traveller, like 'Cowboy' McDonagh, mentioned by S.B. Gmelch (1975, 66), where the match usually involved a teenage couple. The main purpose behind arranged marriages among Travellers today is not to safeguard male interests so much as to safeguard the girl's by securing a man who won't mistreat her. Such men are most likely to be found among 'friends' in the kindred. Men who, with their family, are known and vouched for and are not 'strangers' whose families could turn out to be 'rough'. Brody (1973) found similar reasons for using matchmakers among country people.

How many of the fifteen marriages involving partners from the Westway between 1984 and 1987 were 'arranged' is not known, but one between an 18-year-old boy and 16-year-old girl at St Francis of Assisi's was definitely arranged between the families. Arranged marriages were said to be common, some of them being fixed in childhood, which led some people to say 'We're like the Pakis'. For this reason it is useful to distinguish 'matches' made through independent brokers from 'arrangements' made by families themselves. It should not be thought that Traveller arrangements or matches preclude the option of refusal, but according to Barnes (1975) a girl is advised not to refuse too often if she is to avoid being thought of as 'dirty'. However, for many parents the best marriages are those freely entered into or chosen — even if it *is* after elopement.

Elopement
Known also as 'marriage by capture' to anthropologists, elopement gets around parental objections, especially ones on the girl's side. The wedding follows the girl's 'recapture', the boy's punishment by her close male relatives, and an apology by his family to hers. I counted three such cases under the Westway. In one, the couple knew each other for four months, in another the pair knew each other for less, and in the third case the pair had just fled Ireland. And, except in the first case, weddings followed within weeks of the recapture.

Free marriages and mixed marriages

Travellers do not indulge in public dating or go in for drawn-out engagements. Public displays of affection are discouraged except at large social gatherings like wedding receptions where older relatives can survey what is going on (Helleiner 2000) as well as engage in more relaxed behaviour themselves. Normally, 'interested' couples convey an impression of indifference.

While preferential endogamy is the rule and most on the Westway kept to it, Travellers do marry outside the Traveller community, thereby running the risk of becoming cut off in the long run. This goes especially for females because girls are more likely to leave the immediate company of kin to follow non-Traveller husbands than are boys likely to move away with non-Traveller wives. The girl who moves away also risks falling into the 'dirty' habits of her 'settled' in-laws, whereas the girl who enters the Traveller community can adopt its ways.

In two earlier essays (Griffin 2002a; 2002b) much influenced by Douglas (1973 and 1978), and therefore by Durkheim (1915), I argued that different social structures develop different systems of social classification in which the body becomes a 'natural symbol' or metaphor. Travellers' rhetorical insistence on 'cleanliness' and 'dirt', therefore, reflects more than just a *practical* common-sense concern with hygiene; it also indicates a deep concern for what and who does and does not 'belong', who and what is in place and — as 'dirt' is 'out of place', who and what is 'clean' and who or what is 'dirty'. In other words, a profound concern with the Other and keeping Strangers 'out'.

To be 'clean' is to be 'Traveller'. To be 'dirty' is to be classified an outsider. For their part, settled people use the same words to distinguish themselves from Travellers and, in some cases, to distinguish Irish Travellers from 'real Gypsies'. Either way, classifying the Other as 'dirty' justifies treating Others like 'dirt', and the knowledge of these implications both reinforces the Travellers' own use of these oppositions as tools for defining identity and underpins the stress they put on ritual cleaning practices, which emphasise for them the borderline, the 'difference', between 'inside' and 'outside'. It is this 'part of' but 'being apart from' sense that serves to differentiate them from the surrounding social environment. And because 'cleanliness' is first and foremost women's business it pays men to marry Traveller women if they want to retain their connection with kindred and the wider Traveller society, and see their children grow up as 'Travellers' (see Chapter 10), because unless she is 'reared up' to it or socialised with Travellers, the non-Traveller woman is unlikely to ensure this.

Travellers get their surnames from their father and husband but married women often continue to use their maiden name or their mother's maiden name. Through her husband a woman is joined by *name* to a network of persons with that name and through them to these people's relatives by marriage. At marriage a man and his family of origin become linked to the wife's family of origin and extended kin network — presuming they are not linked already. Children whose parents are both Travellers consequently have access to a large and effective kin network that children of 'mixed' marriages do not.

Two classes of person Westway Travellers have married 'out' to without jeopardy to their identity are English Romanies and Welsh Gypsies. Partly this was because all three groups identified generically as 'Travellers' without any *national* caveat, and partly it was because some Romany families have lived so long in Ireland, where they have married Irish Travellers and adopted Catholicism, that they are no longer regarded on the Westway as 'English' but instead are thought of either as 'Irish Travellers' or as 'Irish Gypsies', their names no longer counting as reliable signifiers of 'Englishness'. Families and individuals with names like Boswell, Grey, Gentle, Hargreaves, Hutchinson, Lee, Loveridge, Smith, Thornton and Whitehouse fall into this category. Conversely, some Westway Irish families have lived so long in England that today they think and speak of themselves as 'English' Irish Travellers to differentiate themselves from 'Irish' Irish Travellers who, depending on circumstances, they may look down on.

Court said mixed marriages between Irish Travellers and country people were 'occasional and shocking' (1985, 34–5), even though some of her informants were the offspring of such unions. On the Westway mixed unions were neither shocking nor occasional; I knew of eight cases of an Irish Traveller marrying either a Gypsy or a 'country person', and systematic questioning of older people would probably have revealed more. It was significant, too, that there was also no special word for non-Travellers who had married-in, or for the children of mixed marriages. Non-Traveller Irish spouses living in the Traveller community were entirely accepted and their children were expected to grow up as 'Irish Travellers', their buffer background eventually forgotten.

Classification of neighbours as 'Irish Traveller', 'Gypsy', or 'country person' was complex. Without exception adults saw the site as dominated by 'Irish Travellers' and this was borne out by the censuses, which regularly showed 80 per cent of households as 'Irish'. These people, for their own part, unanimously described families on three or four pitches at the top as 'Gypsy', 'Romany Gypsy' or 'English Gypsy'. There was also (in 1984) an elderly couple who were described (and saw themselves) in 1984 as neither Romany nor Irish but as English 'travellers' — or itinerant labourers. However, these Irish categories took on a more complex appearance when I talked with the 'English Gypsies'.

Mick, who lived at the top of the site, saw himself and was seen by his wife and children as an 'Irish Traveller'. Irish families at the bottom and in the middle of the site regarded them all as 'English Gypsies' or 'Romanies'. Only the Irish living right opposite and next door to him identified Mick as 'Irish', which says something about levels of privacy and the relative paucity of mutual knowledge across pitches. Mick, now in middle age, had lived in England since a youth, spoke Romani, and with his neckerchief or *diklo* and greased hair passed easily for being a Romany. He and his wife were on their second marriage.

Mick's widowed mother-in-law 'Helen' was the daughter of a Scottish Traveller. Born in Northern Ireland and married to a Welsh Gypsy, she bore a Welsh surname, and like her two married daughters on the site identified herself as a 'Welsh Gypsy' even though most of her Irish neighbours described her as 'English Gypsy' or 'Romany'. As well as the daughter married to Mick, another of her daughters was married to 'George', whose surname is that of a well-known Welsh Romany family. George, who was born in Northern Ireland — part of the United Kingdom — sometimes said he was 'Irish', possibly because he wanted me to see him as no different from most residents, but what is more interesting is the fact that his mother-in-law, a woman who from time to time wore a headscarf and earrings that reinforced her image in Irish eyes as an 'English Gypsy', sometimes also identified herself as (Northern) 'Irish'.

Among the fifteen marriages involving at least one partner from the Westway that occurred during my period as warden, in only one case did a Traveller girl marry a non-Traveller boy and in that particular instance the groom, an Irish boy, already had a brother and sister married to siblings of his bride. So while the union was 'mixed' in the sense that the bride married outside the community, in another sense it was endogamous since the families were already connected by marriage. There was also only one case of a Traveller boy marrying a non-Traveller girl, but here too a 'mixed marriage' was offset by other factors: for while the bride's father was not a Traveller, her mother was, and while her father's father was not a Traveller, her father's mother was. 'Reared up' or raised among Irish Travellers, the bride was hardly an outsider at all. So in both these cases the likelihood of the Traveller spouse remaining in touch with the Traveller community was reckoned very high. It was only when Travellers chose to marry out *and* move into a house early in their marriage that they were seen by other Travellers as being at risk of losing touch with the nomadic community and putting their and their children's cultural heritage and identity at risk.

Other evidence of the close relations between Westway Irish families and English Gypsies often emerged at funerals. For instance, dozens of Romanies attended the funeral at Kensal Green of three young Travellers with relatives at the site, who had been killed in a car crash in Surrey. Observing their presence, one Irish woman remarked, 'Ah, we're all mixed up now.'

Of the fifteen marriages noted above, in only one case were both partners from the Westway, and in all but two cases both husband and wife were 'Irish' — though not necessarily Irish-born or 'Traveller'. Of the two other cases, in one instance the wife was Irish and the husband was Romany, and in the other case both husband and wife were Romanies. In two of the thirteen 'Irish' cases the men (who also happened to be brothers) were sons of an 'English Gypsy' born in Ireland and married to an Irish Traveller, so the men were variously described as 'Irish Gypsies' *and* 'Irish Travellers'.

Most of the fifteen brides appeared to be aged between 16 and 19 years old — families often lost their birth certificates — and most of the grooms between 17 and 21 years. Here, again, I usually felt in no position to pry. Throughout the twentieth century Irish Travellers have tended to marry considerably earlier than non-Travellers, yet several Westway parents, mothers especially, expressed the view that 16 was too young an age for a girl to marry and only 'encouraged' arranged marriages and excessively large families. To illustrate the point, one man told me how, back in 1972, a 15-year-old cousin of his married a 12-year-old girl who, by the age of 27, had given birth to fourteen children.

Free decisions to marry cause parents misery if their son or daughter's choice is not to their liking, whether that choice involves a Traveller or otherwise. On the other hand, the choice of a non-Traveller who is already well known to the family can be a cause for great celebration. Country people who have married-in may be spoken of in glowing terms retrospectively, if not actually at the time. In one case I heard about a Traveller girl who married a 'Paki' whose family subsequently showed her more respect than she would probably have got if she had married an ordinary settled Irish person. In similar vein, though it was possibly a case of the *post facto* rationalising of shame, a father spoke approvingly of Traveller girls (including, I suspected, one of his own) who 'married' men of Caribbean descent and raised the children as 'Travellers'. Remarks like this almost certainly gloss over more complicated realities, nevertheless they do suggest that some Irish Travellers — immigrants and the second and later generations — have greatly changed their attitudes towards 'blacks' as they have grown more familiar with them.

Teenage Doyles

In the end Travellers recognise that they are ultimately all related while also insisting that some ties are much closer than others, and that in most cases individuals and families have no effective or recognisable connections whatsoever, even when their surnames are the same. The total Traveller network that exists in theory comes down in practice to a fragment of *partial network* that is boosted periodically by new marriage alliances. As a result, some families in a partial network, more than others, see themselves and are seen by other people as constituting a strong web reinforced over several generations by endogamy that itself often involves sibling exchange. Furthermore, both from inside and outside perspectives these webs and partial networks are usually identified with place. For example, the Westway Wards, who originally came from County Galway, have close marriage alliances with Mongans, Maughans (Mohans), Collins and Doherties. Families named Cash, Connors and Doran, with eastern county ties, including Wexford and Carlow, are closely connected with McCanns and Murphys. Doyles from County Offaly enjoy generational ties with McInerneys and Tooheys. O'Driscolls from County Cork have close ties with non-Traveller O'Donoghues. McDonoughs from County Galway are closely related to Collins, McGinleys and Stokes. One must simply remember that fragments or partial networks are not in themselves *groups*, they merely have the makings of groups and for short periods may function as groups.

Cousin marriage and sibling exchange
Okely found three first-cousin marriages among the sixty-nine 'Traveller–Gypsy' families she studied in southern England, and three occurred among the poorest 'Gypsy' families (Okely 1983, 157). This is consistent with Bittles's (2001) summary of research on consanguineous marriages in sub-Saharan Africa, India and the Middle East. Yet because Okely is not always as clear as she might be about which aspects of her descriptions apply to Romanies, and which aspects apply (or do *not* apply) to the Irish Travellers who formed part of her study, we should put a little space between ourselves and her work when it comes to Hammersmith.

Thirty years ago Gmelch (1977, 31) found nearly one-in-three first-cousin marriages among Irish Travellers in the Republic, 12 out of 37 unions, the same ratio as I found (16 out of 49) among families who at some time in my tenure stayed at the Westway. On this evidence it would seem that Irish Travellers marry first cousins far more than did Okely's Romanies. Hypothetically, this could be linked both to a greater number of relatively poor families among Irish Travellers and to larger consanguineous partial networks due to a higher birth rate.

Many Travellers said that first-cousin marriage was 'not nice', that it was 'too much like a brother and sister marrying'. Perhaps they said it for my benefit, out of a misplaced sense of decorum. If so, a few points would have saved them embarrassment.

To start with, partial but operative kindred networks are often very large and geographically widely dispersed. Second, it is not unusual for an individual to have seven or more siblings; in the course of two years I came across many with far more than that, and here simple calculations turn up some important hidden facts. If eight married siblings produce six children each, any one cousin among the latter grows up to have forty-seven first-cousins of whom approximately half are of the opposite sex. Allowing for the fact that some of these people are going to be of widely differing ages, one might deduce that half that number (eleven or twelve) are approximately the same age and thus potentially in the same marriage cohort. Third, because of the geographically dispersed nature of Traveller nomad households and the consequent brief and intermittent relationships occurring between same-age first cousins whose families (for reasons already discussed) nevertheless value consanguineous marriage, then it is clear that not all opposite-sex first cousins are in fact 'like brother and sister'; rather, they are at once familiar (in the sense of 'family' or 'friend') and yet sufficiently foreign (in the sense of 'stranger') to make for a 'safe' marriage (see also Helleiner 2000, 181–9). Moreover, there is that relatively large string of first cousins to choose from. To be sure, this does not stop some Travellers sometimes speaking disparagingly of first-cousin marriages, or even comparing such breeding habits to those of rabbits.

There is little scientific evidence to support the view sometimes expressed by Travellers, and very often expressed by non-Travellers, that first-cousin marriages and breeding run the risk of producing congenitally disordered progeny. It is true, of course, that 'The very high ratios of metabolic disorders and congenital problems in Traveller children are partly explained by the practice of Travellers marrying within their own community' (Barry *et al.* 1987, 23); however, the genetic predisposition must first exist (Bittles 2001), which is why, in March 2003, Professor Bittles put this argument on behalf of Travellers to a gathering of fifteen Irish bishops in Dublin, thirteen of whom immediately agreed to request their archbishops to rescind the Church's insistence on first cousins having to seek dispensations to marry.[3]

A marriage alliance type that reinforces the strategic potential of partial networks and increases the probability of the woman's wellbeing is what we call *sibling exchange* (Helleiner 1990), in which siblings marry siblings from other families, either at the same wedding or otherwise. Some sibling exchanges involve first cousins.

When first cousin marriages involve individuals whose parents are themselves first cousin spouses, Travellers speak of a 'double first cousin' marriage. In the following diagrams, triangles represent males and circles represent females; the = sign denotes marriage; horizontal lines represent persons connected in the same generation (in this case two sets of brothers) and verticals represent descent.

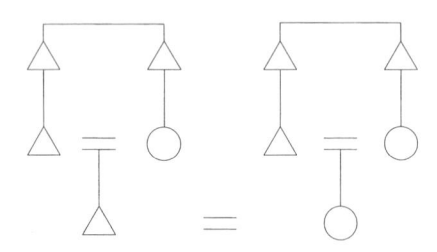

Double first cousin marriage I

In this second example the parents of first cousin spouses (lower line) are again presumed to be first cousins; in this case the younger couple's parents married as a result of sibling exchange: two brothers for two sisters. The paternal uncle of the young man is the father of his wife. His father-in-law is his uncle. Similarly, from the younger woman's perspective, her mother-in-law is her aunt or mother's sister.

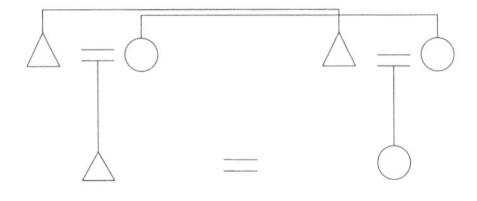

Double first cousin marriage II

Thirdly we see a simple variation on the above situation. The parents of the younger couple (presumed for our purposes to be first cousins) married as a result of a sibling exchange: in this case a brother and sister for a sister and brother.

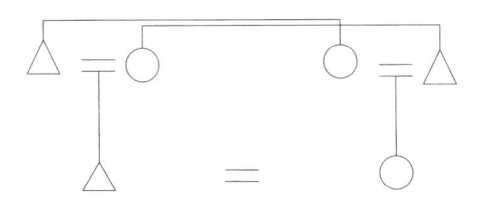

Double first cousin marriage III

In the 1980s both first- and second-cousin marriages required Church dispensations. However, an elderly parish priest in south Dublin in 1987 declared he had never heard of Travellers marrying first cousins. This was all the more surprising since Arensberg and Kimball note that first and second cousin marriages were not uncommon in farming families and happened wherever it was desirable to keep 'farms and dowries within the extended family group, or where the introduction of an outsider is difficult because of class and regional antagonisms' (Arensberg and Kimball 1968, 86). These authors also mentioned niece/uncle marriages of a kind not uncommon in India, and my own mother recalled the sororate where a widower married his dead wife's sister.

Dowry
There are a couple of Traveller sayings, 'Get rid of daughters, hold on to sons' and 'Keep the boys and marry the girls' that reflect important concerns. Although we must not appear adamant (for there are many exceptions and in passing I have mentioned some already), wives tend to follow their husbands' side of the family (or else as couples strike out on their own) daughters are 'lost' to parents. By the same token, of course, sons (or rather one or two of them in a family) tend to remain near their parents, so new 'daughters' (in-law) are acquired. 'Girls', they say, 'are like buses, there's always another coming along'.

For this reason finding suitable husbands for daughters is a bigger parental worry than finding good wives for sons be the latter 'good' or 'bad' (or for that matter relying on sons to find 'good wives' for themselves).

As in buffer society, a girl's family usually bears most of the entail wedding costs and this may entail borrowing money from other sections of the family, such as the father's brothers. The bride's family usually also provide her with a 'bottom drawer' of linen and china, which I very loosely call 'dowry', while the boy's family meet the cost of pre-nuptial pub celebrations and see the couple get a trailer-caravan. Where there are clear economic disparities families may negotiate how the costs are borne.

Weddings
Like the Gypsies, with whom, according to William Bulfin in 1907 (but not John Sampson), the Tinkers had 'little in common ... outside the mania for vagrancy' (Bulfin 1981, 205), Travellers married at one time without religious or civil ceremony. Cohabitation was enough, and, not surprisingly given their 'apartness' and strictures on courting, it was considered wholly adequate that other Travellers witnessed it. In this respect they were no different to Romanies who, according to Westway Gypsies, at one time only conducted public rites following the birth of the first child, which in a qualified way is congruent with Westway Irish views that it is children who 'make' marriages and 'family', not officials. Nowadays few Irish Travellers fail to marry in Church, where the meaning of the rite for most of those attending is social rather than sacramental, since ritual and religion are predominantly private rather than public affairs.

Every Traveller is expected to marry and few stay single for long. Similarly it is expected every marriage will quickly bring forth children. Couples who remain childless for longer than expected may therefore adopt a child — a brother or sister's or some other close relative's. In some cases a childless couple will 'buy' a baby off 'poor' relatives who have other children, or even from 'strangers'. However, the idea of 'purchase' can be misleading and is probably better thought of as 'compensation'. In any case, it calls for closer inquiry.

Travellers frequently declared they would not hesitate to adopt an unwanted child, Traveller or non-Traveller, rather than see it go in need, and some said that they had done so, though they were not Westway families. In this light the threats once made by country parents to their errant children that they would be 'given away' to the Gypsies begin to make sense. Travellers may have also adopted children born out of wedlock to country girls.

Weddings, like funerals, are important settings for the gathering of Travellers who would normally deal more circumspectly with one another. For this reason weddings and funerals are also settings for potential dispute and the settling of old scores within and between extended families. Because of this some Westway residents chose to stay away from weddings even when they were welcome to attend. Besides, formal invitations *per se* are a foreign idea. Whoever wanted to attend either the church ceremony or reception — or both — simply turned up, so weddings were generally large affairs except in the case of those 'on the road', with fewer obligations.

A north London wedding
In April 1985 I attended a small wedding in north London. My wife and I had been invited by the bride's parents who had been travelling around north London since leaving the site in August 1984, and over the course of the next five months we met up several times so that I could pass on letters and official correspondence I had collected for them from a sorting office in North Kensington. The family group normally consisted of three pairs of married siblings — two brothers and a sister — and their children, plus the sibling's parents and maternal grandmother. However by the time news of the wedding and a spoken invitation came just before Christmas 1984 the group had been joined by a fourth sibling along with his wife and children.

On the morning of the wedding we made our way to a church on a busy street in Marylebone. In the churchyard the bride's mother, grandmother, unmarried brothers, married uncles and their families were already gathered with a small number of people I'd never seen before, including a photographer, awaiting the arrival of the bride. The only people obviously absent were the groom and his best man.

The bride's brothers wore dark suits except for one in a light zipper jacket. Her mother, grandmother, and sisters were also dressed formally, though hatless. Only one of the bride's aunts and a cousin, neither of whom I'd seen before, wore hats. All the other women were more informally attired, some of them in jeans. Later I learnt that the hatted aunt had given up the 'travelling life' at the age of 16, had gone back to education and, in due course, married an English 'country man' and settled down in the country 'like normal people', going on to realise her childhood dream of 'living in a house and carrying a bag'. Her daughter, the other female in a hat, had gone to university, taken a degree, and now ran a business exercising horses; her longer-term ambition being to work in Traveller education.

Fifty people were sitting in the church when the bride, in white, arrived in a white Rolls Royce, attended by her father and bridesmaid sister. Only the groom was now missing and it would be another half hour before he arrived, a tousle-haired young man of 20 who, like his best man, looked a little flustered.

The Catholic service was short and simple; wisely so, given the minor distraction caused by the antics of twenty-five young children. In contrast, the groom, bride, their parents and their siblings remained focused and intense. And when one of the bride's sisters, a woman not much older than the bride, faltered with emotion as she read the Lesson, the bride instructed her to pull herself together. With the formalities ended, the little congregation then moved outside for photographs and prepared for more in nearby Regent's Park.

The photo session in the churchyard had barely finished when smiles were suddenly replaced by grimaces as the air was filled with the high-pitched roar of a car engine, the sound of squealing tyres and the acrid scent of burning rubber. Billy, the bride's 17-year-old brother, along with some cousins, had just propelled a car into a stream of traffic coming down the High Street. And it was at this point that someone standing next to me told me why the groom was late: he had collided with a street lamp on the 'wrong' side of the road while scrambling to avoid a head-on collision with a truck. A few minutes later, en route to the Park, I saw the buckled thirty-foot street lamp.

Regent's Park, with its well-kept lawns and beds of late spring flowers, softened this corner of north London. Inside the main gates a smattering of cars moved slowly down drives full on one side with parked cars. Here and there people strolled, soaking up the early summer sun. What happened next is something I will not easily forget. With headlights blazing and hand on horn, Billy sped down the road swerving from side to side to avoid the cars parked on one side and, seconds later, executed a 360-degree turn at a crossroads. He then repeated the exercise in the other direction as his youngest brother Miley hung from the front passenger window, yelling at passers-by and an unfortunate motorist who happened to get in the way. Performance, display, call it what you may, this was a public statement of identity, though few, if any, except the Travellers themselves, knew it. A few minutes later, as the bride and groom posed for photographs next to their Rolls Royce, a second car got between the camera and the couple. The bride's instant invective surprised me, but it was not an act of malice so much as the dramatic performance of identity. Even then, the show was not over.

A 1934 Austin Seven trundled by at walking pace as the man behind the wheel took in the nuptial scene. As the tiny vehicle passed by, three youths crept up behind it and lifted it off the ground by its back wheels and bumper, preventing further passage, and offered the bewildered driver 'ten quid' to take it off his hands entirely. Not to be outdone, Miley then decided it was his turn and, nudging me to watch, pretended to step in front of another slow passing car, causing it to brake suddenly, whereupon he fell flat across the bonnet — harmlessly, as it happened, though the driver didn't know it at first.

The reception was less robust than some I'd been to. One in the East End, attended by over 300 guests and which was estimated to have cost the bride's father over £7000, had involved a sudden enormous rush to laden tables that startled the official caterers who stood by. On reflection, the cultural insignificance of the 'table' and Mauss's description (1979, 72) of Inuit winter feasts involving large crowds whose scramble for food often ended in serious injury helped to put this observation in proper perspective. By contrast with that wedding, the north London occasion was as cooperative and gentle as one would expect at a strictly family feast, and yet it was the opportunity for a lot of good-humoured male teasing and aggression.

A brother of the bride playfully head-butted his son of just 4 months. Billy hit his younger brother Miley over the head for no apparent reason, other than to assert himself. The bride's father, with a chuckle, told his baby grandson to 'f*** off' and then watched, amused, as the child tried to strike back. Two 7-year-olds smashed each other harmlessly with balloons with increasing force, until the smallest one backed off. A husband, much to his wife's annoyance, dipped his baby son's dummy in beer before giving it to him to suck. A young man playfully throttled a female cousin by the neck. The bride got nineteen bumps because it was her birthday and people urged me to lend a hand. Men lifted, nursed, teased and hugged baby sons under 2 and encouraged them to spar. One man balanced an 18-month-old nephew on his upturned hand, raised above his head, where the child stood motionless, a sure sign of future athleticism and male prowess. In all of this and more one saw the nurturing of assertion and risk-taking, 'Aggression' in the broadest sense, if you will, basic to the development of Traveller 'character', no matter how disinclined the individual is to violent aggression or anger.[4]

Marital residences
Ideally Traveller newlyweds pass their first few months with or near the wife's family and then move close to the husband's, but when children on the Westway come to get married, they don't have that choice. Restricted space and overcrowding prevent it. This angers parents who have lived there years. They believe their children deserve more consideration and that the site could be self-managing if it were restricted to a few families. There are, however, two objections to this

argument: first, such arrangements would mean reserving pitches in a way that is both impractical and unworkable on equity grounds; second, the difficulties facing young Travellers wanting to live close to their parents is not unique to them. It is one most working-class couples in London face when confronted by rising house prices and embourgeoisiement. Nor was it only newlyweds and parents who desired site co-residence. Widows or widowers who wanted children or other close relatives to join them could usually only achieve this by getting them to double-up on their pitch as 'squatters' in the hope they would soon get a plot of their own. Another important basis for site co-residence was the sibling bond, and the mutual social and economic aid that comes with it in times of need. Indeed, the sibling bond lies behind a lot of travelling and is one reason why Irish Travellers came to the site, which is only a short way from Shepherds Bush, North Kensington, White City, East Acton, Willesden and Harlesden, where siblings live in houses, and Ealing, where others live on the borough site.

Children

Travellers cherish their children and indulge the small ones hugely. Physical chastisement is generally considered unnecessary and undesirable: the world 'out there' is considered punitive enough. Scolding is another matter; yet florid threats of dire physical retribution rarely fail to have the desired effect no matter whether it comes from a parent or a sibling. Persistent or serious offenders between the ages of 10 and 16 may be 'grounded' or confined to the trailer. Young children are guarded from harm originating outside the trailer site, where child molestation is seen as the greatest danger.[5] Partly because of this, and partly because it is essential to their future success, children quickly learn the importance of being watchful, silent and assertive with strangers. Children are not, however, and cannot be, shielded from the adult realities that exist 'inside' the site. Nor as adolescents are they punished for running the gauntlet with authorities and strangers 'outside', for it is widely understood that risk-taking, confrontation and danger are things they will have to face perpetually as adults, so the sooner they learn how to handle these things the better. When parents grumble about their children and offer apologies for their bad behaviour, they rarely mean it. In fact they usually do so with a touch of fondness in their voice and barely concealed pleasure, for the child who is 'bold' is learning how to survive.

Dressed for St Patrick's Day, 1987

For the same reason, male adolescents are expected to run 'wild'. It is their principal time of risk-taking and freedom from responsibility, which marriage will end. Even the wildest can expect to be 'tamed' to some degree by marital responsibilities. One of Court's informants put it beautifully when he said, 'The happiest time in a man's life is from ten to twenty years. That's the time he is learning how' (Court 1985, 97). With minor modifications the situation still holds, even though Court's informant was speaking of his youth in the 1940s and 1950s. Interestingly, too, if Maurice O'Sullivan's 1930s (1970 reprint) account of growing up in the Blasket Islands, off the coast of Kerry, is anything to go by, it is also how it was for the sons of peasant-farmers.

No boy who has spent his years at the Westway site is likely to look back on it as free and happy, still less the 'time of learning how' that growing up in Ireland, or even Britain, was for his father and his grandfathers. For the Westway boy summer no longer spells the certainty of time spent travelling and meeting other boys his own age at fairs, on farms, commons or in the hedgerows. Instead it means hanging around, suffering days and weeks of boredom and getting into trouble. Moreover, the loss of traditional skills means that they have less chance today of learning particular things from watching older men at work.

Most youths, if they attended school at all, and many did not, had given up by the age of 14. Small wonder, then, that they presented a challenge to youth workers at the North Kensington Amenity Trust, who tried including them in their activities, and to those at the Harrow Club and Rugby Club, where some boys did boxing. In the final analysis, what was most remarkable about these young men was not their serious brushes with the law — which were confined to a few bachelors in their late teens and early twenties, and friends from other sites[6] — but how most of them succeeded in staying out of trouble.

Sex, sexuality and sexual 'deviance'

Teenage Traveller and Romany girls always behaved decorously in public with male Travellers their age. Even when dressed in 'sexy' attire, such as tight jeans, high heels, micro-mini skirts, plunging back or necklines and (by 2004) bare midriffs, their behaviour spoke of family respectability and propriety. In fact such dress meant even more careful behaviour than normal.[7] If, as Court once observed, a Traveller woman's fertility was a source of compensation for her lack of opportunity to publicly display her sexuality (Court 1985, 35), then on the evidence of the Westway we can say such days are over. Higher family incomes, the spread of consumerism and the impact of the popular media have seen to that. 'Glamour' is valued as much by young Irish Traveller women as it is by other girls their age. Where they differ is in the emphasis they place on virginity.[8] As far as I know only two unmarried girls got pregnant. For one it was her second illegitimate child and she was compelled to leave the site because of the extreme shame it brought her family. In both her pregnancies the father was a Traveller but to her shame, a different man in each case. In the case of the other girl, where again the lover was a young Traveller, following a beating by her father and threats of family ostracism, she contemplated suicide. At least that is what she told me when she came to unload her problems; virtually the first time we had spoken. Fortunately her parents did not reject her and as her pregnancy advanced she was increasingly reconciled with them. Finally, some three months before her confinement, the entire family upped their trailer and disappeared. How things progressed afterward I have no idea.

Boys of 16 and 17 bragged unconvincingly of sexual conquests with 'country girls'. Younger boys teased each other about being 'queer'. One or two men in their late teens and twenties had girlfriends in the settled community about whom their families knew nothing, and some probably used prostitutes. In the mid-1980s HIV/AIDS had only just become a topic of public discussion and education and Travellers who talked about it to me were largely ignorant of the causes of transmission. Most Travellers saw male homosexuality as a non-Traveller aberration and the only openly gay Traveller I met during my time as warden did not live on the Westway, but was for a time a regular visitor to the site, where all his 'friends' were women. Well-educated and in regular employment, 'Tim' was more at ease in the settled community than he was in the Traveller community, where men, he said, considered him a 'mop' or 'moprodite'; men whom, it should be added, were no more likely than Traveller women to broach the topic of sexual matters with me, than I with them. The few exceptions were older men, who over a drink sometimes recounted tales of Tinker conquests of 'country women' and cuckolding.

Mischief and assertion

As well as learning their domestic roles, girls as well as boys learnt to be assertive with strangers. For example, in terms of family defence where small children and wives in that order provided the first two lines of defence, adolescent girls took up the third line, guarding men and adolescent youths (in that order) from the unwanted inquiries of officials and police. Guard dogs played a lesser role even though years earlier postmen had complained about them. Small children of both sexes, however, were alert when it came to people asking questions and more than once they remarked on my propensity for questioning. Even as late as 1987 a 7-year-old girl whose mother I often spoke to turned on me one day when she sensed I was pushing her mother too hard. Similarly, a 2-year-old boy with whose parents I was on good terms told me to 'f*** off' when he judged I had asked his mother one question too many. His mother chuckled at his precociousness. A few days later she told me her 1-year-old had learnt to tap on the trailer window to wave to people he knew, and poke his tongue out to strangers. Policing the border begins early.

A small minority of girls periodically went in for shoplifting. And as with boys, girls under sixteen (the age of criminal liability) were usually led into it by older kids in order to avoid being charged by the police themselves. When I began work in 1984 adolescent boys stealing tools off visiting site sub-contractors was the main reason these tradesmen refused to come onto the site. I was initially a little sceptical but there was a ring of truth there. The story of how the boss of the firm responsible for repairs on site had the tow bracket of his Mercedes unbolted while his back was turned, and then ended up paying the culprits ten pounds to get it back again, sounded a stereotypical improbability.

Naturally I was keen to check the story at the earliest opportunity, so when the managing director came to the site to meet me, I asked him about it. 'Yes,' he said, 'it was true, they did pinch it,' and even as he said so turned to check his car, which he had parked for safety outside in Stable Way. His face coloured and he let out a roar, for at that moment we saw a youth skim one of the Mercedes Benz's hubcaps, Frisbee-style, to another boy, verbally taunting the businessman. Fortunately I was able to retrieve the hubcap and in the process learned to my satisfaction that some parents had at least told their children to 'go easy' with the new warden.

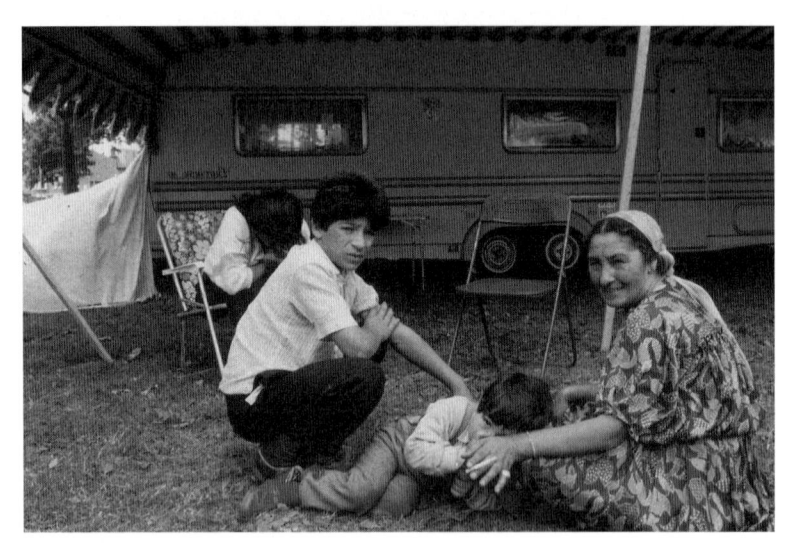

French Gypsies, or Kalderash, camped by North Pole Road, 1987

It wasn't only 'country people' who were the target of Traveller mischief. In July 1986 a family of French Roma drove onto a triangle of grass at the northern end of Latimer Road and a rumour quickly went around that the foreigners were about to pull into the Westway Site. If they did, some Travellers said, they 'would treat them like Pakis'. It was a remark that boldly underlined Traveller ambivalence towards sub-continent Asians. As it happens, the French had no intention whatsoever of moving to the Westway, but on one occasion when I was visiting them they were checked-out nonetheless by Irish Travellers. Loud and jocular, the strangers commented on how 'clean' the French were. I agreed and joked about how I was doing my best with the French to defend the Irish Travellers' reputation. They laughed and said it was futile and with a cheerful wave drove off towards White City.

Formal education

About twenty Traveller and Romany children aged from 2 to 5 years attended the Save the Children Fund (SCF) pre-school.[9] Another thirty-six attended neighbourhood schools: sixteen went to St. Francis of Assisi Primary; eight to Oxford Gardens Primary; five to Avondale Primary; and seven (two of them girls) to Holland Park Secondary. Drawing upon their own experience of school, or lack of it, most parents saw a need of basic numeracy and literacy but not much more. Girls were thus withdrawn from formal education around the onset of puberty and sons a bit later — before they became compliant and unmanly. Few boys remained at school beyond the age of 13 or 14. That pattern may have changed since. The proportion of young people staying on in school has possibly, if not probably, increased. But even if it has not, the situation in the mid-1980s was a great improvement on that a decade earlier when Rosemary Gibb, the Westway Site's first teacher, wrote in a report in 1978 just before she left:[10]

> ... for a variety of reasons, the mothers from the site were not keen to do this [send their children to pre-schools off site]: they are shy; they are sensitive to feelings of not being wanted (some mothers in one group threatened to take their children away 'because of the Gypsies'); they feel different; they feel inadequate; they have not the time ... Many Gypsy families are extremely reluctant to let their small children off the site, to be with people they do not know ... I don't think this reluctance can be solely attributed to fear for the child's safety or to fear of letting their child out among a pack of aliens — there is also a deeper anxiety that has something to do with an un-conceptualised foreboding that the young child's ties to its family will change. There is nothing unusual in a mother's fear of losing the affection of her young child. However, with the Travelling mother it seems to be more intricate and she seems to be more protective

of this bondage. Whatever the reasons, the young-child syndrome is there. I think this attitude should be respected, and the fact accepted that it cannot be suddenly overcome. A mother who is persuaded against her will to send her child to nursery school will instinctually make it impossible for her child to settle: 'Now Tommy, don't you be carrying on today, don't cry when you miss me; don't feel lonely; I'll come out and give you some sweets through the wire; don't run out'. The child who was ready dressed and looking forward to going, never gets there ...

Hans Anderson said that out of reality comes imagination, just as Piaget argued that thinking depends on verbal skills. The Gypsy child's imagination and thought process is exciting in areas he is familiar with, but that area though deep, is very confused. For example, a 12 years old lad, Tommy, could make up wonderful stories about love, marriage, babies, but when it came to imagining and talking about a space rocket he was out of his depth – deprived of construction toys, picture books etc., he had no idea of spatial relationships, shapes; stumbling over descriptions, he could go no further than the bare skeleton of the rocket.

There is no extensive verbal communication between the young Gypsies and their parents, nor are there many stimulating toys to be found in the families' trailers. Stimulation and exposure beyond his home environment, beginning at an early age, could extend the Gypsy child's horizons, sense of reality, and his self-realisation it could reinforce self-identification as well as extending self.

> As far as the Westway Site is concerned, and it is emphasised that the observations are restricted to this site, I am afraid the children are inarticulate about things beyond their own experience, and that experience is limited ...
>
> We (also) have to accept that some Gypsies are far from being angels, and we must work from there. At the same time we have to be quite explicit that they are not all devils ...
>
> My personal, and maybe false, observation of the families on the Westway Site is that they are out of touch with their heritage. In view of this, I think we have two responsibilities, (a) to help them get back into touch with it again; and (b) to help them cope with urbanisation. (Gibb 1978, 7–10)

To meet the needs of reluctant mothers Gibb recommended establishing a play centre on site for the under-5s, and in 1981 the SCF did just that. By 1984 mothers had not only come to value the pre-school for its educational services, in many cases women had learnt to appreciate the psychological support and relief from child-minding the school offered, especially to those among them who experienced depression and other mental illnesses.

Separation and divorce

Several nineteenth-century observers mentioned the Tinker practice of 'wife-swapping' (McRitchie 1889; Sampson 1891; Synge 1992), and later writers have referred to or re-examined this idea (O'Toole 1973; McCarthy 1975; Grene 1975; Court 1985; and for Synge in particular, Helleiner 1990). Suffice it to say, whenever I raised the subject with women they laughed outright at the idea, both as historical and contemporary fact, joking sometimes, 'if only it were true'. Even so, the views of writers like McRitchie and Sampson cannot be dismissed out of hand. Were they duped, were their observations faulty or did they simply misinterpret what they saw? In all probability it was the latter.

Domestic violence and female depression were not uncommon at the Westway and several women at one time or another had gone into refuges or separated from their husbands, some permanently; others probably talked these matters over with the site's visiting social worker. However, none had opted for divorce; their faith a major reason behind this choice. An Irish Traveller in her late thirties, who was married to a Romany for twenty years before he left her for another woman, said she thought the growing problem of separation and divorce was due to changes in 'the structure of the family', by which she meant changes in spouse relations brought about by urbanism and urbanisation, and the greater anonymity and isolation that goes with these things. She said she looked forward to the day 'when someone from the inside, perhaps one of the young educated Travellers' would speak out on behalf of Traveller women. Another woman of about the same age, the mother of two adolescent girls, and someone whose own mother had left her spouse (a non-Traveller) several times during the course of her life but never permanently, went further. 'There has to be more for girls to look forward to than simply getting married early and going through endless pregnancies; there has to be more education and opportunities for work even if it's only working in Tesco'. I suspect this view was fairly widely shared, yet within twelve months her daughter, aged 21, would be married to a Traveller.

Conclusion

To finish this chapter I want to relate what I have said so far about marriage and children to something already touched on in this and earlier chapters, namely 'character'. By 'character' I mean an overarching attitude towards the world that in practice involves a repertoire of culturally embedded behaviours conducive to individual and group survival irrespective of the individual's particular 'personality'. The key features of this 'character' are alertness, secretiveness, discretion, and assertiveness, and they are learnt by imitation and experience. In English to say someone 'shows character' is to say they show spunk or assertiveness.

Throughout these nine chapters I have sought to remind the reader that the history and culture of Irish Travellers is part of the wider history of Irish society and culture. That history, as recalled here, took in colonialism, agriculture and pastoralism, the rural economy, travelling, transhumance, nomadism and emigration, and religiosity and oral tradition. Within this historically viewed landscape I have shown that Travellers choose to remain *apart* (and to 'travel') in order to maintain their culture and identity, but are condemned for doing so. This condemnation, I suggest, is unreasonable.

Little over a decade ago Hutton (1996) described Britain as a '30–40–30 society', thirty per cent 'disadvantaged' for want of work, thirty per cent 'marginalised and insecure' because of deteriorating working conditions, and forty per cent 'privileged' thanks to individuals' increased purchase power. About the same time an OECD survey reported, in the *Guardian Weekly* (5–11 November 1995), rising measures of social inequality fast approaching those in the US. Thus whereas in the 1980s the portion of UK national income accruing to the poorest fifth of the population dropped from 9 per cent to 7 per cent, the top fifth increased its share from 37 per cent to 43 per cent. Presuming this change was linked to changes in the nature of work, one might suppose that in a decade of dramatic globalisation, life for most people became notably more individualistic and less community-minded.

In sum, I suggest that risk-taking has vastly increased, that occupational flexibility has become a priority, that 'portfolio' or 'multi-skilling' careers are deemed the best route to upward social mobility and bespoke 'lifestyles', that social networking ('not what you know but who you know') has come out of the 'closet', and that increased spatial mobility is part and parcel of our global world. As a result, while a greater proportion of people (the 'privileged' 40 per cent) live both more insecure but financially more profitable lives, the remainder (60 per cent) live both more insecure *and* relatively more disadvantaged lives on the social margin. For their part, Travellers, for whom risk, flexibility, multi-skilling, networking and spatial mobility have always been essential and dependent on 'character', actually 'choose' to live apart knowing that they have a safety-net — of family, kindred and their own community — that most in the so-called settled community do not. And these are not the only positive factors with which to reckon the effectiveness of Traveller social organisation.

Not long ago, the journalist Polly Toynbee (*Guardian Weekly*, 16-22 September 2005) reported that the jobseeker's weekly allowance in Britain was £56.20; that 27 per cent of adult Britons had no savings whatsoever; that a quarter of the poorest had debts of at least £200; and that 12 per cent of adults, nationally, had no bank account. The situation in London was said to be even worse, with *half* the capital's children living below the poverty line. On top of this, a report by Professor Paul Gregg of the London School of Economics estimated that a third of British children — over 4 million individuals — lived in poverty, three times the number in the 1970s. The gravity of the situation was further underlined by a 2006 press release relating to Gregg's research, which estimated some 41 per cent of children in London lived in poverty compared with 28 per cent nation-wide.[11] In the light of these stark facts one can truly begin to understand why Travellers and Gypsies to some extent prefer and *choose* to live outside the mainstream, on the margin, for though they bear the costs in bad health and shortened lives, they live their self-directed lives surrounded by 'family'.

In the 1980s and much of the 1990s up until 1997 the number of homeless in London continued to rise. In the year 2000/2001 the inter-agency group Homeless Link received over 252,000 housing applications from homeless people in England, half of which were 'priority need'. On 31 December 2001 an estimated 532 actually 'slept rough' across the nation, a sizeable improvement, admittedly, on the 1,850 estimated on the last day of 1998; meanwhile, the number 'living rough' in London dropped by nearly a third from 621 to 264. Since that time the Greater London Authority's *Homelessness in London 61 report*[12] estimated the total number of homeless families in London, living in temporary accommodation, at the end of December 2004 to be just under 67,000. Of this figure 1,148 were in Kensington and Chelsea, and 1,921 in Hammersmith and Fulham; these figures were only slightly less than the average London borough figure of 2,000. Welcome as these improved figures are, they help us see why Irish Travellers value marriage and children as highly they do, for in the face of homelessness and urban alienation they make for purpose, meaning, and community.

Notes

1. A small number of matchmakers continued working well into the second half of the twentieth century. In 1991, the *Irish Post* (19 January) reported the passing of Tipperary's 'last traditional' matchmaker, Bill Corcoran, 91, a publican, cattle and horse dealer accredited with fixing 200 matches. In the town of Lisdoonvarna, County Clare, matchmaking is now the theme of an annual tourist festival.
2. This situation is changing as Travellers acquire land and houses. The effects on family dynamics remain to be seen.
3. Pers. comm.
4. Turner (1992) in an analysis of Hennis' study (1988) of Weber's sociology shows Weber's indebtedness to Nietzsche and the link between 'character' and 'life-conduct'. See also Mommsen (1989). The 'character' I am describing is reminiscent of that which Berland (1982) details in his study of Pakistani Qalandar nomads.
5. This was the situation even prior to revelations of child molestation by clergy in Ireland and other parts of the world in the 1990s. Though I was unaware of it at the time, a Traveller boy was abducted in Kentish Town some years earlier and not seen again. The police suspected paedophiles. This might explain why child molestation topped the list of gravest deeds whenever I got people talking about 'sin' or 'crime'.
6. Drug dealing, housebreaking, stealing cars (and from cars) were not unknown at the Westway, but nor were they common activities.

7. Short skirts often worn by young Gypsy and Traveller girls on the Westway contrast with the long skirts so often described by ethnographers as worn by Continental Gypsies.

8. Female glamour, propriety, and piety were visible in equal portion at Sunday Mass in Rathkeale, a small town in Limerick, the last time I visited it. According to one long-term resident, a non-Traveller, who unlike some residents saw nothing offensive in the way young female Travellers dressed for Mass, the reason they dressed this way was the general lack of other legitimate opportunities to do so. He may have been right, especially as Travellers at the Mass divided themselves by gender: males on the left, females on the right, the centre of the church being left mainly to non-Travellers of both genders.

9. The Catholic Children's Society (Westminster) took over responsibility of running the school from the Save the Children Fund in 1997.

10. For copies of this and other excellent reports by Rosemary Gibb published in the 1970s, I am grateful to Thomas Acton.

11. Retrieved from www.londoncouncils.gov.uk/doc.asp?doc=16753 on 15 July 2007.

12. Retrieved from www.london.gov.uk/mayor/housing/homelessness_bull/docs/2004_61_2004 on 5 November 2005.

10

'COMMUNITY'

So each knows the other with whom he has to do in a rough and ready way to the degree necessary in order that needed kinds of intercourse may proceed ... It would be a profitable scientific labour to investigate the sort of degree of reciprocal apprehension which is needed for the various relationships between human beings. It would be worth while to know ... how conventional relationships are determined in their development only through that reciprocal or unilateral knowledge, developing with reference to the other party ... [T]he theoretical conception of a given individual varies with the standpoint from which it is formed, which standpoint is given by the total relationship of the knower to the known. Since one never can absolutely know another, as this would mean knowledge of every particular thought and feeling: since we must rather form a conception of a personal unity out of the fragments of another person in which alone he is accessible to us, the unity so formed necessarily depends upon that portion of the other which our standpoint permits us to see ... Accordingly, our situations develop themselves upon the basis of a reciprocal knowledge of each other, and this knowledge upon the basis of actual situations, both inextricably woven ... Our fellow-man either may voluntarily reveal to us the truth about himself, or by dissimulation he may deceive us as to the truth ... The additional trait is that the person deceived is held in misconception about the truth intention of the person who tells the lie. Veracity and mendacity are thus of the most far-reaching significance for the relations of persons with each other.
Georg Simmel, 'The Sociology of Secrecy', 1906

... people meet and mingle together who never fully comprehend one another ... anarchist and the club man, the actor and the missionary ... still live in totally different worlds.
Robert Park, *The city*, 1925

Finally we examine what 'community' meant on the Westway Site, both as a 'community' in itself, and as part of something larger. To begin with, it should by now be apparent that without symbols there is no meaningful communication and therefore no possibility of a 'culture' and 'community'. The system of symbols we casually refer to as 'the media', which constitutes such an important element of what, equally casually, we call 'western culture' is, first and foremost, a system whose basis is gesture and speech. Dress 'code', art, writing, artefacts, goods, and all modern telecommunications technology are thus 'media', which together with their *messages* make for the network of meaning we call 'community'.

This chapter has three purposes. Its first is to explore from emic (the anthropological subject/native) and etic (the anthropologist/observer) perspectives how 'community' is constituted under the Westway, bearing in mind that 'my' (etic) perspective takes in 'their' (emic) one, and that 'theirs' is — and can only be — what as a cultural interpreter I understand it to be. Its second is to present the other Romanies, Travellers and traders who live or work in north Hammersmith and North Kensington and who, by their known presence, contribute to a sense of Traveller community both within and outside the site. Its third is to examine how my awareness of 'them' is the fundamental condition for my claim to know them: to have the sort of knowledge Bourdieu (1977) called 'connaissance'. This may seem unnecessary in a book intended for a broad audience but if we cast an eye back on Simmel's (1906) quote above we will appreciate that a common 'truth intention' is *not* to reveal the truth so much as dissemble and conceal, in which case an examination of the researcher's 'awareness' is important not just for epistemological reasons but because silence, secrecy and concealment are themselves important dimensions of Traveller culture.

'Community' under the Westway

Language and literacy, religion and ideas of cleanliness and dirt (purity and pollution), as well as internal conflict all help demarcate the border of the Westway Site as a little community, so too does stigma. But because stigma (which may be defined as an individual and collective awareness of being tarnished or polluted by other people who by virtue of their taint and taunt one sees as hostile or potentially outsiders) is itself a source of social glue with Travellers and Romany Gypsies stretching way beyond the site's physical parameters, I will deal with it in a section below entitled '"Community" beyond the Westway'.

Language and literacy
For all its modernity, sophistication and global connections Irish society remains profoundly oral; its heroes are still the wordsmith — the poet and musician, and (when it comes to justice and games) the fighter and 'magician'. Conversation (Gannon 1994) and storytelling are important primary art forms in the home, the pub and on the stage of politician and playwright alike. It was the English critic Kenneth Tynan in a review of Brendan Behan's *Borstal Boy*, I think, who said 'If the English hoard words like misers, the Irish spend them like sailors' (or 'waste them like spendthrifts'), and H.V. Morton who declared talk in Ireland 'a game with no rules' (1947). How much truer, then, is this of Travellers who until recently neither read nor wrote, and in a great many cases still don't?

Adult literacy levels varied greatly at the Westway. Some were very proficient but most read and wrote with difficulty, if at all, depending on age and therefore the extent of formal schooling they had undergone. However, I hesitate to describe Travellers as 'illiterate'. Like all unlettered people, their culture is one of 'primary oracy' (Ong 1988) and their 'oral literature', to use Ruth Finnegan's (1988) term, has been studied (Court 1985), as has the oral literature of Scottish Travellers (Williamson and Williamson 1987; Neat 1996). The ways in which formal education and modern media technologies are eroding or, for that matter, helping to reinforce (Carpenter 1974) primary oracy is quite another matter and beyond the scope of this book, but in the light of teacher Rosemary Gibb's 1978 remarks on Westway children it deserves to be researched.

According to Ong (1988), non-literacy (in the conventional sense) results in sound-based cultures that 'unify' people by absorbing them in sound, whereas literacy 'divides' people and makes for analytic sequentialising and detachment. The idea is consistent with Court's observation that 'While settled groups were inclined to adopt and enjoy only the particular strata of literature that affirmed respective group identities — as small farmers favoured patriotic or nationalistic songs, and city office workers read only recently published romantic novels — Tinker literary enthusiasms were not so compartmentalised and self-limiting' (Court 1985, 6). In other words, Traveller 'literature' bridges and borrows from the literature of settled people in a way consistent with their role as self-selected border-crossers. Literacy in the conventional sense is the product of urbanism. Writing, record-keeping, legislation and accounting, which all allow for the creation of bureaucracy, were first developed by humankind in (and for) towns and cities, so become important as the countryside gets more urbanised and nations more industrialised.

Westway Travellers showed little interest in the past, partly perhaps because inheritance counts for nothing; what mattered was today and tomorrow, and their work did not require much reading or writing. With slight print-media influence on their oracy, group conversations tended to be noisy and unconstrained by the logical sequencing literates derive from writing (Finnegan 1988; Ong 1988). What trading requires is quick thinking, verbal facility and an ability to convey confidence. 'Smoothness' and 'glib of tongue' is how Sampson (1891, 205) described Tinker talk. If you see trading as a 'game' then you will see that, like other games, it calls for timing, risk, nerve, bluff and luck every bit as much (if not more) than it calls for linear thinking and cold analysis. At least, it does when the players are amateurs and the line between business and leisure is vague. Aware of this and realising that buffers, especially officials, 'think' and speak differently from themselves, yet reveal their true motives by means other than the writing-based speech they professionally extol, such as verbal tone and body language, Travellers hold outsiders in deep suspicion and deal with them strategically by silence and avoidance, and tactically by playing speech games.

Verbal bombardment and circumlocution empower individual Travellers in difficult situations and unite them as a 'community' under the motorway and as an 'imagined community' beyond. Vocabulary, dialect, volume, tone, tempo and sudden topic switching are all tactically important in speech games; so are interruption, distraction, several people speaking at once, and physical encroachment on the buffer's personal comfort zone. Whether these techniques are used in defence or attack — and the two are not always easily distinguished — the barrage effect causes buffers to beat a retreat. They say the 'pen is mightier than the sword', but when Travellers play speech games the unlettered word is equally effective: 'words' is but an anagram of 'sword' and the 'Tinker's curse' (see Gronförs 1979) is but the most obvious example of verbal warfare.

Cant or Gammon, sometimes known as Shelta,[1] is the secret language of Irish Travellers. The very fact that it is a shared secret in terms of its existence and its meanings also makes it a source of internal social cohesion. For months Travellers denied that Gammon existed on the site and had me fooled in the same way that Scottish Travellers fooled McCormick (1973). Hearing it only when spoken in crisis (and in the early days being uncertain even then that I had heard Gammon *at all*), and only after having given up on learning anything sensible about the language from young people, did one or two Travellers eventually begin teaching me words and phrases, having first sworn me to secrecy for fear of neighbours' reprisals. With the passage of time, however, I picked up and was taught more, and was even encouraged by some to go ahead and write about it when I came to do this book. Some residents said that speaking Gammon meant that they ran the risk of being identified as 'Traveller' when they might otherwise pass simply as 'Irish'. Other people said speaking Cant made you sound 'ignorant': revealing oneself to be a self-confessed outsider. Since the advent of the Internet some Travellers in Britain have put some of their language on websites and as a few scholars have written learned treatises on the subject,[2] I will confine myself here to a few remarks.

Gammon has a tiny vocabulary. I recorded 117 words, compared with the 65 recorded by O'Toole (1973), 150 by Gmelch (1977), and 261 by the Romany linguist Professor Ian Hancock (1973). Small as it is, it is enough for Travellers to be able to communicate among themselves without being understood by outsiders, especially when it is combined with some of the speech games already mentioned above. Most Gammon items are Gaelic words rendered as 'back-slang'. Some are Romani words and others are English cant. Morphology and syntax are English and the delivery, of course, is in an Irish–English dialect. No Westway Traveller spoke Gaelic and, except for 'Mick', none of them spoke more than a few words of Romani. As the purpose of the language is concealment as much as communication *per se*, Gammon is not a domestic language and for that reason not much of it is learnt until late adolescence. Young children, who have already learnt to be guarded with outsiders anyway, therefore make hopeless teachers — something else I learnt the hard way. Common words include the transpositions *alakeen* or *lakeen* for the Irish *cailín* (girl), *tobar* for *bóthar* (road), and the abbreviation *shades* or abbreviated transposition *shaydawg* for *garda siochana* ('guards' or police). *Alamok* is a version of the English 'milk', and *gammy feen* (dirty man) and *gammy beor* (dirty woman) are insulting terms for buffers.

Family names

Surnames are at once an indicator of family networks or kindred connectedness and of internal difference and disconnect, and on both counts serve to define residents as a community and as part of a wider community vis-à-vis non-Travellers.

O'Toole (1973) cited the 1963 Report of the Commission of Itinerancy to identify the sixteen most common Traveller surnames in Ireland as being in this order: McDonagh, Connors, Ward, O'Brien, Maughan, O'Dono(g)hue, Reilly, Mongan, Delaney, Stokes, Cawley, O'Driscoll, Joyce, Collins, Cash and McCarthy. Of these sixteen, thirteen were represented on the Westway at one time or another between 1984 and 1987. Other slightly less commonly found names according to the 1963 report included Coffey, Doherty, Doyle,

Quilligan and McInerney.

In Ireland I counted eighty Traveller surnames,[3] including some (not listed here) identified by Westway residents as 'English'. In Rathkeale, Limerick, the names Brennan, Casey, Gammel, Flynn, Williams, Quilligan and Culligan abound. Under the Westway, as well as names mentioned already, I personally encountered people with the following names: Browne, Coyle (or Kyle), Carty, Casey, Cash, Clarke, (O') Docherty, Dolan, Donovan, Doran, Doyle, Dunne, Faulkener, Gilheaney, Hanrahan, Hogan, Keenan, McCann, McInerney, Murphy, O'Donnel, O'Leary, Purcell, Quinn, Rooney, Ryan, Sherridan, Sweeney and Toohey. Other uncommon names listed by Travellers but which I never came across personally were Corcoran, Cunningham, Craig, Dooley, Goggins, Hegarty, Green, Griffin, Lynch, McGinley, Mahoney, Maloney, Moorehouse, O'Sullivan, Teeland and White. John Sampson (1891) identified the following association between names and provinces: in Ulster, Kane (*Sahon*), Barlow (*Nyakair*), Murray, Banks, Dunley, Watson, Latham and McAllister; in Leinster, McKay, Hynes, Norris, Banks, Reynolds, Connor, Kelly, Brennan, Keegan, Keenan and Costello; in Connaught, McDonnough (*Subol*), Joyce, Mulholland, Gallaher, Simons, Dyer, Cawley, Furie, and Creeney; and in Munster, Donovan, McDunnagh, Mangan, Carty, Cameford, Shinnehan and Rooney.

Christian names and nicknames

At baptism or christening a Traveller child is given two or three Christian (fore)names. In the case of the first-born, the name by which he or she will be formally known is that of the child's grandparent. A first son is named after his father's father, the second son is named after the mother's father, the first daughter after the father's (or mother's) mother, and the second daughter after the mother's (or father's) mother. Subsequent children take their first name from other close relatives, such as uncles or aunts. Where a grandparent's name has already been taken, a younger child may acquire the same name as their second or third baptismal name. Whatever the precise formula, and the above is largely consistent with Helleiner (2000), naming in practice reinforces a sense of 'family' across three, four, even five generations, and in theory connects kindred of an even larger span of generations. In reality, much depends here on the age and gender of the reckoner, since women seem to take more interest in genealogy than men do, and older women have lived and learnt those genealogies more thoroughly than younger women.

A woman in her sixties with grandchildren and memories of two sets of grandparents and their siblings, for instance, would count five generations in which her Christian name recurs. A male of the same age would be able to do the same for both his first name and surname. Even in three adjacent generations recurring Christian names, particularly when reinforced by a godparent/child tie, serve to remind those individuals and the rest of the extended family of their inter-connectedness. Nowadays parents sometimes choose second or third names from lists compiled in books bought from High Street

Kitty Connors

shops, and this name, though not Christian, may take precedence over the first name. 'Helen-Mary', named after the mother's sister and mother's mother, may be better known as 'Holly'. Other children may be addressed and referred to by their second or third Christian name.

Nicknames distinguish individuals in the same family network who share the same Christian name. On a site like the Westway they also help to distinguish people with the same Christian name and/or same surname who are *not* from the same network. In this way nicknames identify individuals as individuals and at the same time — for those 'in the know' — locate them inside a social network wider than kindred alone (see Williams 2003, 5).

Distinctive nicknames of affection given to little girls, like Fairchild and Goodchild, clearly identify them as 'Travellers' and mark them off from non-Traveller children. Perhaps for this reason such names are sometimes dropped when the child starts school, while more prosaic nicknames referring to gender or status in the family, such as Woman, Miss, Son and Brother, may endure and be used as terms of address and reference even by non-Travellers who regularly come into contact with those who bear them.

The basis for nicknames varies. Some are common Irish contractions, such as Tom, Mick, Jim, and Pat (for Patricia and Patrick). Some are diminutives, such as Peggy (Margaret), Nell or Nelly (for Helen, Ellen or Eleanor), Ned (Edward), and Nan or Nancy for Anne. Johnners, Johnno, Jimbo, Hughie and Miley are extensions. Some allude to physical appearance: Long Legs, Shorty, Pinky and Fox (colouring not character). Cliff and Elvis obviously take after celebrities. There are other varieties besides. Whatever their form, nicknames thus demarcate those 'in the know', distinguish individuals *as* individuals, help to differentiate between family networks and signal affection. Women on welfare sometimes used a number of different names to access extra payments, choosing from a combination of baptismal names, nicknames, maiden name and mother's maiden name.

Religion: pure in mind and body

Being Roman Catholics, the Westway Irish saw themselves as 'different' from their Romany neighbours and, at the same time, as members of a global faith-community. Between these two reference points, parents with children attending local Catholic schools had a neighbourhood-based sense of religious 'belonging', especially those with children at St Francis of Assisi Primary. As well as having something in common with other mothers in the neighbourhood, the school also drew parents into parish activities, including, in one case, a parish pilgrimage to Lourdes.

Irish Traveller religiosity has barely been studied and there are inconsistencies and differences of interpretation in what has been written. One reason for this is that outside observers have tended to look at public forms of collective religious activity at the expense of private, personal, and domestic forms. Yet apart from funerals, which provide opportunities for Travellers to show their unity by gathering in large numbers (which topic I deliberately excluded from an earlier essay on private and personal religiosity (Griffin 2002a)), only Sunday Mass provides comparable opportunity for collective expression and even this depends on local circumstances. All other Church rites (including baptism, confirmation, and matrimony) are essentially family-orientated. Since I published that essay Patrick Williams has noted that, when it comes to French Gypsies, 'Manus rites are not public ... These gestures are not collective either. During funerals, which are the only occasions when there are gatherings, nothing happens except that Manus show, both to themselves and the Gadzos, that they are assembled. Likewise, acts of homage to the graves are aimed at ensuring the image of the united group. Each individual does perform these rites but without broadcasting it ... Manus rites allow individual initiative ...' (Williams 2003, 25). For observers to literally not 'see' these private rites is both surprising and not surprising for on the one hand the symbols of private ritual (like holy statues and pictures) are plain for all to see, but on the other the acts of human devotion that go with them over and above the act of display, are not.

One usually only need enter an Irish Traveller's caravan to see a plethora of Catholic symbols and in some cases the symbols or icons are in evidence outside as well, by way of shrines comprising statues of the Virgin Mary (see Plate). Outdoor shrines may be more common than they were when Sharon Gmelch (1975) did her fieldwork but even her photographs provide evidence of a deep religious sensibility. Aside from the passage of time, the real explanation for differences of interpretation or disinterest in Traveller religion come down to tendencies on the part of past writers to have taken Irish Catholicism, with its emphasis on the Mass, for granted and to have then gone on to draw one of three conclusions: that by their absence from Mass (and possibly other sacramental rites) Travellers were *not* religious; that by their individual behaviour at Mass and other rites (including funerals) they were demonstrably less 'religious' than 'superstitious', 'magical', or simply lacking 'real faith'; or that though religious in many cases, Travellers were for this very reason insufficiently 'different' from other Irish people to warrant special study.

Sampson (1891), Synge (1992) and Barnes (1975) thought that Travellers were disinterested in religion. Gmelch (1977) found that they were not concerned with ritual. Bettina Barnes said they were 'action-seeking', thereby seeming to imply that they were not so much 'religious' as 'magical' — orientated more towards pragmatics than 'the actual import attached to religious content' (Barnes 1975, 247). Whether she still holds that view is another matter. The point is that, without proper examination, it is impossible to know what meaning Travellers derive from and bring to Church rites, let alone to individual or family ones like prayer, the rosary, fasting, abstinence, devotional acts, and everyday behaviour.

Although Catholicism was an ethnic boundary marker, Travellers and Gypsies mixed easily. Some Irish had married Gypsies and some of these Romanies had adopted Catholic religious symbols. Indeed, this and the nomenclature 'Westway Travellers' Site' (as opposed to 'Latimer Road Gypsy Site') by which it was known by the early 1980s, was proof of integration. Since then things have changed. The English and Welsh families have gone and their places have been

Westway shrine
Former Westway residents on the Ealing site

taken by more Irish. Moreover, the Catholic Church in England and Wales, as in Ireland, has experienced a massive decline in churchgoing as a result of revelations of sexual crimes by clergy going back several decades. On the other hand, attachment to the Church at the Westway has probably been bolstered by a change of management in the pre-school. No longer run by the Save the Children Fund, the school is now financed and managed by the Catholic Children's Society (Westminster), which also runs adult education programmes on site (Keenan 2005). Whether overall cohesion on site has also improved as a consequence is something else outside the scope of this book. In some ways it would be surprising if it had, for tension and conflict is a universal fact of small communities, especially small egalitarian ones, with or without formal leaders.

Purity and pollution

Much has been written about ritual purity and pollution among the Roma (Sutherland 1975; Miller 1975; Okely 1983). Little or nothing has been said about them in the Irish Traveller community, possibly because, as far as we know, Irish nomads have no ancestral ties with India. Nevertheless, Westway Irish attitudes, beliefs and practices regarding the body went beyond practical concerns with physical hygiene and instead spoke metaphorically of social boundaries, concerns about the 'inside' and 'outside', and the danger of foreign bodies to 'the system'. Over time, and prompted finally by the literature on Roma concerns with ritual purity and pollution, I discerned a pervasive preoccupation with the separation of social categories. Directly and indirectly, Travellers talked a great deal about cleanliness and dirt in ways that often appeared discrepant with behaviour, indicating a high tolerance threshold for 'dirt' of their own making.

Traveller fixations with inner purity may come as a surprise — and provide little consolation — to the many settled people who rebuke Travellers for leaving a mess for others to clean up. It will also surprise those villagers in Kerry who, according Nancy Scheper-Hughes who studied them, 'are equally guarded both about what they take into the body (as in sex and food) and about being "taken in" (as with "codding", flattery, or blarney)' (2001, 212). I use the word 'surprise' here because this tendency among villagers to be wary of what (in two senses) they personally 'take in', suggests that Travellers or 'itinerant tinker-beggars' whose occupations villagers regard as 'polluted' (121), and rank last in terms of prestige compared with twenty other occupations, are in fact no less obsessive than themselves when it comes to guarding the body from impurity. For this reason too, people like myself must be cautious about interpreting these Traveller taboos as indicative of a cultural 'likeness' with Gypsies (which indeed they are), which somehow underwrite Traveller cultural 'differences' from settled people and thus 'prove' their claim to a unique identity. 'Dirt' is 'what is out of place' (Douglas 1978, 50) and for Travellers whose work involves handling settled people's 'dirt' (their old cars, junk and building rubble), dumping dirt or fly tipping is a cheap waste-management solution, as cheap and easy as driving away from one's own domestic waste. Viewed from this angle physical pollution is not a cut-and-dried moral issue. On the other hand, dirtying other peoples' spaces with intentional disregard or malice may well be a more black and white matter, a bold statement about one's attitude towards the Other, and a way of handling stigma. Dirt dumped on Others is here a way of getting even with them for them dumping (metaphorically or literally) on you. Each party 'dishes dirt' on the other and, short of expelling or eradicating the 'dirt' (as in 'ethnic cleansing'), each curses the other and ignores the cursing instead of listening and parleying.

When it comes to laundering let us think of clothes as skins: culture's supplement to nature. Westway Travellers know four rules: garments worn above the waist must be separated from those worn below; men's clothes must be separated from women's; children's clothes must be separated from adults'; and outer or over garments must not be mixed with inner garments or underclothes. Similar rules of separation apply to cutlery and crockery, pots and pans, and teacloths and domestic fabrics. Each category is kept apart when washing by the use of separate basins, bowls or buckets.

The first rule given above concerns the waste/waist line. That worn above the waist is 'clean', that worn below is 'dirty', and never the two shall mix. The border is maintained. The second rule concerns gendered pollution. In Ireland the Church's 150-year obsession with 'grave dangers' of the body and sexual sin (including contraception) are reflected not only in a celibate male clerical hierarchy, but also in a gendered division of labour throughout society (Scheper-Hughes 2001, 205–21), which only began to be challenged some thirty years ago. (In the 1990s charges of paedophilia and other sexual crimes brought against clergy pointed to institutional as well as individual failings and led to a massive erosion of clerical authority and a subsequent significant decline in Sunday congregations.) In the late 1970s a female journalist put it so: 'The old and gritty messages of Irish Catholicism [are] that the whole body business is messy, dirty and sinful' (Sweetman 1979, 17, cited in Griffin 2002b, 121–2). It is therefore not surprising that the first rule, about not mixing clothes from either side of the waistline, is reinforced by the second rule's emphasis on the gendered separation of skins.

As with most mammals, the sexual and reproductive organs of humans lie close to the excretory organs. For this reason humans have constructed taboos about the polluting power of semen, faeces, urine and menstrual blood. Whether the Irish Traveller separation of adult clothes by gender is due to fears like this I am not entirely sure, simply because it is not the easiest subject for a man to investigate. A few women I spoke with on the subject denied that Travellers believed in the inherent danger of menstrual blood, but I am not convinced. For what it is worth, I suspect that at issue here is a gendered division that presumes '*his* organs and emissions [are] as potentially ritually polluting as hers' (Griffin 2002b, 122); semen and menstrual blood both long being deemed dangerous in Ireland.

The third rule concerns innocence and stain. Every Traveller child ideally has its own towel and cake of soap, which are not to be used by adults. The separation of children's clothes from adults' at laundry time is an extension of attitudes regarding children themselves. Remember that children treat adults 'outside' the trailer and the family as equals, while deferring 'inside' to parents, especially to the father and older siblings. Remember, too, that childhood is a short-lived period of innocence and that adulthood comes with early marriage and the arrival of a baby. Inside the trailer, inside the family with older siblings, and in the company of animals like horses and dogs, the young quickly acquire dangerous knowledge of sex and reproduction, and yet the moral imperative to see innocent 'childer' kept pure remains. Faced with this dilemma, parents try to protect their children from as much adult danger originating 'outside' the family, site, and Traveller community at large as they can, knowing that they cannot shield them from the adult dirt and dangers arising 'inside'. Having mothers, who are the principal guardians of purity, separate adults and children's clothes (that at surface level separate the deep intrinsic purity of children from the inherent stain and danger of adults) over-compensates for the inability to separate children from 'dirt' arising within the family, and in the only possible way.

The fourth rule concerns the 'inside' and 'outside': the border between Self and Other. 'Inner' or undergarments (including those worn below the waist) are 'dirtier' in more ways than one than 'outer' or overgarments, including those soiled by 'honest' dirty work. Nature's wastes belong 'outside' the body. Failure to eject them causes the body to sicken and fail. Foreign bodies incapacitate. The body is thus the perfect 'natural symbol' for people's conception of the social system, which in this case is the nuclear and extended family. Seepage of semen, menstrual blood, urine, faeces, mucus and spittle still inside the body (and its protective 'skin' of clothes) not only threatens one's Self, but is thought to sometimes be able to harm others in the course of social interaction. Manifest in the fourth rule, therefore, is a reinforcement of that most fundamental separation of all social categories, the separation of ('clean') insiders from ('dirty') outsiders essential to maintaining the social system's integrity. The same dislike of mixing 'clean' (Self) and 'unclean' (Other) categories was seen in some men's disdain for wearing underpants and their refusal to use sheets and blankets used by other members of the family (preferring instead to use duvets or eiderdowns with removable covers, personally identifiable, and frequently and easily washed). This last bit of information, incidentally, was given to me by a woman, and seems to support the idea of a peculiarly male fear of ritual female pollution.

Pristine interior. The small blue notice pasted on the window for Roma evangelists reads: 'We are Catholics and we aren't going to change our religion. Please do not insist. Our fathers were Catholics and we will always be Catholics. May Our Lady of the Immaculate Conception Pray for you always, Thank you.'

In summary, by attending to categories and boundaries that symbolise their social organisation these nomads reproduce a sense of separate community and identity in a world marked by their own mobility and social proximity to those who threaten to assimilate them. In circumstances of constant flux and changing social boundaries, the body and its associated cleaning practices provide a ritual way of dealing with the contradiction between *ideals* and practical *realities*. As a natural symbol, or metaphor, the body and its treatment speak of family and community: 'ever changing in its structure, its essential identity remains constant' (Griffin 2002b, 126–7). As all about them changes, including their own culture and bodies, their community and identity remain constant.

Conflict

Conflict can *make* community and *break* community. It can be an expression of 'community' every bit as much 'harmony' can. It can arise out of a sense of 'likeness' and 'alikeness' as much as it can arise out of a sense of 'strangeness' or 'strangerness', and nowhere more so than in small-scale egalitarian societies. Faction-fights and sport are ritual forms of conflict expressive of 'community'. Joseph Berland's paper 'We travel together and fight a lot' (Berland n.d.) explored this phenomenon among nomadic Gypsies in Pakistan. Max Gluckman's (1966) essay on the cohesive function of the fear of feuding in Africa did the same and, given Irish Travellers' fear of conflict and feuding under the Westway, it is an apt reminder of the cohesive role paradoxically played by conflict in making the site a community.

Tom McCarthy

Travellers admire fighters even if they are not fighters themselves. Boxing was the only organised sport where young Travellers competed against non-Travellers outside the site, at places such as the Harrow Club. One or two men had boxed as amateurs or semi-professionals. Other Travellers in Ireland and England have made reputations as championship contenders for lucrative titles such as 'King of the Gypsies', fierce and illegal contests where large sums of money change hands in side-bets. The only fight I saw involved two young Irish Travellers who decided to settle an argument over I know not what. The boxers drew a crowd, a man stepped in to referee, and the boys fought clean, bare-fisted and bare-chested. After ten minutes of harmless swings and feints, a lot of circling and a few good strikes, the fight was over. Anti-climactic but honour-saving.

Leaving aside domestic disputes, which were always considered private matters, the most serious conflicts *either* involved close kindred, such as cousins, who might let their problems simmer before allowing them to erupt, leading to revenge-motivated counter-attacks, *or* they occurred between unrelated families, resulting in the weaker party leaving the site permanently. Firebombs, guns and knives had all been used at various times in feuds and vengeance attacks. Not that violent conflict was endemic. What was endemic was the *fear* of violence. To be sure, in the final analysis it was a *fear* of force that held the site together as a community, for in both the above cases (conflict within the kindred, and between non-kindred) conflict had little effect on the rest of the site other than the fact that by bearing silent witness families were bound together by their witnessing and silence. A third type of conflict that bound families as a community was Housing's legal eviction of squatters. On such occasions individuals and families joined as one to impede the work of bailiffs and police. Even then the solidarity was largely ritual: a 'performance' of public sentiment normally missing.

Squatters were a cause of conflict and resentment, and so were evictions — a solution to squatters. As 'strangers', squatters tested the patience of *bona fide* licensees; as 'friends', they tested the patience of their relatives. As warden I was obliged to beat a narrow path between all parties concerned, a path made trickier when the squatters in question claimed to have a sick family member and were supported in this by the site's social worker or members of the Support Group. Fortunately, few evictions were needed. Families issued with court orders usually left before eviction day arrived, and evictions that were conducted never presented me with lasting tensions. On the contrary, after the event Travellers generally acknowledged the necessity of the eviction, with some thanking me for seeing the job done.

A further source of conflict between unrelated families arose from the secret 'selling' of pitches. This occurred when a family leaving permanently 'sold' its pitch to one already on the site who wanted a better pitch or one closer to relatives; in this way extended families aimed to cluster together. If they could not be next to each other they would try for pitches opposite each other, even if it took time to pull off. The resentment came from those who missed out on the opportunity to buy or sell themselves and saw others profit illegally. Actual changeovers took place at night or on public holidays, in the same kind of way that squatters used to suddenly set up shantytowns in Latin America. By the time I had discovered what had happened the situation was practically irreversible since changeovers invariably involved not two players from two pitches but three or four from as many pitches. As in draughts one move had led immediately to another binding players retrospectively in a conspiracy of moves to which I had been oblivious. As my management skills then came under scrutiny, the entire site was momentarily further united in the spectacle.

The other traders

Along the east side of Latimer Road, close to *The Latimer Arms* and a few yards from Stable Way, a number of terraced houses sported lucky horseshoes, horse-head doorknockers, and front-window displays of horse figurines; all minor testaments to the past importance of this animal locally. Directly opposite, on the west side, before they were pulled down to make room for the motorway and some small factories that now stand in this part of the street, there used to be several houses belonging to Gypsy families who were descendants of the first nineteenth-century visitors.

MADAME OLGA
PALM, CRYSTAL BALL READINGS

THIS GIFTED LADY HAS GOD-GIVEN POWER TO CURE ALL OF YOUR TROUBLES. MAYBE YOU ARE ILL OR UNHAPPY, DOES BAD LUCK SEEM TO FOLLOW YOU WHEREVER YOU GO. DO YOU HAVE MARRIAGE PROBLEMS, BUSINESS PROBLEMS,IF YOUR LOVED ONES ARE NOT TRUE TO YOU, IF YOU HAVE BEEN CHEATED OUT OF LIFE – THEN LET HER LIFT YOU OUT OF SORROW – BRING BACK YOUR HEALTH AND HAPPINESS, REMOVE YOUR EVIL AND PUT YOU ON THE ROAD TO SUCCESS AND RESUME YOUR FAITH IN HUMANITY.

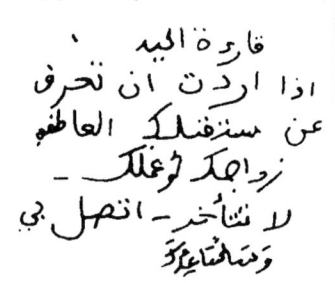

قارءة اليد
اذا اردت ان تعرف
عن مستقبلك العاطفي
زواجك أو عملك –
لا تتأخر – اتصل بي
ومشكلاتك

Handbill (Local address and telephone number here removed). The Arabic says, 'Palm reader. If you want to know about your future: passions, marriage or your work. Don't wait, call me'

A 1980s telephone book covering w10, w11 and w12 showed up no less than fifty surnames in and around Latimer Road that could have belonged to Romanies. So, after checking in Housing records to see if any of the addresses were council properties, I visited some of them to see what observation might tell. Together the telephone directory, direct observation, and Housing records revealed two Hearnes, twelve Lovells, four Boswells, two Loveridges, eighteen Chapmans (one in the motor trade), one Pharoah, and eight Lees — including one with a yard where I found a van laden with scrap iron and a 'London trolley' adorned with the words 'Lees' Seafood' painted on the side, a small reminder that a hundred years earlier C.G. Leland reported Romanies in Hastings selling fried fish way before *gorgios* took over the trade. I also found Lees in a street off Goldhawk Road, near Brackenbury Road, Shepherds Bush, where in the 1990s Irish Travellers from the Westway Site lived in temporary council accommodation. And close by, above a shop in Askew Road, off Goldhawk Road, a 'Madame Olga' told fortunes by appointment according to a neat handbill written partly in Arabic. Madame O was probably one of a Kalderash network that uses names like Morgan, Sterio and Williams, and has links stretching from Balham, south London, to Mexico, the USA, Canada and New South Wales in Australia. Some of the network at times occupied a house in a road off Oxford Gardens, off Latimer Road, which would explain a visit paid by so-called 'Canadian Gypsies' to the Westway Site in the early 1980s.

Mention has already been made in Chapter 9 of a family of fifteen Kalderash from Strasbourg who set up camp opposite Little Scrubs at the junction of North Pole Road and Scrubs Lane, at the northern end of Latimer Road, so one of their women could get hospital treatment at Du Cane Road. The group claimed to come originally from Spain and made their living cleaning and mending big cooking pots in hospitals. They said that they were Churara, not Gitanos, and as if to prove the point brought out a knife which they

Romany flower seller in Nascot Street, off Scrubs Lane, 1986

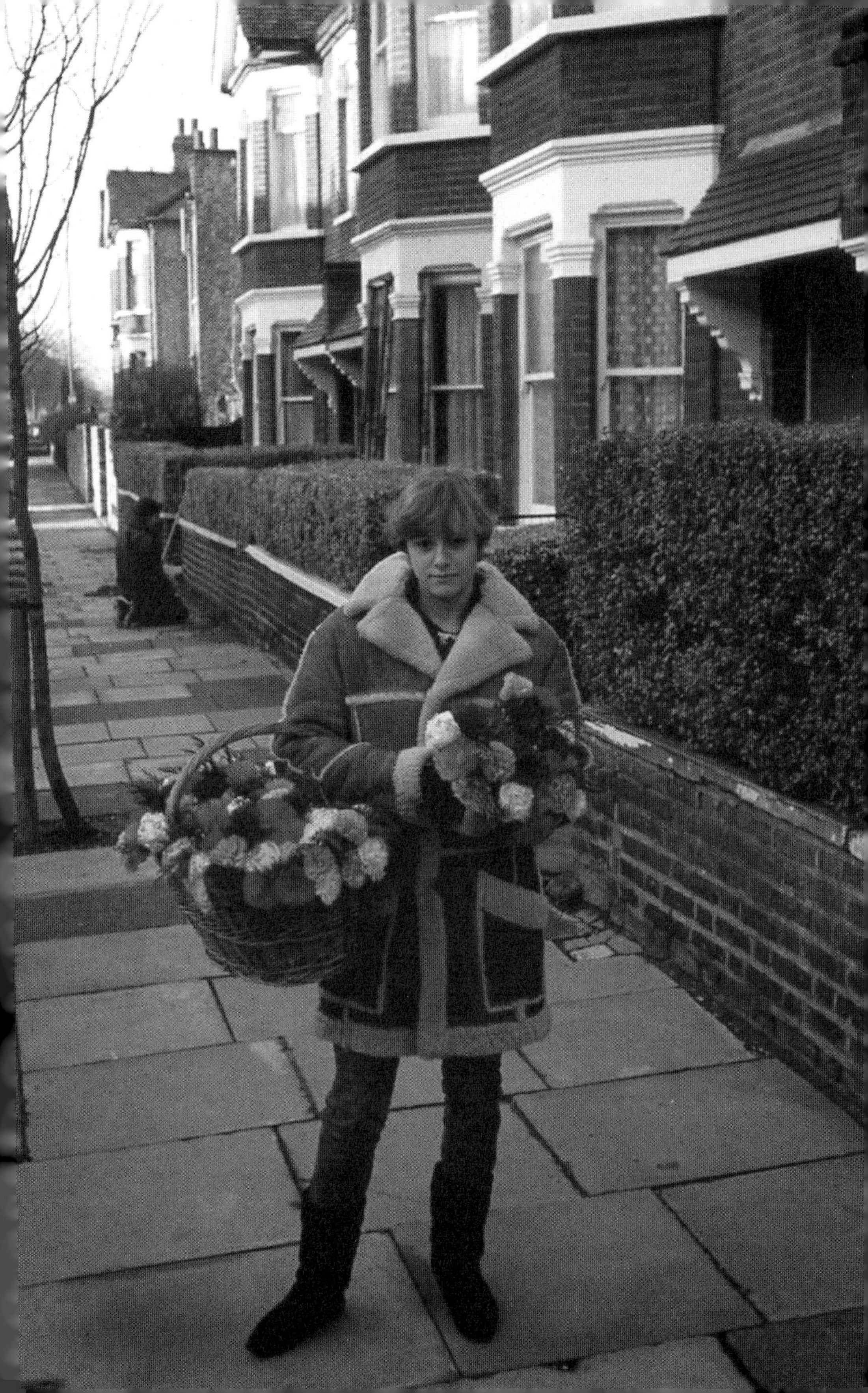

said was their *vitsa* icon, which they would not hesitate to use on any of the rough travellers they had already run into if they gave them trouble. It seemed apparent from their descriptions of these travellers as not 'real Gypsies', more like Sinti and *'vanniers'*, that they were talking about Irish Travellers. Nothing about England pleased them, which in most regards was 'twenty years behind France'. The food was awful, pubs filthy, and English Gypsies with their non-existent Romani little better than the Irish *'vanniers'*. It was hard to convince them otherwise, looking at their two new Mercedes Benzes and fine trailers. To make matters worse, they were running short of money. Would I buy a rug off them for £700? No, but I would buy them Camembert and goat's cheese from the purveyor in the market opposite the Met Underground station in Hammersmith Broadway where old Mrs Penfold, formerly of Latimer Road, used to sell flowers. I could also find wine and decent French bread. By the following day the family's luck had changed. The previous evening they had met up with a Romani-speaking 'gitane' in Balham, named Riccardo, who had kindly lent them money. Riccardo, I found out years later, is a name used by some of the globetrotting fortune-telling Kalderash. After three weeks, when the French left for home, Irish Travellers took over their spot.

In December 1986 in Nascot Street, a minute or two away from where the French had camped, three Romany women from West Drayton, a girl, her mother and grandmother sold artificial flowers door to door, and said they often ran into Gypsies living locally in houses. Nascot Street lay just behind the *Pavillion* pub, which is one of many in the district, some of which cater in a desultory way for Irish tastes — music, as well as food and drink. *The Plough* at Kensal Green, on the Harrow Road (which Gladstone (1969, 118) once described as 'a thoroughfare as drab as it was unending', (a description still accurate in the 1980s), was not particularly 'Irish', but a van often parked outside it with 'Lucky Lady', a horseshoe and 'Staffordshire Belt' painted on it hinted at Gypsy connections. So did a similar van always parked outside the flats opposite the Harrow Club in Freston Road, where English, Afro-Caribbean English, and

English–Irish youth mixed (Burnett 1983, 73, 77), along with young Irish Travellers.

In early 1986, at the Shepherds Bush end of Freston (old Latimer) Road, a Traveller couple named Keenan stopped in a caravan near the Edward Woods Estate. A few hundred yards away, under the Westway, lived Keenans from County Ofally.[4] The young pair eventually secured housing trust accommodation in Norland Square, while another homeless couple were placed in 'emergency housing' in Stebbing House, on the Edward Woods Estate.

Part of the new sports facilities under the M40/M41 interchange, 1994

In 1986 and 1987 New or New Age Travellers (NATS) camped in vehicles on wasteland between Evesham Road, to the west side of Freston Road, and the West Cross Route. One was a Romany man of about thirty, named Lee, who had been raised in a house on the south coast. Others were former members of a group of anarchist eco-warriors called the Mutoid Waste Disposal Company (MWDC), which was into recycling old vehicle parts as giant sculptures. Other former MWDC members lived in a motley collection of ingeniously refitted vehicles in Galena Road, off King Street, central Hammersmith. In January 1991, a few yards up from Latimer Road tube station, near Mike Taylor's City Mission under the flyover, six New Age trailers, an old army lorry, a bus, a transit van and nine other vehicles parked up in Pamber Street near *The Latimer Arms*. Marty Ward said some of the NAT's children told his children they were not 'real Travellers' because they did not travel. Marty was considerably amused. Since that time this area, immediately beside the flyover, has been redeveloped. Shabby streets going nowhere have been transformed, along with the space beneath the interchange, into state-of-the-art indoor and outdoor sports facilities and an enlarged horse ring for the Stable Way totters and riders, who train there oblivious both to traffic above and the fact that it was here thirty years ago that Marty and other pioneers joined Roy Wells' 'rolling campaign' and eventually paved the way for the Westway Site.

New (or New Age) Travellers camped between Evesham Street and the M41, 1986

'Community' beyond the Westway

'Community' or a sense of 'belonging' does not necessarily entail a sharing of physical space (Clifford 1992; Olwig and Hastrup 1997). 'Community' entails the mutual awareness of a sense of belonging with others, although some 'community' is virtual, some 'imagined', and sometimes the latter entails images 'remembered'. Moreover, what is mentally 're-created' is occasionally physically re-constructed — as in the case of 'Little Italies', 'Little Irelands', and the State of Israel.

Awareness of 'belonging' to one community affects one's awareness of belonging in others, and awareness of multiple 'belonging' is always conditional. Emic expressions of 'us' and 'them' and how that awareness gets translated into action are what anthropologists incorporate into their own etic perspectives. In the remaining pages I therefore want to examine Westway Travellers' sense of 'community' over and beyond the site and, in the process, briefly revisit my role as warden, as it is the conditioning factor of my claim to 'know' Travellers, whose specific 'truth intention' (Simmel 1906) is to *not* disclose.

Wary and aware
Awareness of 'difference' presupposes an awareness of likeness. And the awareness of exclusion presumes the awareness of inclusion, or to put it another way, what it means to communicate meaningfully with other people using shared symbols. Symbolic interaction provides the basis for culture and community and is nowhere better observed than in the sort of small face-to-face community that Redfield (1960) called 'the little community'. For example, the village, tribe or nomadic Lapp band whose way of life, according to Ernst Manker, 'pulsated regularly with the seasons, driving the blood — the people — out toward the periphery in the spring and back again to the heart in winter' (cited in Redfield 1960, 9). A description that would equally apply to Irish Travellers, were it not for regulations making it unlawful to park caravans except where local authorities determine. Still, nomadism has far from ceased and, on the Westway and other

sites, awareness of what it means to live in a 'little community' deeply influences the Travellers' view of 'community' or lack thereof beyond these sites. Martin Ward once said, 'On a site you've got your own community. In a flat or house you lose all touch with the Travelling People. Living on a site you have got twenty Traveller families around you'. He was not the only one to say so. This from a man with thirty years' experience of conflict originating 'inside' the site, as well as more 'outside'.

Travellers say Travellers who settle in houses risk becoming confused, disoriented and 'lonesome'. And for those who go one step further by taking up working permanently for Others, they say the risk is even greater, though obviously not all those who have done so agree. Moving out of the Travelling community has its own advantages. According to Pixley, a sociologist, 'a nexus between pay and work is a less decisive political and social issue than the nexus between citizenship and paid work. That is, the basic conditions for political participation in modern societies are strongly linked to *mainstream* employment' (Pixley 1993, 199). Because Westway Travellers, like most nomadic Gypsies, are not 'strongly linked to mainstream employment' they are conscious of not being real 'citizens' and equally aware of belonging primarily to groups and kindred networks of their own making, which, like Mauss (1979), we cannot precisely call 'tribe' or clans, but which are thought of as forming a national community of 'Travellers' or 'Gypsies'.

The philosopher Polanyi (1974) talks of two kinds of awareness: direct or primary, and subsidiary or secondary. 'Primary awareness' involves what he calls *focal attention*; secondary awareness stems from *peripheral attention*. Both as 'anthropologist' and 'warden' my awareness of what was going on in the two districts I studied was direct and focal, especially under the Westway. After a short honeymoon period, however, with the exception of a handful of individuals who in the first few months may have suspected me of being an ex-policeman or serviceman with focal attention, most site residents throughout 1984 considered my awareness peripheral and my knowledge insubstantial, a situation even the friendliest of them encouraged by holding me at a distance. That situation changed after I returned from teaching in January 1986. A growing number of people now came to know me as a 'scholar' and became more 'primarily' aware of me than before (and focally attentive) and less wary of me than previously. This allowed a mutual 'truth knowledge' to emerge, while simultaneously avoiding giving other people the impression that they were becoming over-familiar with the 'warden'. The big exception to this growing candour was Marty Ward, with whom I fell out in 1986, and with whom relations were not repaired until 1987.

Country as 'community'
Defined as a shared place, location, terrain or locality, 'country' is a word Travellers sometimes use to talk of different areas of England; however, it is not essential to Traveller 'community' in the same way that it is in one of its manifestations for settled people, 'country people', and citizens. It *is* important, however, as memory, in the way that it also is for immigrants, refugees and displaced people. In short, locality or 'country' is important to those aware that others see them as strangers, as people out of place.

To be a stranger is to perpetually face others' questions: 'Who are you?' 'Where are you from?' and 'Where exactly *is* your country?' Personal identity and country are presumed to be inextricably tied up. 'We' are 'our' country, 'You' are 'yours' — wherever that might be — or at least 'our' idea of it. And though migration and multiculturalism result in a mixing-up of lands and identities, and make for reconfigurations of community, there remains a sense of native 'being' or 'belonging' to the land, and land itself 'being' native. Australian Aborigines and Fijians constantly say this, but they are not alone. The Irish folk-singer Dolores Keane captures the same idea in a line of a song entitled 'Solid Ground': 'It's the land that owns the people, you cannot own the land, the land owns you'.

To travel with an open mind is to risk reconfiguring one's Self and one's world. Patrick Williams, in his book on Manus Gypsies, expresses the idea succinctly when he says, 'We can often achieve a better sense of a reality we might have pondered for years when we come to peruse new horizons' (Williams 2003, 1). Though hardly a new idea it is still an important one. For the anthropologist 'perusing new horizons' is at the heart of his or her research methodology, just as it is central to what it means to be a Traveller. At the start of this book I went out of my way to say how perusing new horizons in Ireland at the age of ten and thereafter travelling each day to school in Ealing, via Hammersmith, initiated me into the lifelong quest to 'achieve a better sense of reality'. The question I now ask, therefore, is what does the perusal of new horizons mean for 'community' beyond the 'blood' of family for Irish Travelling People who do *not* own land or fixed property and are *not* tied to any particular locality?

One hears it said that Irish Travellers traditionally followed 'family' routes. Nevertheless, there are some long-distance Travellers who have visited almost every corner of Ireland and done so many times over. Yet even these families identify with particular country, the country in which they were born and the country where they bury their dead. Here, memory and talk of place reinvigorate identity, call Travellers back, and serve to create for them 'community' beyond the here-and-now, and beyond the Westway. Relocation is the essence of commercial nomadism and so is enforced dislocation. Relocation takes many forms, but as 'return to country' it is a return to community. Enforced dislocation of the kind that comes from being ordered to 'move on' involves awareness of meaningful location, of 'locality', where land and Self entwine. One very important reason certain Westway Travellers revisited country in Ireland was to bury kin, attend graves, and conduct memorial rites around the eve of All Souls Day, 31 October, the last day of summer. The dead embed nomadic roots and lend scattered kindred a sense of community beyond the horizon. Travellers with dead buried in west London, on the other hand, feel more attached to the area.

History as 'community'
History is a matter of memory, recall, or the memorialisation of other people's memories. As an Australian historian recently pointed

out, archives are but a form of memory awaiting the professional historian's fabrication of 'collective memory'.[5] On the Westway, beyond the immediacy of family and the memorialisation of the dead on tomb headstones, Travellers had little or no knowledge of their collective history. Academics have their own theories about the origins of Travellers as a distinct ethnic group (Gmelch and Gmelch 1974; Acton 1974; Ní Shúinéar 1994), and in Chapter 2 I presented my own. Some argue that Tinkers or Travellers can be traced back over millennia, others say to the twelfth century (see Murphy and McDonagh 2000), some to the days of Elizabeth I and Cromwell, and none exclude additions made at the time of the Famine and land clearances. What is clear is that, like any other 'nation', what Travellers represent today as a culture and community has no single point of origin. It is the result of long-term evolution and will continue to evolve.

Most Westway adults I talked with on the subject thought that their ancestors were probably peasant farmers who came onto the road during the Famine years. A few, with names like McCarthy and O'Brien, toyed with the idea of being descendents of the Irish kings of that name, 'knights of the road' vanquished by the English (see Woodham-Smith 1991, 26), an idea that has been around some time. O'Toole (1973), Barnes (1975), and Weidel and O'Fearadhaigh (1978) all reported Travellers using the self-description 'knights of the road'. By contrast, Martin Ward thought his ancestors could have been indigenous smiths from far earlier times, and the notion is not implausible. It is possible that some families, whether they realise it or not, *are* the biological descendents of Celtic itinerants and nomads of the early Christian or even pre-Christian era. It is even possible that some of them have unbroken inter-generational links with them across the centuries by way of an evolving discrete culture. The surname Ward, for example, is common in County Galway, where Martin Ward's ancestors come from, and is an Anglicisation of *Mac an Bháird*, meaning son of the poet or bard (Grenham 1993), an itinerant occupation once closely associated with precious-metal working.

Academics have not been able to establish with certainty the origins of the first Irish Travellers or Tinkers, but others broadly agree on the origins of the master metalworkers and nomadic warriors we know now as 'Celts' who emerged as an identifiable but variegated group in central Europe around 800 BC. Their finest metalwork — classified as 'Hallstat' — flourished on the Continent between 800 and 600 BC and from there made its way to Ireland, notably to Ulster, though by which route and whether carried by immigrants or traders is still open to question (Harbison 1994), as is the more fundamental question about whether Ireland was identifiably 'Celtic' at all before the late Iron Age. The earliest identifiable 'Irish Celts', the Gaels, surfaced in the first millennium, probably well after 500 BC (Roberts 1995), having possibly arrived from Spain (Markale 1993). In their new country the Gaels were the catalyst for what Hawkes (1961), cited by Harbison (1994, 171), calls the country's 'cumulative Celticity', out of which we can say 'a cumulative Irish Traveller ethnicity' would in time evolve. Among La Téne-style[6] artefacts left behind by Iron Age Celts at places like Attymon, in Galway, were numerous swords, bronze spear-butts, horse-bits and remnants of harness (Harbison 1994, 161), for in Ireland as on the Continent the Celts held the horse in the highest esteem (Harbison 1994, 164–5) and, judging from their brilliant bloodstock and racing industries, still do.

John Doyle

In the end, like the scholars themselves, Travellers are woefully short on historic detail. They see themselves as 'different' from other Irish people and presume they are also 'different' from Gypsies. Yet because Traveller identity at the family and kindred level is tied to 'country' as well as to nomadism and a 'way of life', they are also aware of belonging in a qualified way with other 'Irish' as citizens, and with those other 'Travellers' they call the Gypsies.

Stigma as 'community'

It should now be clear that, despite its singular location and residents' deep concern with borders, the Westway Site is not a 'closed' community. Rather, it is part of the outside community and this is due largely to modern technologies and media. Yet *because* and not just *despite* this, residents are also strongly attached to notions of the family and kindred, extensive social networks, and to maintaining the boundary between themselves collectively and non-Travellers. Moreover, this attitude is bolstered by their awareness of stigma.

The Traveller's principal field of social interaction with outsiders is in the market, where trading rules prevail. Here the Traveller is the hunter and collector and settled people are 'game'.[7] Like Hermes and Autolycus, the Traveller conducts his business quietly and usually under cover, save when it comes to hard bargaining or defending his position. Williams says the Manus, his dog, and the hedgehog 'understand each other without the need for speech — and that is the Manus ideal' (Williams 2003, 30). As hunters, the Manus consider hedgehogs 'clean' and good to eat, as well as stealthy foragers living around the margins (in this case fields and hedgerows) like Manus themselves. All trade involves *stealth*, drama, magic and a touch of deception or enchantment. The original Greek word for theatre alludes to the work of the gods. Traders, especially self-employed street-traders, play to the balcony more than most. With props and performance they turn street markets into theatre, and the Irish, with their oracy and history of fairs and markets, know the art of acting/trading better than most. Henry Mayhew found a lot of London's costermongers were Irish, and Westway Travellers often said they found it easier dealing with English people than with the Irish at home or market-savvy 'Pakis' in the suburbs who both know the art and tricks of trading.

In *The Winter's Tale* (Act II), the pedlar Autolycus fools the Clown — whose occupation is fooling — into thinking he has been robbed by footpads. A 'wolf' in clothing, this dealer's 'traffic is sheets', his 'revenue the silly-cheat', and his father 'a snapper up of unconsidered trifles'. By stealth he picks the Clown's pocket and later deludes him into thinking he is a courtier (IV.III). When the Clown responds meekly by saying 'We are but plain fellows', Autolycus pounces, using all his insider knowledge and awareness of trade stigma. 'A lie; you are rough and hairy. Let me have no lying; it becomes none but tradesmen, and they often give us soldiers the lie: but we pay them for it with stamped coin, not stabbing steel; therefore they do not give us the lie.'

Traveller and Gypsy traders or general dealers know the stigma attached to their ethnic identity, as well as sometimes to their work. For these reasons (unless ethnicity is deemed a positive enhancement — as in the case of fortune-telling) they hope their ethnicity passes unnoticed so it does not spoil their chances as traders. Indeed many second- and third-generation Irish Travellers, and some of the longer domiciled first generation, now consider themselves more 'English' or 'British' than 'Irish',[8] even though their dialects betray an enclosed community and hint at being 'in' but not 'of' the wider community, culturally insulated in the same sort of way that some sociologists have come to regard certain kinds of tourist (see Jacobsen 2003).

At-one-two-people

Travellers and Gypsies are aware of the complex, layered, interwoven, nature of community and cultural identity and the need of insiders to express it and record it for posterity. 'Gypsies and Travellers are all the one race,' a Doyle from Ofally said to me. 'Who is a Romany today, anyway'? asked the woman of mixed Welsh, English, and Scottish Traveller ancestry, related by marriage to Irish Travellers, who normally described herself as 'Romany'. 'A Gypsy, a Tinker, and proud of it, we're proud of who we are, but hide our identity and haven't a voice,' said an O'Driscoll from Cork. 'Yes, it's a good life,' said Marty, 'We have need for our nationality ['identity' as Travellers] and want to keep our culture. We've kept it going all these centuries, so why change it now?' 'Well, we *remember* it,' put in his wife, 'but we Travellers ourselves have *changed* it.' History then is memory, and culture is as much a part of history as is history a part of culture, and culture is always changing because people themselves change it.

The opinions above are consistent with John Sampson's observation a century ago of the 'many striking coincidences of life which link the Celtic to the Romani vagrant' (Sampson 1891, 204). He continued: 'in Ireland at least, [the Tinkers are] as distinct a caste as our English Gypsies' (Sampson 1891, 204), a view shared by Vesey-Fitzgerald (1944, 33), who thought Irish Travellers 'Quite distinct: and yet obviously closely allied, so closely in fact, that they are a branch of the Romanies ... not just Irishmen who have taken to the road ... a race'.

No Irish Traveller claimed links either ancient or modern with Scottish Travellers. Nor, of course, were any aware of Lucas (1882, 102) recalling a traditional account of how 'In the reign of James II of Scotland', fifty years before Romanies were reliably reported in Scotland (see Fraser 1995), 'it happened a company of Saracens or Gypsies from Ireland [almost all Scottish Gypsies say their ancestors came by way of Ireland to Scotland, and they still call those coming from Ireland Getr'ns, kindred, Sanscrit, Gotra, kindred] infested the country of Galloway, whereupon the King emitted a Proclamation, bearing That whoever should disperse them and bring in their captain, dead or alive should have the Baron of Bombie for his Reward'. McCormick (1973, 405–6), writing in 1907, refers to the same report, as does Fraser, who makes clear the story referred to '"Saracens" or "Moors"' (Fraser 1995, 111).

If this story is reliable then we must wonder whether the 'Saracens' from Ireland were 'Romanies' and, if so, how long they had been in Ireland and whether they married indigenous nomads. We really don't know. Thomas Acton (1974) has criticised MacAlister's claim (1976, 132-3) that Irish Travellers are people of peasant background who first presented as a distinct ethnic group in the late medieval period by seizing on MacAlister's too-easy dismissal of the many Romani words in Irish Traveller speech. '[To] say that on the evidence of their non-Romani language, the Irish Travellers must be Irish in origin, and that because they are Irish in origin any Romani words they may have cannot be 'theirs', is to circularise the argument. It would be no less plausible to suppose there might have been, in the formation of the Shelta/Gammon speaking group, a Romani element, *possibly of a different immigration* from that which formed the English and Welsh Gypsy communities' (Acton 1974, 66-7, my emphasis). Court (1985, 22) also reckons that in the absence of a 'comprehensive, exacting study' of Irish Travellers it is possible that some are of Romany descent. I think she is right.

Aside from language and formal Church-based religion, both of which differentiate thousands of Roma from one another without making one lot more 'Gypsy' than the rest, I saw no essential social or cultural differences between the Irish Travellers and Romanies on the Westway; nor does my reading of the literature suggest otherwise. To all intents and purposes the British Roma and Irish Travellers are so alike culturally and socially that we can think of them as constituting a single community, albeit one which, like every other community, is apt to internally self-differentiate according to particular circumstances. Therefore, in 1989, when an English High Court declared that 'Gypsies' were an ethnic group but excluded 'Travellers' on the grounds that no matter who used the word it did not adequately indicate a distinctive ethnic identity, the Irish Travellers missed out on achieving ethnic status and the rights in the UK that flow from it. The most likely reason behind this decision was the court's fear of similar claims being made in future by New Age Travellers. In 2000 that position changed when a British court faced with allegations of discrimination brought by five Travellers against several London pubs (some of them in Harrow just north of the Westway) ruled they *were* an ethnic minority as defined by the Race Relations Act. Yet, to this day, in Irish law Travellers are regarded merely as a distinct 'social group' or 'community'.

Conclusion

Concealment and disclosure are parts of normal social intercourse (Simmel 1906). Secrecy and silence are not peculiar to Travellers, it is just that Travellers practise these behaviours more assiduously than most, and as long as they continue to 'travel' both as families and as itinerants within nomadic families, and go on maintaining their kindred networks while valuing autonomy, occupational flexibility and adaptability, secrecy and silence will continue to help them maintain their identity.

F.G. Bailey, an anthropologist who did fieldwork in India and northern Italy, once wrote, 'If peasants seemed to the outsider to be mean, self-interested and suspicious, that must to some extent have been because experience with outsiders taught them to protect themselves by such attitudes. This, of course is, not the whole story: it is one of our contentions that those who live in a close-knit community are invariably suspicious of those beyond its boundaries' (Bailey 1971, 31). How much more, then, should we expect the same of small travelling groups of Travellers and Gypsies? Conrad Arensberg said that 'blood and land' went together in Ireland and that to say someone had 'bad blood' was to declare him a 'stranger to the land' (Arensberg 1937, 85–9), while to say that someone had Tinker blood was to damn him by descent. On all three counts it is therefore not surprising that Irish Travellers have been stigmatised and have learnt to be supremely wary of outsiders.

The late Thomas McCarthy once remarked to me that 'Most outsiders don't know anything about Travellers because they don't even try. The man on the ground is the one who knows them best. Not like the politicians. People is afraid of Gypsies'. Another friend, John Doyle, said, 'You could live twenty years among Travelling People and still know little about them'. Neither exaggerated, and so it has been with their help and the help of others like them, not least Martin Ward (with whom my relations were for a long time testy before coming good in the end), as well as with the unwitting help of others that I have tried to give an unbiased account of life under the Westway. I know that some parts may annoy and others will be contested for the reasons Simmel (1906) and Park (1925) well understood, but my hope is that is that this book goes some way to seeing Travellers win that 'leave to live' of which the Bard spoke and to which they unquestionably have the right.[9]

> If tinkers may have leave to live,
> And bear the sow-skin budget,
> Then my account I well may give
> And in the stocks avouch it.
> (*The Winter's Tale*, IV.II.19–22)

Martin Ward and the author, 1994

Notes

1. Most scholars use these terms interchangeably.

2. See Harper and Hudson (1971), Acton and Davies (1979), Hancock (1984).

3. A tapestry hanging in the Dublin Travellers' Education & Development Group headquarters in 1995 showed the districts associated with an even longer list.

4. In the sixteenth century Thomas, Lord Offaly, who the Irish called Tomás an tSioda or 'Silken Thomas', had a harper called O'Keenan (Curtis 1985, 162).

5. Professor Peter Edwards, in 'Manufacturing Memory', The Geoffrey Bolton Lecture, Perth, Western Australia, November 2006.

6. The name comes from a Swiss archaeological site.

7. Chatwin claims this likeness between Gypsies and Aborgines in *The Songlines* (1998), his 'ode' to nomadism.

8. On different and sometimes dubious grounds I have heard 'British' or 'English' Irish Travellers at the Westway talk scathingly about 'Irish' Irish Travellers.

9. In 1984 the National Council for Travelling People adopted a Charter of Rights, prepared for it by the Irish Centre for the Study of Human Rights, University College Galway. Article 2 lays down the right to free movement and the proper provision of sites.

The Westway Site, 2004, looking north west

Epilogue

Since 1984, when I took on the job of warden, and indeed, since 1987 when I left, there have been many changes large and small on the site, within the neighbourhood, and in Barnes and Mortlake, as well as in the wider London area and for that matter more generally in the United Kingdom and the Irish Republic. In the course of these pages where I have adopted an historical purview I have referred to some of these changes and their implications for Travellers and Romanies I knew at the Westway, and we would do well to recall them.

Firstly, beginning in the late 1980s, that dramatic leap of the Irish economy, the so-called 'emerald tiger', and consequent rebirth of immigration to Ireland, the first of any magnitude for centuries, which saw many Irish living in Britain, including Irish Travellers, return home. Helped by bucket airfares, the continued expansion of international air travel, and coincidental dissolution of national borders as a result of the growth and closer integration of EU member countries, it has continued apace.

Secondly, Britain has a more multicultural society in fact and ethos than ever before, and this is nowhere more evident than in London, ancient shelter of foreigners. Much more remarkably, the same is true of Ireland. In twenty years Dublin and other cities have become multi-ethnic places, and even country towns and small villages harbour 'new Irish' of African, Asian, and mid or eastern European origin – Roma included.

Thirdly, negative images of the Irish and Ireland once common in England have not just disappeared they have been largely replaced by extremely positive ones stemming from the growing economic success of the Irish. Even agonistic views in and of Northern Ireland and the damage inflicted on Anglo-Irish relations at state level, as well as upon individuals and local communities in the aftermath of the IRA's 1996 bombing of Manchester and London, have largely faded, especially with the establishment of a power-sharing agreement in Northern Ireland in January 2007. The Republic is now a favourite haunt for British tourists and numerous Britons have gone to live there: 'West Brits', some Irish call them. However, all this is not to imply that Irish Travellers no longer face hostility in England, or that settled English people no longer dread their sudden appearance and efforts to develop sites. Far from it.

Throughout this book I have tried to capture some of the different and at times conflicting perspectives non-Travellers have of Irish Travellers. I have made a point of not casting Travellers as 'victims' (even when at times they are) for I believe they have grown weary of that angle, besides which, the advocacy path is best left to others more qualified. Instead, I have made every effort to examine Travellers social organisation and culture as objectively as possible, realising, as Travellers themselves do, just how complex such matters are and how hard it is for anyone to do justice to that complexity without distorting it or else appearing to speak about or for *all* Travellers when in no position to do so. And yet without some level of qualified generalisation no valid and reliable record is possible, which returns me to the idea of opposing perspectives. Irrespective of individual disposition, most Travellers are tricksters. Yet, in this regard, as in so many others, Travellers are little different from much of the wider Irish population. For the trickster's art is not only confined to nomads, it is found wherever people, regardless of their station in life, compete aggressively in commerce.

This is not the time to begin an exegesis on humour, but few of us would dispute that humour helps shape a realistic perspective and assists in the toleration of trying personal circumstances or social disadvantage. This appreciation of the role of humour therefore helps to explain why trickery amounts to besting or beating one's opponent: making a mug of someone, 'taking the Mickey', or coming out best. Seen alongside his mostly transient commercial connections with sedentary people, humour lights the trickster's fuse to the dismay (or perhaps bemusement) of victim or bystander. In the interests of truth, victimology or the rational explanation of victim-hood, should therefore apply even-handedly. For as Travellers themselves *know*, but liberal self-censorship often prevents us revealing, there are at least two sides to a story. Those who know, and especially those who claim to pursue the truth professionally, must therefore acknowledge openly that social responsibility involves two sides: Travellers and settled people alike. Cycles of deceit practised on both sides, sometimes for understandable reasons, need to be broken. Fortunately, judging by the proliferation of Traveller and Roma conferences, organisations, local and national government meetings, reports and papers, websites and internet information, a more open dialogue has already begun in the UK, Ireland and the EU more generally on a scale unimaginable twenty or even ten years ago. Better yet, Travellers and Gypsies themselves now figure significantly in policy-making.

When last in England and Ireland, in 2004, I observed many changes. Some were extensions of processes I have already described; some were part of the unfolding process of other matters; some had taken place on the site, others outside it, yet the changes in one were not separate from changes in the other, and it will continue to be that way. So it is appropriate to end this book by briefly mentioning some of these developments. Here I should explain that those on the site in 2004 were mostly observed without recourse to interviews, although I did speak with the few Travellers still there from earlier times, to a leading newcomer, Tom Sweeney, and to the Housing officer charged with daily management of the site.

For a start, I witnessed further signs of that neighbourhood urban renewal already apparent in the 1980s. The sports centre and other leisure facilities under the A40 had greatly expanded and the totters' yard and training ring were busier than ever. One of these entrepreneurs seemed to have branched out to provide pony lessons to the affluent, itself (perhaps) a sign of galloping gentrification. Close to where *The Latimer Arms* once stood, venue for so many Traveller evenings, an all-weather surface, hockey-cum-football pitch served earnest amateurs. A few feet away under the concrete pillars of the A40, behind high steel mesh fences, people played basketball and tennis. In St Ann's Road, council town houses built by Kensington & Chelsea in the 1990s added style to an area once filled with abandoned workmen's cottages and the occasional squatters' dive, despite fresh coatings of dust from passing traffic. In Freston Road below the Harrow Club, south of the railway viaduct, I discovered tall elegant red brick offices whose rear premises, bordering upon the West Cross Route where New Age Travellers had camped among buddleia bushes twenty years earlier, were given over to company parking and other mundane activities. More significantly, against a backdrop of high cranes on the west side of the West Cross Route (A3220), an overpass with slip roads connected the A3220 more directly with White City, though not with the heavily built-up area of Notting Dale on the east side. I suspect this development may have had a considerable effect on the collective psychology of the Westway Site residents located further up the Cross Route, where the site itself showed signs of transformation.

The site's infrastructure was less decrepit than I knew it and the place was clean and tidy. Much money has been invested in the site. Chalets, a wholly new departure that hint at an increased sense of site and resident permanency, occupied many plots, most of them now fenced off. There were still plenty of small- to medium-sized caravans but most of the mobile homes had gone. The wasteland of the triangle had also disappeared, overtaken by some kind of commercial enterprise. There was also evidence of demographic change.

Nearly all the families I knew in the 1980s had long moved away, some to other parts of London and some I imagine back to Ireland. Either way it is likely their younger members will have remained mobile and in some instances (if other evidence is an indication) travelling widely abroad. Only a cluster of Wards remained at the top of the site where they had always stayed, and the elderly Connors couple continued to occupy their old spot. New people occupied the bottom and most of the middle reaches and the fulcrum of power had shifted accordingly, from 'top' to 'bottom', involving a new dynamic turning on Martin Ward and relative newcomer Tom Sweeney. Sweeney struck me as a man at home with officials and policy makers, with rules and rule-makers, and, mindful of the need to work with other minority ethnic groups, was moving fast in that direction. Shortly before I left England in October I bumped into him at a mid-week academic conference in central London. A new breed of leader, seemingly confident with the parlance of middle-class officials, Sweeney's arrival opens a new chapter in the old story of Travellers and Gypsies in west London. That chapter, however, calls for another chronicler, one far closer to the events in time and place than I, someone who can situate it in the fast unfolding narrative of fresh Roma arrivals in Britain and Ireland, the biggest intake of Gypsies from the Continent to occur in these islands for a century.

Perth, Western Australia, February 2007

Bibliography

Advisory Committee for the Education of Romany and other Travellers/National Gypsy Education Council [ACERT/NGEC], *Swann Report and Travellers* (London, 1986)

Ackroyd, P., *Hawksmoor* (London, 1985)

Ackroyd, P., *London: the biography* (London, 2001)

Acton, T.A., *Gypsy politics and social change: the development of ethnic ideology and pressure politics among British Gypsies from Victorian reformism to Romany nationalism* (London/Boston, 1974)

Acton T.A., 'Reacting to Swann – some difficulties for ACERT and the NEC', in ACERT/NGEC, *Swann Report and Travellers* (London, 1986)

Acton, T. and Davies, G., 'Educational policy and language use among English Romanies and Irish Travellers (Tinkers) in England and Wales', in *International Journal of the Sociology of Language. Romani Sociolinguistics* 19 (1979)

Adams, E. and Bartlett, L. (eds), *Going down the Lane: memories of Portobello Road* (London, 1990)

Albera, D., 'Open systems and closed minds: the limitations of naivety in social anthropology – a native's view', *Man/Journal of the Royal Anthropological Institute*, N.S. 23 (1988)

Alexander, S., 'St Giles Fair, 1830-1914', in R.J. Morris and R. Rodger (eds), *The Victorian city: a reader in British urban history, 1820-1914* (London/New York, 1993)

Allsop, K., *Hard travellin': the story of the migrant worker* (Harmondsworth/Ringwood, Australia, 1972)

Andereck, M.C., *Ethnic awareness and the school: an ethnographic study* (London/Delhi, 1992)

Anderson, B., *Imagined communities: reflections on the origins and spread of nationalism* (London/New York, 1994)

Anderson, J.E., *A history of the parish of Mortlake*, facsimile by Mary Grimwade (London, 1983 (orig. 1886))

Anderson, J.E., *A history of the parish of Barnes*, facsimile by Mary Grimwade (London, 1983 (orig. 1900))

Anderson, N., *The hobo: the sociology of the homeless man* (Chicago, 1961 (orig. 1923))

Arensberg, C., *The Irish countryman* (Gloucester, Mass., 1937)
Arensberg, C.M. and Kimball, S.T., *Family and community in Ireland* (Boston, Mass., 1968)
Attwell, M., *Childhood memories of Barnes village* (Chippenham, 1996)
Bailey, F.G., *Tribe, caste and nation: a study of political activity and political change in Highland Orissa* (Manchester, 1960)
Bailey, F.G., *Gifts and poison: the politics of reputation* (Oxford, 1971)
Barnes and Mortlake History Society, *Barnes and Mortlake remembered* (Hendon Mill, n.d.)
Barnes and Mortlake History Society, *Vintage Barnes and Mortlake* (Hendon Mill, 1983 (orig. 1979))
Barnes and Mortlake History Society, *Barnes and Mortlake as it was* (Hendon Mill, 1983 (orig. 1977))
Barnes, B., 'Irish Travelling People', in F. Rehfisch (ed.), *Gypsies, Tinkers, and other travellers* (London/New York, 1975)
Barrett, S., *Paradise: class, commuters and ethnicity in rural Ontario* (Toronto/London, 1994)
Barrett, S., *Anthropology: a student's guide* (Toronto, 1996)
Barry, J., Herity B. and Solon, J., *The Travellers' health status study: vital statistics of Travelling People* (Dublin, 1987)
Barth, F. (ed.), *Ethnic groups and boundaries: the social organization of cultural differences* (Boston, 1969)
Barton, N., *The lost rivers of London: a study of their effects upon London and Londoners, and the effect of London and Londoners upon them* (New Barnet, 1982)
Becker, H.S., *Outsiders: studies in the sociology of deviance* (New York, 1996 (orig. 1973))
Becket, J.C., *A short history of Ireland* (London, 1986)
Bennett, A., *A man from the north* (London, 1973 (orig. 1898))
Benyon, J. and Dunkerley, D. (eds), *Globalization: the reader* (New York, 2000)
Berger, P.L. and Luckmann, T., *The social construction of reality: a treatise in the sociology of knowledge* (New York, 1967)

Berland, J.C., 'We travel together and fight a lot: conflict and disputing activities in a peripatetic community' (unpublished, n.d.)

Berland, J.C., *No five fingers are alike: cognitive amplifiers in social context* (Cambridge, Mass./London, 1982)

Bittles, A., 'Consanguinity and its relevance to clinical genetics', *Clinical Genetics*, 60 (2001)

Bochner, A.P. and Ellis, C., *Ethnographically speaking: autoethnography, literature, and aesthetics* (Walnut Creek, Ca., 2002)

Booth, C. (ed.), *Life and labour of the people of London*, vols 1–3 (London, 1889)

Borrow, G., *Romano Lavo-Lil: A book of the Gypsy* (Gloucester, 1982 (orig. 1874))

Boswell, S.G., *The book of Boswell. Autobiography of a Gypsy*, ed. John Seymour (Harmondsworth, 1973)

Bounds, M., *Urban social theory: city, self and society* (Melbourne/London/New York, 2004)

Bourdieu, P., *Outline of a theory of practice* (Cambridge, 1977)

Briggs, L.C., *Tribes of the Sahara* (Cambridge, Mass., 1960)

Brody, H., *Inishkillane: change and decline in the west of Ireland* (London/Boston, 1973)

Brown, M., *The market gardens of Barnes and Mortlake* (Richmond, 1985)

Brown, M., *Barnes and Mortlake past with East Sheen* (London, 1996)

Brown, N., *Hermes the thief: the evolution of a myth* (Great Barrington, MA, 1990 (orig. 1947))

Bulfin, W., *Rambles in Eirinn*, vols 1 and 2 (London, 1981 (orig. 1907))

Burnett, M., *History of the Harrow Mission and Club in Notting Dale: one hundred years of service to the community* (London, 1983)

Burton, Sir Richard *The Jew, the Gypsy and El Islam* (London, 1898)

Cairns, D. and Richards, S., 'What ish my nation?' in B. Ashcroft, G. Griffiths, H. Tiffin (eds), *The post-colonial reader* (London, 1995)

Campbell, J.J., *Honour, family and patronage: a study of institutions and moral values in a Greek mountain community* (Oxford, 1964)

Camus, A., *The outsider* (New York, 1946 (orig. 1942))

Carpenter, E., *Oh, what a blow that phantom gave me!* (New York, 1974)

Chambers Biographical Dictionary, eds J.O. Thorne and T.C. Chambers (Edinburgh, 1990)

Chambliss, W.J., 'A Sociological Analysis of the Law and Vagrancy', *Social Problems* (Summer 1964)

Chatwin, B., *The songlines* (London, 1998)

Chesney, K., *The Victorian underworld* (Harmondsworth, 1972)

Clifford, J., 'Traveling Cultures', in L. Grossberg, C. Nelson and P.A. Treichler (eds), *Cultural studies* (New York, 1992)

Clifford, J., *Routes: travel and translation in the late 20th century* (Cambridge, Mass./London, 1997)

Clifford, J. and Marcus, G.E. (eds), *Writing culture: the poetics and politics of ethnography* (Berkeley/Los Angeles/London, 1986)

Cobbett, W., *Cobbett in Ireland: a warning to England*, ed. Denis Knight (London, 1984 (orig. 1834))

Cockin, M. and Gould, D., *Mortlake Parish Register 1599–1678* (Barnes, 1954)

Cohen, A.P., *The symbolic construction of community* (Chichester/London, 1985)

Cohen, A.P., *Whalsay: symbol, segment and boundary in a Shetland Island community* (Manchester, 1987)

Cohen, A., *Masquerade politics: explorations in the structure of urban cultural movements* (Oxford/Providence, 1993)

Coleman, T., *The railway navvies* (Tiptree, 1972)

Commission for Racial Equality, *Discrimination and the Irish community in Britain* (London, 1997a)

Commission for Racial Equality, *The Irish in Britain* (London, 1997b)

Connell, K.H., *Irish Peasant Society: Four Historical Essays* (Dublin/Portland, 1996 (orig. 1968))

Coogan, T.P., *Wherever the green is worn: the story of the Irish diaspora* (London, 2002)

Court, A., *Puck of the droms: The lives and literature of the Irish Tinkers* (Berkeley/Los Angeles, 1985)

Curtis, E., *A history of Ireland*, 9th reprint (London, 1985 orig. 1936))

Davies, W., *The autobiography of a supertramp* (London, 1951 (orig. 1908))

Davis, G., *The Irish in Britain 1815–1914* (Dublin, 1991)

Delaney, C., *The seed and the soil: gender and cosmology in Turkish village society* (Chicago, 1991)

de Paor, L., *Portrait of Ireland past and present* (New York, 1985)

de Paor, L., *The peoples of Ireland: from pre-history to modern times* (London/Melbourne, 1986)

Diamond, J., *Collapse: how societies choose to fail or survive* (London, 2005)

Dickens, C., *Household Words: A Weekly Journal*, 1 (1850)

Donnan, H. and Wilson, T.M., *Borders. frontiers of identity, nation and state* (New York/London, 1999)

Douglas, M., *Natural symbols: explorations in cosmology*, 2nd edn (Harmondsworth, 1973)

Douglas, M., *Purity and danger: An analysis of concepts of pollution and taboo* (London, 1978)

Draper, W.H., *Hammersmith: a study in town history* (London, 1989 (orig. 1913))

Duncan, A., *Taking on the motorway: North Kensington Amenity Trust 21 Years* (London, 1992)

Durkheim, E., *The elementary forms of the religious life*, 2nd edn (London, 1915)

Engels, F., *The conditions of the working class in England* (Harmondsworth, 1987 (orig. 1845))

Evans, E.E., *Irish folk ways*, 3rd impression (London, 1966 (orig. 1957))

Evans, E.E., *The personality of Ireland: habit, heritage and history* (Cambridge, 1973)

Evans, G., *Kensington* (London, 1975)

Evans, S., *Stopping places: a Gypsy history of south London and Kent* (Hatfield, 2004)

Evans-Pritchard, E.E., *The Nuer: a description of the modes of livelihood and political institutions of a Nilotic people* (Oxford, 1940)
Evans-Pritchard, E.E., *Essays in social anthropology* (London, 1962)
Fielding, S., *Class and ethnicity. Irish Catholics in England 1880–1939* (Buckingham/Philadelphia, 1993)
Finnegan, R., *Literacy and orality: studies in the technology of communication* (Oxford/New York, 1988)
Finnegan, R., *The hidden musicians: music making in an English town* (Cambridge, 1989)
Firth, R., *We, the Tikopia* (London, 1936)
Firth, R., *Elements of social organization: a sociological study of kinship in primitive Polynesia* (London, 1971)
Fletcher Jones, P., *Richmond Park: portrait of a royal playground* (London/Chichester, 1972)
Foote-Whyte, W., *Street corner society: the social structure of an Italian slum* (London, 1973 (orig. 1943))
Forrester, B., *The Travellers' handbook: a guide to the law affecting Gypsies* (London, 1985)
Frankenberg, R., *Village on the border: a social study of religion, politics and football in a north Wales community* (London, 1957)
Fraser, A., *The Gypsies*, 2nd edn (Oxford/Cambridge, Mass., 1995)
Fried, A. and Elman, R.M. (eds), *Charles Booth's London: a portrait of the poor at the turn of the century, drawn from his Life and labour of the people in London* (Harmondsworth, 1971)
Gannon, M.J., 'Irish Conversations', in M.J. Gannon, *Understanding global cultures: metaphorical journeys through 17 countries* (London, 1994)
Geertz, C., *The interpretation of culture* (New York, 1973)
Geertz, C., *Works and lives: the anthropologist as author* (Cambridge, 1988)
Geertz, C., *Local Knowledge* (London, 1993 (orig. 1983))
George, D.M., *London life in the eighteenth century* (Harmondsworth, 1966)

Gerhold, D. (ed.), *Putney and Roehampton* (London, 1994)

Gibb, R., *Gypsy education in North Kensington: a first report by Rosemary Gibb* (London, 1977)

Gibb, R., 'Teacher's report on social and educational matters on the Westway Gypsy Site', unpublished, London, 1978

Gladstone, F., *Notting Hill in bygone days* (London, 1969 (orig. 1924))

Gluckman, M., 'The Frailty in Authority', in M. Gluckman, *Custom and Conflict in Africa* (Oxford, 1966)

Gmelch, G., 'The effects of economic change on Irish Travellers' sex roles and marriage patterns', in F. Rehfisch (ed.), *Gypsies, Tinkers, and other Travellers* (London/New York, 1975)

Gmelch, G., *The Irish Tinkers: the urbanization of an itinerant people* (Menlo Park, Ca., 1977)

Gmelch, S.B., *Tinkers and Travellers: Ireland's nomads* (Dublin, 1975)

Gmelch, S.B. and Gmelch, G., 'The emergence of an ethnic group: the Irish Tinkers', *Anthropological Quarterly*, 49, 4 (1974)

Godfrey, A., *Old Ordnance Survey Maps: Notting Hill 1914* (Gateshead, 1986)

Goffman, E., *Stigma: notes on the management of spoiled identity* (Harmondsworth, 1968)

Golden, H., 'Urbanization and the growth of cities in England and Wales, 1800–1900', in H. Golden (ed.), *Urbanization and cities: historical and comparative perspectives on our urbanizing world* (Lexington, 1981)

Goudie, F. and Stuckie, D., *Railways and transport of Hammersmith and west London* (Wokingham, 2000)

Greater London Council, *Policy report on the Irish community* (1984)

Green, M.J., *Celtic myths* (London, 1993)

Green, P. (aka Macgréine, P.), 'Irish Tinkers or "Travellers": some notes on their manners and customs, and their secret language or "cant"', *Bealodeas: Journal of the Folklore of Ireland Society*, 111 (1931–2)

Grene, N., *Synge: a critical study of the plays* (London, 1975)
Grenham, J., *Clans and families of Ireland* (Dublin, 1993)
Griffin, C.C.M., '"Space, the final frontier": Gypsies and England's New Age Travellers' (unpublished paper, Conference of the Gypsy Lore Society, 1995)
Griffin, C.C.M., 'Wardening, witnessing, words and writing: rights of passage, passages to write', *Journal of Australian Studies*, 6, 1 (1999)
Griffin, C.C.M., 'The religion and social organisation of Irish Travellers on a London caravan site (part 1)', *Nomadic Peoples*, N.S. 6, 1 (2002a)
Griffin, C.C.M., 'The religion and social organisation of Irish Travellers (part II): cleanliness and dirt, bodies and borders', *Nomadic Peoples*, N.S. 6, 2 (2002b)
Grimwade, M. and Hailstone, C., *Highways and byways of Barnes* (Barnes, 1992)
Grönfors, M., *Blood feuding among Finnish Gypsies* (Helsinki, 1979)
Hailstone, C., *Alleyways of Mortlake and East Sheen* (Barnes, 1983)
Hall, G., *The Gypsy's parson: his experiences and adventures* (London, 1915)
Hancock, I.F., 'Shelta: a problem of classification', *Journal of the Gypsy Lore Society*, 3rd series, 52 (1973)
Hancock, I.F., 'Shelta and Polari', in P. Trudgill (ed.), *Language in the British Isles* (Cambridge, 1984)
Harbison, P., *Pre-Christian Ireland: from the settlers to the early Celts* (London, 1994 (orig. 1988))
Harper, J. and Hudson, C., 'Irish Traveler cant', *Journal of English Linguistics*, 5 (1971)
Hawkes, C., 'Gold ear-rings of the Bronze Age, east and west', *Folklore*, 72 (1961)
Helleiner, J., '"The Tinker's Wedding" revisited: Irish Traveller marriage', in M.T. Salo (ed.), *100 years of Gypsy studies. Publication No. 5* (Cheverly, Maryland, 1990)
Helleiner, J., *Irish Travellers: racism and the politics of culture* (Toronto/London, 2000)

Hennis, W., *Max Weber: Essays in Reconstruction*, trans K. Tribe (London, 1988)
Herzfeld, M., *Anthropology: theoretical practice in culture and society* (Malden, Mass./Oxford, 2001)
Hibbard, G.R. (ed.), *Bartholomew Fair/Ben Jonson* (London/New York, 1977)
Holroyd, M., *Augustus John: a biography*, 1987 reprint (Harmondsworth, 1976)
Hope, C., *Darkest England* (London, 1996)
Hoppen, K.T., *Ireland since 1800. Conflict and conformity*, 2nd impression (London/New York, 1990)
Hughes, T.P. and Hughes, A.C., *Lewis Mumford: public intellectual* (New York/London, 1990)
Hussey, G., *Ireland today: anatomy of a changing state* (London, 1995)
Hutton, W., *The state we're in* (London, 1996)
Jackson, A. (ed.), *Anthropology at home* (London/New York, 1987)
Jacobsen, J.K.S., 'The tourist bubble and the Europeanisation of holiday travel', *Journal of Tourism and Cultural Change*, 1, 1 (2003)
Jenkins, T., 'Fieldwork and the perception of everyday life', *Man*, N.S. 29, 2, (1994)
Johnston G.B. (ed.), *Poems of Ben Jonson*, 3rd impression (London, 1962)
Jones, G.S., *Outcast London: a study in the relationship between classes in Victorian society* (Oxford, 1971)
Jusserand, J.J., *English wayfaring life in the Middle Ages*, 8th edn (London, 1891)
Keaney, B., *Don't hang about* (Oxford, 1985)
Keenan, R., 'Tall travellers' tales', *The Tablet* (26 March 2005)
Kennedy, L., *10 Rillington Place* (London, 1995 (orig. 1961))
Kenrick, D. and Bakewell, S., *On the verge: the Gypsies of England* (London, 1990)
Kenrick, D. and Clark, C., *Moving on: the Gypsies and Travellers of Britain* (Hatfield, 1995)

Kyriacou, S. et al., *The forgotten lives: Gypsies and Travellers on the Westway Site*, Ethnic Communities Oral History Project (London, 1989)

Leach, E., 'Anthropological aspects of language: animal categories and verbal abuse', in P. Maranda (ed.), *Mythology* (Harmondsworth, 1973)

Leblon, B., *Gypsies and Flamenco* (Hatfield, 1995)

Lees, L.H., *Exiles of Erin: Irish migrants in Victorian London* (Manchester, 1979)

Leland, C.G., *The Gypsies* (London, 1882)

Leland, C.G., *The English Gypsies and their language*, 4th edn (London, 1893)

Lévi-Strauss, C., *Tristes tropiques* (Harmondsworth, 1976)

Lévi-Strauss, C., *The view from afar* (London/Harmondsworth, 1987)

Lister, R., *The craftsmen in metal* (London, 1966)

Lonergan, D., *Sounds Irish: the Irish language in Australia* (Adelaide, 2004)

Loose, J., *Roehampton: the last village in London* (London, 1979)

Lovell, M.S., *A rage to live: a biography of Richard and Isabel Burton* (London, 1999)

Lovrick, T., *Metropolitan Sewers: A Preliminary Report by Associate Surveyor on the Potteries, Kensington* (London, March 12 1849)

Lucas, J., *The Yetholm history of the Gypsies* (Kelso, 1882)

MacAlister, R.A.S., *The secret languages of Ireland* (St Helier/Amsterdam, 1976 (orig. 1937))

McCarthy, P., 'Life with the Travelling People', in V. Bewley (ed.), *Travelling People* (Dublin, 1975)

McCormick, A., *The Tinkler-Gypsies* (Wakefield, 1973 (orig. 1907))

McDonagh, M., 'Origins of the Travelling People', in E. Sheehan (ed.), *Travellers, citizens of Ireland* (Dublin, 2000)

McGahern, J., *Amongst women* (London, 1991)

McLuhan, M. and Fiore, Q., *The medium is the massage* (Harmondsworth, 1967)

McMahon, S., *A short history of Ireland* (Dublin, 1996)

MacNeill, M., *The festival of Lughnasa* (Oxford, 1962)

McRitchie, D., 'Irish Tinkers and their language', *Gypsy Law Society Journal*, Old Series 1 (1889)

Malcolmson, P.E., 'Getting a living in the slums of Victorian Kensington', *The London Journal* 1 (1975)

Marcus, G.E., *Ethnography through thick and thin* (Princeton, 1998)

Markale, J., *The Celts: uncovering the myths and historic origins of Western culture* (Rochester, Vermont, 1993)

Mauss, M., *The gift: forms and function of exchange in archaic societies* (London, 1974)

Mauss, M., in collaboration with Beuchat, H., *Seasonal variations of the Eskimo: a study in social morphology* (London, 1979)

Mayhew, H., *London Labour and the London Poor* (vols 1–3 first published 1861, vol. 4 1862, vols 1–4 1865) (Harmondsworth, 1985)

Messenger, J.C., *Inis Beag: isle of Ireland* (New York/Chicago, 1969)

Miller, C., 'American Rom and the ideology of defilement', in F. Rehfisch (ed.), *Gypsies, tinkers and other travellers* (London, 1975)

Mills, C.W., *The sociological imagination* (Oxford, 1959)

Mommsen, W.J., *The political and social theory of Max Weber* (Oxford, 1989)

Morton, H.V., *In search of Ireland*, 21st edn (London, 1947 (orig. 1930))

Murphy, F. and McDonagh, C. (comp), Sheehan E. (ed.), *Travellers: citizens of Ireland* (Dublin, 2000)

Neat, T., *The summer walkers. Travelling people and pearl fishers in the Highlands of Scotland* (Edinburgh, 1996)

Newby, E., *A traveller's life* (London, 1983)

Ní Shúineár, S., 'Irish Travellers: ethnicity and the origins question', in M. McCann *et al.* (eds), *Irish Travellers: culture and ethnicity* (Belfast, 1994)

North Kensington Community History Series, *Multi-racial North Kensington*, no. 2 (London, ?1987)

O'Connor, K., *The Irish in Britain* (London, 1972)

O'Connor, P., *Britain in the sixties: vagrancy, ethos and actuality* (Harmondsworth, 1963)

O'Faolain, S., *The great O'Neill: a biography of Hugh O'Neill, Earl of Tyrone, 1550–1616* (London, 1942)
O'Faolain, S., *The Irish* (Harmondsworth, 1981)
Okely, J., *The Traveller Gypsies* (Cambridge, 1983)
Old Inhabitant, *Kensington, Notting Hill, and Paddington* (London, 1882)
Olwig, K.F. and Hastrup, K., *Siting culture: the shifting anthropological object* (London/New York, 1997)
Ong, W.J., *Orality and literacy: the technologizing of the world* (London/New York, 1988)
Orwell, G., 'Why I Write', in G. Bott (ed.), *George Orwell: selected readings* (London, 1947)
Orwell, G., *Down and out in Paris and London* (Harmondsworth, 1963 (orig. 1933))
Orwell, G., 'Hop picking', in S. Orwell and I. Angus (eds), *The collected essays and letters of George Orwell, volume I, an age like this, 1920–1940* (Harmondsworth, 1970 (orig. 1931))
O'Sullivan, M., *Twenty years a-growing* (London, 1970 (orig. 1933))
O'Toole, E.B., 'An analysis of the life style of the Travelling People of Ireland', *Journal of the Gypsy Lore Society*, 3rd Series 52, 3–4 (1973)
Owen, K. (ed.), *Our homes, our streets*, North Kensington Community History Series no. 3 (1987)
Owusu, K. and Ross, J., *Behind the masquerade: the story of Notting Hill Carnival* (London, 1988)
Oxford Dictionary of Quotations, The, ed. A. Partington (Oxford, 1992)
Oxford English Dictionary, The, eds J.A. Simpson and E.S.C. Weiner (Oxford, 1989)
Pálsson, G. (ed.), *Beyond boundaries: understanding translation, and anthropological discourses* (Providence, R.I./Oxford, 1994)
Park, R.E., *The city* (Chicago, 1925)
Parker, E., *Highways and byways in Surrey* (London, 1919)

Parsons, T., 'Culture and social system revisited', in L. Schneider and C. Bonjean (eds), *The idea of culture in the social sciences* (Cambridge, 1973)

Pearson, J., *The profession of violence: the rise and fall of the Kray twins' vicious empire* (London, 1976 (orig. 1972))

Peterson, N., *Tribes and boundaries in Australia* (Canberra, Australia/Atlantic Highland, New Jersey, 1976)

Pixley, J., *Citizenship and employment: investigating post-industrial options* (Cambridge, 1993)

Pocock, D., *Social anthropology*, 2nd edn (London, 1977 (orig. 1961))

Polanyi, M., *Personal knowledge: towards a post-critical philosophy* (Chicago, 1974)

Power, P.C., *Sex and marriage in ancient Ireland* (Dublin/Cork, 1976)

Power, C., 'Irish Travellers: ethnicity, racism and PSRs', *Probation Journal*, 50, 3 (2003)

Puxon, G., *On the road* (London, 1968)

Raban, J., *Soft city* (London, 1988)

Rao, A. (ed.), *The other nomads: peripatetic minorities in cross-cultural perspective* (Koln/Wien, 1987)

Redfield, R., *The little community* (Chicago, 1955)

Redfield, R., *Peasant society and culture* (Chicago, 1960 (orig. 1956))

Redfield, R., *The little community and Peasant society and culture* (Chicago, 1960)

Rehfisch, F. (ed.), *Gypsies, Tinkers, and other Travellers* (London, 1975)

Republic of Ireland Commission of Itinerancy, *Report of the Commission of Itinerancy* (Dublin, 1963)

Roberts, R., *The classic slum: Salford life in the first quarter of the century* (Harmondsworth, 1971)

Roberts, T.R., *Celtic Myths and Legends* (New York, 1995)

Rooks, C., *The hooligan nights* (Oxford, 1979 (orig. 1894))

Rorty, R., *Objectivity, relativism and truth* (Cambridge, 1991)

Ross, M., 'Off the road: the changing face of the Travellers', *Magill* (July 1990)

Salgado, G., *The Elizabethan underworld* (London, 1977)

Sampson, J., 'II – Tinkers and their talk', *Journal of the Gypsy Lore Society*, 1st Series 2 (1891)
Samuel, R., 'Comers and goers', in H.J. Dyos and M. Wolff (eds), *The Victorian city: images and reality, volume 1* (London, 1973)
Samuel, R., *Village life and village labour* (London, 1975)
SBS World Guide, 9th edn (South Yarra, Australia, 2001)
Scally, R.J., *The end of hidden Ireland: rebellion, famine, and emigration* (Oxford/New York, 1995)
Scarman, Lord, *The Scarman Report: the Brixton disorders 10–12 April 1981* (Harmondsworth, 1982)
Scheper-Hughes, N., *Saints, scholars, and schizophrenics: mental illness in rural Ireland* (Berkeley/Los Angeles/London, 2001 (orig. 1979))
Sheehan, E. (ed.), *Travellers, citizens of Ireland: our challenge to an intercultural Irish society in the 21st century* (Dublin, 2000)
Sheppard, F.H.W. (ed.), *Survey of London, vol. xxxvii, North Kensington* (London, 1973)
Simmel, G., 'The sociology of secrecy', *American Journal of Sociology*, 11, 4 (January 1906)
Simmel, G., 'The Stranger', in K.H. Wolff (ed. and trans.), *The sociology of Georg Simmel* (Glencoe, Illinois, 1950)
Sjoestedt, M.L., *Gods and heroes of the Celts* (Berkeley, 1982)
Smith, R., *Gypsy Smith: his work and life: by himself* (London, 1902)
Spencer, B. and Gillen, F.J., *The native tribes of central Australia* (Oosterhout, 1969 (orig. 1899))
Squillace, R., *Modernism, Modernity and Arnold Bennett*, (Lewisburg/London, 1997)
Stanley, J. and Griffiths, B., *For love and shillings: Wandsworth women's working lives* (London, 1990)
Steinbeck, J., *Travels with Charlie* (London, 1965)
Stewart, M., 'True speech: song and the moral order of a Hungarian Vlach Gypsy community', *Man*, 24, 1 (1989)
Stewart, M., *The time of the Gypsies* (Boulder, Colorado/Oxford, 1997)

Stocking, G.W., *Delimiting anthropology: occasional essays and reflections* (Madison, Wisconsin, 2001)

Stokes, F.G., *A dictionary of the characters and proper names in the works of Shakespeare* (New York, 1970)

Sutherland, A., *Gypsies: the hidden Americans* (London, 1975)

Sweetman, R., *On our backs: sexual attitudes in a changing Ireland* (London/Sydney, 1979)

Synge, J.M., *The Tinkers' Wedding and other plays* (London/Rutland, Vermont, 1992 (orig. 1904))

Taylor, M., *A brief survey of the history of the Travelling People in North Kensington and Hammersmith* (private publication, 1983)

Tennant, K., *The battlers* (Sydney, 2002)

The Irish and Employment Conference, draft paper, c.1986, no other details available

Thomas, S., *St Francis of Assisi, Pottery Lane: a London parish 1860–1985* (Godalming, 1985)

Thompson, E.P., *The making of the English working class* (Harmondsworth, 1968)

Thompson, F., *The illustrated Lark Rise to Candleford: a trilogy by Flora Thompson* (London, 1983 (orig. 1939))

Todorov, T., 'Knowledge in social anthropology: distancing and universality', *Anthropology Today*, 4, 2 (April 1988)

Turner, B., *Max Weber: from history to modernity* (London/New York, 1992)

Turner, V., *The ritual process: structure and anti-structure* (Harmondsworth, 1969)

Van Gennep, A., trans. M.B. Vizedom and G.L. Caffee, *Rites de passages* (Chicago, 1960 (orig. 1909))

Vaughan, A.T. and Vaughan, V.M., *Shakespeare's Caliban: a cultural history* (Cambridge, 1991)

Vesey-Fitzgerald, B., *Gypsies: an introduction to their history* (London, 1944)

Vogel, J.O. (ed), *Ancient African metallurgy: the sociocultural context* (New York/London, 2000)

Walford, E., *Greater London: a narrative of its history, its people, and its places. Vols II, V, VI* (London, 1885 (orig. 1883/4))
Walford, E., *Village London: the story of Greater London. Part 4, South West* (London, 1985 (orig. 1883/4))
Walsh, J., *The falling angels: an Irish romance* (London, 1999)
Weidel, J. and O'Fearadhaigh, M., *Irish Tinkers* (New York, 1978)
Whitting, P.D. (ed.), *A history of Hammersmith based upon that of Thomas Faulkener in 1839* (London, 1965)
Williams, P., *Gypsy world: the silence of the living and the voices of the dead* (Chicago, 2003)
Williamson, D. and Williamson, L., *A thorn in the King's foot. Stories of the Scottish Travelling People* (Harmondsworth, 1987)
Woodham-Smith, C., *The Great Hunger: Ireland 1845–1849* (Harmondsworth, 1991 (orig. 1962))
Worsley, P. (ed.), *The new introducing sociology* (Harmondsworth, 1992)

Also consulted

Acton, T.A., 'The Social Construction of the Ethnic Identity of Commercial Nomadic Groups', in J. Grumet (ed.), *Papers from the fourth and fifth annual meetings, Gypsy Lore Society, North American Chapter* (New York, 1985)
Adams, B., Okely, J., Morgan, D. and Smith, D., *Gypsies and government policy: a study of the travellers' way of life in relation to the policies and practices of central government* (London, 1975)
Barnes, J.A., *A pack of lies: towards a sociology of lying* (Cambridge, 1994)
Begbie, H., *Broken earthenware* (London, 1909)
Bewley, V.E.H. (ed.), *Travelling people* (Dublin, 1975)
Borrow, G., *Lavengro: scholar, Gipsy, priest* (London/Glasgow, 1851)
Brent Irish Mental Health Group, *The Irish experience of mental ill-health in London* (London, 1986)
Cloake, J., *Cottages and common fields of Richmond and Kew: economic and social history of the manor of Richmond up to the mid

nineteenth century (Chichester, 2001)

Commission for Racial Equality, *Common ground: equality, good race relations and sites for Gypsies and Irish Travellers. Report of a CRE inquiry In England and Wales, Summary* (London, May 2006)

Connolly, S.J., *Priests and people in pre-Famine Ireland 1780-1845* (Dublin/New York, 1982)

Curtin, C., Donnan, H., and Wilson, T.M. (eds), *Irish urban cultures* (Belfast, 1993)

Dyos, H.J. and Wolff, M. (eds), *The Victorian city: images and reality*, vols 1 and 2 (London, 1973)

Feldman, D. and Jones, G.S., *Metropolis London: histories and representations* (London/New York, 1989)

Fitzpatrick, D., *Irish emigration, 1801-1921* (West Tempest, 1985)

Flood, A.C., *The Irish in Camden* (London, ?1990)

Flower, R., *The Western Island or The Great Blasket* (Oxford, 2000 (orig. 1944))

Fowler, S., *Richmond in the Census of 1851* (Richmond, 1988)

Gilley, S., 'Catholic faith of the Irish slums 1840-70', in H.J. Dyos and M. Wolff (eds), *The Victorian city: images and realities*, vol. 2 (London/Boston, 1973)

Gmelch, S.B., 'A fieldwork experience: Irish Travellers in Dublin', in G. Gmelch and W.P. Zenner (eds), *Urban life: readings in urban anthropology* (Prospect Heights, Illinois, 1988)

Goffman, E., *The presentation of self in everyday life* (London, 1969)

Hasker, L., *Hammersmith and Fulham through 1500 years. A brief history* (London, 1992)

Hastrup, K. and Hervik, P. (eds), *Social experience and anthropological knowledge* (London, 1994)

Helleiner, J., 'Traveller settlement in Galway City: politics, class and culture', in C. Curtin, H. Donnan and T.M. Wilson (eds) *Irish urban cultures* (Belfast, 1993)

Irish in Britain Representation Group, *Report on the position of the Lambeth Irish community* (1985)

Kiely, G., O'Donnell, A., Kennedy, P. and Quinn, S., *Irish social policy in context* (Dublin, 1999)

Long, G., *The Folklore Calendar* (London, 1996 (orig. 1930))

Marriott, M., *Village India: studies in the little community* (Chicago, 1955)

Mayall, D., *Gypsy identities 1500-2000, from Egicyans and Moonmen to the ethnic Romany* (London, 2004)

McCann, M., Ó' Siocháin, S. and Ruane, J. (eds), *Irish Travellers: culture and ethnicity* (Belfast, 1994)

Packard, R.M., 'The study of historical process in African traditions of genesis: the Bashu myth of Muhuyi', in J.C. Miller (ed.), *The African past speaks* (London/Hamden, Conn., 1980)

Power, C., *Room to roam: England's Irish Travellers* (London, 2004)

Seaman, L.C.B., *Life in Victorian London* (London, 1973)

Smith, D.H., Fraser, A., Reeve, D., Boswell, S. and Wade, R., *Gypsies and Other Travellers*, Ministry of Housing and Local Government and the Welsh Office (London, 1969)

Taylor, N., *The village and the city* (London, 1973)

The Irish and Employment Conference, 'Extracts from the "Irish in London" research project: Irish Employment profile: evidence from the 1966 Sample census and 1981 Labour Force Survey', draft document for The Irish and Employment Conference, c.1982

White, J., *The worst street in London: Campbell Bunk, Islington, between the wars* (London, 1986)

Index

Reference to illustrations in italics

Aborigines 305
Ackroyd, P. 166-7, 172
Acton, T. xiii, 48, 112, 276n10, 312
Adams, Kate 76, 89, 101
Allen, Florence 76, 98-100, 103-4, 121n7, 154
Allen, George 99, 101, 154
Allsop, K. 10
Alton estates 7, 127, 132
Andersen, N. 10
Anderson, B. *see* 'imagined community'
Anthropology xvi-xvii, 1-4, 10-12, 166 *see also* culture, ethnography, fieldwork, theory
  and history 1-2, 19
  and memory 25, 41, 165, *165*
  at home 14, 27n1, 142, 171
Arensberg, C. 10, 211, 246, 313
Armstrong, Louis 9
Ascot 100
Autolycus 35, 159n16, 309-10
  see also Hermes, Shakespeare
Avondale Park 72, 99
Awareness 223, 278, 303-6
  see also stigma
Bailey, F.G. 21, 27n4, 313
Ballard, Ethel 145
Ballard, Percy 145

Ballinasloe *see* fairs
Bard Road 102, 104
Barnes, B. 247, 287, 307
Barnes Common 128, 131, 136-8, *141*, 142
Barrett, S. 27n1
Barth, F. 124
Becker, H. 26
Begging 163, 212, 232-3
Behan, Brendan 279
Bennett, Arnold 16-18, 19, 20, 24, 27n3, 166-7
Berland, J. 11, 275n4, 294
Beverley Brook 127-8, 138
  see also borders
Bittles, A. 254-5
Black Death 31, 41
Black Hill 72, 76
Boas, F. 20, 124
Booleying 31, 185, 197-8, 201-6 *see also* nomadism, transhumance
Booth, C. 43, 71
Border (boundary)
  crossers 15-16, 26, 133, 280
  crossings 123-6
  Hammersmith & Kensington 69, 72, 122n16 *see also* Hammersmith Bridge and Hammersmith & Fulham 130n18

Mortlake & East Sheen 45, 158n7, 126–32
    Mortlake & Richmond 5
    porous 167
    see also community, identity, purity, rites of passage
Borrow, G. 47, 48, 75–7, 79–82, 133
Bosvil, Ryley 64–5, 86n2 *see also* borrow
Boswell, Plastoe 84
Bourdieu, P. 278
Brody, H. 247
Buckinghamshire 83–5, 154
Buckinghamshire, Nobby 101–2, 107, 121n10
Builder 69–70
Bulfin, W 245, 258
Burton, Sir Richard 12–13, 45, 146
Bushey *see* Hertfordshire

Campbell, J.J. 240
Cant *see* Irish languages
Caravan Sites Act 1968 26–7 *see also* designation
Carnival 95, 97, 108
Carson, Sir Edward 52
Carts *see* vehicles
Catholic Children's Society (Westminster) 276n9, 289
Cattle 204, 220 *see also* booleying, infield, fairs, markets
Ceards 32–4 *see also* Celtic Smiths
Celtic calendar 204–7
Celtic Smiths 307–8 *see also* Irish Travellers
Cemeteries *see* graves
Character 148, 154, 199, 203, 262, 272–5n4
Chamberlain, Joseph 52
Chertsey Court 140, 146
Cheney, K. 34–5
China 85, 102–3, 140, 152–5
City missions *see* Harrow School, Rugby School, Mike Taylor
Clark, C. 222
'Clash of civilisations' 30
Class
    Barnes, 137–8, 15
    conflict 20
    Epsom 136
    Ireland 205, 257
    Mortlake & Sheen 45, 129–30, 138
    Notting Dale/Hill 64, 89, 93
    Roehampton 8, 131
    see also equality, honour, Irish in England, racial discrimination, socio-economic disadvantage, stratification
Cleanliness 248 *see also* purity
Clifford, J. xv, 22, 124
Coal trade 102, 137, 142, 144, 152–5

Cobbett, W. 38–9
Cochrane, Kelso 94–5
Cohen, A.P. 124
Coleman, T. 46
Collins, Michael 58
Coloured People's Progressive Association 95
Community *see* Chapter Ten
  xiv–xvi, 15–16
  and conflict 21
  and railways 64–5, 128, 129
  as 'sites of travel' 22, 72
  development 61, 108
  European (EU) 217
  imagined xv, 281
  Irish in Britain 217–221
  'little'
    Redfield's 23–4
    Barnes & Mortlake's 150
    Latimer Road as 62
    Bangor Street as 97
    London's many 60, 134, 162, 172–3
    Notting Dale's 62–72, 86, 101
    Westway Site's 59, 177
    Ireland's 205–7
  see also awareness, border, identity, Irish Traveller, rites of passage
Conflict *see* Community, Feud
Connors, Johnny 112
Connors, Kitty *284*, 320
Construction companies 55, 220

Costermongers 71, 97–8, 102, 134
  Mayhew's Irish 82, 309
Counter's Creek 69, 122
Cousin marriage *see* marriage
Court, A. 25, 32, 33, 249, 265, 280
Cromwell, Oliver 37, 307
Cromwell, Thomas 37, 126
Cultures xv
  anthropological approaches 16–19
  of bureaucracy 183–4
  of professions 183–4
  shock 7, 162, 167, 217
  see also anthropology, multiculturalism
Curtis, E. 51

Day's Cottages 83, 86n7
Delaney, C. 1, 4
Designation 26–7, 109–10
  Kensington & Chelsea's application 111–2
  Hammersmith & Fulham's application 113, 119, 189
  see also Caravan Sites Act 1968
De Valera, Eamonn 54, 90, 210
Dickens, Charles 67–9, 163
Dickerson, Albert 122n13, 144, 147, 150–1
Dirt *see* purity
Diseases 67–9, 71, 138 *see also* Westway Travellers Site
Divorce 271–2
Domesday Book 7, 123

Domvile, Admiral 131
Dover House Road Estate 131, 149
Donnan, H. 124
Douglas, M. 8, 248 *see also* purity
Dowry 258
Doyle, John 53, *136*, *308*, 313
Drugs 229, 275n6
Durkheim, E. 17, 19, 20, 21, 125, 248

Eades, J. 9
Ealing 6–7, 263, 306
Easter Rising 53, 90
Edelman, C. 57n5
Education 2, 16, 112, 181, 218–9, 269–71 *see also* Catholic Children's Society, Inner London Education Authority, Rosemary Gibb
Edward Woods estate 98, 107, 165–6, 301
Egalitarianism *see* Equality
'Egypt' ('Egyptians') 34, 36–7, 57n7, 83, 145 *see also* Buckinghamshire, Pharo
Eire 54 *see also* Irish Free State, Republic of Ireland
  Neutrality 90, 120n2
Elopement *see* Marriage
English in Ireland 30, 37, 51–2, 318
Epsom 134, 135, 138, 208
Equality 222, 240–1

Commission for Racial 218, 240
Eskimo 221n7, 215–6, 249 *see also* Mauss
Ethnography *see* Chapter Six, xvi, xvii, 3–4, 22–3, 162
  see also Anthropology, Fieldwork
Evans, E. Estyn 184, 215, 241
Evans-Pritchard, E.E. 22 *see also* Nuer
Evesham Road 301

Fair 35, 210, 265
  Appleby 208
  Bangor Street 99
  Barnet 102, 210
  Bartholomew 57n7
  Goose 209
  Ireland 208–9, 214n8, 233, 309
  Pinner 100
  St Giles 77
  Wormwood Scrubs 77, 99, 100, 227
  see also Ascot, Epsom
Familism 199, 203, 205
Family 236–40
Fares, Mick 151–2
Fascism 92, 94, 120n5 *see also* Moseley
Feud 196, 210, 234, 265, 294–5
Fieldwork 3–4, 9–12, 15–16, 20, 22, 174–5
  Author's Irish limits 214n8

serendipity 146
turning points 180
see also anthropology at home, friendship, S.B. Gmelch
Fiji(ans) 11–12, 119, 305
  nostalgia 165
Finch, Margaret *see* Sarah Skemp
Finnegan, R. 27n1, 279
Firth, R. 1, 20, 239, 244n10
Forrester, B. 110
Fortune telling 107, 213n6, 232, 297, 310
France
  bidonvilles 119
  Kalderash *268*, 300 *see also* Manus
  radicalism 39
Frankenberg, R. 125
Fraser, A. 35, 37
Freston Road 98, 102, 192, 300–1, 319 *see also* Latimer Road
Frestonian Republic 104 *see also* New (Age) Travellers
Friendship
  animals 211
  Gypsy 98–105, 139
  in fieldwork 3, 174–5, 178, 179
  pub 155
  Traveller 225, 229, 234, 238–40
Fruit and veg trade 151–2 *see also* costermongers

Galena Road 104, 302
Gammon *see* Irish languages
Garrett Lane 134, 147
Geertz, C. 22, 24, 25, 184n3
Gender *see* Marriage, Sex
Gentleman's Magazine 48, 135
Gentrification *see* Urban renewal
  Mortlake 130
  North Kensington 108, 319
George, D. 47
Gibb, Rosemary 114, 269–71, 279
Gifford, Lord 114
Gillen, F. 124
Gipsy Lane 137, 159n13
Gladstone, F. 67
Gladstone, William E. 52, 211
Globalisation xv, 14, 21, 26, 216, 242, 273
Gluckman, M. 20, 294
Gmelch, G. 31, 232, 254, 282, 287
Gmelch, S.B. 31, 178, 233, 247, 287
Godfrey, Queenie 134
Graves 234, 306
  and borders 172
  Manus 286
  Mortlake 145–6
  Sir Richard Burton 12–13
Greene, Graham 10
Gregg, P. 274
Griffith, Arthur 52 *see also* Sinn Féin

Gryce, Frederick 149
Gypsies *see* nomads, travellers, Travellers, Welsh Gypsies
Gypsey Corner 140
'Gypsyry'
  Notting Dale 48, 71, 80–2, 86
  Wandsworth 79, 133
Gypsy Council 112
Gypsy Lore Society xv

Hall, George 72, 105
Hambro, Baron 131
Hamilton, Patricia 116
Hampton Square 45, 103, 140, 142
Hammersmith
  Bridge 139, 169
  'inner city' 61, 218
  'migratory tendency' 72, 77
  Palais 9
  Sacred Heart School 10
Hancock, I. 282
Harbison, P. 308
Harris, 'Eddie' 144, 147, 152–5
Harrow Club 102, 265, 295, 300, 320
Hawkes, C. 308
Hearne, Joe 98–101
Hearne, General Anne ('Mary-Anne') *96*, 99–100, 103–6
Hedges, Hesther 138
Helleiner, J. 271, 283
Hemmingway, Ernest 10
Herefordshire 83
Hermes 32, 35, 309 *see also*
Autolycus, tricks(ter)
Hertfordshire 27, 83, 85, 99
Herzfeld, M. 124
Hesketh Place 98
High Street, Roehampton 131, 132
History *see* Ackroyd, anthropology, ethnography, memory and meaning 21, 24
  as 'community' 306–9
  Barnes & Mortlake History Society 138, 142
  of habitats 202–3
  oral/written 20, 25, 91
Hobbes, Thomas 39
Holocaust Centre xiii
Homelessness *see* racial discrimination, socio-economic disadvantage
Home Rule 52–4
Homosexuality *see* Sex
Honour 240–1
Horses 35, 46, 98, 136, 260
  and masculinity 208–9, 211
  and the young 229, 292
  Celts 308
  dealers 49–51, 54–5, 84, 213n6, 228–9, 246
  figurines 296
  Irish love 214n12
  see also Rag and Bone Men, markets
Howard, Michael 1
Human Rights Act xiii

Hunt, Billy 102–3, 151
Hussey, G. 216–7
Hutton, W. 273

Identity *see* Chapter Ten
   and culture 3, 6, 59, 107–8, 124–5, 273
   and ecology 195–6
   and locality 24, 26, 128
   and marriage 249, 251
   author's ethnic vi
   biology/physiognomy 105, 107–8
   'black British' 95
   community and 2, 14–16, 126, 293
   'English' 93
   'Gypsy' 115, 250–1
   hidden 101, 106, 155, 156, 231–2
   'Irish' ethnic status 161, 218–9
   Londoners 24, 128, 162, 172–3
   performance 259–61
   see also borders, community, culture, memory, partial-network, Irish Travellers, purity and wardens
Inner London Education Authority 218 *see also* education
Infield 196, 197, 198, 204 *see also* Openfield
Inuit *see* Eskimo
IRA 53, 55–6, 90, 194
Irish Civil War 53–4

Irish Famine 42, 43, 47, 69, 307
   and marriage 245–6
Irish in England *see* Chapter Two
   employment 1980s 219–21
   ethnic 'minority' 217–8
   Cockneys 43
   'ghettoes' 43–44
   interfaith marriages 91
   in war 46, 53, 57n10, 62
   'navigators' 46
   professional ghettoes 91
   returning to Ireland 1970s 55
   social characteristics of 1980s immigrants 55–6
   social mobility 51, 91
   slums 34–5, 41, 44, 45, 80 *see also* Notting Dale
   spatial mobility 44, 91
   see also identity, stigma
Irish in Ireland 52–4 *see* Famine
   agriculture 211, 216–7
   unemployment 1980s 55
   urbanising 216–7
Irish Free State 54, 211 *see also* Eire, Republic of Ireland
Irish Languages 56n4
   and literacy 279–80
   cant/Gammon/Shelta 34–5, 80, 97, 280–2
Irish Travellers *see* Ceard, Celtic smiths, identity
   as immigrants xiv, 29
   as nomads xvii, 25, 54
   as 'tinkers' 31–7, 79–80

as traders xiv
as 'Travellers' (or 'Gypsies')
    25-6, 249-51
assertion 262, 267-8 see also
    character
as victims see also stigma,
    racial discrimination,
    socio-economic
    disadvantage, ridicule
ethnic status 203, 218, 312-3
health 263 see also diseases,
    Westway Site
identity 48, 51, 98, 195, 242-3,
    248-9 see also identity
in america 228
in war 53, 57n10, 79
in the making 47-51 see also
    Mayhew
language see Irish languages
names 247, 253-4, 282-5
population 222-3
tin plate workers 39
Itinerant 198-201

Jackson, A. 27n1
Jacobs, 'Alan' 148
Jenkins, T. 164,172, 184n2
Jews 12, 92, 107, 120n2, 149
Jennings Building 42-3, 70
    see also Irish in England,
    slums
John, Augustus 159n19
Jonson, Ben 36, 57n7

Kalderash 155, 268, 298, 300

Keane, Dolores 305
Kennedy, Patricia 8
Kenrick, D. 75, 106, 112, 138,
    222, 243n4
Kilsby, Ron 147-8
Kimball, S. 211, 257
Kray twins 93-4

Lake, Samuel 65
Larkin, Admiral 131
Lapps 241, 303
Latimer Road 75, 76-7, 82, 98
    see also Freston Road
    and A40(M) 62
    Caravan Site 59, 61-2 see also
        Westway Travellers Site
    Gypsies 1800s 63, 72, 76
    Travellers and Gypsies in
        flats/houses 86, 98, 102,
        105, 193, 298
    Semi-isolated 109
    'Soapsud Island' 67
Lee, 'Prince' Gypsy 107
Leigh, Vivian 8
Leland, C.G. 34, 54, 105, 121n8,
    298
Lévi-Strauss, C. xvi, 10, 18-19
Literacy 79, 188, 239, 269,
    278-81 see also Irish
    Languages, oracy
Livingstone, Ken 95-6
Lobjoit, William 137
London
    docks 46-7, 78
    inner/outer boroughs 13, 60,

61, 65, 218, 223
Irish population 1801 51
many Londons 172-3
multi-centred 42
population movement 46
population 1801 60
population 1901 46
suburban villages 156, 162
suburbanisation 129
suburbs 64, 75, 93, 128, 163
   'concussion' 167
   seamlessness 131
   'science of' 16-19
   Southall 229, 310
see also Irish in England, community, identity
London Anthropological Society 12
London Corresponding Society 39
London Illustrated News 63, 86
London University 164, 233
Lonergan, D. 56n4
Lovell, Mignonette 137-8, 142

Macalister, R.A.S. 42, 312
Macmillan, Harold 94-5
MacNiell, M. 206, 207, 233
Malinowski, B. 20
Manresa 8, 132
Manus 286, 305, 309
Marcus, G. 4, 22
Markets 44, 102, 231, 179
   Covent Garden 134
   French 184n2
   Hammersmith 102
   Portobello 98
   see also fairs, horses
Market gardens 134, 137, 144, 155
Marriott, M. 27n5
Marriage 250-271
   Romany 59
   Irish Traveller 247, 259-61
Mary Place 84-5, 86, 99, 104, 121n7
Matches see marriage
Mayhew, H. 43, 47, 79, 97, 163, 309
Mauss, M. 215, 216, 262, 304
McCarthy, Thomas 53, *294*, 313
McInerney, 'Son' 229
McKenzie, Bruce 114, 117
McKenzie, Compton 191
McLuhan, M. 223
McMahon, S. 42
McRichie, D. 271
McTernan, O. 107, 114, 115
Medfield Street 5, 126, *127*, 131-2, 134
Memory 25, 171, 179
   see identity
   and history 122, 165, 306-7, 311, 315n5
   of country 215, 305
Mischief 267-8 see also Autolycus, Hermes, tricks(ter)
Mitchell, Charles Henry 155
Mongols 241
Moonmen 36

Morton, H.V. 245, 279
Mosely, Oswald 88, 92, 94
Muirhead, Tim 114
Multiculturalism 56, 95, 218, 243, 305, 316
Mumford, L. 60

New (Age) Travellers 77, 104, 58n11, 301, 302, 312
Newby, Eric 167–71
Ní Shúinéar, S. 307
Nomad(ism)
   author's early interest 10–11, 22, 34
   'commercial' 25, 46, 58n11, 80, 198–202, 306
   'grey' 28n6
   'industrial' 46
   pastoral 198–202
   restrictions 110
   see also booleying, transhumance, travel
North Kensington Amenity Trust 119, 186, 229, 265
Notting Dale *see* slums
   culture shock 162
   deprivation 43, 71 *see also* diseases, slums
   'gypsy emporium' 72–5
   laundries 168
   recent changes 109, 320
   'travellers' 83–6
Nuer 198

O'Connor, P. 10, 57n10
O'Faolain, Sean 30
O'Fearadhaigh, M. 307
Okely, J. 179, 254
Ong, W. 280
Openfield 195–6
Oracy 239, 279–81, 309 *see also* literacy, Irish languages, reputation
Orwell, George 1, 4, 10, 82
O'Sullivan, Maureen 8
O'Toole, E.B. 282, 307

Palaces 42, 61, 64, 81, 98, 101
Park, R.E. 1, 29, 277
Parnell, Charles Stewart 52
Parsons, Ivor 142, 144
Parsons, Janet 142, 144, 151
Parsons Joan 142, 144, 146, 150–1
Parsons, Patience 144–5
Parsons, T. 125
Parsons, Tom 142
Penfold, Frank 102
Pharo and variations 145, 147, 150–2, 298
Pharo, Ellen 145
Phao, George 144
Pharo, Lol 148
Pharo, Reginald George 145–6
Pharo, William 137–144
Pierpont, John 131
Pitches 186–9 *see also* 'little community'– Westway Site
Pixley, J. 304

Pocock, D. xvi
Polanyi, M. 304
Pollution *see* Purity
Poor laws 40 *see also* vagrancy
Portobello Road 98, 107, 120n3, 121n5, 165, *231*, 232
Positivism 17-21, 167
Pottery Lane 81-2, *see also* St Francis of Assisi
Poverty *see* socio-economic disadvantage, racial disadvantage, slums
Power 183-4, 186-8
Priests Bridge 128, 141 *see also* Beverley Brook, border
Prison 160n23, 226
'Private troubles' 195
Princess Royal 182
Profumo, Jack 94
Pubs 9, 94, 121n11, 134, 300
  Bull's Head 160n22
  Charlie Butler 142, 147, 229
  Discrimination 312
  Duke of Northumberland 160n22
  Earl Spencer 126
  Hare and Hounds 15, 147-8, 155
  in fieldwork 9, 179
  Jolly Gardeners 103
  Kings Head 132
  Latimer Arms 113, 178, 229, 296, 319
  Manor Arms 138, 150
  Montague Arms 132

  Pavillion 300
  Queen of the Gypsies 135
  Red Lion 137
  Rose of Denmark 150
  Strugglers 137
  Sun Inn 148
  Wheatsheaf 45
Puck Fair *see* fairs
Punch 43
Purity 189, 278, 289-94
Puxon, Gratton 47, 112

Queen 73, 75

Raban, Jonathan 172
Race Relations Act 92, 94, 313
Race riots 47, 93-5, 120n5, 163
Rachman, Peter 94
Racial discrimination 91-2, 94, 218-23, 312
  see also ridicule, socio-economic disadvantage
Radcliffe-Brown, A.R. 19, 20
Rag and bone men 150-1, 210, 214n10 *see also* Steptoe and Son, totters
Railways 128 *see also* navigators
  dividing communities 64-5
  underground – 'transport' not 'travel' 164
Rao, A. 199
Rathkeale 54, 225, 233, 276n8, 283
Redfield, R. 22, 59, 303
Redmond, John 52

Rehfisch, F. 179
Religion 278, 286–9 *see also* purity, weddings
Rent Act 1957 93–4
Republic of Ireland 54 *see also* Eire, Irish Free State, Irish in Ireland
Reputation
　Westway Site 193–4 *see also* Martin Ward
Respect(ability) 194, 211, 228, 240–1 *see also* honour, respect, respectability
Richardson, Benjamin Ward 138
Richmond Park Road 13, 45, 142, 147, 148–9, 152
Ridicule 43–4 *see* racial discrimination, stigma
Rillington Place 63
Risk xiv, 262, 264, 273–4, 280
Rites *see* religion, purity, rites of passage
　of passage 6, 15, 125, 207
Roberts, R. 43, 58n12
Roehampton University 9
Rooks, Clarence 43, 171
Roots
　and graves 12, 306
　author's 4–6
Routes
　and 'habits of action' 164, 173
　author's 6–11
　Travellers 4, 210, 306
Rugby Clubs 70, 99, 265
Rundale *see* Openfield

Sacred Heart Convent 8–9
Sampson, J. 159n19, 258, 271, 280, 283, 311
Saracens 311
Save the Children Fund 177, 269, 276n9, 289
Scally, R.J. 185, 205–6, 214n12
Scheper-Hughes, N. 289
Schicker, F. 114
Secrecy 27–8, 281, 313–14 *see also* silence
Sex 265–6 *see also* purity
Scottish Travellers 203, 250, 279, 310, 311
Shakespeare, William 34–7, 57n5, 57n6, 159n16
Sharp family 123, 147, 151, 154–5
Shelta *see* Irish languages
Sickness 212, *see also* diseases, Westway Travellers Site
Silence 176–7, 278, 280, 294 *see also* secrecy
Simmel, G. 27n2, 223, 277, 278, 314
Sinn Féin 52, 54, 90
Skemp, Sarah 135
Slattery, Roger 113, 122n17
Smith, Cornelius 71
Smith, George 51, 58n12, 86, 246
Smith, George 'Feathers' 142, *143*, *144*, *146*
Smith, Lemonelia 137, 142, *143–4*, *146*, 148
Smith, Rodney 11, 98

Slums 58n12 *see also* Irish in England, reputation movement from 70, 92
Notting Dale 63, 65–7, *68*
Snake Alley 140–1, 159n18
Spencer, B. 124
St Anne's Road 82, 98, 107
St Francis of Assisi 69, 72, 82, 133, 286
St Mary Magdalene 5, 12–13, 44, 145–6
Steinbeck, John 10, 161
Socio-economic disadvantage 220, 242, 318 *see also* racial discrimination, stigma
1990s Britain 273
Social theory xvii, 4 *see also* anthropology, ethnography, fieldwork
native 20
Southall *see* markets
Spalpeen 198, 202, 213n4
Stable Way 62, 97, 102–3, 296
see also totters
Stanley Road 151, 155
Steptoe and Son 97, 151
Stevenson, Robert Louis 164
Stewart, Michael 103, 116–7, 122n19
Stigma
and 'community' 279, 309
Irish xiv, xvi, 161
Irish Traveller 173, 290, 310–13
see also purity
itinerant 213n4, 290

townland use 205
trade 310 *see also* autolycus
see also racial discrimination, reputation, ridicule
Stratification *see* class, equality, respect(ability)
Suburbs *see* London
Suddaby, Terry 114
Sussex University 15
Sweeney, Tom 319–21
Synge, John Millington 202, 271, 287

Tapestry 44, 126, 315
Taylor, Mike 121n70, 302
Tent 72
 Barnes Common 138, 142
 bender 202–3
 Burton's tomb 12–*13*
 Kew Meadows 139–40
 Notting Dale 72–4, 77, 83–6n7, 98
 1980s homelessness 163
Tew, Mary *see* M. Douglas
Thatcher, Margaret 56, 95, 162–3
Thomas Street 84–5, 86n7
Thompson, Flora 159n19
Tinman 32, 57 *see also* Ceard
Tin Plate Workers Company 47
Tiv 239
Totters 97–8, 101, 144, 319
 see also rag and bone men, Steptoe and Son
Todorov, T. 19

Tonniës, F. xiv–xv
Toynbee, P. 274
Trailers *see* Caravans
Transhumance 15, 213n5, 273 *see also* booleying, nomadism
Transport *see also* caravan, New Age Travellers (NATS), railway, vehicle
Travel
  author's 120, 171
  for health 234
  global 15, 25, 242, 316
  sense of 126, 164
  'sites of' xv, 22, 72, 77–8
  'travelling cultures' xv, 72
  unplanned 10
  'undesirable' 39 *see also* vagrancy
  vis à vis commuting 128, 164, 172
  vis à vis settled 78
  with open mind 305
Travel writers 10, 12 *see* Burton, Morton, Newby, Steinbeck
  writing and anthropology 22
Travellers 58n13, 77, 86n5, 236 *see also* 'wandering tribes' Newby Travellers 25, 78, 82, 106 *see* New (Age) Travellers, Irish Travellers, Itinerant, Scottish Travellers, Travellers, Welsh Gypsies/Travellers
'Travelling Irish' 79 *see also* 'travelling men'

'Travelling men' 202
  wider 'traveller' Irish community 198, 209
Travelling people
  author's early curiosity 11
Travelling tinkers 159n15, 159n19
Treadgold Street 76, 84
Tricks(ter) 32, 209 *see also* Autolycus, Hermes, mischief
  of trade 210, 310, 318
Tynan, Kenneth 279

Unemployment *see* socio-economic disadvantage, racial discrimination
Urban renewal 108, 319
'Urban village' 91, 162, 164 *see also* 'little community'
  Barnes 137, 148, 154
  Mortlake 44, 130–2
  Roehampton 7, 126, 131
Urbanisation 23, 38, 212, 217, 271
Urbanism 217, 272

Vagrants 35, 40, 44, 48, 77
  Bulfin's 259
  laws against 31, 39, 40
  Mayhew's 48
  O'Connor's 10, 57n10
  Sampson's 311
Vandalism 109, 190–1
Van Gennep, A. 15, 125, 207–8 *see also* rites of passage

Vaughan, A.M. & Vaughan, A.T. 36
Vessey-Fitzgerald, B. 34, 57n9, 311
Vine, E. 149, *157*
Vehicles 197, 202–3 *see also* caravans

Walford, E. 123, 133, 159n10
Walmer Road 71, 72, 82, 99, 106
'Wandering Tribes' 79 *see also* travellers
Wandsworth *see* 'gypsyry', Roehampton
Ward, 'Billy' 229, 231, 234
Ward, Martin *314*
   ancestry 307
   author's relationship 178, 305, 314
   authority 187–8, 320–1
   campaign 113
   legal battles 26, 117–19
   on 'community' 304
   on New (Age) Travellers 302
Ward, Winifred *230*
Warden
   author as xvi, 13, 26–7, 162, 174–8, 303–4
   author's difficulties with professionals 176–7, 181–3
   court orders 118–9
   predecessors 114–17
Watford *see* Hertfordshire
Waugh, Evelyn 10
Wealth *see* class, equality, honour, respect
Weber, M. 21, 275n4
Weddings *see* marriage
Weidel, J. 307
Wells, Roy 111–13, 302
Welsh Gypsies/Travellers 236, 249, 250–1, 287, 310, 312
West Indians 89, 93–5, 193, 218, 225 *see also* carnival
Westway Traveller Site
   demography 233–6
   ethnic composition 350
   households 236–40, 243n7
   lead levels 117–8, 192, 213n3
   spatial mobility 233–6
   see also Irish Travellers, reputation
Westway Travellers Site Inter-Agency Group 181–3, 274
Westway Travellers Support Group 27, 114, 118, 182, 192, 296
Williams, P. 286, 305
Wimbeldon Common 126, 131, 133–4
Woolf, Justice 119
Wormwood Scrubs *see* fairs
Worsley, P. 20–1